Liberation
Theology
and Its Critics

Liberation
Theology
and Its Critics

Toward an Assessment

Arthur F. McGovern

ORBIS ✖ BOOKS

Maryknoll, New York 10545

The Catholic Foreign Mission Society of America (Maryknoll) recruits and trains people for overseas missionary service. Through Orbis Books, Maryknoll aims to foster the international dialogue that is essential to mission. The books published, however, reflect the opinions of their authors and are not meant to represent the official position of the society.

Copyright © 1989 by Arthur F. McGovern
Published by Orbis Books, Maryknoll, NY 10545
All rights reserved
Manufactured in the United States of America
Manuscript editor and indexer: William E. Jerman

Library of Congress Cataloging-in-Publication Data

McGovern, Arthur F.
   Liberation theology and its critics: toward an assessment/
Arthur McGovern.
      p.   cm.
   Includes bibliographical references.
   ISBN 0-88344-595-6
   1. Liberation theolgy. I. Title.
BT83.57.M38   1989
230'.046 — dc20   89-38805
                                                              CIP

Contents

Introduction

Theological controversies often remain within the confines of seminary classrooms or academic journals. This can hardly be said of Latin American liberation theology. It has stirred public controversy almost from the outset. It continues to evoke passion, especially among its enemies. In the fall of 1988, I received three separate copies of a popular, "nonsectarian" magazine aimed at alerting Christians to the grave dangers and evils of liberation theology. The entire issue focused on this. The magazine cover conveyed the message dramatically: the half-figure of a peace-loving Jesus juxtaposed with the half-figure of a snarling guerilla fighter. A few weeks prior, both the *Wall Street Journal* and the *New York Times* carried full-page ads with warnings about the danger of a communist takeover in Mexico. A lengthy section of the ad was directed against liberation theology. It began: "The Latin American political process of the last twenty years has been injected with the harmful influence of the so-called 'theology of liberation' which proposed to install Communism in the name of Christianity, and which has been the seedbed of more terrorists in the region than any outright Marxist parties."[1]

These examples express rather extreme forms of propaganda, but in doing so they only emphasize the need for more serious assessments of liberation theology. Many legitimate questions can and should be raised about liberation theologians' use of Marxist concepts, their stress on the socio-political dimensions of the Bible, their views on social change and related issues. But assessments should be based on what liberation theologians have actually said, with an effort to understand the different contexts in which they have written.

As my work progressed on this book, it became increasingly apparent that many judge liberation theology simply by the identity it took on in the early 1970s. That original identity, moreover, was shaped not just by what liberation theologians wrote at the time, but by interpretations of their writings based on projected fears about the influence of leftist ideas or on statements and actions on the part of radical Christian groups and individuals. So in attempting to assess different positions expressed in liberation theology I have made special efforts throughout the book to distinguish between liberation theologians and other groups, and to note some significant changes within liberation theology.

In its origins liberation theology formed a part of a wider movement that marked a dramatic change within the church in Latin America. The Catholic Church, perceived over the centuries as a politically conservative force in Latin America, began to shift ground in the 1960s and 70s. Vatican II influenced this change, but social unrest within Latin America itself contributed significantly. As happened in the United States, student movements became radicalized and universities became centers of protest. But a new awareness of Latin American problems arose also from church efforts to evangelize the poor more effectively. Through a variety of contributing influences, a new generation of bishops, priests, religious, and laity became deeply concerned about the massive poverty that afflicted so much of Latin America. Many in this new generation took on apostolic work that involved living with and working with the poor directly, and this experience made them deeply conscious of both the misery and the hopes of the poor. They committed themselves to change, a change they believed would require a radical restructuring of Latin American society. A new group of Catholic theologians, joined from the outset by Protestant colleagues, gave voice to this new spirit in liberation theology. It set a new agenda for the church in Latin America, a call for the church to lend its power and influence to the cause of the poor.

The new agenda received considerable support from the Latin American bishops' meeting at Medellín (Colombia) in 1968, but in succeeding years divisions within the church over the new theology became more pronounced. The conflicts between the bishops of Chile and the Christians for Socialism gave intensity to the controversy over liberation theology in the early 1970s; Vatican pronouncements on liberation theology brought new attention to it in the 1980s. Conservative-liberal conflicts have troubled the Catholic Church since the Second Vatican Council, but the conflicts in Latin America have touched on far broader and deeper struggles within the whole of Latin American society.

The *political implications* of liberation theology will provide the principal focus of this work. Liberation theology must certainly be studied and judged as a theology, and the theological method and themes of liberation theology form an important part of this present book. Theological interest alone, however, would not explain the amount of attention and controversy that liberation theology has engendered. As its very name suggests, liberation theology has as an ultimate goal the "liberation" of the poor in Latin America. This liberation, if broader in meaning than politico-economic change, certainly envisions a restructuring of society itself.

The theology of liberation has drawn attention dramatically to the situation of the poor in Latin America. Many in the United States owe their awareness of conditions in Latin America to church involvement with the poor and the influence of liberation theology. Official Catholic Church documents now openly espouse an "option for the poor," and recognize the need for structural changes in society. The ways of expressing this option and effecting change, however, remain issues of sharp dispute. Liberation theologians believe that the church should become much more directly and openly involved in politics. Many church authorities claim that this would subvert the primary "religious" mission of the church. Liberation theologians read the Bible as a powerful witness to a God who acts in behalf of the poor in order to liberate them. Critics charge that liberation theologians overemphasize the political and threaten to "reduce" faith to politics. Liberation theologians have found Marxist analysis useful in determining the root causes of poverty and misery in Latin America. Critics fear that use of such analysis leads to an oversimplification of the problems of Latin America, but more importantly that the use of Marxism for purposes of analysis will lead to an espousal of Marxist-Leninist strategies of violent class struggle, and ultimately to Marxist-dominated governments.

The Marxism issue certainly awakened my own initial interest in liberation theology. This interest led first to a book on Marxism and Christianity, which included chapters on liberation theology and on the Christians for Socialism in Chile.[2] The book, in turn, spurred an ongoing interest in liberation theology and in Latin America. Dwelling on Marxism, however, creates its own special problem in writing about liberation theology. Not to address this issue would mean evading the questions most frequently raised about liberation theology. At a press conference in Maryknoll, New York (July 1988), almost all the questions asked of Gustavo Gutiérrez by U.S. reporters dealt with political issues related to Marxism: the use of Marxist analysis, the stances of liberation theology with respect to socialism, capitalism, and democracy. These political issues, all related to Marxism, are uppermost in the minds of many in the United States. The concerns of church authorities range more broadly to questions of use of scripture, faithfulness to church teachings, and the mission of the church. But church critics of liberation theology, even in raising these broader issues, often focus as well on the question of Marxist influence in liberation theology.

All this attention on Marxism, however, can unwittingly serve to exaggerate its very restricted role in liberation theology. Concern for the poor and their liberation arises from a profound *Christian* motivation. The Bible itself condemns "exploitation" of the poor and domination of the rich over the poor. Much that liberation theologians denounce as sinful in the structures of Latin American society could be stated without any recourse to Marxism. In fact, the cloud of Marxism often causes the clarity of harsh conditions in Latin America and the clarity of God's concern for the poor to be obscured. In the early years of liberation theology, social analysis played a very important role. Most often the analysis focused on dependency theory, but references to Marxist analysis occurred frequently enough in the writings of some liberation theologians. Even in studying this period, the important issue is not "whether" Marxism formed part of liberation theology, but "how" it was used. In recent years, themes related to Christian spirituality, drawn from experiences of the poor, far outweigh any details of social analysis, with references to Marxism very infrequent and carefully modified.

Given the importance of "political issues" in liberation theology, and of the Marxism issue in particular, this book does address them in some detail, especially in the middle chapters (chapters 6–9). But it strives as well to give a true "overview" of liberation theology and to devote special attention to important theological themes (theological method, christology, spirituality, ecclesiology, etc.). Throughout the book, special attention is also given to "critics" of liberation theology. Chapter 3 offers a composite discussion of critics and criticisms; later chapters include criticisms related to specific points.

When I first began work on this book, despite the long-standing controversy over liberation theology, relatively few studies in English offered any complete overview or evaluation of liberation theology. Robert McAfee Brown had introduced many U.S. readers to liberation themes in his *Theology in a New Key,* but he wrote this in the mid-1970s. Then, as I made plans for my own research, new works began to emerge. Phillip Berryman's fine *Liberation Theology* appeared in 1986. It offers a very readable and insightful introduction, valuable especially for placing various stages and aspects of liberation theology in their cultural and historical context. Two prominent liberation theologians, Leonardo and Clodovis Boff, published their short but compact *Introducing Liberation Theology.* Ricardo Planas has a *Liberation Theology* dealing especially with the use of Marxist analysis, and Princeton scholar Paul Sigmund will soon publish a broad overview-commentary on liberation theology with respect to issues of democracy. Other works offer introductions to different liberation theologians or liberation themes.[3]

Though most of these works include some criticisms of liberation theology, I felt the need for a study that would attempt to assess liberation theology overall in the light of a variety of criticisms raised against it. The term "assessment" can sound quite pretentious, as if one could stand above the controversies and render an impartial judgment based on a thorough comprehension of all the data available. I have no such illusions. The qualifier "toward" an assessment implies the limits of such an effort. Much of the assessment in this book focuses on social analysis. On theological issues, especially on some issues of biblical exegesis that lie outside my competence, I have more often simply presented contending views or offered outside assessments and some limited personal evaluations. The issues involved in studying liberation theology are extraordinarily broad and complex because they involve not only efforts to understand its theology and use of social sciences but also some understanding of conditions in Latin America as well as Latin American history and culture.

Two separate, three-month trips to Latin America (1981 and 1988), involving visits to ten different countries, made me keenly aware of the difficulties one faces even in speaking of "Latin America." Each country has its own distinct history, culture, and problems; the status of liberation theology in each country differs considerably also. Interviews with liberation theologians, as well as with a number of social scientists, historians, pastoral workers, and critics of liberation theology in Latin America have warned me of the dangers of sweeping generalizations. While I have striven for objectivity and for a fair presentation of opposing views, I am quite aware that one's values inevitably color any effort of assessment. Whatever the limitations of this particular effort, liberation theology has achieved prominence and merits a study and assessment of its positions and those of its critics.

An Overview of the Book

This book represents an effort by a North American to understand better the world of Latin America and the culture and conditions that prompt a liberation theology, while giving expression to some of the misgivings that many North Americans experience when reading about liberation theology. After an initial chapter on the development of liberation theology in its historical context, the book focuses on three sets of issues with respect to liberation theology: theological issues, socio-political issues, and ecclesial issues. These correspond roughly to the three points that Phillip Berryman presents as the principal elements of liberation theology.[4]

Chapter 1, on the history of liberation theology and the events that influenced its development, will serve also as an overview of the book as a whole, for it introduces some of the main themes in liberation theology and the criticisms that arose in opposition to it. The second chapter looks chiefly at what liberation theologians see as most distinctive in their work—a new method of doing theology. In discussing the method of liberation theology I have summarized the contributions of specific liberation theologians (Gustavo Gutiérrez and Carlos Mesters, Clodovis Boff, and Juan Luis Segundo) to show their distinctiveness. This use of writings by individual theologians to illustrate a general theme characterizes the approach used throughout the book. The third chapter offers an overview of some of the major critics and criticisms of liberation theology. Chapter 4 looks at some major biblical themes: God as liberator and the mission of Jesus. Chapter 5 takes up two special theological themes on spirituality and on women and liberation. It concludes the discussion of theological themes with an important defense of liberation theology by Gustavo Gutiérrez (in a book not yet available in English as I write).

The middle chapters of the book deal with the use of social analysis in liberation theology, and with economic-political positions that arise out of this analysis. Liberation theologians view social analysis as integral to their work. Liberation theology seeks not simply to explain but to assist in changing the world, and change requires guidance from social analysis. Chapter 6 takes a look especially at two modes of social analysis that have stirred the most controversy: Marxist analysis and dependency theory. But the chapter begins with a historical account of Latin America's colonialist heritage, a heritage that in my judgment explains the roots of most current problems in Latin America. Chapter 7 explores statements by liberation theologians on four related economic-political issues: dependency, Marxism, capitalism, and socialism. The chapter concludes with a presentation of some criticisms directed specifically at liberation theology's use of social analysis. Chapters 8 and 9 attempt assessments of the major political issues that have created conflicts between liberation theology and its critics: the use of Marxist analysis, the use of dependency theory to explain Latin American problems, and the option for socialism. Under this last heading, the option for socialism, I also take up the issue of "violence and class struggle" and deal in some detail with Nicaragua whose revolution many hoped would provide a model for social change.

Chapters 10 and 11 deal with some important ecclesial issues. Chapter 10 deals with the development, special characteristics, and political significance of "base communities" in Latin America. It gives special consideration to base communities in Brazil but includes a discussion of communities in Nicaragua and offers an overview of the "praxis" of liberation theology in other countries as well. Chapter 11 takes up "ecclesiology," with special attention to the works of Leonardo Boff and his reflections on the experience of the base community movement. The final section of the chapter discusses the important question of how liberation theologians and their critics believe liberating social change can and should be effected.

The conclusion to the book will treat briefly of the present status of liberation theology in Latin America, its promise for the future, the obstacles that threaten its continued growth, and some "suggestions" about its strengths and weaknesses. An appendix gives some identification and background for the many liberation theologians cited in the book.

The book seeks to help the reader gain a better understanding of Latin America and of liberation theology in Latin America. It does not include the development of liberation theology in other Third World countries, nor does it study parallel liberation theologies in the United States (e.g., black theology, feminist theology). Similarly, the book does not attempt to explore how liberation theology fits or could fit into a more universal theological system—as does Roger Haight's *An Alternative Vision.*[5] Again, my major interest lies with the political implications and political issues generated by liberation theology. I have attempted to study the more properly "theological" aspects of liberation theology, and have noted some assessments made by reputable biblical scholars. The chapters on theology proper, however, may only lay the groundwork for more professional assessments by theologians.

The book could have followed a somewhat different plan—for example, following the three "mediations" that Leonardo and Clodovis Boff present as basic to liberation theology. The three sets of issues I deal with do correspond somewhat to the "socio-analytic," "hermeneutic," and "practical" mediations used by the Boffs.[6] I began, however, with the theological issues (the "hermeneutic" mediation) because I am dealing with a *theology* of liberation and because I deal so extensively already with socio-economic issues. I have devoted four chapters to these latter issues, on the other hand, because of liberation theology's own emphasis on "liberation" from dependent capitalism, and the major critics' focus on issues such as the use of Marxist analysis, dependency theory, and advocacy of socialism. In the course of my investigation and travels, however, I came to realize that liberation theology does not exert great influence on the "macro" level of policy-making in Latin America (for example, whether a given country will opt for socialism); yet these are the areas where many controversies about liberation theology arise. Liberation theology has raised political consciousness about the failures of capitalism and about values expressed by socialist ideals. But its immediate effect has been to mobilize the church's concern for the poor and to help generate actions at a "micro" level—for example, in defense of peasant rights, in protest against human rights violations, and in promoting land reform.

One Liberation Theology or Many?

Throughout the book I treat liberation theology as *one* movement, and liberation theologians as *one* group. The Boffs in their introductory work and almost all liberation theologians in their writings refer to liberation theology as a common venture. Yet differences certainly exist. Liberation theology includes a wide spectrum of theologians with very different styles and emphases, ranging from the very biblical spirituality of Segundo Galilea to the very polemical, aggressive analyses written by Franz Hinkelammert.

Those who divide liberation theology into different currents or types usually imply value judgments, considering some type or types "acceptable" and others not. In the 1970s, one of the major critics of liberation theology, Cardinal Alfonso López Trujillo, contrasted a current of liberation theology (judged good) that bases itself on the Bible and church teachings, with a current (judged bad) that bases its theology on Marxist analysis and practice. While he considered the Christians for Socialism as the worse offenders in this second camp, López Trujillo included leading figures like Gutiérrez and Leonardo Boff as well. (He did, however, qualify his judgments, saying that Gutiérrez differs from some of his sympathizers and collaborators, and may have modified his views, and that Boff's views on the "popular church" do not have the same belligerency as the Christians for Socialism statements.)[7]

Paul Sigmund speaks rather of two "phases" of liberation theology: an earlier Marxist phase and one now focused on base communities. Thus he finds not so much a division between liberation theologians, but rather an evolution of liberation thought (as exemplified in Gutiérrez's earlier and later writings).[8]

Even Juan Luis Segundo, from within the ranks of liberation theology, distinguishes two approaches in liberation theology. In contrast with other distinctions I note in this section, Segundo does not reject either form he describes. Both lines work for the same liberation goals, but they do differ in their emphases. The first approach, Segundo observes, uses a critique of ideologies to challenge long-standing expressions of Christianity and of so-called Christian societies. This first line, which clearly represents Segundo's own position, dominated in the initial stages of liberation theology and continues into the present. It works to delegitimize ideologies that claim to speak in the name of Christianity. It speaks to intellectuals, students, church authorities, and middle-class Christians to "convert" them to new ways of thinking and acting. The second approach to liberation theology, more prominent in recent years, seeks to work more directly with the poor in base communities. It emphasizes, says Segundo, learning from the poor, giving voice to their beliefs, and helping them to mobilize their own efforts at liberation.[9] In my judgment, the Brazilian theologian Carlos Mesters would most clearly represent this type of liberation theology, though Gustavo Gutiérrez might exemplify a shift from the first to the second types with his recent works on the spirituality of the poor.

An Argentinian philosopher-theologian, Juan C. Scannone, sees liberation theology as *one* movement, but he also describes in some detail four currents he finds in liberation theology. Other writers on liberation theology, including some liberation theologians, have cited his distinctions and found them useful.[10] The first current, he notes, proceeds "from the pastoral praxis of the church." It starts with the praxis of the institutional church; it stresses the integral and evangelical character of liberation; it does not use social analysis as a constitutive part of its theology. In short, this represents the thinking of many bishops in Latin America and would certainly constitute the most "acceptable" form of liberation theology from an official church perspective.

A second current starts "from the praxis of revolutionary groups." This current Scannone identifies especially with the Christians for Socialism and the early writings of Hugo Assmann. It relies strongly on Marxist analysis (but separated from its atheism) and is committed to revolution (not necessarily violent). It is highly critical of the church and sees the Christian faith as coming too late to criticize the revolutionary program of the left. It puts the faith at the service of revolutionary ideology and class struggle, in Scannone's judgment.

The third current starts "from historical praxis," and Scannone would identify most of the best-known liberation theologians (Gutiérrez, the Boffs et al.) with this approach. Though it uses elements of Marxist analysis, it consciously attempts to be faithful to the church and its theological tradition. Unlike the second current, which tends toward elitism, this third form stresses the poor themselves as subjects of their own liberation and it works closely with base communities.

The fourth current represents Scannone's own position and that of a fellow Argentinian theologian, Lucio Gera. It proceeds "from the praxis of the peoples of Latin America." Scannone criticizes those who use Marxist analysis, because it treats "the people" in socio-economic class categories, whereas the current he favors stresses the people as a historical-cultural identity. This type of liberation theology focuses on what is specifically Christian in liberation praxis with special attention given to popular religiosity.

One obvious problem with Scannone's set of distinctions: almost all the best-known liberation theologians seem to fall into the third current — though Segundo and perhaps some others might not accept Scannone's description as defining their method. The first current would most likely not exist without the impetus of this third group, and Scannone's own fourth type seems representative of only a small group in Argentina. (Some critics see it as a defense of Peronism.) But the distinction Scannone makes between the second and the third group, together with his judgment that it would be "unjust" to identify Gutiérrez and others with the second group, appears to me quite critical in any assessment of liberation theology. Segundo Galilea, using an almost identical description of four tendencies in liberation theology, indicates the importance of these distinctions. Many liberation theologians (the third group), he says, stress economic factors, the influence of ideologies and class conflict. But they are not Marxist. The activists (second group, or in his division a fourth tendency) who give primacy to Marxism and who promote an "ideology of liberation" now constitute a dwindling number and do not really do theology as such. Yet their thinking, Galilea asserts, is what many critics present as the "theology of liberation."[11]

These various currents of liberation theology are more helpful in locating where *critics* stand in respect to liberation theology. Readers of any book on liberation theology will almost certainly assume that it deals with the writings of those most commonly identified as liberation theologians (Gutiérrez, Boff, Segundo, Sobrino, Míguez Bonino et al.) and not with statements by militant groups nor with official church versions of liberation theology. Hence while recognizing differences among these theologians, I shall speak of the common body of their writings as liberation theology.

This liberation theology, however, is not a static entity. It has changed and evolved over the years since its inception, and the changes it has undergone often reflect the spirit of a particular period in recent Latin American history. Liberation theology first developed in a time of radical confrontations and challenges. In the 1960s and early 70s, Cuba and Chile seemed to offer hopes for a radical break with dependent capitalism; repressive military dictatorships presented a dehumanizing alternative. Social analysis focused on "ultimate" causes — capitalism and dependency. Some Christian radicals joined ranks with revolutionary groups and criticized sharply the church's perceived alignment with ruling powers and its reluctance to commit itself to revolutionary change.

Liberation theology did not create this context, but not surprisingly it did reflect the spirit of these times. Some critics, on the other hand, tend to attribute to liberation theology the worst excessives of this period, charging liberation theologians with reading Marxism into the Bible, encouraging violence, and showing disdain for traditional church teachings. Again I would emphasize the importance of treating objectively what liberation theologians actually said, even in this initial period, as opposed to what Christian activists proclaimed or what critics perceive as implied in liberation writings. Moreover, even the writings of liberation theologians during this initial period should not be taken as "final statements." Liberation theology has evolved over the years, often reflecting changes within society and within the church.

As I hope to discuss in more detail in chapter 1 and in subsequent chapters, liberation theology in the late 1980s operates in a very different historical context. The problems facing the poor remain very much the same, but few Latin Americans today anticipate any soon-to-come, radical break with existing structures. Formal democracies, whatever their limits, have replaced military dictatorships in several countries. This new context has significantly influenced the social analysis used in liberation theology and more especially the kind of "praxis" it encourages in base communities. These changes also complicate the task of assessing liberation theology, for significant time-lags often exist between the original composition of works in liberation theology, their translation into English, and the responses of critics.

As these introductory comments should suggest, this present work tries to weigh carefully the historical context of liberation writings, though its chapters focus on major themes in liberation theology rather than historical stages of development. The effort to point up historical context and development within a framework of key elements of liberation theology (theological themes, social analysis, and church-related issues) has inevitably led to some repetition of important events. Some events or positions noted in one chapter appear again in later chapters with greater detail or emphasis. Three chapters deal explicitly with history: chapter 1 gives a general history of liberation theology and its background; chapter 6 deals at some length with the overall history of Latin America; chapter 10 includes a history of base communities. The repetition of certain points serves also to underline facts or ideas that I perceive as especially important for understanding liberation theology.

Polarizing Terms: Capitalism and Marxism

The history of Latin America differs significantly from the history of the United States. The differences will emerge at various points in this book, but they make especially difficult the use of certain terms that can arouse polarized reactions from the outset. The term "capitalism," for example, connotes something far different to most Latin Americans than it does to the average U.S. citizen. While critical of many features of the capitalist system, few U.S. Americans would vote to change over to socialism. They might resonate more with the expression "free enterprise," but most would acknowledge the opportunities and the actual achievements that U.S. capitalism has bestowed on most of its own people.[12] The "peripheral capitalism" that Latin Americans have experienced carries sharply negative connotations for the vast majority of Latin Americans. Ricardo Antoncich, speaking as a Latin American, notes this striking divergence of feelings:

> There is an enormous difference between our Latin American experience of capitalism and that of the average citizen of the United States. For example, North American society is characterized by an extensive middle class. There is no parallel here with the miniscule middle class of Latin American peripheral capitalism, in which the condition of very wealthy minorities stands in stark and shocking contrast to that of the very poor majorities.[13]

Capitalism has a dismal record in Latin America. Even the staunchest critics of liberation theology do not attempt to defend it. Bishop Alfonso López Trujillo asserts: "We are convinced that capitalism is a human failure."[14] Roger Vekemans, S.J., called for a Christian socialism to avoid the evils of capitalism and Marxist socialism.[15]

The word "Marxism," in turn, has almost entirely negative connotations for most North Americans (and for many Latin Americans). For them, Marxism means simply Marxist-Leninist totalitarian regimes. They judge as naive anyone who cannot recognize that Marxism, despite its alluring appeal of liberation, has in fact brought repressive rule without its vaunted promises of growth and equal distribution of wealth. They hold suspect anyone who would trust Marxist analysis as a guide. Liberation theologians and many of their supporters view Marxism differently. They believe that Marxist analysis correctly perceives the exploitative consequences of capitalism. They believe that one can use Marxist analysis without succumbing to its atheism and philosophical materialism, and that one can learn from it without espousing hatred and violence. They see Marxist analysis as distinctive in Latin America, shaped not by Lenin or Stalin, but by creative Marxists like Antonio Gramsci in Italy and by indigenous Marxists like José Carlos Mariátegui in Peru. They believe that Latin American Marxist movements should be judged by their own policies and actions, not by what Marxists elsewhere have done. Whatever one's political views, arguments should look beyond labels in an effort to discern the reality of a situation. My concerns in this regard should be quite evident as the book unfolds.

Inasmuch as my own personal values, concerns, and predispositions affect the assessments made in this book, it may help the reader to have some principal ones expressed openly at the outset. In other writings I have been quite critical of capitalism and tried to present what I thought Christians might learn from Marxism. But these writings were intended to counter the U.S. proclivity to view Marxism simply as evil, without distinguishing its various aspects and forms, to view socialism as either utopian or as simply another name for Marxism-Leninism, and to view capitalism as the only rational economic system. When I read works by some liberation theologians that deal with social analysis I sometimes found, in contrast, rather sweeping indictments of capitalism without any distinctions about the complexities of its structures. In many early works I found an almost unquestioned faith in socialism without a sufficient critique of Marxist-Leninist socialism, which I see as most often destructive of freedom and less than adequate in achieving the economic productivity required for the welfare of society.

As later chapters of the book will indicate, however, I have found in my research that nearly all the liberation theologians have developed more nuanced political-economic views, and that some were quite nuanced in their positions from the outset. In my judgment, any system, capitalist or socialist, where economic and political power are concentrated in a few hands (or in one country), will almost inevitably lead to injustices. The world needs economic democracy as much as it needs political democracy; both require a just *access* to ownership and participation. Michael Novak claims that those who call themselves "democratic socialists" are in principle really democratic capitalists.[16] I would reverse this and say that a *truly* democratic capitalism would differ little from democratic socialism.

Some Added Reflections

In the area of theology proper, I have been personally enriched by theologians who have developed the "human side" of Jesus, and I am convinced by liberation theology's judgments that the socio-political dimensions of the Bible were overlooked through much of the history of Christianity. At the same time, as my personal comments in later chapters will indicate, I believe that some liberation theologians have dwelt almost exclusively in some works on the socio-political dimension, or have drawn inferences from scripture that do not cohere with the whole message of the Bible. On this score, however, as on political issues, I find liberation theology coming to a better balance with a great number of works in recent years on Christian "spirituality" (see chapter 5).

In short, I find some of the criticisms lodged against liberation theology as valid. Far too many criticisms, however, are based on distorted interpretations of liberation thought. Too many critics "read into" liberation theologians positions they do not hold. (Some liberation theologians are guilty of doing the same with those they oppose.) I have made a special effort in some places to point out where this misrepresentation has occurred. Liberation theology is too important to leave to polemics. It deserves an honest effort that presents as fairly as possible the views both of liberation theologians and their critics. This book may fail to achieve this fairness, but it seeks it as a goal.

Of the many liberation theologians discussed in this book, Gustavo Gutiérrez receives the most extended treatment. Through most of its history liberation theology has been most associated with his name (though Leonardo Boff has gained equal prominence in recent years). As I rewrite these introductory pages, it appears that Gutiérrez may again become a target of special attack by church authorities. This I find deeply disturbing. While perhaps wishing he had qualified or clarified some statements in his earliest works, I find his theology thoroughly Christian even in its earliest formulations. In addition to reading most of his works, I have attended some twenty or thirty of his lectures over the past two years. His message is *profoundly* spiritual, and he personally demonstrates wonderful qualities of humor, compassion, and humility. One might complain that he now gives too little attention to social analysis, but hardly that he promotes Marxism (which he rarely even mentions). Despite the attacks made on him, I have never heard him utter a single word of even implied criticism of any church authority or any other person. It seems almost inconceivable to me that anyone would seek to condemn his work at this stage. But he has come under attack again, as I will indicate at the end of chapter 1.

In conclusion to this introduction, I am indebted to a number of persons for their criticisms and suggestions in reading over different drafts of the book or specific chapters: to Roger Haight and J.J. Moeller for comments on the whole manuscript; to Matt Garr, Dean Brackley, and Garth Hallett for comments on a first draft of the book; to Jeff Klaiber for suggestions on the history of Latin America and the church, and to Al Hennelly for comments on chapter 1; to Joe Mulligan and Juan Hernández Pico for sections on Nicaragua; to Barbara Butler and John Donahue for reflections on chapter 4; and to Joe Daoust for helpful criticisms on chapter 8. I am especially grateful to the liberation theologians who gave their time in sometimes lengthy interviews: Gustavo Gutiérrez, Ricardo Antoncich, Juan C. Scannone, José Míguez Bonino, Juan Luis Segundo, Pablo Richard, Tereza Cavalcanti, Ana Maria Tepedino, María Clara Bingemer, María Teresa Porcile, J. B. Libânio, Clodovis Boff, Carlos Mesters, Juan Hernández Pico, Jorge Pixley, Jon Sobrino, and Ignacio Ellacuría.

I thank Frank Chamberlain, Joan Hastreiter, and many others who work with the poor for their insights into the pastoral work of the church. I thank also Javier Iguíñiz, Carmen Lora, and other social scientists (in Peru especially), and a number of critics of liberation theology (in Brazil especially) who shared their views. I am thankful to Robert Ellsberg for his editorial guidance and his compilation of the appended "profiles of liberation theologians," and to Clayton Schario who helped solve computer problems.

Tom Schubeck merits a special note of gratitude for comments on various parts of the manuscript but more especially for arranging many of the interviews and much of the 1988 trip to Latin America that we shared together.

Chapter 1

A Brief History
of Liberation Theology

History figures prominently in liberation theology on at least three scores. First, the history of Latin America, its colonial heritage especially, profoundly affects contemporary conditions in Latin America; I have devoted a special part of chapter 6 to explaining its impact. Second, history holds a prominent place within liberation theology itself because it sees God as acting "in" history. Third, the history of liberation theology evokes special interest because it expresses a very dramatic break with the past and mirrors all the unrest that has developed within the church and within Latin America over the past few decades.

A thorough and comprehensive history of liberation theology remains to be written. Some good, readable overviews of liberation theology and of the contemporary church in Latin America do exist, however, and I have borrowed from them in writing this opening chapter.[1] A historical introduction serves an important purpose of situating liberation theology in its context, a context needed for any assessment of it. This chapter will call attention to some of the important political and ecclesial events that influenced the development of liberation theology, and will note some of the moments of support and opposition experienced by liberation theology. Hence the chapter will serve also as an overview of the book as a whole. I refer at times to "liberation movement" and not simply to liberation theology because the theology is part of a much broader succession of changes within the church and within Latin American society. When I speak of the church I have the Catholic Church primarily in mind, though Protestant churches and theologians have become an increasingly significant factor in Latin America. The church involves the whole people of God, but at times, usually prefaced by some word like "institutional" or "official," I have referred to the church in a more restricted sense of official church leaders.

The Church of the Past

The history of the church in Latin America includes many valiant stands taken by individual church leaders who resisted injustices and defended

1

the poor. But most historians present the institutional church overall as playing a very conservative political role in the past, aligned for the most part with the landowning class. Much of the initial drama surrounding liberation theology, and the liberation movement it reflected, sprang from its opposition to this predominant heritage from the past.

In the United States, though some colonies had dominant religions initially, the Constitution made separation of church and state a cardinal principle so that no one church could claim a position as "the official" religion of the nation. In contrast, a crusading zeal to bring "the one, true Catholic faith" to the new world characterized the conquest of Latin America. The Spanish conquistadores planted the cross alongside the flag of Spain and often justified their conquests in the name of establishing a new Catholic Christendom.

The Spanish and Portuguese colonizers, Enrique Dussel observes, viewed themselves as elected by God. The Roman papacy, too weak to act independently, entrusted itself to Catholic rulers. It issued decrees granting Portugal the right to possess any land it had discovered, or would discover, in Africa and America. To Spain and Portugal it gave a *jus patronatus*: a patronage that entrusted to them the propagation of the faith, and gave them the right to nominate bishops and to share in the benefices and tithes the church would receive in these lands.[2] Even on issues of church policy, the bishops and religious could not communicate directly with Rome but had to deal with Spanish and Portuguese officials. The aims and purposes of the church and state thus tended to be indissolubly linked. The church, while it lost almost all autonomy, gained protection and support for its missionary efforts as well as control over education. Its privileged status enabled it to play a significant role in shaping culture as well. Churches or cathedrals dominated the new city squares. Celebrations revolved around the church calendar: fiestas in honor of the patron saints of a city or region; the feast day of one's own baptismal name figured more prominently than birthdays; Sundays became days of communal gathering.

The Spanish and Portuguese came to the lands of America with dual goals: to dominate and to evangelize. The goal of domination clearly gained the upper hand. The conquerors sought precisely to conquer, to subdue the Amerindians and force them into tilling the soil and extracting ore from gold and silver mines. Often, with the support of some church officials, they justified their conquests and domination by considering the Amerindians as inferior humans, and even as subhuman.

Attitudes toward the conquered Amerindians evoked sharp disputes, however, from the outset. If some missionaries acquiesced in treating the Indian natives as innately inferior, many others did not. A number of Dominican and Franciscan missionaries protested treatment of the Indians and defended them as truly human beings endowed with souls and equal under God. Antonio de Montesinos, one of the first Dominicans in the new world, aroused great animosity among the colonists when he denounced them for their abuse of the Amerindians. "You are in mortal sin ... for the cruelty and tyranny you use in dealing with these innocent people."³ Montesinos was called back to Spain, but his battle was taken up by another Dominican, Bartolomé de Las Casas. Initially, even as a priest, de Las Casas had Amerindian slaves of his own. But in 1514, at the age of forty, he took on their cause and fought for them until his death fifty-two years later. He succeeded in getting the king to pass laws protecting the Amerindians, though the laws themselves proved ineffective in holding back soldiers from preempting Amerindian land and slaves.⁴

Some missionaries sought to protect Amerindians by bringing them, under the protection of the law, into settlements or "reductions." The most famous of these, the Jesuit reductions in what is now Paraguay and Argentina, flourished for nearly one hundred fifty years until the Jesuit order was suppressed. Jesuit supervision of the reductions was often paternalistic and sometimes authoritarian, but the reductions protected Amerindians against enslavement and trained them to be self-sufficient in agriculture and crafts. At least one historian believes that the Amerindian of the reductions "probably fared better than any Indian of America before or since."⁵ The same could not be said of black slaves in Latin America. The Jesuits and other religious orders, while they may have treated blacks with more benevolence than some other colonists, nevertheless maintained large numbers of slaves themselves.

After the sixteenth century, zeal in defense of the Amerindians diminished. The church became institutionalized. "It was more interested in dominating the creole society of Spanish Americans than in harvesting Indian souls."⁶ A study made in Lima at the end of the colonial period (1750–1821) showed that only ten of fifty-seven pastors, when asked about their motivation for becoming priests, put service of God and others as a primary motive. Most acknowledged that they viewed the priesthood as an opportunity to achieve a higher social status.⁷ Petty feuds developed between the religious orders, between the lower clergy and their bishops, and between the church and the state. The churches gained immense wealth from lands, though they left much of their land unproductive. According to one historian, the church controlled over half of the property in Mexico by the end of the colonial period.⁸ Throughout the colonial period, however, the church was one of the few institutions that reached all classes and races.

When the struggles for independence from Spain erupted in the early decades of the nineteenth century, some lower clergy became political leaders in the new movement. Fr. Miguel Hidalgo y Costilla and Fr. José María Morelos led the first battles for independence in Mexico. They armed poor mestizos and Amerindian peasants, and fought for an independence that would address the needs of the poor. Priests in Argentina and Central America likewise shared in the battles for independence. Most of the hierarchy, however, remained loyal to the monarch until Latin American independence brought Spanish rule to an end.[9]

The church fell into disarray with the coming of independence, and its decline continued throughout the nineteenth century. It had already lost all its Jesuit missionaries (2,200 expelled in 1767) whom Dussel believes "represented the most capable, educated, and committed of the missionary force."[10] The new independent governments still recognized Roman Catholicism as the official church, but many exercised their own new *patronatus* system aimed at divesting the church of its wealth and power. In Peru, for example, all Spanish priests were suspended, novitiates and convents were closed, and the churches were made to pay taxes.[11] The number of priests declined dramatically, from one priest per 1,000 persons in 1800 to one priest per 3,000 in 1890, and one per 5,000 in 1930.[12]

In the second half of the nineteenth century, the Liberals came to power in many Latin American countries. They generally represented new interests in commerce and industry, and espoused ideas from the European Enlightenment. They enacted legislation in many countries separating church and state, and in some instances confiscating church property. The church sought to protect itself through alliances with the Conservatives, representative of the traditional landowning class. By the end of the nineteenth century, the church had fallen into a sense of "tragic hopelessness."[13] In earlier periods most Latin Americans simply accepted Catholicism as their cultural heritage without developing any special loyalty or adherence to the church. Now the church had to win support if it hoped to survive.[14] But it did begin to experience a resurgence as it moved into the twentieth century. It sought especially to gain new strength through Catholic education, and several new Catholic universities were founded in the first half of the twentieth century. New youth groups and Catholic action groups, some of them begun in the 1930s, gained momentum in the decades following World War II. Protestant missionary efforts, however, also met with increasing success, providing still another challenge.[15]

A Changing Church

Significant changes in the Catholic Church in Latin America began well before Vatican II. Pastoral concerns about the shortage of priests, about losing the faithful to Protestantism, and about the influence of Marxism, prompted some of the first moves. Bishops in Brazil drew up a national plan (1955–1960) to counter the shortage of priests with more involvement by the laity. The training of lay coordinators, Cursillo retreats, Catholic action groups modeled after the Young Christian Workers in Europe, the Better World Movement brought over from Italy, and a plan for radio teaching of religion, all formed part of revitalized efforts to reach more of the faithful and to involve them more actively. These efforts, along with the educational work of Paulo Freire in northeastern Brazil, laid the groundwork for the "base communities" that would become prominent in the years following.

Many other areas of Latin America experienced the same dynamism, with similar growths in Catholic student movements and the development of Christian Democratic political parties. The diocese of Panama City became a leading training area for lay "delegates of the Word" to serve in areas where priests were lacking. The bishops of Latin America moved to establish a General Conference of Latin American Bishops (CELAM) which held its first general assembly in 1955. In the early 1960s, again to counter the shortage of priests and religious, Pope John XXIII sent out an appeal calling on religious orders to give 10 percent of their members to the work of the church in Latin America. The subsequent influx of foreign missionaries, though it never reached 10 percent, brought new ideas and new spirit to the church in Latin America.[16] The work of Maryknoll missionaries became especially significant in some countries.

The Second Vatican Council (1963–1965) unquestionably provided a tremendous impetus for change, though Latin American bishops did not figure prominently in its debates. The Vatican Council covered a vast range of issues, most of them aimed at adapting the Christian message to modern men and women. Its most profound effects would result from its new emphasis on the church as "the people of God," and from its statements about "transforming the world." *Gaudium et Spes* called on the church to identify the joys, hopes, griefs and aspirations of humanity, and especially of the poor, as its own. It made greater use of scripture and encouraged Bible reading by the laity. It spoke of Christ's mission as breaking the power of evil "so that this world might be fashioned anew according to God's design and reach its fulfillment."[17] It affirmed the importance of human activity in carrying out Christ's mission and its new eschatology stressed no longer heaven alone but "a new earth where justice will abide." These emphases laid the groundwork not only for liberation theology but for social activism in the church in the United States and throughout the world.

The papal social encyclicals of the 1960s contributed to the spirit of change as well. John XXIII's *Mater et Magistra* (1961) expanded the church's traditional concern for the worker to include treatment of poor nations. His *Pacem in Terris* (1963) included an important discussion of socio-economic rights (for example, the right to food, to employment, to education, to medical care). Paul VI's *Populorum Progressio* (1967) focused its main attention on trade relations between rich and poor nations. The encyclical included some points of analysis that liberation theologians would also underscore: that colonialism, while it provided some beneficial results, often left colonized countries with one-crop economies dependent on fluctuating world prices; that within these countries a small group often dominates while the remainder of the population is left poor and powerless.[18]

Liberation theology would take on a distinctive approach of its own, but many of its theologians studied in Europe where Jürgen Moltmann, Johannez Metz, and other "political theologians" had already developed theological ideas used later in liberation theology: God is revealed in history and promises a new future; the future God promises is a new heaven *and* a new earth; the church must act for the sake of the world, not for its own interests; the church must become "an institution of social criticism" confronting injustice in the world.

Liberation theology, with its stress on social analysis of conditions in Latin America, would benefit from the efforts of François Houtart of Louvain University in Belgium, the French Dominican Louis Joséph Lebret, and others who worked to establish institutes in Latin America devoted to delineating and analyzing social conditions in Latin America. Centers for research were set up in Bogotá, Rio de Janeiro, Montevideo, and Buenos Aires; the Jesuits set up centers for social investigation and action (CIAS) in various countries.[19]

Social and Political Unrest

If these "church events" helped pave the way for liberation theology, stirrings to bring about economic changes in Latin America had an equally great impact. The United Nations declared the 1960s a "decade of development"; Latin America became a special focus of attention. How to achieve true development became an area of sharp disputes. The classic U.S. American way involved infusing U.S. know-how, technology, and capital to spur development. With this in mind, and to stave off the threat of communism, President John F. Kennedy launched an Alliance for Progress. Many Latin Americans, however, believed that Latin America already suffered from too much "dependency" on the United States and Europe. Convinced that Latin America suffered in its trade relations by relying too much on the export of raw materials (e.g., coffee, sugar, copper), some countries developed a policy of "import substitution" to encourage Latin Americans to produce their own manufactured goods. When these policies appeared ineffective, many in Latin America, including the new liberation theologians, looked for more radical solutions.

In 1959 forces led by Fidel Castro in Cuba overthrew the dictatorship of General Batista and undertook a new socialist way that involved "breaking away" from U.S. dependency. If many North Americans view Castro's efforts in a negative light, his efforts spurred new hopes in many Latin Americans. Castro's attempt to break capitalist dependency, and to assure food, education, medical care, and employment to the lowest sectors in Cuba, stirred the enthusiasm of many. The Cuban revolution, a historian of liberation theology observed, "marked the beginning of a new era in Latin American history."[20] Che Guevara sought to implant the same revolutionary spirit and organization in other countries of Latin America. Student groups became militant, endorsing Marxist revolutionary goals. Many

Catholic Action groups, both student groups and workers, became more radicalized and disenchanted with the ineffectiveness of reforms and the hesitancy of the institutional church to take more decisive stands.

Encouraged by the Vatican II call for the church to become more involved in the struggles and aspirations of the poor, and led by the church's own efforts in the 1950s and 60s to reach the "masses" more effectively, a great number of priests and religious had begun to work with, and live with, the poor. Living and working with them brought new awareness of the wretched conditions of the poor, which in turn led to anger directed at the structures and oppressing groups they saw as causes of this misery. Groups of priests, reflecting a wide range of more radical perspectives, formed in the middle and late 1960s: the Priest Movement for the Third World in Argentina, Golconda groups in Colombia, and ONIS in Peru. They denounced capitalism, criticized the church for its reluctance to break with the ruling classes, and called for more revolutionary change.

Camilo Torres, a Colombian priest, decided that only through armed revolutionary struggle could Christian love be made truly efficacious. He joined with a guerilla group, was killed, and became a hero in death. When Pope Paul VI came to Colombia in August 1968, he received a mailbag of letters from radicalized Christians, some regretting his coming to a country whose rulers justified the killing of Camilo Torres, others urging him to denounce injustice and to support the revolutionary changes underway.[21]

If the years leading up to liberation theology witnessed this swell of small but militant revolutionary groups, it also marked the beginning of repressive military rule in many countries of Latin America. The military had often intervened in the past to establish order when a particular civilian government appeared to have lost control or threatened to introduce too much change. In the 1960s and 70s, beginning with a military coup in Brazil in 1964, the military began to impose their own plans of development and national security on many Latin American countries. The repression only further intensified the calls for revolutionary change.

The Inception of Liberation Theology

Though most of the world came to know of liberation theology only after the publication of Gustavo Gutiérrez's ground-breaking work, *A Theology of Liberation*, its distinctive features began to take shape nearly a decade before. Leonardo and Clodovis Boff, in *Introducing Liberation Theology*, draw a compact picture of this formative stage. While some of the first meetings of Latin American theologians preceded even Vatican II, the Boffs credit the council with encouraging these theologians to think creatively and freely about the pastoral problems affecting their countries:

> This process could be seen at work among both Catholic and Protestant thinkers with the group Church and Society in Latin America

(ISAL) taking a prominent part. There were frequent meetings between Catholic theologians (Gustavo Gutiérrez, Segundo Galilea, Juan Luis Segundo, Lucio Gera, and others) and Protestant (Emilio Castro, Julio de Santa Ana, Rubem Alves, José Míguez Bonino), leading to intensified reflection on the relationship between faith and poverty, the gospel and social justice, and the like. In Brazil, between 1959 and 1964, the Catholic left produced a series of basic texts on the need for a Christian ideal of history, linked to popular action, with a methodology that foreshadowed that of liberation theology; they urged personal engagement in the world, backed up by studies of social and liberal sciences, and illustrated by the universal principles of Christianity.

At a meeting of Latin American theologians held in Petrópolis (Rio de Janeiro) in March 1964, Gustavo Gutiérrez described theology as critical reflection on praxis. This line of thought was further developed at meetings in Havana, Bogotá, and Cuernavaca in June and July 1965. Many other meetings were held as part of the preparatory work for the Medellín Conference of 1968; these acted as laboratories for a theology worked out on the basis of pastoral concerns and committed Christian action. Lectures given by Gustavo Gutiérrez in Montreal in 1967 and at Chimbote, Peru, on the poverty of the Third World and the challenge it posed to the development of a pastoral strategy of liberation were a further powerful impetus toward a theology of liberation.[22]

The meeting of the Second General Conference of Latin American Bishops (CELAM) gave the newly-developing theology its greatest impetus. The bishops met in Medellín, Colombia, in the late summer of 1968, to implement Vatican II teachings and to relate them to the major issues facing the church in its mission in Latin America. The bishops appropriated some of the methods used at the Vatican Council: thus they adopted a method of beginning with factual descriptions and analyses of conditions in Latin America and then reflected on these theologically.[23] They called for reports from different pastoral sectors; they drew upon position papers presented by theologians and social scientists. José Comblin, an advisor to Dom Helder Câmara, focused on the class structure of Latin American society. An aristocratic white elite has always controlled wealth and power in Latin America, said Comblin, excluding the vast majority from any real economic, political, or cultural development. The church reinforces this domination. Its priests and bishops find their natural associates in the upper classes; Catholic education serves primarily the same upper classes.[24]

Gutiérrez first proposed a "theology of liberation" in a talk given in Chimbote, Peru (July 1968). Looking toward the upcoming Medellín assembly of bishops, he urged the church to speak of liberation rather than of development in addressing the problems of Latin America. Social scientists had introduced the concept of liberation to emphasize Latin American dependency. Gutiérrez combined this socio-political sense of liberation with a biblico-theological meaning: God acted in history to save a people from every form of enslavement. Liberation became an important concept in subsequent Medellín documents.

In addressing the issue of justice the bishops charged that the misery besetting large masses in Latin America was an "injustice that cries to the heavens." God intended that all should share in the goods of the earth, and sent the Son "that he might come to liberate" all peoples from the slavery to which sin had subjected them, from hunger, misery, oppression, and ignorance. The bishops affirmed: "The church—the people of God— will lend its support to the downtrodden of every social class so that they might come to know their rights and how to make use of them."[25]

In addressing peace the bishops decried the extreme inequality that exists between social classes. They attacked international imperialism and placed the principal guilt for the economic dependence of Latin American countries on foreign monopolistic powers. They warned against the use of violence but recognized that situations of injustice were so grave as to constitute "institutional violence." In speaking of "poverty of the church" they called for solidarity with and commitment to the poor.[26]

As later commentaries on Medellín would note, the bishops' documents sometimes stressed the liberation theme with its bolder challenge to existing structures, but in other places retained the more reformist concept of "integral development."[27]

In 1970 several works from a liberation perspective emerged. All of them emphasized the importance of the social sciences in interpreting Latin American reality. Juan Luis Segundo, in a series of articles compiled in *De la sociedad a la teología*, avoided Marxist language but accepted the insights of dependency theory as important for guiding the church's pastoral practice. He echoed the dependency thesis that rich industrial nations of the North had grown prosperous at the expense of peripheral nations in the South. He argued that Christianity is not simply a religion of otherworldly salvation. Even St. Paul speaks of salvation from *all* evil, material as well as spiritual. Rubem Alves, in his work *Religión, opio o instrumento de liberación?* and in his *A Theology of Human Hope* stressed the inadequacy of First World sources for dealing with the problems of the Third World. He criticized U.S. optimism about technology as the sure path to progress, and he criticized Moltmann and modern German theology for not providing a theology to deal with the most pressing problems of poverty and oppression. Gutiérrez, in 1970, published his "Notes for a Theology of Liberation," setting out theses he would develop more thoroughly a year later. Hugo Assmann, in 1971, published his *Opresión-liberación, desafío a los cristianos*, stressing the centrality of liberation from dependency, the necessity of praxis as a measure of truth, and criticizing European political theologies as lacking a basis in concrete analysis and praxis.[28]

Gutiérrez's *A Theology of Liberation* was published in Spanish in 1971 and appeared in English translation two years later. It remains the best-known work in liberation theology and the best overall statement of its position. I might, therefore, recall briefly its principal arguments. Though Gutiérrez would be criticized for "reducing" liberation to socio-political changes, he insisted from the outset on the need for liberation in three different spheres: (1) socio-politico-economic liberation from poverty, oppression, and dependency; (2) liberation in history of all dimensions of human freedom, with humans becoming responsible for their own destiny and living in solidarity; (3) liberation from sin, which is the ultimate root of injustice.[29]

Gutiérrez's initial chapters dealt with the problem of the dependency of Latin American countries on countries in the North. He described at length the "praxis" of liberation already underway in Latin America, and he compared more traditional ways of doing theology with the method proposed by liberation theology. This new method he defined as "a critical reflection on Christian praxis in the light of the Word." Theology had to address itself to the pressing political and social concerns of Latin America and do so by learning from the ongoing efforts of the poor and their supporters to liberate themselves from structures that caused these problems.

In later chapters of the book, Gutiérrez took up several biblical themes that would become more fully developed in subsequent works of liberation theology. He addressed first the meaning of "salvation." He insisted that it should not be conceived as otherworldly only. It embraces all of human reality: body and spirit, the individual and society, time as well as eternity. History is one; the history of salvation began with creation. God's concern for the physical well-being and salvation of all peoples became dramatically evident in the story of the exodus. The exodus showed God acting in history through a *political* action, which liberated the people from misery and oppression in Egypt, formed them as a people, and led to the construction of a new and more just society.

Jesus Christ brought this saving work to a new fulfillment, offering liberation from sin and from all its consequences (oppression, injustice, hatred). Jesus' preaching of the "kingdom" proclaimed the liberating action of Jesus (though Gutiérrez in this first work dealt less directly with scriptural studies about the kingdom and more with Vatican II statements about the relation of the kingdom to earthly progress). Gutiérrez then dealt with the many ways in which scripture reveals our encounter with God in history. The prophets taught that God could be known only through doing justice (Jer 22:13-16). Jesus stressed knowing God through love of one's neighbor; he identified himself with the poor (Mt 25). While Jesus rejected the Zealots' approach to political revolution, his actions involved a clear political dimension. He confronted the groups in power that oppressed the Jewish people; he died at the hands of political authorities who saw him as a threat.

Gutiérrez then challenged the church to accept the demands of God's word and to become involved in the struggles of the poor. He argued that the church's alleged "neutrality" in political affairs covered over the fact that the church had often explicitly given support to ruling governments and that "saying nothing," when conditions of injustice prevail, amounts to an implicit support. The church could not avoid being political. The church, then, should become poor in its own lifestyle and "opt to struggle with the poor," by denouncing the present order and announcing what should be in the light of Jesus' message about the kingdom of God.

In time, Gutiérrez's concern would find expression in many official church documents about an "option for the poor." But his statements about "opting to struggle with the poor" as a social class would evoke strong criticism. In addressing the troubling issue of "class struggle" Gutiérrez stressed the reality of the conflict and sought pastorally to show young Christian activists how to retain a sense of universal Christian love in spite of the conflict. But critics would focus on the Marxist connotations of the expression "class struggle" and this point would form part of a more generalized critique about the influence of Marxist thinking in liberation theology.

Sources of Support and of Conflict

In its initial years, liberation theology could draw upon numerous church documents to support at least its principal thrust of Christian involvement in behalf of the poor. Vatican II recognized the importance of working to transform the world; papal social encyclicals drew attention to the plight of poor nations and criticized rich nations; Medellín had espoused a number of the principal ideas in liberation theology. Paul VI in his *Octogesimo Adveniens* (1971) made some cautious distinctions about socialism and even about Marxism, which liberation theologians would cite.[30]

The most striking example, however, of official church acceptance of liberation themes appeared in a document on "Justice in the World," emanating from a worldwide synod of bishops in 1971.[31] The bishops asserted that action on behalf of justice and participation in transforming the world appeared to them as "a constitutive dimension" of the preaching of the gospel (n. 6). The bishops used the language of "liberation" repeatedly (nn. 4, 6, 30–35, 77). Numerous points stressed in liberation theology came into the synod document as well: violence and oppression caused by unjust systems and structures (n. 5); the failure of development policies (n. 10); "international systems of domination" (n. 13); "the obstacles which social structures place in the way of conversion of hearts" (n. 16); the need for self-determination by poor nations (n. 17); "the intervention of God's justice on behalf of the needy and the oppressed" (n. 31); a mission of preaching and witnessing to justice as proper to the church's mission (nn. 39–48); education for justice and raising consciousness (nn. 49–58); hope in the coming kingdom and "the radical transformation of the world" (n. 76).

Liberation theology made an impact on other areas as well. Other Third World regions began to develop their own liberation theologies. Theologies of liberation developed in the black church and among women's groups. "Theology of the Americas" conferences were later held in the United States in 1975 and 1980, and some well-known North American theologians — Robert McAfee Brown, Rosemary Radford Ruether, Gregory Baum, and Frederick Herzog, among others — wrote in defense of the new theology.

Some bishops, on the other hand, were alarmed by the new liberation theology; some apparently regretted Medellín even before it concluded. They liked even less the workshops and studies being conducted by Segundo Galilea and others under CELAM sponsorship. They lobbied for changes and succeeded. In November 1972, at a meeting in Sucre, Bolivia, Bishop Alfonso López Trujillo was elected secretary-general of CELAM. Other conservative opponents of liberation theology won important posts also. López Trujillo cut back on many CELAM projects and sought to use its agencies to check the rising popularity of liberation theology. The Belgian Jesuit Roger Vekemans joined López Trujillo in Bogotá, Colombia, set up a research center (CEDIAL), and established a new periodical *Tierra Nueva* to counter the liberation trend.[32] López Trujillo viewed the new liberation theologians as militants who paint Jesus as a proponent of violent revolution. "Is Christ a Zealot who seeks radical change by means of violence? . . . Does he impatiently seek the 'kingdom,' and does he want to speed his mission by means of violence?"[33]

The sharpest early clash, however, came in 1972–1973 in Chile. The Marxist candidate Salvador Allende won the election of 1970 and became president. The bishops respected the electoral process and remained neutral; Cardinal Raúl Silva Henríquez even spoke favorably about the potential of socialism. But a group of priests, ministers, and religious wanted more from the church than neutrality. They formed a group called Christians for Socialism in 1972. In their assembly documents they sharply criticized church social teachings and called for a more radical, revolutionary Christianity. Shortly before Allende fell victim to a military takeover in 1973, the bishops prepared a prohibition against clergy membership in the Christians for Socialism.

While recognizing some positive contributions, the bishops criticized the Christians for Socialism on the following scores: (1) its members reduce Christianity to one dimension — namely, politics — and use the gospel to espouse a particular political option — namely, socialism; (2) they use Marxism to reduce religion to an ideology of class struggle, and they treat all opposing Christian views as "bourgeois ideology"; (3) they claim to speak for true Christianity and the true church.[34]

The conflict between the bishops and the Christians for Socialism greatly affected church attitudes toward liberation theology. The criticisms raised against liberation theology eleven years later, in the 1984 Vatican instruction on liberation theology, reflect almost point for point the charges made by the Chilean bishops against the Christians for Socialism (CFS). The CFS documents were more Marxist, more aggressive, and more sharply critical of church social teachings than the theological works of the liberation theologians (though some of them did contribute to the CFS documents). But all the failings of the CFS documents became attributed to liberation theology itself. Numerous critiques written against liberation theology cited the CFS documents as examples of offending points.

This linking of liberation theology with the Christians for Socialism did not simply occur by coincidence, at least not in the judgment of German theologian Norbert Greinacher, who claims that the connection formed part of a deliberate, carefully orchestrated plan to discredit liberation theology. Included also in this plan initiated by López Trujillo and Vekemans were contacts made in Germany, with Bishop Franz Hengsbach of Essen and others, to promote theological critiques of liberation theology and to enlist Opus Dei as an ally against liberation theology.[35]

At the Vatican, Pope Paul VI issued no special documents on liberation theology, but his 1975 address on evangelization, *Evangelii Nuntiandi*, contained both affirmation and warnings about the use of the liberation theme. The exhortation affirmed liberation as a legitimate biblical notion, but was careful to place it in a context of evangelization. "As the kernel and center of the Good News, Christ proclaims salvation, this great gift of God, which is liberation from everything that oppresses man" (EN, n. 9). The letter, noting the poverty and injustices in the world, recognized the church's duty to proclaim liberation from such evils and to assist in the birth of its liberation (EN, n. 22). But the encyclical issued warnings that anticipated the Vatican instructions of the 1980s: the liberation effort must not be reduced to a simply temporal project or restricted to one dimension of life (the socio-political); while human liberation and salvation by Christ are linked together, they should not be identified as the same (EN, nn. 32–35).[36]

When many liberation theologians met in Mexico City in 1975 they entitled their proceedings *Liberation and Captivity*. The theme of captivity reflected significant political changes in Latin America: the military overthrow of Allende in Chile, a reactionary military coup in Uruguay, the ouster of a reform-minded leader in Bolivia, an impending military takeover in Argentina, and the failures in Peru of the one military government that had been more leftist and reformist. Some liberation theologians, however, believed that the concept of captivity weakened the hope and sense of commitment expressed by liberation. Focus on captivity proved a brief and passing phase.

Theological reflection, on the other hand, deepened and broadened. Gutiérrez's *The Power of the Poor in History*, Leonardo Boff's *Jesus Christ Liberator*, Juan Luis Segundo's *The Liberation of Theology*, and Jon Sobrino's *Christology at the Crossroads* made their appearances in Spanish and Portuguese editions, along with works by Enrique Dussel, José Míguez Bonino,

Ronaldo Muñoz, Pablo Richard, José Comblin, and numerous others. Base communities continued to grow and thrive. Many bishops, in Brazil especially, but in Chile and other countries as well, became more outspoken in condemning human rights violations in their countries.

A New Pope and a Significant Year: 1979

The 1970s ended on several dramatic notes affecting liberation theology. In 1979 John Paul II spent his first year as pope and traveled to Mexico to address the third CELAM conference in Puebla. The Puebla conference itself debated many of the issues and trends set in motion at Medellín. The same year also marked the overthrow of the Somoza regime in Nicaragua and the beginnings of an internal war in El Salvador. Each of these merits some comment.

John Paul II does not fit neatly into liberal-conservative political categories. When he addressed the opening session at Puebla he warned that "the church's mission is not political" and that Jesus should not be presented as a revolutionary. But when he spoke the next day to Mexican Amerindians he championed their struggle for rights. In subsequent trips to Latin America he gave warnings about political involvement, but again spoke sharply on social issues. His own talks in visits to Poland were weighted with clear and strong political implications. The pope clearly rejects Marxism and has warned liberation theology about using "false ideologies," but his own encyclical *Laborem Exercens* (1981) used elements of Marxist analysis. He approved the 1984 Vatican instruction on liberation theology, but has stated that liberation is an authentic biblical theme (and I will note later his comments on liberation theology in 1986 after a trip in Brazil). It appeared quite clearly that the pope wanted any social message spoken within the church to follow two important guidelines: social principles used to help construct a new society should be based on truly authentic Christian doctrines, and not on any secular ideology; and the official, hierarchical church must be the guiding force in determining the social mission of the church.

The Puebla Conference, at the outset, appeared quite threatening to liberation theology and to all that the bishops had previously stated at Medellín.[37] Bishop López Trujillo did indeed try to select delegates and to promote a document that would clamp down on the liberation movement. He did not succeed, though the conference proved to be a stand-off between radical-progressive and conservative-reactionary forces. The socio-economic analyses and the theological perspectives enunciated at Puebla lacked the forcefulness of Medellín. But concern for injustice and liberation language continued to be used. No explicit discussion was taken up in the documents about liberation theology as such. But the concept of "integral liberation," of a liberation that embraces the political, spiritual, and personal, emerged as a key notion. The most positive aspects of the Puebla

Conference, from a liberation viewpoint, were the declaration of a preferential option for the poor and the approval and encouragement of base
communities. Gutiérrez was quoted as saying that the future of these communities was more important than liberation theology itself. Liberation
theologians were excluded from the conference proper, but they made
themselves available to bishops who consulted with them and used their
suggestions. By taking this tack, rather than waiting to criticize the results,
the liberation theologians hoped to show that they were committed to working in and for the church.

In July 1979 the Somoza government fell and the Sandinistas took power
in Nicaragua. For many supporters of liberation theology, the changes in
Nicaragua inspired great hope. Nicaragua gave promise of much that the
Christian liberation movement stood for. Unlike most previous revolutions,
it renounced violence against its previous enemies. It proclaimed as basic
human rights that every citizen had a right to food, to employment, to
decent medical care, and to an education. It sought to make these rights
realizable through land reform, priority given to basic staple foods, the
building up of medical facilities, and a mass literacy campaign. Though
most of the Sandinista leadership fit under different categories of Marxism,
the new revolutionary government began with popular Christian support,
especially from base communities. Four priests held important government
positions.

Any attempt to cover the subsequent turns of events in Nicaragua—U.S.
hostility toward the Sandinistas, the funding of the Contra war, the opposition of Cardinal Obando y Bravo to the government, the visit of John
Paul II—would carry us far beyond the purpose of providing a summary
overview of the development of liberation theology. It seems evident, however, that the pope's tense visit to Nicaragua in 1983 contributed to his
approval of Vatican instructions warning about certain tendencies in liberation theology.

In El Salvador, Fr. Rutillo Grande was killed in 1977 for his efforts in
organizing peasants on the issue of land reform, and a death threat was
issued against all Jesuits by a right-wing death squad. The military stepped
down in 1979 but a coalition "reform" government failed to agree, leading
to guerilla war on the left and massive killings of civilians by right-wing
squads and government forces. The deaths of Bishop Oscar Romero and
four American women dramatized the human suffering involved in living
out the commitment to the poor expressed in liberation theology. Romero
had pleaded with Salvadoran soldiers to stop killing their civilian sisters
and brothers. Romero's death and his homilies on behalf of social justice
and in condemnation of repressive violence expressed, Phillip Berryman
believes, "the core of liberation theology."[38]

Vatican Statements on Liberation Theology

In subsequent chapters we will take up various criticisms of liberation
theology. But two official documents from the Vatican, in 1984 and 1986,

received so much public attention that they merit a special summary presentation in this chapter. Giving this summary presentation will also permit me to separate specific points later, as they apply. In September 1984, Cardinal Joseph Ratzinger, representing the Congregation for the Doctrine of the Faith, issued an "Instruction on Certain Aspects of the Theology of Liberation."[39] It stated a very limited and precise purpose: to draw attention to "the deviations and risks of deviation, damaging to the faith and Christian living, that are brought about by certain forms of liberation theology, which use, in an insufficiently critical manner, concepts borrowed from various currents of Marxist thought."

The document did not make clear, however, which theologians should be included under these "certain forms." As a warning against misuses of liberation theology, the document might have won a stronger hearing by liberation theologians and their supporters. The document appeared, however, to be aimed against some of the leading theologians. This intepretation of the document's "intent" appears supported by several related facts. In a critique of liberation theology published a few months before the instruction was issued, Ratzinger cited Gutiérrez and Jon Sobrino as explicit targets.[40] He also sent a list of charges against Gutiérrez to the bishops of Peru; Sobrino was investigated; Boff was called to Rome in 1984 to answer charges, and then silenced for a year (see chapter 11, on Boff's silencing).

As noted earlier, Ratzinger's major criticisms of liberation theology echo closely the criticisms of Chilean bishops directed against the Christians for Socialism eleven years before. The Vatican statement acknowledged that "liberation" is a legitimate theological theme, and that God does defend the poor and speak out against injustice. It criticizes "certain forms" of liberation theology, however, on several scores. First, liberation theology (certain forms of it) reduces faith to politics. It turns the political dimension in scripture into "the principal or exclusive component" leading to "a reductionist reading of the Bible" (V, 5); "every affirmation of faith or theology is subordinated to a political criterion" (IX, 6). It tends also to reduce sin to bad social structures, neglecting the root of all evil, personal sin (intro.; IV, 2, 12, 15).

Second, the Vatican document asserts that liberation theology adopts Marxism uncritically and allows its theology to become captive to Marxist ideology. Liberation theology rightly draws attention to conditions of poverty and injustice but adds on a "pathos which borrows its language from Marxism, wrongly presented as though it were scientific language" (VII, 12). It is misguided in believing that one can separate Marxist analysis from the rest of Marxist ideology (VII, 6), and makes Marxist analysis the guiding force of "praxis" and the sole criterion of truth (VIII, 1–5). This liberation theology, moreover, accepts Marxist class struggle as "the fundamental law of history" (X, 2–3), a class struggle that leads to hatred and to "systematic and deliberate recourse to blind violence" (IX, 5–7).

Third, this liberation theology attacks authority in the church. "The social doctrine of the church is rejected with disdain" (X, 4) and the hierarchy is discredited as belonging to the class of oppressors (IX, 3; X, 1). Liberation theology also opposes a church of the poor to the hierarchical church, by promoting its ideas in base communities whose members lack the theological preparation and capacity to discern (X, 13; XI, 15).

When the Vatican published the 1984 instruction, it also indicated that a more positive statement of the church's own teaching on liberation would follow. This subsequent "Instruction on Christian Freedom and Liberation" (1986) did not treat liberation theology directly but presented its own version of what a theology of liberation should or should not include. One theme runs throughout the 1986 instruction: freedom, which is primarily personal and spiritual, is more fundamental than any social, earthly liberation. This view gets expressed in various ways in the course of the document.[41]

Liberation movements, while they have been beneficial in some instances, have often proved a delusion and led to new forms of servitude (nn. 10–19). Temporal liberation can only create better *conditions* for authentic freedom; it does not create freedom itself (n. 31). Even the exodus does not deal with just thisworldly liberation, but involved obedience to the laws of the Covenant (nn. 44–45). True freedom comes through grace and the sacraments, from being liberated from personal sin, and reunited with God (nn. 52–53). Personal sin is the root cause of evil; "social sin," in reference to unjust structures, is sin only in a derived, secondary sense (n. 75).

At one point the instruction changed the language of Medellín and Puebla from a "preferential option for the poor" to the poor as "the object of a love of preference on the part of the church" (n. 68). Later in the same section, however, it speaks simply of a "special option for the poor." The initial change may have been intended to counter use of "option for the poor" to justify a partisan political commitment or, worse yet, class struggle (nn. 46–48 and the final sentence of n. 68), but it may simply have been inserted to stress Christian motivation for the option. The Vatican use of "object" of love, along with references to the poor as "the little ones" who "endure poverty and affliction" (nn. 46–48), unfortunately suggest that the poor are indeed viewed as objects of compassion. Such an attitude would appear in sharp contrast to Pope John Paul II's stress in *Laborem Exercens* on workers as "subjects" of their own destiny.

Gutiérrez and Leonardo Boff, nonetheless, spoke quite favorably of the new instruction.[42] If the instruction clearly stressed the subordination of the socio-political to the personal-spiritual, it did recognize liberation as an important theme of Christian theology; it left application of this theme to local churches (n. 3); it recognized the need to change unjust structures in society (nn. 60, 68, 75); and it affirmed base communities as a "source of great hope" and a "treasure for the whole church" (n. 69). At least one statement, moreover, asserted that the poor themselves were justified in taking action, through morally licit means—including even armed struggle as a last resort—to secure structures that would protect their rights (nn. 75, 79).

The most heartening document for liberation theologians during this period came in the form of a letter (April 9, 1986) from John Paul II to the bishops of Brazil. The pope praised the bishops and their collaborators for their solidarity with the people of Brazil, and he commended them for not hesitating "to defend with courage the just and noble cause of human rights and to support courageous reforms," to better distribute wealth, land, education, health, housing. Most importantly, however, he affirms: *"We are convinced, we and you, that the theology of liberation is not only opportune, but useful and necessary."* This affirming statement is preceded by and followed by lengthy statements on uniting this liberation theology with the perennial magisterium of the church. The pope calls for a "new stage" in liberation theology, one that will relate it to the social doctrine of the church, and he calls on the bishops "to keep constant vigil" so that the correct and necessary liberation theology will be developed in Brazil and in Latin America, "in fidelity with the doctrine of the church."[43]

The pope did not withdraw the two Vatican instructions; he called attention to them explicitly. He did not suggest, however, that the major works and leading lights of liberation theology fall outside "approved" liberation theology (an impression given by the 1984 Vatican instruction); he strongly affirmed that liberation theology as such is useful and necessary. Nor did his letter suggest that he intended to substitute a "Vatican form of liberation theology" for the theology that had actually developed in Latin America. At least his comment about a "new stage" in liberation theology seemed clearly to refer to Latin America's own liberation theology. Finally, however, the pope made it quite clear that continued affirmation of liberation theology in general, and of works by individuals, would depend on their faithfulness to church doctrine. The letter constituted, nevertheless, a new bridge between liberation theology and the official church, and it gave new hope.

For a time it appeared that relations between liberation theologians and church authorities had improved significantly. In fact, Enrique Castillo Morales, adjunct secretary of CELAM, stated in early 1988 that "the problem with liberation theology has passed for Latin Americans." The letters of the pope to the bishops of Brazil and Peru, together with the two Vatican instructions, had achieved "the balance which had been lacking." Moreover, he noted, Gutiérrez had been asked to collaborate with CELAM in organizing seminars for Latin American bishops.[44]

A very different attitude, however, was conveyed by Pope John Paul II when he addressed the bishops of Peru during a visit in May 1988. In extremely sharp language the pope spoke of "the obstinate persistence of doctrinal and methodological views that sow seeds of confusion among the faithful and attack the unity of the church." He mentioned in particular views that talk of "permanent class struggle," and he called upon the bishops to denounce these deviations and errors, and to take whatever measures necessary to correct them and make sure that the directions contained in the 1984 and 1986 Vatican instructions are observed.[45] The pope's comments seemed clearly directed against Gutiérrez, for he represents the voice of liberation theology in Peru. The pope's reference to "obstinate persistence" will seem baffling to anyone who has read Gutiérrez's writings or attended his lectures over the past several years, for they contain nothing that could even possibly be construed as Marxist or as doctrinal errors. But an attack on Gutiérrez by Bishop Ricardo Durand (Callao, Peru) may possibly explain the thinking behind the pope's comment. Durand claims that whatever Gutiérrez may now say, his *A Theology of Liberation* and *Power of the Poor in History* contain statements about class struggle and other views which Durand interprets as clearly Marxist.[46] The logic underlying this seems to be that as long as these books remain in print and their positions have not been explicitly repudiated by Gutiérrez, he shows "obstinate persistence" in holding incorrect views. This view of Gutiérrez appears also to reflect the position of the influential papal nuncio in Peru who reportedly composed the pope's address to the bishops there.

New conflicts emerged in Brazil as well. In 1988 the Vatican attempted to silence one of the leading supporters of liberation theology, Dom Pedro Casaldáliga of São Felix in the Brazilian Amazon, and "warning letters" were apparently sent also to eight other progressive Brazilian bishops.[47]

On the level of socio-economic conditions, the situation of the poor remains as deplorable now as it was twenty years ago; in some respects conditions are worse, exacerbated by the crushing burden of national debts. The political context in which liberation theology operates, however, has changed significantly. Many countries in Latin America have moved from military rule to civilian rule. This has influenced a new type of praxis in the liberation movement. While many remain still skeptical about trusting the new Latin American "democracies" to effect any significant social changes, liberationists have used the greater freedom provided by the new political context to encourage the buildup of popular movements to give the poor greater strength and voice in the life of their nations.

The work of liberation theologians themselves continues to expand, with greater emphasis on spirituality, the emergence of a feminist perspective in liberation theology, and exploration into many new areas of theology. By 1988 a dozen or more works had already been published in a projected series of fifty books by a variety of liberation theologians on all areas of theology.

Liberation theology's swift emergence onto the scene in Latin America made it the object of both adulation and intense opposition. Its path in the future may prove less dramatic but it has shown its staying power as a significant theological movement. Its lasting and continued points of identity thus merit the exposition and assessment that follow.

THEOLOGICAL ISSUES

Chapter 2

A New Way of Doing Theology

New methods in some field of study almost invariably begin with a conviction that prevailing ways of understanding and dealing with problems no longer suffice. Thomas Kuhn developed this insight in his *The Structure of Scientific Revolutions*. In science, for example, the older Ptolemaic conception of the universe proved insufficient to account for the movement of stars and planets, and Copernicus introduced a new paradigm to replace it. Darwin challenged creation accounts of the universe and introduced the concept of evolution. Kuhn's insight into scientific revolutions could also apply to the history of philosophy. The Greeks were discontent with the use of myths to explain the universe and sought to develop causal explanations derived from inductive and deductive reasoning. Descartes wrestled with the failure of philosophy to deal with the questions raised by skeptics and proposed a new method to resolve them. Hume, Kant, Husserl, Heidegger — each of their philosophies was characterized by some distinctive method.

This same process appears in theology as well. Aquinas used Aristotelean and Platonic categories to create a new systematic understanding of Christian truths. Modern biblical studies have relied on new paradigms (form criticism, redaction criticism, etc.) to gain new insights into scripture. Karl Rahner drew upon transcendental Thomism and existentialist philosophy to create a new theological method. Not surprisingly, then, liberation theology has created its own distinctive method of doing theology, a method that challenges traditional interpretations of the Christian message and discovers new meaning by looking at scripture from the perspective of the poor.

Liberation theologians believe that the more dominant, established methods of doing theology have failed to address the most pressing problem in Latin America: the poverty and misery of the majority of its people. Traditional faith perspectives had encouraged charity along with acceptance of suffering. They did not, in the view of liberation theologians, provide real inspiration or hope for changing society, nor did they give any indication of God's power and grace at work on behalf of the poor. Liberation theology sought to establish a new method of theology that would respond to these issues.

Without some sense of the dehumanizing conditions faced by the poor in Latin America, and of the faith response that these conditions have elicited, liberation theology would have little meaning. This chapter begins, therefore, with a discussion of conditions in Latin America and Christian responses to them. The second and longest part of the chapter takes up the question of methodology proper. The introduction to this book noted distinctions that some have drawn about different currents of liberation theology. We should expect, then, some variances in method as well. The differences, however, more often involve questions of emphasis rather than of conflicting approaches. All the major liberation theologians include some mention of praxis, of the use of social analysis, and of the need to question ideological elements in traditional presentations of the Christian message. This chapter will highlight each of these three points, using Gutiérrez on the importance of praxis (with some added comments about the work of Carlos Mesters), Clodovis Boff on the role of the social sciences, and Juan Luis Segundo on the questioning of ideologies.

CONDITIONS, CONSCIENTIZATION, AND COMMITMENT

Liberation theology arose out of a profoundly disturbing experience, the experience of Christian faith confronted by the misery of massive numbers of poor in Latin America, a misery which the bishops at Medellín said "cries to heaven for justice." A new awareness of conditions in Latin America and a response of commitment to change them led to the creation of the new theology of liberation. Before studying its more formal methodology, it may prove useful to consider conditions in Latin America, the conscientization they evoked, and the commitment to change they engendered.

Conditions in Latin America

Leonardo and Clodovis Boff begin their work, *Introducing Liberation Theology*, with two stories that illustrate the agony of poverty in Latin America. The first incident tells of a woman who confessed that she received communion, even though she came too late for Mass, because she had not eaten for three days and she literally hungered for the host. The second story tells of a bishop who vowed to assist some hungry person each day after he met a woman who tried to nurse her baby from a bleeding breast that contained no more milk.[1] Statistics lack the poignancy of such personal stories, but they give some sense of the level of poverty. Families in the United States enjoy a median income of more than $30,000 a year. A few years back a Detroit newspaper estimated that the average high school teenager in a wealthy Grosse Pointe school spent over $300 per month on luxury items alone—designer clothes, entertainment, junk food, alcohol, and drugs. That matches the total annual income of the average family in Haiti. Most countries in Latin America fall a few hundred dollars below or above the $1,000 a year GNP per capita mark: for example, Bolivia, $470; Honduras, $720; Nicaragua, $770; El Salvador, $820; Peru, $1,010; Colombia, $1,320; Chile, $1,430.[2]

The most "prosperous" newly industrialized countries, Brazil and Mexico, have achieved per capita GNPs of $1,640 and $2,080, respectively. Behind these relatively higher incomes, however, lies another story. Brazil stands out as a nation of jarring contrasts, with luxury hotels, skyscrapers, and brilliant architectural projects, all surrounded by massive slums. Of all countries in the world listed by the World Bank in its *World Development Report 1987*, Brazil shows the worst record in disparity of income distribution. The lowest 20 percent of the population receive only 2 percent of the national income; the top 10 percent account for over 50 percent of the income.[3] These figures cited by the World Bank come from a 1972 study; a more recent study shows an even worsening pattern of wealth and income distribution; the share of the bottom 50 percent declined by more than a third between 1970 and 1980.[4] The children of Brazil have suffered most. Nearly one-third of the youth of Brazil, *Time* magazine reported, have become hopelessly deprived. Millions have been abandoned by destitute parents; the rest live in such poverty that abandonment almost seems preferable. "They rove in gypsy bands, sleep in construction pipes, in rat-infested cellars of abandoned buildings, or on street corners in miserable heaps."[5]

One finds the same strong contrasts in Mexico, as my own first visit to Latin America in 1981 confirmed. The tourist in Mexico City finds spacious avenues, beautiful mansions, luxury hotels and restaurants, and modern department stores. As in most Latin American cities, most of the poor live on the outskirts of the city, in slum barrios with unpaved mud roads and dilapidated housing. Yet immigrants from the rural areas flood into the cities because the economy of the countryside offers even less hope. I visited Ojo de Agua, a rural Mexican village typical of much of Latin America. The parish census counted 271 families. All but six families earned less than $150 a month. Ninety-one families averaged between $20 and $40 a month, or less than $500 a year in family income. The median family income for the parish stood at $80 a month. None of the homes had running water; the nearest clean drinking water was two miles away. None of the homes had electricity. Most families subsisted on a diet of beans and tortillas, with some soup and rice at the main meal. Because I was a special padre guest, one family added to the meal for me a special treat—two eggs. The family living behind the parish rectory—a family considered "better-off" because it owned a small plot of land and a few livestock—crowded its eight members into a small hut with only two beds.

One could add to these images countless others: women and children scavenging through garbage for food or trying to make a living by salvaging cans and pieces of metal to sell for recycling; half of Bolivia's children suffering from malnutrition; tens of thousands of Peruvians living in huts along mile-long stretches of grassless, treeless land in Lurigancho outside Lima; Chilean families living on the banks of a garbage-dump "river" outside Santiago; masses of landless peasants in northern Brazil and in many parts of Latin America; jobless workers everywhere.

Later chapters will take up the issue of social analysis aimed at investigating the causes of such conditions. But landless peasants and jobless or low-paid workers comprise an essential part of the conditions themselves, so that one can hardly describe situations without some reference to one obvious cause. An estimated 1.3 percent of the landowners in Latin America control 71.6 percent of all land under cultivation.[6] Little wonder, then, that so many accounts of Latin America speak of landless peasants. A report by the *New York Times* dwells on the land crisis in Central America as the underlying cause of its current political crises. Vast inequities in land ownership have characterized Latin America from the outset (see chapter 6, below). In Central America the concentration of ownership was further broadened in the mid-to-late nineteenth century, when communal peasant lands were taken over to enlarge plantations growing sugar, coffee, bananas, and cotton for export. In the 1950s still more land was taken over for cattle ranches to supply U.S. markets. Each takeover meant less land for producing staple foods to meet domestic needs; cattle-raising in particular demanded much land but little labor.[7]

Efforts to reverse this situation, and to make land available for more peasants to produce more staple food products, have led to political conflicts, as the *New York Times* study goes on to explain. Only Costa Rica has managed to achieve some significant reform without major conflict. Nicaragua has inaugurated much broader land reforms, but the Contra attacks and some peasant resistance to cooperative or state farm ventures have created conflict there. In Guatemala, in the early 1950s, the Arbenz government attempted a far-reaching land reform program. But a U.S. sponsored overthrow of the Arbenz government brought a quick and thorough reversal of the land reform. In El Salvador, tens of thousands of peasants were massacred in a 1932 peasant uprising. In 1976 wealthy landowners blocked a modest reform that would have affected only 3 percent of the land. Protests calling for land reform met with violence; Fr. Rutilio Grande was assassinated in 1977 for backing peasant demands.

Urban workers in Central America face similar problems. The lack of opportunities in the rural area has forced increasing numbers of peasants into the cities. But some 50 percent of the urban labor force are unemployed or underemployed. This vast pool of labor permits owners to obtain cheap labor—with almost no raises over the past decade—and to resist efforts of workers to unionize. (In most of Central America only 8 to 15 percent of workers are unionized.) Without unions many firms manage to avoid paying even minimum wages. The average family of four in Central America lives on $90 a month.[8]

These same conditions prevail in most of Latin America and other abuses follow. In Colombia some 3 million children under the age of 14 work in violation of labor laws; some 100 children there die each day of malnutrition.[9] Moreover, efforts to bring about change have met with severe repression. In Guatemala, 90 percent of the Indian population have either no land or less than the seventeen acres required to support a family. Their efforts to protest have led to thousands of executions by military forces and tens of thousands of refugees.[10] Brutal repression has characterized all too many regimes in Latin America.

Penny Lernoux's *Cry of the People* graphically relates stories and statistics of repression throughout much of Latin America. It tells of the thousands "disappeared" in Argentina and of the thousands arrested, tortured, and executed in Chile and Brazil. The stories of repression include some eight hundred fifty sisters, priests, and bishops, along with countless Christian lay leaders, who have been arrested, tortured, executed or deported.[11] More than sixty thousand persons have died in El Salvador in the past decade, most of them in the early 1980s at the hands of right-wing death squads or the military. In Brazil, the official records of some seven thousand trials, nearly a fourth of which involved testimonies about torture, have become public. How nearly one million pages of documents were obtained, with Cardinal Paulo Evaristo Arns playing an important role, constitutes a remarkable story of courage and ingenuity.[12] But the Brazilian official documents themselves record testimonies involving some 283 types of torture, including electric shocks, rape, parrot perches, forcing a victim to drink urine, and beating a 4-year-old child to make its mother talk. Vast numbers of Latin Americans have thus suffered not only the oppression of poverty itself, but many also have suffered from the violent repression of governments resistant to change.

Conscientization

A new or heightened awareness of such conditions triggered the responses that led to liberation theology. Without such awareness, and without the compassion and indignation such conditions evoke, liberation theology would never have developed. We would romanticize liberation theology, however, if we assumed that each liberation theologian gained this awareness initially through some jarring personal encounter with the poor. Several factors within the church and within society at large conspired to create a more general awareness of the misery afflicting the poor in Latin America. In the 1950s and 60s the social mission of the church became more activated through groups like the Young Christian Students and Young Christian Workers. In Brazil, Paulo Freire launched his educational movement among the poor, and the institutional church inaugurated a grass-roots movement of education (MEB) to evangelize the poor. The political climate in several countries greatly affected the awakening of new awareness. Brazil and Argentina had "populist" governments that attempted social reforms. Universities and student groups became centers of political activism. The Cuban revolution (1959) stirred Latin American patriotism and lent weight to more radical political strategies.

Juan Luis Segundo claims that the university context most influenced the initial development of liberation theology. Christian students, influenced at the outset by Marxist students and professors, began to call into question the whole social order and the ideologies used to support it. Theologians working with these students began to question the non-Christian ideologies built into theology itself and into society as a whole. The "first line" of liberation theology, as I noted in discussing Segundo's views in the Introduction, stressed conversion of the middle class. It sought to awaken Christians to commit themselves to liberating activities for and with the poor. Out of this first line a second line of liberation theology developed, one in which theologians have sought to learn from the poor, especially in work with Christian base communities.[13]

Other liberation theologians with whom I spoke in Latin America would challenge this explanation. They attribute the development of new awareness more to the influx of priests and religious working and living directly with the poor, and to the conscientization experienced by lay "delegates of the Word" once they began to reflect with their communities on the conditions in which they lived. Still others may have simply found the writings of other theologians or church documents, such as Pope Paul VI's *Populorum Progressio* or the documents of Medellín, as giving the initial impetus to their own process of conscientization.

Gustavo Gutiérrez has given us an account of his own reactions when he first began to work with the poor years ago:

> I discovered three things. I discovered that poverty was a destructive thing, something to be fought against and destroyed, not merely something which was the object of our charity. Secondly, I discovered that poverty was not accidental. The fact that these people are poor and not rich is not just a matter of chance, but the result of a structure. It was a structural question. Thirdly, I discovered that poor people were a social class. When I discovered that poverty was something to be fought against . . . it became crystal clear that in order to serve the poor, one had to move into political action.[14]

Part of the process of conscientization involved the second step noted in Gutiérrez's account, an awareness of the "causal" factors that produce poverty. This led to the adoption of different methods of social analysis, including the controversial use of Marxist analysis and of dependency theory, to find more effective ways of analyzing conditions in order to respond to them effectively.

Commitment

In the process leading from conscientization to commitment, faith plays an essential role. Even the strongest critics of liberation theology will generally acknowledge that liberation theologians have acted with good — though critics might add "misguided" — intentions, and that Christians *should* be concerned about the poor. Awareness of the extensiveness and destructiveness of poverty triggered responses of Christian compassion and indignation. These responses would lead to theological reflection, to "judging" situations in Latin America in light of the Christian message. Liberation theology would ask how the Bible speaks to these situations and how Christians ought to respond to the world of poverty, suffering, and oppression that surrounds them. The response, they realized, must involve more than contemplation. It involves "acting." Jesus asked for a response of action: "I was hungry and you gave me food" (Mt 25:35). Christians must seek, the Boffs assert, effective actions that will eliminate injustice and poverty: "We can be followers of Jesus and true Christians only by making common cause with the poor and working out the gospel of liberation."[15] Liberation theology thus involves from the outset a commitment to the poor, to a liberating praxis. The aspirations of the poor for change, and the engagement of many Christian groups in their behalf, were, it should be added, an important part of the experience that prompted liberation theology.

Theology itself should contribute to bringing about needed changes. An essential purpose of knowledge, many liberation theologians would say, is to transform the world. Jon Sobrino, in introducing his *Christology at the Crossroads,* makes this point by distinguishing two phases or aspects of response to the Enlightenment in Europe. The first response aimed at understanding the world; the second, made famous by Marx, stressed changing the world.[16] Hugo Assmann and Rubem Alves go even further. Assmann insists that the task of transforming the world is so intimately linked to the interpretation of the world that the latter is seen to be impossible without the former:

> Reflection ceases to have a world of its own and becomes simply a critical function of action; its world and its truth are experience itself, and there is no more flight to a verbal world decked with ontological considerations that reflect man's inability to deal with the real problems.[17]

Or in the words of Rubem Alves, "Truth is the name given by the historical community to those actions which were, are, and will be effective for the liberation of man."[18]

Commitment should manifest itself in time spent working directly with the poor in the struggle for liberation. The Italian Marxist Antonio Gramsci spoke of "organic intellectuals" who engage directly in helping workers to educate and organize themselves.[19] Some liberation theologians have adopted this expression to define their own role. Thus Leonardo and Clodovis Boff describe liberation theologians as organic intellectuals with one foot in centers of study and the other foot within the community.[20] The Boffs also see liberation theology as a phenomenon much broader than the work done by professional theologians. Liberation theology operates at three levels: the professional work of theologians; the pastoral work of bishops, priests, religious, and lay pastoral agents; and the popular expression and building of faith in base communities. The Boffs believe, however, that theologians must have *some* contact with the poor to do liberation theology effectively. Here too they make use of a triple division to indicate different forms or levels of contact: a somewhat restricted level with periodic visits to base communities or advising them; alternating periods of scholarly work with periods of pastoral work in a community; living and working permanently with the people.[21]

This threefold level does appear to cover the actual practice of most liberation theologians. Some with whom I spoke in Latin America have Masses in poor barrios on weekends; three married women theologians, with families in Rio de Janeiro, manage to meet regularly with the poor in Bible groups or with pastoral workers; some theologians like Clodovis Boff spend part of the year working directly with the poor; Gutiérrez lives in a lower-class barrio in Lima and helps run a parish there. Some may have quite minimal contact; Segundo does not view liberation theology as requiring this direct participation (see the Introduction); he has, however, met weekly to discuss theology with a group that includes teachers and social workers who work with the poor.

One might, of course, question whether "contact" with the poor really constitutes a "praxis" of liberation, for praxis suggests involvement in community organizing and political struggles. (Even this involvement does occur, however; Leonardo Boff was arrested for participation in a demonstration during my 1988 visit to Brazil.) One might also ask whether liberation theologians have created for themselves a set of criteria nearly impossible for any one person to fulfill adequately: expertise in theology itself, active involvement in the praxis of liberation, and the competence in social sciences needed to do careful social analysis—in addition to writing, teaching, conferences, and speaking engagements. We shall see in the following section how praxis and social sciences form a part of the methodology of liberation theology.

METHODOLOGY IN LIBERATION THEOLOGY

Liberation theologians see themselves, in Gutiérrez's words, as proposing "a new way to do theology."[22] I will explore this new way more formally now. All theology involves reflection on scripture and formulating its message in a more systematic way, using different unifying concepts such as salvation and redemption. In order to be relevant, theology must also address human needs and aspirations. Theology thus brings to scripture certain questions drawn from life's problems. It also often borrows from other disciplines—traditionally, most often from philosophy—certain categories or modes of thinking that may help to illuminate and systematize the data given in revelation.

The lived experience that has most shaped liberation theology we have already noted: the experience of massive poverty in Latin America together with new aspirations and efforts to bring about a change. Gutiérrez made this experience of responding to the sufferings and struggles of the poor the basis of his theological method. We will take up first his definition of liberation theology, adding to it a discussion of the distinctive contribution of Carlos Mesters.

Liberation theology also challenged the traditional reliance of theology on methods drawn from philosophy. To understand the situation of the poor in Latin America, and to guide an effective praxis leading to liberation, philosophy no longer seemed an adequate tool. Liberation theologians turned instead to the social sciences. For an understanding of their role in liberation theology we will look especially at the work of Clodovis Boff. The use of social analysis and the experiences related to praxis triggered from the outset suspicion and questions about the way in which theology and other expressions of Christianity have traditionally been presented. Segundo has formulated in greatest detail this method of questioning, so I will examine his thought on this third aspect.

As noted earlier, these do not constitute separate models, nor do they represent stages in the process of doing theology. All three form an integral part of the same general process; but in separating them we can see more clearly how each contributes. In the first part of this chapter I included, without formalization, some reference to "seeing, judging, and acting"—a formula borrowed from Young Christian Worker groups of the 1930s–1960s. Some liberation theologians have used this formula as a popular way of presenting the methodology of liberation theology: seeing—by recognizing and then analyzing conditions; judging—by faith and theological reflection; acting—through commitment to liberating praxis. I have avoided using this formula more extensively because, as a borrowed expression, it explains less effectively the distinctiveness of liberation theology's methodology, and because it suggests a neatly ordered thought process that I suspect rarely occurs in the way theologians or ordinary Christians operate. It may prove helpful as a group technique, but even for this use it risks the danger of oversimplifying analysis or choosing some one or two biblical texts as the basis for actions. Serious theologizing and serious efforts of liberating praxis require much more.

Critical Reflection on Praxis

In *A Theology of Liberation,* Gutiérrez offered what still remains the best-known statement of the method of liberation theology. He begins this work with a discussion of the purpose and method of this new way of doing theology. The book, he says, will attempt to reflect on the experiences of men and women who have committed themselves to a process of liberation from exploitation and oppression. The classical tasks of theology involved first an attempt to gain wisdom that would guide Christian spiritual development. Then, from the twelfth century on, theology began to establish itself as a science, to present the faith in clear rational categories. Liberation theology recognizes these as permanent functions of all theological thinking. But, Gutiérrez continues, it gives more stress to the importance of "praxis," of actively living out one's faith.[23]

"Confronted by an unjust society, Christians feel keenly that they cannot claim to be Christians without a commitment to liberation."[24] More formal theological reflection may then follow, but faith itself calls first for commitment. Thus Gutiérrez observes:

> The Christian community professes "a faith which works through charity." It is—at least it ought to be—real charity, action, and commitment to the service of men. Theology is a reflection, a critical attitude. Theology *follows:* it is the second step.[25]

Gutiérrez then defines liberation theology as "a critical reflection on Christian praxis in the light of the Word."[26] Controversy would focus on the importance given to "praxis" in this definition. In the pages preceding this definition, Gutiérrez gives eight different reasons for the stress on praxis. The centrality of charity in Christian life expresses a commitment to praxis by emphasizing living out one's faith through actions. But other developments have also pointed to the importance of relating faith to action: developments in spirituality ("the contemplative in action"), new attention in theology to revelation as illuminating the human situation, the life and activity of the church as a focus of theology, the Vatican II method of reading "the signs of the times," Maurice Blondel's philosophy of human action, the influence of Marx's idea of praxis, and finally the place of "historical praxis," of Christians seeking to "do" the truth. All these dimensions merit noting, though critics focus only on the last two: on the Marxist connotations of praxis, and on using historical praxis, rather than Christian doctrines, as the starting point for theological reflection.

Gutiérrez does not define praxis, though in a later work he says that it involves "a transforming activity marked and illuminated by Christian love."[27] Praxis does not mean simply activism; it connotes transforming activity *guided by* theory and goals. Gutiérrez emphasizes the motivating force (Christian love) behind praxis; Marxists stress the social analysis that guides revolutionary activity. But social analysis also constitutes an integral part of liberation theology, as the next section on Clodovis Boff's formulations will make evident.

Commenting on the evolution of the use of praxis (or practice) in liberation theology, Pablo Richard observes that Gutiérrez first used it (1964–1968) to refer to the pastoral activity of the church: from a Christendom model of relating the church to the world, to a New Christendom, to maturity in faith, and to the prophetic pastoral approach favored by liberation theology. Then critical reflection on praxis became focused on the political practices of Christians, especially the militant involvement of priests, religious, and lay leaders, and on the questions their involvement evoked. Finally, says Richard, critical reflection concentrated more on the activity and movements of the popular classes, for liberation theology believes that the poor must become agents of their own history.[28]

The prepositions used to describe "critical reflection on (de) praxis" also underwent various transformations to emphasize involvement "in" as well as reflection "on" praxis (en y sobre), or "from" (desde) praxis, to emphasize the place from which theological reflection develops. In his own exposition of liberation theology, J.B. Libânio uses all these prepositions and others. Liberation theology, he says, is involved in practice; it is a theology of praxis; it is directed for praxis; and it operates from praxis, such that the poor influence theology itself.[29] In the early 1980s, Gutiérrez began also to speak of practice and contemplation as sources for theological reflection. I will defer discussion of this change, however, to the final pages of chapter 5.

Critics of liberation theology focus on the Marxist connotations of praxis and on using praxis as a criterion of truth. Gutiérrez most often uses praxis to connote a Christian living out of the faith and he clearly says that praxis must be reflected upon "in the light of" the word of God. But his use of the expression "historical praxis" creates problems because it covers such a broad extension of activities.

When Gutiérrez begins to treat historical praxis more concretely, in chapters 6 and 7 of A Theology of Liberation, he describes a wide array of movements and groups that fall under the general heads of "the process of liberation in Latin America" and "the church in the process of liberation." These processes involved ranges of events from the formation of guerilla groups to bishops speaking out against injustices. As a basis for generating some new theological concepts, such as liberation, such a broadly-based praxis might suffice. But in determining concretely the direction that liberating praxis should take, this same broad base seems hardly adequate. It may suggest some very general goals (for example, economic and political participation of the poor in determining their own destiny), but actual praxis also involves conflicting strategies of change (for example, nonviolence versus armed struggle, or pragmatic short-term gains versus uncompromising demands), in addition to addressing conditions in very different political situations. The Boffs offer a schematic example of how critical reflection on praxis could be used in reference to struggles concerning land distribution.[30] More pointed reflections seem to occur among Christian groups in specific situations. But one finds few concrete examples of critical reflection on specific problems and strategies in liberation theology itself. A move in that direction, along with the development of some explicit ethical criteria for judging the best actions to take, would greatly advance the work of liberation theology, in my judgment.

The discussion above assumes use of the term "praxis" in a socio-political sense as activities that serve to transform society. Gutiérrez's own works, in recent years, on spirituality and understanding the world of the poor, have implicitly broadened the meaning of praxis to include all that the poor "experience" in their lives—their sufferings, their joys, and their experiences of God in the daily struggle to survive. The word "experience," on the other hand, could suggest passivity. What Gutiérrez and other liberation theologians reflect upon, in their growing emphasis on learning from the poor, is the "action" of the poor in confronting their lives. Active involvement in decisions comes closer to the meaning of praxis as transforming activity.

In this broadened sense of praxis, the work of Carlos Mesters merits special mention. Mesters, a Dutch Carmelite who has spent most of his priestly life in Brazil, has pioneered in efforts to present the Bible in a language accessible to the poor, and to give voice to their experience of God through the Bible. I might have waited to discuss his efforts in a later chapter on base communities. But his work does involve a very distinctive methodology, one that involves reflection on the lives and actions of the poor. It would seem, then, to fit justifiably in this chapter.

In his *Defenseless Flower* Mesters provides an explanation of the elements he believes must be present for the Bible to attain its objective: enabling God to speak to the people, to give an understanding of events in human lives, and to instill in them new power to live in hope and love.[31] The first element involves reflection on reality (pre-text). God's "first book" is life itself; God communicates God's self through nature, history, and our personal lives. Without this reality the Bible would be like a seed outside the ground or a branch without a trunk. The sin we created in society, however, impedes us from finding God in this first book of life, so God gave us a second book, the Bible, so that we can decipher our world and transform it.

The second element focuses on study of the Bible itself (text). The Bible must be studied with great seriousness and discipline. We must find what God means, not what we want to hear. We must guard against manipulating the text to favor our own views. The third element involves a communitarian lived experience of faith (con-text). Without this communal sharing, the Bible's words will never become "music in the hearts of the listener." The Bible was born within a community of faith; it is a book of the community and for the community; so within the community will its message be fully understood. Understanding the Bible does not flow simply from study. It depends far more on the inspiration and action of the Holy Spirit within the listening community, inspiring a disheartened, oppressed people to experience the power and strength it needs to seek freedom and liberation.

Mesters illustrates these elements at work in Luke's story of the disciples of Emmaus (Luke 24). Reflection on reality (pre-text): Jesus got the disciples to talk about their problems, about the frustration, sadness, and disheartedness they had experienced with the death of the one they hoped would be their savior. Study of the Bible itself (text): Jesus then used the Bible to show the real meaning of these events "in the light of the word of God." This demanded a deep knowledge of scripture and respect for *its* meaning, not manipulating the text to fit one's own ideas, as the Jewish leaders too often did. Communitarian living of faith in the resurrection (con-text): Jesus walked with the disciples, conversed with them, and created an ambiance of openness. Then he stayed with them, gave thanks with them, and shared eucharist with them (the breaking of the bread). Within this community that Jesus formed, the disciples' eyes were opened, their hearts burned within them, and they experienced the joy of the resurrection.

Mesters then turns to the experiences of various Christian base communities. They live in conditions of oppression, but after reflecting on Mark's account of Jesus walking on the water (Mark 6:45–51), members of one group witnessed to their personal experiences of Jesus empowering them. "I got courage to speak to the police." "A neighbor gave me money to buy medicine for my sick daughter." "Fr. Henrique visited me when I was sick; I started feeling better and had the strength to get up when he left."[32] These examples of "popular exegesis" indicate a great liberty taken with the Gospel text, but a faithfulness to its essential meaning nonetheless. They speak to personal needs (pre-text). They emerge as inspirations and grace from within a community sharing (con-text). They nevertheless reflect faithfulness to the Bible (text), because they focus on the courage, power, and hope that the Gospel story was intended to inspire.

Mesters' work illustrates the method of "critical reflection on Christian praxis in the light of the Word" if praxis is taken in the broad sense of the experiences and active engagement of the poor in confronting the oppressive conditions in which they live. It involves critical reflection in setting down criteria (pre-text, text, con-text) for evaluating the response of the poor to the word of God, and it provides a distinctive approach for understanding the Christian message from a perspective of the poor.

The Role of Social Sciences in Liberation Theology

Clodovis Boff, in *Theology and Praxis,* seeks to explain how liberation theology, or more generally political theology, makes special use of the social sciences. *Introducing Liberation Theology,* which Boff coauthored with his brother Leonardo, offers a more popular presentation of his overall description of the method used in liberation theology. We might begin with this more introductory work to show first how the use of social sciences fits into the whole process of doing liberation theology.

Like Gutiérrez, the Boffs insist that commitment to liberation and participation in the liberation process must precede theology proper. "Before we can do theology we have to 'do' liberation."[33] Without a living link to living practice, liberation theology would be simply a matter or words. But given this involvement, liberation theology proceeds in three main stages, which correspond to the stages used in pastoral work: seeing, judging, acting. The Boffs designate the main steps in liberation theology as three mediations (i.e., three ways by which we gain an understanding of God's word and presence in relation to conditions in human life):

> Socio-analytical (or historico-analytical) mediation operates in the sphere of the world of the oppressed. It tries to find out why the oppressed are oppressed. Hermeneutical mediation operates in the sphere of God's world. It tries to discern what God's plan is for the poor. Practical mediation operates in the sphere of action. It tries to discover the courses of action that need to be followed so as to overcome oppression in accordance with God's plan.[34]

The socio-analytical mediation used by liberation theologians asks about the causes of poverty and oppression. This mediation looks first at socioeconomic poverty. It rejects explanations that attribute poverty to laziness or to backwardness. It sees "dialectical" explanations as most accurate: poverty results from an economic system (capitalism) that exploits workers and excludes others (the unemployed or underemployed) from the whole productive process. It uses Marxism, but "purely as an instrument," which offers certain "methodological pointers" for understanding the world of the oppressed: for example, the importance of economic factors and the power of ideologies. But this mediation also looks to other forms of social oppression, such as discrimination against blacks, against indigenous Indians, and against women.[35]

The hermeneutic mediation looks at "what God has to say" about conditions of oppression, what faith and scripture tell us about oppression and liberation. The hermeneutic used by liberation theology does not give the only legitimate reading of the Bible, nor does it claim to focus on all the most important themes in the Bible. It gives its attention to those themes most relevant to the situation of the poor. Thus it favors certain books of the Bible—for example, Exodus, which recounts the liberation of the Israelites and their formation as the people of God; the prophets, for their vindication of the rights of the poor; the Gospels, because of the centrality of the divine person of Jesus and his liberating message and actions; the Acts of the Apostles, for their portrayal of a free and liberating Christian community; and Revelation, for its symbolic expression of the struggles between God's people and all the monsters of history.[36]

Practical mediation, the Boffs observe, stresses the importance of action flowing from the other two mediations. Liberation theology begins with commitment and involvement, and it leads back to action for justice and love, for renewal of the church, and for transformation of society. This action for the poor will involve a faith that is "above all else political," but a faith that cannot be *reduced* to politics because faith always includes moments of contemplation and thanksgiving that transcend political realities. This practical mediation incorporates several factors: deciding what is historically possible or viable in a given situation; defining strategies and tactics (favoring nonviolent methods); coordinating micro-actions with a macro-perspective; linking with other historical forces in society; and drawing up programs for action.[37]

These three mediations form the major divisions in Clodovis Boff's *Theology and Praxis*. Boff's penchant for often abstruse academic terms and distinctions — sometimes dozens of them in a chapter — makes reading his work unnecessarily tedious and difficult. (Some readers may wish to skip over the next several paragraphs). It addresses, however, an issue that goes beyond the description of the three stages given in *Introducing Liberation Theology*. Boff's longer work strives to show how a theology of the political is produced, and how in particular such a theology makes use of social sciences.

Boff begins by distinguishing between first theology, which deals with specifically religious realities such as grace and the incarnation, and second theology, which deals with secular realities such as sexuality, culture, or politics. Liberation theology, or a theology of the political, falls under the heading of second theology, but Boff insists that it should not be treated as just one aspect of life, as one might do in a theology of marriage. The liberation theme affects the whole of theology.[38]

The socio-analytic mediation involves the use of social sciences to define and describe the "political" upon which theology will reflect. Liberation theology grows out of a political praxis aimed at transforming society. But this political praxis must be mediated through assimilation of the social sciences, through an understanding of the socio-political world. Thus theologians must use social sciences if the theology of the political is to be "rigorously scientific."[39]

Boff insists, however, that theology must be vigilant to retain its autonomy. Though social conditions influence theology, it must use its own principles and seek its own goal of truth. To discuss the political, theology must know what it is discussing; hence social science becomes intrinsic to second theology and to the theology of the political. Theology must retain its autonomy, however, by resisting two pitfalls: first, the danger of reducing faith to politics, and second, the danger of an apolitical escapism. Theology becomes ideological when it presents itself as *the* theology, as legitimate and true for all times. Boff believes that European theology failed to recognize its historical, cultural context and hence presented itself as "theology itself."[40]

Boff then looks at concrete theories within the social sciences that might serve as the needed socio-analytic mediation. Since, says Boff, most mediations in Latin America are connected with Marxism, theology must consider its claims. He rejects Marxism's philosophical aspect, its dialectical materialism, as reductionist and dictatorial. He accepts, on the other hand, Marxist social analysis as legitimate in principle, though he notes that its status as a "science" remains quite problematic. Boff believes that a "dialectical" view of society, which recognizes the fact of struggle and conflict in society, as does Marxism, corresponds more accurately to conditions of oppression in Latin America than does a "functionalist" social science, which stresses order and equilibrium of social forces.[41]

Boff then turns to the hermeneutic mediation, which deals with interpreting scripture. He uses a model drawn from the French Marxist Louis Althusser to explain how theology proceeds methodologically to reflect on the political. Althusser himself sought to correct a "vulgar" Marxist view that ideas simply copy or reflect reality. Science, Althusser argued, involves the *production* of knowledge. When social scientists use basic data to construct theories, even the basic data have already been conceptualized. For example (my own): even to speak of the "poor" involves conceptualizing one group by way of comparison with other sectors of society. Theology also uses concepts to explain the basic data of faith. Thus, Boff notes, St. Thomas Aquinas used first principles drawn from faith to develop a deductive science of theological reflection.[42]

All scientific thought, whether in the social sciences or in theology, involves reflection on a basic set of data (1st generalities) through the use of a set of concepts (2nd generalities) to produce a general theory (3rd generality). Thus in first theology, which deals with specifically religious issues, one might reflect on Christ's preaching and actions (lst generalities) using the concept of "savior" (a 2nd generality) to develop a theory of salvation (3rd generality). In the social sciences one might reflect on the situation of workers (lst generality) using the concept of "social class" (2nd generality) to develop a theology of class struggle (3rd generality).

Boff then explains how hermeneutic mediation draws upon socio-analytic mediation. Theology looks at a social situation (lst generality) as mediated by the social sciences (2nd generality). In Latin America use of social sciences has led to a theory of dependency as that which best explains conditions in Latin America. Dependency calls for a strategy of liberation. The theologian makes use of this socio-analytic explanation or mediation to develop a *theology* of liberation. In first theology, which deals with specifically religious realities, the concept of liberation does not appear. Theologians take from first theology the concept of salvation, which appears *like* human liberation, and from the social sciences they take the concept of liberation. In second theology, the socio-analytic concept of liberation is translated into a theological category so that liberation is seen *as* God's salvation. Through this linking of a socio-analytic category (liberation) to a first theology concept (salvation) a theology of liberation is "produced." Theologians do not begin with a theological concept of liberation, for it is not given in first theology; rather they work *upon* the socio-analytic concept of liberation to produce liberation theology.[43]

In combining these mediations Boff calls for "creative fidelity" in interpreting scripture. A theologian must remain faithful to scripture; one cannot fasten upon some meaning simply because it fits one's interests. Moreover, one cannot find a *direct* correspondence between scripture related to its historical context and present-day concerns related to their context. For example, says Boff, one cannot establish a direct correspondence between the liberation of the Israelites out of Egypt and liberation of the oppressed in Latin America. But scripture remains open to new meaning, "pregnant with all the virtual senses that will come to light upon contact with historical currency."[44] Theologians need, then, to interpret scripture to fit present situations, just as the evangelists and St. Paul interpreted the teachings of Jesus to fit their situation.

In dealing with the third mediation, practical mediation, Boff offers some comments about "praxis" that will prove important in assessing a criticism directed against liberation theology. Commitment and engagement, Boff notes, do not guarantee the quality of one's analysis or theology. They do, however, condition what one selects as objects of study and concern.[45] Moreover, the theologian who truly shares in the life of the poor can better articulate their faith and problems. But praxis itself cannot be the criterion for theological truth; theology remains autonomous.[46] Praxis shows the capacity of faith for social transformation, but it must always be tested by moral criteria, by an ethico-critical determination. "All practice must be evaluated."[47]

Most of the controversy over the use of social sciences in liberation theology relates to the use of Marxist analysis especially, and also to the use of dependency theory. These issues I will take up in detail in chapters 6–9. I might simply note at this point that the Boffs defend some uses of Marxist analysis but do not give great prominence to use of Marxism. Clodovis Boff's comment about praxis, however, merits an immediate reflection. Hugo Assmann, cited earlier in this chapter, seemed to identify truth and praxis, and critics of liberation theology have attacked this identification. Boff's comments provide an important corrective; he argues that praxis does not justify itself but must be subject to critico-ethical evaluation. His comments on the autonomy of theology, having its own truth, also bears upon this issue.

By way of an immediate assessment, I would like to have seen Boff also stress the autonomy of the social sciences with objective truth as their goal. Boff "opts" for dialectical over functional analysis. As a starting point one could justify this choice, but options tend to reinforce the selection of one set of data to the exclusion of others. The search for truth requires openness to critiques of any given form of analysis. Most liberation theologians, including Boff, would accept this principle, and significant changes have occurred in respect to the use of dependency theory (see chapter 7). Search for truth, however, should supersede the value one places on any given form of analysis.

Boff's analysis of the three mediations used in liberation theology provides a very useful overview of important elements in liberation theology's method. His description, however, could give the impression that liberation theologians use these mediations in the successive order that Boff presents, as progressive "stages" of reflection. But some liberation theologians begin with praxis; others with suspicion of prevailing hermeneutics; they do not all simply proceed from the first to the third mediation. Also missing from Boff's account is any explicit attention to the discernment required to use these mediations. The mediations need themselves to be mediated. The use of social sciences does not simply "tell us" how social reality should be interpreted; we must weigh competing explanations. Biblical hermeneutics often point to conflicting interpretations of a given biblical passage, and adapting revelation from the past to the present requires its own mediating discernment. Gutiérrez's concept of "utopia" expresses this need to go beyond any "givens" in social sciences or in hermeneutics and to use imaginative and prudential judgments in determining Christian practice.

Questioning Ideologies

For Juan Luis Segundo liberation theology has as its major task challenging the non-Christian ideological elements in theology and in traditional presentations of the Christian message. The very title of his book, *The Liberation of Theology,* expresses this goal. I will consider it first and then look at his *Faith and Ideologies,* noting also how he applies his method in studying the historical Jesus. In the latter book Segundo defines ideology as any system of means to reach some goal; in *The Liberation of Theology* he tends to follow the more common use of ideology as the ideas and symbols that express and promote the interests and values of some given group or culture (as, for example, the ideological expression: "In the United States everyone has an equal opportunity to succeed").

Traditional theology, says Segundo, presented itself and still presents itself as independent of present-day conditions and ideologies. It recognizes its dependence on the past because Christian truth depends on the Bible. But it believes that it can apply divine revelation to the present world without being influenced by the ideologies and struggles of that world.

Segundo challenges such a view. The liberation theologian believes that all ideas, including those in theology, contain ideological elements that often reflect the language and the values of the dominant, prevailing culture. Theology therefore requires the use of disciplines that not only look to the past but help to explain the present as well. Segundo calls the methodology that combines these disciplines the *hermeneutic circle*. "Hermeneutic" means having to do with intepretation. The "circle" involves interpreting the word of God afresh in the light of present conditions, striving to change reality, and then reinterpreting the word of God again.[48]

This hermeneutic circle involves especially a "suspicion" of ideological elements in prevailing interpretations of the Christian message. Liberation theology thus strives to uncover these elements, to "deideologize" theology, and then to look at revelation anew. Segundo notes four decisive factors in this methodology. First, a new experience of reality (for example, new awareness of the conditions of the poor) leads one to suspect ideologies operating in society (for example, in the way some Latin American governments present themselves as defenders of Christian civilization). Second, this suspicion leads one to question and analyze the whole ideological structure of society, including its theology. One begins to suspect that the church's alleged neutrality in politics masks a support for the status quo, and that the church's pastoral ministry ignores social conflicts that divide society. Third, this new sense leads one to suspect the way the Bible has been interpreted, for example, seeing only charity and not justice in its message. Fourth, this exegetical suspicion leads to a new understanding of the Bible, one that shows a God very much dedicated to liberating the poor.[49] The first two steps deal more with analysis of political and religious ideologies and institutions, and the latter two with biblical hermeneutics.

This method borrows, to some extent, from Marx's critique of ideologies. Marx viewed the socio-cultural ideas dominant in a particular society—for example, the defense of self-interest and profit-seeking in capitalist society—as reflecting the special interests of a dominant class in society. He viewed religion as an escape from social misery on the part of the poor, and as a justification for the status quo on the part of the rich. Segundo, however, sees Marx's critique of religion as inadequate because it failed to "complete the hermeneutic circle." Marx saw *only* the ideological element in religion. He failed to appreciate the positive values and potential of religion, and consequently he did not go back to religion to interpret it anew.[50]

In explaining the hermeneutic circle Segundo uses the idea of "suspicion" to question ideological elements that have come to mask the authentic message of the gospel. In *Faith and Ideologies* he seeks to distinguish faith from ideology to show how values of faith may not be effectively expressed in the means or ideology used to actualize them. Segundo rejects definitions that present faith and ideologies as contending forces. All faith expresses itself in some ideology; all ideologies presuppose some underlying faith. Segundo rejects, therefore, any viewing of Christianity simply as faith, or of Marxism simply as an ideology.

Faith is constituted by the *values* that structure and give meaning to our life. We derive these values from others, from referential witnesses whom we trust and believe in, for we value persons above all. Faith is anthropological—that is, it is a dimension in every human life and is not religious per se. Ideology is any system of means to some goal. An ideology builds on faith values and expresses these values in principles or modes of action.[51] This distinction establishes Segundo's basis for examining Christianity. Christianity involves more than faith; it expresses itself in ideologies that may not be Christian. Segundo uses this same distinction to argue that Marxism is not simply an ideology but also includes faith.[52]

He makes an important distinction also between faith and religion. Faith is anthropological; it deals with absolute human values. Jesus made the promotion of human welfare an absolute value. Religion, in contrast, often considers its own maintenance and growth as its principal values. It tends to "sacralize" its own tenets, structures, and traditions. Jesus challenged the Pharisees on this score. They made observance of laws and traditions more important than the good of humans.

Placing human welfare over the structures of religion does not mean, however, putting human concerns over God's will. For "the welfare of human beings is always *God's* cause and God's work." Hence "God's commandment, ultimately, is to love human beings."[53] We can therefore also say that Jesus' faith, if anthropological, was also religious in the sense that it was directed to God and to the values that God holds dear.

God's own central concern or value finds expression in the prayer that Jesus taught us: "Thy kingdom come." We pray and work for the coming of a just society marked by loving relationships between all persons. The call of the kingdom appeals to preexisting values in us, for example, the value of love; but it demands that these values become priorities over concerns like money and security. All faith involves a transcendent element, something not yet achieved but which we believe can be—for example, the kingdom of God. Faith also involves trusting in persons who witness to values and hope in their realization—for example, believing in Jesus and his apostles. The transcendent element in Christian faith does not come from believing that the words of the Bible are divine, or from miracles and other proofs, but from faith in Jesus and his apostles who lead us to affirm that "in the end" it will prove better to act as Jesus did and taught.[54]

The values expressed in Christian faith remain constant. The means of effectively actualizing these values can change. Giving alms to the poor may have been efficacious in Jesus' time. Today, says Segundo, it is not. To love effectively today requires changing unjust systems and structures. Living out Christianity involves a "learning process," finding in each age the ideology (means) needed to make Christian faith (values) effective.

Segundo uses these distinctions in his study, *The Historical Jesus of the Synoptics.* The heart of the gospel message lies in the faith it offers: its values and the meaning it gives to life. When Jesus preached the kingdom he appealed to the value of human welfare, of living in solidarity with the poor of the world, and seeking to create a more just and humane society.

Segundo repeats his views on the dual elements involved in any faith: a transcendent hope and believing in those who witness to certain values.[55] He repeats as well his distinction between faith and religion, again noting that Jesus judged religion by the value of human welfare. "Man was not made for the Sabbath." He acknowledges that the ideology or means embraced by Jesus focused on conversion of the heart and on interpersonal relations, and not on socio-political changes in structures. But again he argues that Christian faith today should look to new means, to make Jesus' faith values truly effective.[56]

The faith-ideology distinction appears distinctive of Segundo's own theology. Its very distinctiveness, however, creates a problem. In his more recent works noted above, Segundo uses ideology as a neutral term, as "any" means. But in most of liberation theology, and in his own earlier works, ideology had primarily negative connotations, as a set of ideas that impede recognition of the true Christian message. In fact, one could very well summarize the distinctive method of liberation theology as a challenging of ideological elements in traditional modes of expressing reality and Christian truths, leading to a new understanding from the perspective of the poor.

Critics of liberation theology accuse it of succumbing to "false ideologies" (with Marxism as the primary temptation) or as distorting the teachings of Christianity. Ironically, one of the major impetuses for liberation theology came from a conviction that the church itself had succumbed to false ideologies by supporting unjust and repressive rulers, or that it had distorted the Christian message by presenting it as apolitical. While some military rulers or dominant oligarchies may have consciously manipulated the message of Christianity by presenting themselves as "defenders of Christian civilization," most of the ideological elements in church teachings have developed unintentionally. They simply reflect the dominant culture, liberation theologians would say. The very strength of these ideologies comes from the "appearance" of being what Christianity has always taught or what seems best for society. Almost all the major themes in liberation theology deal with some form of deideologizing prevailing ways of thinking and replacing them with new perspectives.

FROM CRITIQUE OF IDEOLOGIES TO NEW PARADIGMS

As a conclusion to this section on methodology, and as a prelude to discussing critics, I might illustrate this questioning of ideologies and discovery of new understanding with several examples grouped under the headings of Boff's three mediations. The examples will offer also an overall picture of some of the most important issues treated in liberation theology.

The Socio-Analytical Mediation. First, in looking at Latin America's problems, liberation theologians became convinced that the causes of poverty and oppression are structural. Hence many came to speak of "sinful structures" and "social sin." Though in recent years church documents have recognized the existence of unjust structures (for example, concentration of wealth and power), they have more traditionally viewed change as a matter of personal conversion. *Rerum Novarum* and the first social encyclicals clearly emphasized "moral appeals"; change would occur when rulers and wealthy owners returned to Christian moral principles and did their duty as Christians. Questioning the adequacy of such appeals and asserting the need for structural changes have become key positions in liberation theology.

Second, liberation theologians from the outset identified these structures as an exploitative capitalist system and as Latin America's situation of dependency in respect to Europe and the United States. On this point the prevailing modes of analysis came not from the church but from leaders in society. The prevailing wisdom viewed Latin America as "backward" and in need of the "developmental" models that had proved successful in Europe and North America. The questioning of this model became all but constitutive of liberation theology. The very term "liberation," while used also in a biblical sense of God acting to liberate the poor, gave special importance to socio-political liberation from dependency.

Third, underlying most of the other positions taken by liberation theology one finds a critique of ideologies and attempts to show that doctrines and practices in the church are historically and socially conditioned. The church has traditionally presented its teachings and its own structure as "unchanging truths." Indeed certain truths, like the divinity of Christ, do remain constitutive of Christian faith. But many interpretations of doctrines and structures in the church appear products of socio-historical conditions. For example, much in the hierarchical structure of the church—formal addresses like "your excellency," robes and mitres, and hierarchical levels (pope, cardinals, archbishops, bishops, etc.)—seem clearly to reflect the social structures of the Middle Ages. For liberation theologians a more serious issue concerns the use, and sometimes manipulation, of Christianity by wealthy classes seeking to defend their own privileges: for example, claiming the "right to private property" as a Christian principle that justifies rejection of reforms calling for redistribution of land. Many liberation theologians also question "Christendom" and "New Christendom" attempts to make the institutional church the guardian of traditional values in society in return for protection by the state.

The Hermeneutical (Biblico-Theological) Mediation. First on this score came a challenge to traditional teachings that centered the concept of "salvation" almost entirely on eternal salvation in heaven. A response to massive poverty in Latin America required more than a hope for eternity. Liberation theologians found in the exodus account especially a paradigm of God's saving action *in* history and from *physical* oppression. In Jesus' preaching of the kingdom of God they found a vision of the kind of society

God intended, a reign of justice and love in which the poor would have a privileged place.

Second and closely related to this first point, liberation theologians would question the "spiritualization" and "individualization" of the gospel message. The kingdom of God became interpreted over time as a spiritual development within each person, or as a growth of the church. St. Matthew's statement of the first beatitude, "Blessed are the poor in spirit," gained precedence over St. Luke's "Blessed are the poor." God's strong defense of the poor and sharp warnings of "woe to you rich" were reduced to encouraging the rich to give alms to the poor.

Third, liberation theologians challenged the method and assumptions in European theology.[57] As Gutiérrez especially would stress, modern theology in Europe had as its fundamental question: "How can the gospels speak today to the modern, middle-class, and educated Christian?" Latin American theology must ask rather: "How can the gospels speak to the poor, to a marginalized people considered as 'nonpersons' in the modern world?" Interpreting the Bible from the "underside," from the perspective of the poor, became central to the work of the liberation theologian.

The Practical Mediation. First on this point, liberation theologians questioned priorities in respect to expressing one's faith. Following St. Thomas Aquinas who defined faith as an "assent to the truths of Christianity," traditional Christianity stressed orthodoxy as the test of one's faith, though certainly charity always held an important place. Liberation theologians believe that orthopraxis, how one lives out one's faith, should receive priority. Working with the poor to eliminate injustices should take precedence over educating the rich.

Second, the mission of the church became an important issue. While the church recognizes its responsibility to speak out on socio-political issues, even Vatican II insisted that the proper mission of the church is religious, not political.[58] The church should offer guidance and inspiration to the laity but should avoid direct political involvement. Liberation theologians believe that long-standing injustices in Latin America demand from the church a more active political involvement. Here too they see ideology at work. Political "neutrality" often operates as an implicit endorsement of ruling powers, especially when bishops and cardinals offer prayers at the inaugurations of repressive military rulers. This call for greater political involvement, and most especially Gutiérrez's call for the church to "opt for the poor in their class struggle," would evoke considerable criticism and controversy.

Third, the very nature of the church came under question. The Catholic Church has traditionally presented itself as a hierarchical church, with the mission of the church entrusted to the pope and bishops. Priests, religious, and laity "collaborate" in helping the hierarchy to carry out *its* mission. Some liberation theologians, and Leonardo Boff in particular, have challenged this top-down view of the church. They call for greater initiative from the bottom-up with the bishops serving, rather than controlling, the "people of God."

Because most of these points will come up again in later chapters, I have stated them briefly without textual citations. They give an overview of liberation themes, but they illustrate especially the kind of dialectical questioning that I see as most characteristic of liberation theology. Its challenging of traditional views has made it controversial; its development of new interpretations has gained for it attention. Most liberation theologians, in common with reform movements in the past, would see its new themes rather as a "retrieval" of the true spirit of the gospels and of early Christianity.

One could find elements of Marxism in many of these positions. Certainly the challenge of the Marxist critique of religion, religion seen as an ideological force used to pacify the poor and to justify the status quo, caused liberation theologians to look critically at prevailing views and practices in the church. But this challenge also influenced the official church; many of the papal social encyclicals were written as a response to the Marxist challenge. Liberation theologians themselves acknowledge that they have "borrowed from" Marxism. What they borrow, however, does not involve a "baptizing" of Marxist analysis and much less of the whole program and ideology of Marxism.

The Boffs speak of borrowing "methodological pointers" from Marxism. I have found Bernard Lonergan's category of "heuristic structures"—insights that prove fruitful in engendering more insights—as the best expression for the borrowing. Ricardo Planas states liberation theology's use of Marxism in almost identical terms. Marxism is used, says Planas, not in its dogmatic political aspect or as a strict scientific method, or even as a philosophy. "Instead, Marxism is seen in its broadest sense as a cultural current, and as a heuristic approach in scientific analysis and praxis, capable of inducing or stirring up new ideas."[59]

This brief discussion of the use of Marxist insights will serve as a lead into the next chapter, an initial presentation of some of the major critics and criticisms of liberation theology.

The use of Marxism by liberation theologians has quite obviously triggered some of the main charges against it.

Chapter 3

The Critics: An Overview

Even within science, new paradigms initially meet with resistance. Within theology, however, the issue involves more than just resistance to new ideas or resistance to social change. These factors undoubtedly have influenced some criticisms, but Christianity, unlike science, draws its very meaning from the past, from the scriptures and tradition that have shaped it. Faithfulness to God's word is an essential criterion for any theology. Liberation theologians recognize this and seek precisely to show that themes of liberation constitute the true meaning of God's word. Many critics, in turn, feel that liberation theology risks emptying the faith of its fullness and using it for questionable political goals.

This chapter studies briefly some critics of liberation theology, critics from Latin America, Europe, and the United States. If we cannot discuss all the liberation theologians, even less can we hope to consider all their critics. As we shall see, critics tend to repeat each other (as do the liberation theologians). But this chapter will consider representatives from each of these parts of the world. The conclusion of the chapter also offers a synopsis of the many criticisms lodged against liberation theology and makes some comments about difficulties in assessing them.

Liberation theology has not suffered from inattention; the critical books and articles in Latin America alone almost match the voluminous literature written from a liberationist perspective. In presenting the thought of liberation theologians I have tried to note some changes in their thinking over the years. A complete investigation of recent periodicals in various languages might indicate similar changes on the part of some critics. But the major criticisms first raised in the early and mid-1970s still persist, as critiques published in more recent years indicate. Many of the strongest criticisms originated in Latin America.

Latin American Critics

Cardinal Alfonso López Trujillo, past president of CELAM, stands out as the most prominent Latin American critic of liberation theology. His

1980 work *De Medellín a Puebla* combines several essays written in the course of the 1970s about various church issues. He begins with an essay about the "crisis in the priesthood," which he attributes to several causes (impatience with the implementation of Vatican II, problems with celibacy, loss of a sense of the supernatural with horizontalism put in its place, etc.). He then discusses the church, which he sees defined by communion and mystery (raising issues I will return to in chapter 11 on ecclesiology).

In a second essay he deals with the issue of conflict and reconciliation; it bears on liberation theology because he sees its stress on conflict as Marxist, in opposition to the centrality of reconciliation in Christianity. In an essay on the conference of Latin American bishops (CELAM), he defends the priority CELAM has given to the church's mission of evangelization. Evangelization does not mean regressing to the past or so spiritualizing the message of Christianity that it excludes social commitment.[1] López Trujillo presents CELAM's stance as a reasonable, moderate position between right-wing reactionary ideologies, such as Catholic "integrism" or national security ideology, and leftist liberationist groups. CELAM stands, he says, for an "integral Christian liberation," in contrast to a liberationist perspective politicized and penetrated by Marxist analysis.[2] As we will see repeatedly in critiques from the 1970s, he designates the Christians for Socialism (CFS) as the chief expression of this Christian-Marxist liberation trend. He deals also with two tendencies among base communities: one integrated into the church, the other in tension with the hierarchy.

In an essay on ecclesiological tendencies in Latin America, he blames Paulo Freire and his method of conscientization for using (as did Marx) the idea of the poor as an oppressed "social class" — a language, says López Trujillo, one does not find in the documents of Medellín. Hugo Assmann likewise converts the concept of the "people" into the poor as a class, and even into the poor as the proletariat.[3] He accuses Giulio Girardi, an Italian Christian-Marxist whom he considers one of the principal leaders of the Christians for Socialism, of subordinating faith to Marxist ideology and of creating antagonism in the church by presenting the hierarchy as representatives of the bourgeoisie.

López Trujillo includes Gutiérrez and Leonardo Boff as part of this same tendency. He blames Gutiérrez for texts that created the "atmosphere" leading to conflict in the church, but he acknowledges that Gutiérrez differs from some of his sympathizers and collaborators. Quite possibly, says López Trujillo, Gutiérrez felt obligated to use combative language and did not see all its implications. Probably today, he adds, Gutiérrez would modify his views.[4] As for Boff, López Trujillo observes that he does not speak "with the same belligerency" as the Christians for Socialism, but he uses the same ideas about the popular church.

In an essay on different theologies of liberation in Latin America, López Trujillo distinguishes Medellín's method from that of the more leftist liberation trend. The bishops at Medellín did start with reality; they recognized socio-political problems as requiring attention. But they insisted that theology be done from a faith basis (*desde la fe*). They acknowledged the need for changing structures but stressed the "call for conversion" and the need for reconciliation as more essential. The struggle for justice should not promote or add to class conflict; it should not be violent; it requires conversion of hearts and transforming attitudes.[5] In contrast, the liberation theology of Gutiérrez, Assmann, Comblin, and the CFS makes political change the whole concern of liberation theology. Hence their slogans: "All is political"; "The gospel is political"; "The church is political."[6]

López Trujillo thus distinguishes two forms of liberation theology, one an acceptable form, the other a danger to the faith. The first one (Medellín) emphasizes conversion from sin, reconciliation, and the religious mission of the church without neglecting the political. The second form, in which López Trujillo includes Gutiérrez, Assmann, Comblin, and Segundo, stresses the political-conflictive dimension of society through a reading of Marxist analysis and its imperative.[7] The remainder of the essay deals with the implications of using Marxist analysis.

Cardinal López Trujillo writes in a much more polemical style in his *Liberation or Revolution?* He answers his title question unequivocally: the liberation theology movement promotes Marxist revolution, not true Christian liberation. While he cites Gutiérrez and other liberation theologians, the quotations used most often to "verify" his criticisms originated with various activist groups like the Christians for Socialism. He charges liberationists, and by implication liberation theology, with a portrayal of Christ as a revolutionary, the exaltation of guerillas as heroes, a presumed advocacy of violence (for they accept Marxism), and denunciations of the hierarchy as bourgeois enemies for not supporting revolution.[8] Some theologians, he adds, seem to accept without hesitation Lenin's view that anything that supports the cause of class struggle and revolution is moral.[9]

As a presentation of the most extreme views made by Christian activist groups and individuals, this latter polemic might have some merit. It also indicates the extent of tensions and conflict within the church in the 1970s. It does not serve well, however, as a description or assessment of liberation theology itself.

Because I have dealt in some length with López Trujillo's critique, I will treat more briefly just one other notable critic. Roger Vekemans, S.J., works closely with López Trujillo in Colombia. Vekemans's *Teología de la liberación y cristianos por el socialismo* again underscores by its very title how much critics linked liberation theology in the 1970s with the Christians for Socialism movement. Vekemans's book begins with a brief history of the church in Latin America. He concludes the chapter by noting how liberation theology emerged from a concern to liberate the exploited masses. Its proponents felt that the church's social teachings, which urged a "third way" between capitalism and socialism, no longer had validity and that Christians must ally with existing movements. Hugo Assmann, he adds, went so far as to claim that Christianity had nothing of its own to contribute to the revolutionary process.[10]

Vekemans then takes up the various theories of social change prominent in the 1960s: modernization or development, dependency theory (which Vekemans claims really expresses only neo-Leninist views on imperialism), and the theory of marginality (which he used). The theory of marginality viewed the basic problem in Latin America as the exclusion of masses of persons (the marginal) from the resources and advantages enjoyed by privileged "inside" groups. The needed change would thus involve integrating the masses into society and enabling them to participate more fully.[11] Liberationists rejected this position; their analysis stressed Latin American dependency on Northern capitalism. They called for a class analysis of humanity's division into oppressed and oppressing classes, and saw a socialist break with world capitalism as the only solution. These positions, said Vekemans, amounted to establishing theology on errors of social analysis.[12]

Vekemans then spends some eighty pages, much of it bibliography, showing the similarity of liberation views to views of theologians and social scientists in Europe and the United States. His main theological criticisms of liberation theology deal with its use of praxis and its use of biblical texts.[13] It ultimately reduces truth to the efficacy of praxis, and the logic of this leads to a neo-Leninist ethics. It makes praxis central but says little about the content, form, or nature of praxis. Who decides, he asks, what praxis to follow and on what basis? Vekemans charges that the biblical foundations of liberation theology are based on weak and faulty hermeneutics; he cites various European theologians to make this point.

For a briefer summary of criticisms (in English) by a Latin American theologian, one might also read Bonaventure Kloppenburg's pamphlet on the eleven *Temptations for the Theology of Liberation*.[14]

European Critics

The International Theological Commission, appointed by the Vatican and made up predominately of European theologians, set up a committee in 1974 to study and evaluate the new theology of liberation. The commission met in October 1976 and formulated a document on "Human Development and Christian Salvation," which the commission viewed as a central theme in liberation theology. The commission document made no judgments about individual liberation theologians but noted "difficulties" raised by the theology as a whole. Gutiérrez had written that history is one; there are not two histories, one sacred and one profane; rather the history of salvation touches the very heart of human history. The commission focused on this issue. It acknowledged a profound link between world history and salvation history. To change inhuman conditions does form part of God's plan and Jesus did come to free us in every way. The construction of a just society "in a sense" does anticipate the inauguration of God's kingdom. But, the commission continued, in some theological movements these data come to be interpreted in a one-sided fashion such that the gospel loses its supernatural character and becomes consolidated with secular history. God's saving plan does unfold in history "but not in such a way that the force and dynamism of God's word consists totally in its function of stimulating social and political change." Faith's practice cannot be reduced to changing conditions in society; it involves also conscience formation, changes of attitude, and adoration of God.[15]

The commission issued several other cautions. Political controversy should not obliterate work for peace and reconciliation. Stimulating praxis does not constitute the main work of theology; "its more prominent function is to seek understanding of God's word." Social theories used in theology should be critically tested, especially Marxist-Leninist analyses, which harbor ideological elements that rest on debatable philosophical assumptions.[16]

The commission then took up issues relating to biblical interpretations. In respect to the exodus story the commission anticipated points that the 1986 Vatican instruction would repeat a decade later. Liberation did not mean simply escape from oppression in Egypt; it involved covenant worship solemnized on Mount Sinai. The Old Testament stresses that it is not the human being but Yahweh who effects change. Similarly, while the prophets lashed out against oppression and injustice, they did not call for revolt against oppressors. They saw unjust structures but stressed individual responsibility. The New Testament calls for change but "is not primarily concerned about the social sphere and human togetherness." It speaks primarily of liberation from death and from sin. It stresses that no genuine change in society will occur except through conversion, unless men and women are reconciled with God and with one another.[17]

Finally the commission discussed the relation between God as liberator and human liberating action. God does not replace the need for human action; God works through the hearts and minds of men and women. But full liberation deals with the whole person and hence must involve an effective change of mind and heart. We may argue, says the commission document, about how legitimate it is to speak of "institutional sin" or of "sinful structures," for the Bible speaks of sin in the first instance in terms of explicit, personal decisions. Sin does, however, penetrate social and political institutions. There does exist a clear link and unity between human development and divine salvation—but not an identity. God's promises go beyond human progress and the kingdom goes beyond anything human efforts can achieve. The commission recognizes that class differences exist and that they produce conflict, but it insists that counterviolence does not resolve the issue.[18]

If the international commission did not specify names or even specific movements, most of the points noted would be used by critics as charges against liberation theology and against Gutiérrez especially. In chapter 5, after I have considered liberation writings on theological themes, I will conclude with a note about Gutiérrez who has responded, almost point for point, to the issues raised by the commission and by later Vatican instructions.

Cardinal Joseph Ratzinger quite obviously remains the most prominent critic of liberation theology and the most influential through his position as head of the Sacred Congregation for the Defense of the Faith. In chapter 1 on the history of liberation theology, I already spelled out the main points of the 1984 and 1986 Vatican instructions. Since from all reports Cardinal Ratzinger was the primary author of these instructions, I have treated the criticisms they contain as representing his views. The 1984 instruction distinguishes between an "authentic" theology of liberation, "one rooted in the word of God, correctly interpreted," and theologies of liberation "that reduce the gospel to an earthly gospel" and propose a novel interpretation of the faith, which constitutes a practical negation of the true faith of the church. This novel interpretation, the instruction says, springs from "concepts uncritically borrowed from Marxist ideology" and from a rationalist type of biblical hermeneutics.[19]

The 1984 instruction gives several examples of what it sees as a reductionist reading of the Bible: for example, treating the exodus as a principally or exclusively political liberation; giving an exclusively political interpretation of the death of Jesus.[20] It contains numerous criticisms of the uncritical use of Marxism: claiming it is truly scientific; using its analysis as *the* guide for praxis; believing this analysis can be separated from Marxist atheism-materialism; adopting Marxist class struggle as a means of social change. I have noted these only briefly here because they come up for fuller discussion in chapters 7–8. The same instruction also criticizes unjust attacks on the hierarchy and tendencies to create a separate "popular church."

Two special criticisms by Ratzinger merit a fuller discussion at this point: one deals with the use of Marxist concepts in interpreting scripture, the other with the concept of social sin. His comments about using Marxism in interpreting scripture are most pronounced in an address published in the Italian magazine *30 Giorni* in March 1984. His views on "social sin" figure more prominently in the official Vatican instructions published later in 1984 and in 1986.

In the March 1984 article, Cardinal Ratzinger singles out what he considers most basic in liberation theology. It views all reality as political, "so liberation is a political concept and the guide to liberation must be a guide to political action." The later official instructions would avoid mentioning any theologians by name, but the cardinal's March address does cite specific theologians. He quotes Gutiérrez as saying: "Nothing remains outside political commitment. All exists with a political coloration." He then adds that he finds it difficult to imagine how we can "seriously empty the global reality of Christianity into a scheme or study of the socio-political practice of liberation."[21]

Because the Gutiérrez quote serves as a thesis statement for Ratzinger's attack, I might step back for a moment to comment upon it. Ratzinger has Gutiérrez saying that "nothing remains outside political commitment." As it stands this statement asserts a very reductionist view of faith. The article gives no page references to this or other quotes, but I did track down what clearly appears to be the source of the position attributed to Gutiérrez. Gutiérrez wrote, in *A Theology of Liberation*: "Nothing lies outside the political sphere understood in this way. Everything has a political color."[22] The first sentence looks somewhat similar to the quote given by Ratzinger (and the second sentence differs only in words), but Gutiérrez's actual quote is far more nuanced. The "political sphere understood *in this way,*" he explains carefully earlier in the paragraph, refers to the Aristotelean concept of *polis*; all that we do is influenced by, and influences, the society in which we live. The quote says nothing about "political commitment." Possibly the Gutiérrez quote, as cited by Ratzinger, came from some other source; or translations could differ (but hardly, it would seem, that much). At any rate this example illustrates how one can "read into" a statement far more than the theologian actually says (if indeed the quote I cited from Gutiérrez is the one Cardinal Ratzinger was commenting upon).

Ratzinger moves on from this point to discuss how this (seemingly) politicized view of Christian faith developed. After the Second Vatican Council new efforts to interpret scripture gave rise to a naive faith in science, treating it as a new gospel of truth. Those who experienced a void of meaning in the Western world looked to neo-Marxism as a way of achieving new meaning. This in turn led to the acceptance of Marxism as a model for meeting the moral challenge of poverty and oppression in the world.

Repeatedly (at least a dozen times in his address), Ratzinger criticizes so-called scientific methods that claim to offer truth. This tendency began with the acceptance of Rudolf Bultmann's exegesis of scripture as truly scientific. "The figure of Jesus was uprooted from its position in the tradition by means of science, considered as the supreme method."[23] Then, in the late 1960s, the Marxist analysis of history was judged as "the only one with scientific character." This then led to the positions adopted by liberation theology, which interpreted the world in terms of class struggle and political conflict, and consequently read the Bible in this light.

In his essay, Ratzinger notes numerous examples where he believes liberation theologians fuse (or confuse) biblical images with Marxist dialectic: the poor in the Bible are interpreted in terms of Marx's concept of the proletariat; the "people of God" expressed in Vatican II becomes a popular church engaged in class struggle with the hierarchical church; the history of salvation becomes fused with a Marxist view of history, and the magisterium's insistence on permanent truths of faith is viewed as hostile to progress.

In the final pages of his March article, Ratzinger singles out Jon Sobrino for criticism. He sees Sobrino as reading scripture against a background of Marxist hermeneutics and he cites several examples. Sobrino, says Ratzinger, speaks of the faith of Jesus as fidelity to the Father but then substitutes "fidelity to history" for faith. He makes love consist in an option for the poor but liberation theology then interprets this in a Marxist sense of class struggle. He makes the kingdom of God fundamental in the preaching of Jesus, but this is understood "in a party form and turned toward praxis." He gives a "fearful interpretation" of the death and resurrection of Jesus by making those who suffer and struggle for liberation exercise a lordship over history, which the Bible attributes to God alone.[24] I will consider Sobrino's christology in chapter 4; in my reading of Sobrino I have not encountered such things as substituting fidelity to history for faith, or making any reference to party praxis; his works contain almost no references to Marx. But the absence of any page references (at least in the English version of Ratzinger's address) makes assessment difficult.

The specific theological issue that Ratzinger deals with most extensively in both the 1984 and 1986 instructions concerns the relationship of personal sin to social sin and social change. The 1984 instruction takes up the question of sin in the opening paragraphs of its Introduction: "liberation is first and foremost liberation from the radical slavery of sin." Liberation involves freedom from economic and political forms of slavery, but some so emphasize temporal liberation that they seem to "put liberation from sin in second place and so fail to give it the primary importance it is due."[25]

For Christians the most radical experience of liberation comes through Christ who freed us from sin and slavery to the flesh. It is the new life of grace that makes us free. "This means that the most radical form of slavery is slavery to sin." Other forms of slavery find their deepest root in slavery to sin.[26] The New Testament teaches us that sin is the greatest evil. To show that Christ's deliverance applies even to slaves, "the New Testament does not require some change in the political or social conditions as a prerequisite for entrance into freedom." Consequently the full ambit of sin cannot be restricted to "social sin." One cannot localize evil principally or uniquely in bad social, political, or economic structures as though all other evils come from them. There are structures that are evil and that we must change, but structures "are the result of man's actions and so are consequences more than causes." The root of evil lies therefore in free and responsible persons who have to be converted.[27]

The 1986 instruction makes this point fundamental to its whole treatment of "freedom and liberation." Personal freedom is more fundamental than social earthly liberation. Liberation movements have often led to new forms of servitude (nn. 10–19). Temporal freedom can create only better conditions for authentic freedom; it does not create freedom itself. Even under conditions of servitude, humans never lose their spiritual freedom.[28] We gain true freedom through grace and the sacraments, by being freed from sin and restored to communion with God.[29] Inner conversion is essential for social change to become truly human; to give priority to structures over persons runs counter to human dignity. Personal sin is the root cause of evil; "social sin," in reference to structures, is sin only in a derived, secondary sense.[30] The instruction does recognize that we should be active in changing unjust social structures. Appeals to inner conversion should be given priority, but this "in no way eliminates the need for unjust social structures to be changed."[31]

Selected essays by other European critics can be found in James V. Schall's *Liberation Theology in Latin America*. Hans von Balthasar offers criteria for judging Catholic theology, criticizes the politicizing of biblical texts, stresses the universality of the kingdom of God (it does not exclude the rich), and challenges the use of the expression "sinful structures" (only persons are sinful). Jean Galot argues that love and changes of heart reflect the true spirit of the gospel, which teaches that no degree of social change will ever end the disparity of wealth and poverty in the world. Inequities will be compensated for, however, in eternity. PH.-I. André-Vincent charges liberation theology with using a Marxist hermeneutic of the bible to "reinvent" Christianity.[32]

North American Critics

Thomas G. Sanders, writing in September 1973 for *Christianity and Crisis,* proffered one of the earliest critiques of liberation theology by a U.S. theologian. He viewed liberation theology as a form of the "soft utopianism" criticized by Reinhold Niebuhr. Liberation theology, said Sanders, uses categories quite similar to those of Marxism to interpret society: history as conflict, humanity divided into oppressors and oppressed, class struggle, etc. It does not advocate Marxist-Leninist hard-line tactics of violent revolution, but embraces socialism as a utopian hope. So Niebuhr's criticisms of soft utopianism apply. Socialism envisions a world without exploitation and of just, cooperative, and loving relations. Its advocates fail, however, to account for human sinfulness, which creates conflicts in all forms of society. All systems remain imperfect and ambiguous; the problems of Latin America involve many complex factors. Utopianism, Sanders concludes, does not offer a solid basis for social change.[33]

The use of Niebuhr's "political realism" in contrast to Latin American "utopianism" would be reasserted by many other U.S. critics. Dennis McCann develops at length this type of criticism in his *Christian Realism and Liberation Theology*. Political theology, if it is to remain truly Christian, must have criteria for distinguishing religious transcendence from political enthusiasm. Niebuhr crafted such criteria, says McCann; liberation theology has not. Niebuhr insisted that a practical, political theology must graft "astute intelligence" onto "vital religious idealism" to move toward an ethical reconstruction of society.[34] Marxism, though it does not see itself as a religion, provides a vital religious idealism, but one too easily embraced with utopian fanaticism. Marxism's success in recent decades derives from its "emotional appeal" to impoverished nations, an appeal that blames others for their situation of poverty and oppression.[35] McCann joins Niebuhr in stressing the *reservations* that politically involved Christians must bring to any movement of political enthusiasm. Hence they reject both bourgeois liberalism and Marxism on account of their utopianism—"their naive optimism about the chances for a perfect society."[36] Christianity should be prophetic; it should have an ideal standard toward which it works. But it must also have a realistic sense of what is possible.

Stalinism influenced Niebuhr's disillusionment with Marxism, but Roosevelt's New Deal provided a positive experience on which to base Christian realism. The New Deal had mitigated class struggle by providing an "organizing center" (the government), which achieved a balance of power through the use of political reforms.[37] This democratic experience Niebuhr and McCann clearly view as the model that will also provide the greatest hope of success for Latin America.[38]

McCann believes that liberation theology lacks the criteria needed to establish a truly Christian political theology. Gutiérrez defines liberation theology as a "reflection on praxis in the light of the Word of God." But, in McCann's judgment, Gutiérrez does not resolve a critical ambiguity in this definition. Either one makes praxis the ultimate criterion, in which case the word of God becomes only a theological justification for praxis; or if one does make the word of God the ultimate criterion, liberation theology differs little from Vatican II or progressive European theology. McCann claims that Gutiérrez does not and cannot resolve this dilemma. He believes that Juan Luis Segundo opts for a method based on praxis and effectively rules out a decisive judgment derived from faith. Jon Sobrino opts, in contrast, for content derived from scripture, but in doing so his work simply repeats the work of progressive European theologians.

The force of McCann's arguments would appear to depend on the linkage of several assumptions. First he sees Paulo Freire's method of conscientization as *the* distinctive methodological principle in liberation theology.[39] This method, according to McCann, promises not merely to challenge prevailing ideologies, but to eliminate theological reflection entirely. For it does not believe in any limit-situations (for example, human createdness, finiteness, and sinfulness). Hence it includes no reservations or provisos. Freire's method, moreover, assumes the Feuerbachian humanism of the young Marx, with its belief that all obstacles to complete human self-realization can be achieved without God.[40] For McCann, then, liberation theology rests on Freire's method of conscientization, which involves a Marxist-humanist view of history in which humans become the responsible agents of history such that God (logically at least) plays no part. If liberation theologians choose the method of liberation theology, with its stress on praxis, then the message of Jesus no longer serves as a final word. If, says

McCann, liberation theologians choose the content of the word of God, then nothing distinguishes it from progressive Vatican II theology.[41] McCann's argument, however, depends on its linking of some highly questionable interpretations (e.g., that liberation theology rests on Freire's method and that Freire's method rules out God). Matthew Lamb, in a review of McCann's book, offers a rather devastating critique of these assumptions.[42]

Michael Novak's *Will It Liberate?* uses similar "Niebuhrian criteria" in his criticisms of liberation theology. Since Novak's critique focuses almost entirely on the perceived failures of liberation theology's social analysis and its subsequent rejection of capitalism in favor of socialism, I will treat his critique separately, at the end of chapter 7. Richard Neuhaus, in *The Catholic Moment*, shares in Novak's defense of capitalism and his disdain for socialism. Neuhaus cites Peter Bergers's work (*The Capitalist Revolution*), which he says demonstrates conclusively that democratic capitalism is the best hope for the world.[43] He also challenges the supposed originality of Latin American theology (an argument made by numerous other critics). "There is hardly a prominent concept in liberation theology that cannot be directly traced to a European source."[44]

Neuhaus's book was published in 1987 but his criticisms focus entirely on liberation works written in the late 1960s and early 70s. More specifically the texts he cites come almost exclusively from Segundo's "A Theology for Artisans of a New Humanity" series. Neuhaus ignores all the works published by Segundo and other liberation theologians since that time. On this score, one might well imagine Neuhaus's reactions to a study of Reinhold Niebuhr's work that studied only the writings of Niebuhr's socialist period and ignored all his later writings.

On the basis of these limited, early Segundo texts, Neuhaus does not hesitate to make sweeping generalizations about liberation theology as a whole. "The dominant liberation theologians exclude the transcendent as a matter of principle."[45] Liberation theology, as reflected in Segundo, involves a "denial of original sin" and a Pelagian "insistence upon human self-justification."[46]

In comparison with Gutiérrez's more cautious and nuanced statements, Segundo does indeed express his positions in stronger terms. Neuhaus, however, attributes positions to Segundo that go beyond what Segundo actually states. For example, Neuhaus claims that Segundo holds that "anything that hinders the work of liberation is by definition false," but the reference Neuhaus gives would not support this. Segundo says that truth "would seem to *include* efficacy in its very essence"; Neuhaus inserts the word "only" in citing Segundo's views on truth as that which is efficacious.[47] Neuhaus's critique focuses on what he sees as a "reductionism" of faith to politics in liberation theology, but he uses his own form of reductionism in selecting and interpreting texts that support his critique.

Schubert Ogden, in *Faith and Freedom*, offers a far more sympathetic critique of liberation theology. His purpose, he says, is not to refute liberation theology but rather to offer corrective points so that it can truly encompass a concern for human liberation in the world. For theology to do this, it must first be appropriate to Christian faith and God's revelation. It must also, however, be appropriate to understanding human history.[48] Ogden believes that most liberation theologies (Latin American, black, feminist) have typically offered a "witness" rather than theology proper, and he feels that they tend to rationalize positions already taken.[49] Liberation theology must ask not only whether it serves praxis, but must ask *how*—critically—it serves such praxis. While McCann stresses the necessity of a dualism that keeps God's action in history distinct from human efforts for liberation, Ogden moves in an opposite direction. He calls on liberation theology to adopt the idea of God found in process theology, a God whose very being depends in part on the response of other beings.[50]

Ogden does, however, underline a distinction between two aspects of God's acting that he believes liberation theologians should keep separate: a distinction between redemption and emancipation. Redemption comes from God alone; it expresses God's acceptance of all. Yet even redemption requires a response; without faith we cannot be saved. Sin constitutes a rejection of God's loving acceptance; hence we participate even in God's work of redemption.[51] Redemption retains the personal aspect of salvation between God and each person. Emancipation, in contrast, pertains more to the collective efforts of humans to transform the world. If God's redemptive love comes from God alone, God's work of emancipation *depends* on the cooperation of those created. God acts in the world to optimize and fulfill the greatest potential of all persons; but to achieve this, God needs our work. If God establishes the cosmic order of things, God leaves to us the work of establishing society and culture. Hence emancipation does involve work to bring about needed systemic changes.[52] Ogden also argues that liberation theology must look to all forms of bondage (for example, environmental issues). He ends with the same warning raised by other critics. Liberation theologians must always retain a *critical* reflection on social praxis. Theology can result in solidarity, but it cannot rest upon it.[53]

We cannot anticipate all of the responses of liberation theologians to these criticisms at this point. Major issues will be addressed in subsequent chapters. But we might note in response to Ogden's useful distinction between redemption and emancipation that Gutiérrez's discussion of the gratuity of God's love (under spirituality in chapter 5) addresses this problem. I might at this point also offer a synopsis of the criticisms raised against liberation theology.

A Summary of Major Criticisms

Reducing Faith to Politics. The most militant critics of liberation theology accuse it of reducing faith to politics; other critics believe that it "risks" such a reduction. (I have stated most of the summary criticisms in their stronger forms). Liberation theology, and Gutiérrez specifically, argue for "one history" of salvation. Critics generally acknowledge that God does act "in history," but they contend that this formula tends to reduce salvation to earthly progress alone (horizontalism), neglecting eternal life, transcendence, and many aspects of personal spiritual growth (the vertical). They use this same argument to question the interpretation given by liberation theologians to various biblical passages. Exodus is seen as socio-political liberation only, without reference to the religious laws of the covenant. The prophets appear as social critics only. The kingdom of God preached by Jesus is equated with earthly progress. Jesus' death is given an exclusively political sense.

Ratzinger and some other critics give much attention to the issue of sin. They see liberation theology as focused on "social sin" to the neglect of personal sin, which the instruction views as the ultimate source of evil in the world. The liberationist claim that all life is political, and that the church must involve itself politically, runs counter to the primary religious mission of the church, critics argue.

The Uncritical Use of Marxist and Socialist Ideas. The most polemical critics of liberation theology see it simply as an effort to "baptize" Marxist revolution. Other critics would acknowledge the Christian "intentions" of liberation theology, but believe that its reliance on Marxist concepts and its advocacy of socialism create grave risks for the faithful.

Cardinal Ratzinger and others believe that many liberation theologians operate from a Marxist fundamental option and employ a "Marxist hermeneutic" in interpreting the Bible. Hence not only the social analysis they espouse, but their theology proper reflects Marxist thinking. Some critics charge that the use of Marxist concepts implicates liberation theology in an espousal of Marxism. Thus one critic argues that once Gutiérrez introduces the concept of "class struggle" he has placed himself in the camp of Marxism.[54] Some believe that the emphasis on praxis leads in this same direction.

Many critics question the accuracy and adequacy of Marxist analysis as a tool for understanding conditions in Latin America. Many challenge dependency theory on the same score. A great number of critics, including some quite sympathetic to liberation theology overall, feel that its advocacy of socialism is uncritical. Liberation theologians, they claim, have only utopian ideas about socialism; they do not spell out the institutions needed to establish justice *and* freedom, and they do not criticize sufficiently the deficiencies and failures of existing socialist regimes.

Creating a Separate Church. In the early stages of liberation theology especially, church authorities attacked what they felt was an attempt to create a "popular church" in opposition to the institutional, hierarchical church. Some critics continue to view the base community movement as still tending in this direction. They consider unjust many criticisms made of the hierarchy—for instance, that church authorities are allied with the status quo if they do not espouse liberationist views. Some claim that liberation theologians reject the social teachings of the church, replacing them with the Marxist views noted above.

Some Concluding Reflections about Critics and Criticisms

The large number of these criticisms makes assessment difficult enough. Each separate point would require pages, or even chapters, of attention. Sometimes the criticisms take the form of generalized indictments without reference to any specific text of a theologian. (I generalized also in the summary account above, but my purpose was simply to outline, and not to judge, the major criticisms). Even when specific references are cited, however, criticisms sometimes appear based on what the critic "sees implied" in the text rather than what it actually states.

I have already indicated examples of this last problem, but it may merit citing another example of critiques of this type. The periodical *Tierra Nueva* (Bogotá, Colombia) has served as a major center for critiques of liberation theology. In one issue (in 1988) Enrique Colom Casta offers a critique of Gutiérrez's *The Power of the Poor in History*. The article purports to show why Gutiérrez's theology falls under the forms of liberation theology condemned by the 1984 Vatican instruction.

The author presents a series of "theses" that he attributes to Gutiérrez, and in each case he offers quotations from Gutiérrez to illustrate the thesis. The first of the theses Casta puts forward does indeed correspond to the quotations assumed under it: that Latin America requires social revolution, not reform. But subsequent theses state positions that go far beyond what the quotations from Gutiérrez actually say. Gutiérrez rejects bourgeois analysis and defends the usefulness of Marxist analysis; Casta translates this to mean Marxism represents *the* social analysis needed. Gutiérrez cites Marx's famous thesis "the point is to change the world"; for Casta this means that Gutiérrez accepts Marx's whole epistemology. Gutiérrez states that the poor must struggle as a social class; Casta presents him as saying that class struggle is "the structure of reality itself and the motor of history." Gutiérrez says that Jesus died as a consequence of his defense of the poor; Casta translates this into Jesus died "as a revolutionary."[55]

Fair critics will base their criticisms on an objective reading of what a given theologian actually says. Some critics of liberation theology have not done this; some liberation theologians have also failed in this regard, as we shall see later.

One final specific issue I might comment upon briefly by way of conclusion. Many U.S. critics, I have noted, use criteria from Niebuhr's political realism as a way of critiquing liberation theology. To a significant degree, in recent years, liberation theologians have become more pragmatic and critical in discussing the goals of liberation. This will become evident in later chapters. But the pragmatic tendencies of U.S. thought and the more utopian thinking of liberation theologians involve more than simple cultural differences. The achievements of the New Deal influenced Niebuhr's thinking significantly. He felt that the democratic process, with its balance of powers, had achieved in the United States some real approximations of Christian ideals of social justice. If Niebuhr had done his theology in Haiti, or in the Soviet Union under Stalin, it seems quite unlikely that his writings would have taken the same turn, stressing the imperfections caused by sin that one must accept in any socio-economic system. The values and criteria one stresses depend greatly on the situation one is confronting.

Chapter 4

Biblical Themes

Liberation theologians believe that God has spoken and continues to speak, clearly and forcefully, about the liberation of the poor from misery and oppression. While awareness of conditions in Latin America and commitment to change them may precede questions about God's revelation, critical reflection constitutes liberation theology as theology proper. The reflection may begin, as we have seen, with "suspicion" about the ways in which the Christian message has been traditionally interpreted. Or it may simply proceed from the question: "What does the word of God have to say about the poverty-oppression of the poor and their longing-striving for liberation?"

Asking that question and probing scripture for answers have unquestionably led to a new awareness in theology about God's concern for the poor, for justice and liberation. The biblical perspectives presented in the U.S. Catholic bishops' letter on the U.S. economy testify to the impact of biblical themes made prominent by liberation theologians: the exodus and covenant that shaped Israel's history, the prophets' proclamations of God's concern for justice, Jesus' identification with the poor and preaching of the kingdom.[1] More and more theologians have also recognized that theological reflection throughout the ages has been prompted by human concerns in a given epoch. But if new concerns lead to new insights into scripture, the insights must always be tested by their faithfulness to scripture. U.S. theologian John Shea stresses this mutuality:

> It is necessary for each generation of believers to bring their concerns to Jesus; but it is also necessary for the totality of concerns which constitute scripture to talk back to each generation of believers. The relationship between experience and tradition must be a mutual dialogue.[2]

Any assessment of liberation theology's use of scripture will involve testing both parts of the relationship between experience and biblical revelation. Prompted by new concerns, liberation theologians have clearly uncovered or recovered important dimensions of God's revelation. Most of the issues raised by critics concern the faithfulness of these new interpretations to what Shea would call the "totality of concerns" that constitute scripture. At the outset, liberation theologians seemed at times to present new interpretations as giving *the true* message of Christianity; they did so in part because justice-liberation themes had become lost in the ways the Christian message came to be interpreted over the centuries. More recent works in liberation theology acknowledge the incompleteness of some liberation themes in giving a full picture of revelation. Thus the Boffs, in noting the special perspective of liberation theology (scripture viewed from the perspective of the oppressed), add: "We must say straightaway that this is not the only possible and legitimate reading of the Bible." Liberation theology stresses themes that speak to the poor, "but not to the exclusion of everything else." "They may not be the most *important* themes in the Bible (in themselves), but they are the most *relevant* (to the poor in their situation of oppression)."[3] The Boffs also stress the importance of "fidelity" to God's word. This fidelity will serve as an important criterion in the assessments that accompany the discussion of the biblical themes treated in this chapter.

This chapter will take up two major themes. The first has to do with God as liberator. It deals especially with liberation perspectives on the story of the exodus and then with the prophets and their concern for the poor. Some critical assessments also form part of this first section. The second section deals with christology and the mission of Jesus. It considers three representative treatments of christology: by Leonardo Boff, Jon Sobrino, and Juan Luis Segundo. It makes some note of criticisms directed against these theologians, and it concludes with reflections about different "images" of Jesus in Latin America.

Subsequent chapters will treat of other theological themes. Chapter 5 studies the important theme of spirituality, and an emerging theme about women and liberation. Chapter 11 takes up issues related to ecclesiology. All of these involve biblical reflection, but I want to concentrate in this chapter on the two major themes of God as liberator and Jesus' mission to the world. As liberation theology develops, it continues to expand its scope of theological themes, with reflections on the Trinity, on Mary, and other topics. I will not attempt to cover all these, but this very expansion reflects efforts to take on the "totality of concerns" mentioned by John Shea.

GOD AS LIBERATOR: EXODUS AND THE PROPHETS

The biblical themes treated in this chapter all form part of the whole history of salvation. I might preface this section, then, with some comments by Gutiérrez about salvation history. In *A Theology of Liberation,* Gutiérrez begins his study of biblical perspectives by relating the traditional category of "salvation" with the new category of "liberation." In past centuries Christians came to view salvation as the attainment of eternal happiness in heaven, made possible by Christ's forgiveness of personal sins. In this context theology turned often to the question of how unbelievers might be saved. The new questions to be addressed by theologians ask how an unjust world can be transformed, how humans in all the dimensions of their life can be saved, and how sin as a socio-historical reality can be overcome. God's saving power, Gutiérrez asserted, deals not just with our souls in acts of forgiveness that lie outside, or above, history. God's saving power underlies all our experiences in "one history." God is revealed through saving actions in history and through human events.[4]

The history of Israel, presented in the Old Testament, provides a richness of sources for liberation theologians to reflect upon. It tells the story of a God who indeed did act "in" history to establish a people by liberating them from oppression in Egypt, forming a covenant with them at Sinai, and leading them into a promised land. Many liberation theologians, including Gutiérrez, have reflected on these salvific events.[5] I will focus first on J. Severino Croatto's *Exodus*. His work merits special attention for several reasons: he is a biblical scholar; he focuses on the most controversial paradigm of liberation, the exodus, and ties in other biblical reflections with this paradigm; and his opening chapter formulates clearly the problem of relating revelations from the past with a contemporary reading of the Bible.

Biblical exegesis, says Croatto, deals with what the Bible tells us about the salvific events lived by the people of Israel, but it also includes what one can explore from our own (Latin American) perspective. The Bible contains a "reservoir of meaning," which surpasses the historical meaning of the text. Hence the hermeneutic Croatto employs involves rereading the biblical message on the basis of Latin Americans' experience as oppressed peoples. As the liberating experience of the exodus led toward entrance into the promised land, so do oppressed peoples now engage in a process of liberation in search of freedom as a more final goal.[6] A dual perspective—the significance of biblical events for Israel, and the significance of the same events for oppressed peoples today—runs throughout Croatto's work.

The Bible begins with the book of Genesis and its story of God's creation of the world. While the book of Genesis, says Croatto, makes no mention of liberation and rarely uses the word freedom, it does clearly establish freedom as a human vocation. A profound representation of the essence of human beings comes with the Genesis designation of humans as made in the image and likeness of God (Gn 1:26). If other ancient religions viewed their kings as images of God, only Genesis asserts that *all* human beings are created in God's image. Genesis describes Yahweh as a creator God, and humans share in likeness to God through their creativity. The creator God fashions a human being in the image of the divine—as a creator. From this human beings receive their mission "to build up the world." "Human beings are called to freedom for themselves and for others."[7]

The Exodus

Croatto sees the exodus as a central paradigm of God's acting in history. Hence he looks not only to its significance for the people of Israel but also as a "promise" for the oppressed in today's world. He examines the exodus account on several scores. First he looks at the *situation* of the Hebrews in Egypt. They were enslaved; their broken spirit left them incapable of even hoping for salvation; they groaned and cried, and Yahweh heard them (Ex 3:7, 9; and 6:5). They seemed unaware of the promises Yahweh had made to Abraham. Their situation was one of political oppression, and God began the process of liberation not by forgiving personal sins but by physical, social liberation.[8]

Croatto then looks at the *words* spoken in the face of this situation of oppression. The oppressed themselves could only speak in groanings and cries. The word of Yahweh came as a response to Moses: "I have visited you and seen all that the Egyptians are doing to you, and I have resolved to bring you out of Egypt where you are oppressed ... to a land where milk and honey flow" (Ex 3:17). God's word not only reveals a plan to work liberation through Moses, but it also "conscienticizes" the people. The word of the oppressor, however, shows refusal to listen. The pharaoh hardens and refuses to liberate the Israelites. Croatto draws from this a contemporary lesson: "The oppressor can never free," because oppression serves his interest and aggrandizes his power. Only through the power and force of Yawheh can liberation be achieved.[9]

After dealing with the *events* of liberation (the passover, the departure, etc.) Croatto turns to the *message* of Exodus and what it might mean for the present. The exodus story, Croatto observes, shows that God acted as a liberator. God did something for the historical, thisworldly liberation of a people, and did it through a leader, Moses. Latin America has also had, and still has, Moses-figures who utter liberating, conscienticizing words. The history of the exodus also speaks of violence. "If the oppression is carried to the extreme of repression, the liberating action is necessarily violent" (for example, God's destruction of the pharaoh's army, the plagues sent, etc.). God had to resort to violence when persuasion failed. Croatto adds: since oppression is never justifiable, nor resignation to oppression tolerable, "justice is a radical good that demands of love ... a violent action."[10]

Pablo Richard includes some reflections on the exodus in a commentary on idolatry. He begins with some rather strained, hyperbolic assertions about capitalism and religion: for example, that the economist Milton Friedman is also "an eminent theologian," and that "religion is an obligatory theme in any journal of international importance."[11] But he addresses primarily the issue of idolatry in relation to the exodus account. Wanting God as a consoler-in-oppression is idolatry; God transcends this alienation and gives a self-image as a liberating leader-out-of-slavery. Like Croatto,

Richard draws attention to violence in the book of Exodus: for example, when Moses becomes enraged with the idolatry of the Israelites, he orders the Levites to kill the offenders and some three thousand died that day (Ex 32:27). Richard concludes: "Processes of liberation are always violent, not only to the oppressor, but also to the oppressed, who must undergo an internal transformation to liberate themselves from their oppressed and alienated consciousness."[12] The same emphasis on the necessity of violence occurs when Richard treats of the first book of Maccabees:

> In this situation, the oppressed people could profess its faith in God only by violent struggle against the politico-religious system imposed by Antiochus. . . . The people struggled for thirty years after that, first in a guerilla war, and then in total warfare, against domination and idolatry.[13]

For critics who charge liberation theologians with advocating violence, these commentators on exodus would provide one of the very few pieces of evidence they might use. Neither commentary, however, goes from the biblical context to argue for use of violent means to effect change in Latin America.

In an interview (July 1988), Pablo Richard spoke out strongly *against* violence, especially against all forms of terrorism or reliance on military might to control a population. He would allow for armed struggle only if the vast majority of the people supported an insurrection (as in Nicaragua against Somoza) and if the likelihood of victory was strong.

Jorge V. Pixley, a Protestant U.S.-Nicaraguan biblical scholar, has also written an important work on the exodus. While agreeing with Croatto on the need for popular appropriation of the exodus message, Pixley emphasizes the need for scholars to establish the truth of any biblical account. While the Bible itself must remain the highest authority, establishing its truth requires attention to the text itself and a study of its historical context.[14] Drawing upon the works of other biblical scholars, Pixley discusses the three versions of Israelite history found in the Pentateuch (the Yahwist, the Eloist, and the Priestly accounts) and he gives special attention to the different stages of Israel's history, each with its own differing social context. He describes four important periods in the history of Israel. First, with respect to the people in Egypt who experienced the exodus, scholars can offer only a hypothesis. Those who left with the exodus appear to have comprised a heterogeneous group of peasants, along with immigrants from Eastern regions, and with leadership assumed by Levites. Scholars place the exodus between 1230 and 1250 B.C. Contemporaneously (13th to 11th centuries) certain tribes of "Israel" formed in Canaan where they were joined by those who came out of Egypt. They were peasants who struggled against the kings and lords of the cities who demanded tribute. These peasants sought to live as a classless society with allegiance to Yahweh alone. This group would thus appropriate the exodus account as a revolutionary struggle against kings and the monarchy, with the pharaoh viewed as a paradigm of unjust oppressors. The tenth to the sixth centuries B.C. constituted the third period, one in which the Israelites had their own monarchs to protect them against the Philistines. This new situation, in which new class differences developed, stressed nationalism with Moses viewed as the paradigm of a national leader. The fourth period (6th century) marked the ascendancy of the priestly class. Israel's identity was viewed as religious; the exodus and Sinai accounts were interpreted as the foundation of a religious community.[15]

This historical excursus helps to explain in part the conflicting emphases given in readings of the exodus account. The liberation theologians stress rebellion against oppressors (reflecting the 1st and 2nd historical periods); the Vatican and other critics stress the religious dimension of laws and worship (the 4th period). Or, as Pixley writes about this fourth period: "Sinai was transformed from the place where a free people was constituted to the place where God revealed the ordinances of his legitimate worship."[16]

The body of Pixley's work deals with the exodus texts. We might briefly highlight some points he makes. He sees Moses as a member of the elite class in Egypt; he broke with his social class when he recognized God on the side of the oppressed. Aaron appears not to have played a significant role in the exodus (and was possibly not even a distinct person) but he takes on importance in the later priestly accounts.[17] Pixley confronts a problem that some other liberationist accounts slide over: victory is attributed to Yahweh alone, not to any human efforts. "By sheer power Yahweh brought us out of Egypt" (Ex 13:14); "Yahweh will do the fighting for you; you have only to keep still" (Ex 14:14). Pixley answers this problem on philosophic rather than textual grounds. God works through human agents; God initiates change but is not an exclusive agent. Humans and God work together as co-creators of change in history.[18]

Pixley stresses that the exodus story involved much more than the liberation struggles of Hebrew tribes. It involved the formation of a new people, which strove to establish a classless society, but later fell back into class divisions and monarchical rule. And while Pixley speaks of the special emphasis on religious observances in the priestly fourth period, he also asserts that loyalty to Yahweh and trust in Yahweh remained constant in each period. A secular revolution was never an option for the people of Israel.[19]

An Assessment: Comments and Critiques concerning Exodus

Theological interpretations of the Bible should speak to contemporary concerns but should also remain faithful to the biblical text. Pixley's work on exodus shows care in staying with the text while providing background from various scholars to show the social significance of events and of the formation of Israel as a nation. Perhaps one could quarrel with the use of the expression "classless society" to describe the antimonarchical phase of Israel's history, but Pixley's approach appears sound overall (professional exegetes may have a different opinion). Croatto's desire to find "meaning for today," on the other hand, seems at times to force the text. Both Croatto and Richard "draw lessons" about the role of violence in bringing about social change. But the overarching message of the Bible, including the Old Testament, is one of reliance on Yahweh, not on force of arms. Moreover, the exodus account does not present a story of armed resistance by the Israelites. The violence comes through acts of God (the plagues, etc.), even if we assume these acts of God were actual historical events, an assumption many exegetes would not accept.

Liberation theologians are certainly justified in looking to the exodus as a biblical paradigm for a suffering people yearning for liberation. J. Andrew Kirk, a Protestant biblical theologian working in Argentina, acknowledges this point in his commentary on liberation theology's use of the exodus story.[20] The exodus was the central event in Israel's history; it does show God responding to the cries of the poor; it did involve liberation from physical suffering and oppression, and not just salvation from personal sin. But Kirk questions both the method used by some liberation theologians to interpret the text and some of the specific conclusions they reach. In respect to method, he finds too little effort to verify exegetically their use of a given text, and too much reliance on the present situation in Latin America as a controlling factor in interpreting the text.[21] (Kirk's critique did not include Pixley's work, which came later.)

With respect to the conclusions they reach, Kirk challenges two assumptions that operate in many of their interpretations: one, that Israel became conscious of its identity as a people only after being liberated; two, that Moses and the people initiated and organized the struggle for liberation with the religious factor coming as a later interpretation. Kirk claims that liberation theologians simply make these assumptions without arguing them, and that they would prove unconvincing if they did argue them. For example, the texts uniformly present Yahweh as the initiator and agent of Israel's emancipation.[22]

Norbert Lohfink, a prominent scholar at the Pontifical Biblical Institute in Rome, includes lengthy comments about liberation theology's use of the exodus story as part of an overall assessment of liberation theology's option for the poor. Lohfink agrees with liberation theologians that the Bible shows God's will as clearly concerned with human society and this world. The prayer of Jesus, the Our Father, quite clearly says "Thy will be done *on earth* as it is in heaven." "Thy will be done," says Lohfink, does not mean simply keeping the ten commandments. It means realizing the plans that God has for this world.[23]

Like Jorge Pixley, Lohfink stresses the formation of a new society as essential to an understanding of the exodus. God's plan for the world,

Lohfink argues, takes the form of calling a people together and having it create a "contrast-society" where humans deal justly and equitably with each other, so that no one is ever poor or oppressed. Other Near Eastern religions had commandments about love for the poor, but they also defended the established political order and its social structures. Yahweh, the God of Israel, differed from other gods not only by bringing the people out of slavery in Egypt but by forming them at Mount Sinai into a new society: a society without social stratifications, a divinely willed "contrast-society" to serve as a model of just human relations in contrast to all other existing societies. Lohfink believes that this idea of a contrast-society also explains Jesus' preaching of the kingdom and the early church's sharing goods in common (Acts 4:32).

Lohfink disagrees with liberation theologians, however, on some other points. He does not see joining with secular liberation movements as expressing God's plan; loyalty to Yahweh was an essential bond in the exodus. Lohfink recognizes base communities, however, as embodying many characteristics of a contrast-society: joined in faith, transforming themselves, and reaching out to transform society. In respect to the liberation from Egyptian oppression, Lohfink challenges many liberation theology interpretations. Yahweh did not work through political change but *removed* the Israelites from Egypt; they were taken outside the system. Moreover, the Israelites themselves did *not* use violence against the Egyptians or even fight against them. "Yahweh will do the fighting for you; you have only to keep still" (Ex 14:14). The violence done (the plagues, the destruction of the Egyptian army) was brought on by Yahweh, not by human actions; the Israelites viewed the exodus as a miracle, as the work of God alone.

The evaluations we have been discussing demonstrate the difficulties of translating revelations from the past into specific guidelines for the present. An analogy may help to pinpoint this problem. A parable tries to convey a basic message (with possibly different levels of meaning). Treated as a parable, the exodus account conveys clear meanings about God's desire to liberate the oppressed and to form them into a new and just society. On this point agreement can be found. An allegory, in contrast, contains numerous details, each with some potential significance. Theologians fail when they treat the exodus account as one would an allegory, matching past actions or situations with specific applications for the present. Critics of liberation theology may justly argue that we cannot draw "organized fighting against oppressors" as a lesson from exodus, but the conclusions Lohfink reaches about the exodus would leave the poor of Latin America with a set of very unrealistic options (for example, leaving their countries for some promised land, forming exclusively Christian societies, or expecting God to work miracles without human effort).

The Prophets, Justice, and the Poor

Christians have traditionally recognized God's concern for the poor as expressed in charity. "I was hungry and you gave me to eat. . . . Whatever you did for the least of my brethren [and sisters] you did unto me" (Mt 25). Liberation theologians insist that God's concern goes far beyond compassion and charity; it involves justice. The prophets make this point clear: to know the Lord is to do justice. José Míguez Bonino cites Jeremiah 22:16, where Josiah is praised for doing justice: "He judged the cause of the poor and the needy; then it was well. Is not this to know me? says the Lord." Hosea 4:1–2 makes the same point by equating lack of knowledge of God with failure to do justice.[24]

José Porfirio Miranda's *Marx and the Bible* argues vigorously the connection between knowing God and doing justice. Miranda claims that Western translations of the Bible, since the sixth century A.D., robbed biblical texts of their force. In the Hebrew text assisting the poor was considered a work of justice (*sedaqa*) but it became translated as almsgiving, which connotes an act of charitable supererogation.[25] To know Yahweh is to achieve justice for the poor. Miranda insists, moreover, that the Bible does not just mean that justice is one sign or manifestation of knowledge of God. It is *the* way. Amos, Hosea, Isaiah, and Micah know only one decisive theme: justice and right.[26]

Croatto speaks at length also about the prophets. He begins by asking why the prophets did not appear until centuries after the exodus. He believes that the people of Israel did not require prophets at first, because they truly *lived* as the type of community that God had planned. But with the rise of power structures in Israel (their own kings and alien rulers), conflicts and special interests emerged destroying the spirit God intended.[27] The prophets speak repeatedly of sins of injustice. Amos criticizes those who "trample the heads of ordinary people and push the poor out of their path" (Am 2:7). Isaiah chastises the rich and powerful: "Take your wrongdoing out of my sight. Cease to do evil. Learn to do good, search for justice, help the oppressed, be just to the orphan, plead for the widow" (Is 1:17). Isaiah attacks especially those who take control of the land, depriving others: "Woe to those who add house to house and join field to field until everywhere belongs to them and they are the sole inhabitants of the land" (Is 5:8). Jeremiah denounces the kings of Israel for their criminal conduct, insisting as we noted above that to do justice is to know Yahweh. While one might argue that even the prophets of Israel did not organize the poor to take action, they did "raise the consciousness" of Israel. God's demands for justice to the poor seem unambiguously clear.

Julio de Santa Ana, a Methodist theologian from Uruguay, examines the history of religious attitudes toward "the poor and poverty" from Old Testament times to the present. In the Old Testament one finds some views that seem to attribute poverty to laziness (for example, Proverbs) or as a punishment from God. But the prophets denounce poverty as an evil and view it as the result of the *injustice* of the rich and powerful. They denounce various forms of oppression and injustice: taxes and suffocating tithes, fraudulent trading, seizures of land, selling as slaves those who cannot pay debts, and the use of violence. But we also find, in Zephaniah and in the Psalms especially, a more spiritual sense of the poor as those who humbly submit to God's will and who wait upon God with quietness and confidence.[28]

As both a complement to these works by liberation theologians and as an assessment we might conclude this section with some reflections by George M. Soares-Prabhu, a Catholic biblical scholar from India. His study of the biblical poor confirms much that Santa Ana and other liberation theologians have written about the poor and about God's special concern for the poor. But he examines also the question whether the biblical poor fit, or do not fit, into a Marxist category of the poor as the working proletariat. His enriching study seemed worth presenting in some detail.

The word most often used to designate the poor in the Bible is the Hebrew *anawim*. It probably derives, says Soares, from a root meaning "to be bent, bowed down, afflicted," and it suggests persons who have been dehumanized and reduced by oppression to a condition of diminished worth. In a later, secondary form *anawim* also took on a religious meaning; those who are in poverty and powerless "bend before God" and put their trust in God. Soares then notes other words also used to designate the poor: *ebyon*, connoting a person in material need; *dal*, whose roots mean low, weak, and powerless; *rash*, which has an unambiguous sense of economic poverty. Of these, *anawim* offers the most significant meaning, embracing the aspects contained in the other terms.[29] The Bible sees the *anawim* as victims of oppression but also as those through whom history is redeemed.

Soares spells out the role of the poor in three propositions that show an analogy between the biblical poor and Marx's proletariat. First, the poor in the Old Testament are primarily the sociological poor, comprised of several groups: impoverished and indebted peasants who live in distress without being wholly destitute; the destitute, including unemployed and landless workers, bonded laborers, and beggars in the city; all who are afflicted or oppressed, not just the economically needy; and in postexilic times, the spiritually poor. In the New Testament the Greek word *ptōchos* is used most often to designate the poor; it describes persons who are destitute and must beg to eke out an existence. Many exegetes in the past have tried, says Soares, to spiritualize the meaning of poor (as those who trust in God), but increasingly exegetes are coming to recognize the poor as a sociological category. The poor to whom Jesus announces "good news" include the destitute (the indebted, those subsisting on daily wage labor or by begging), the illiterate, and the socially outcast. "All these are 'poor' because all are seen as victims of an oppression . . . which reduces them to a condition of diminished capacity or worth."[30]

Second, while wisdom literature sometimes attributes poverty to internal factors (laziness, drunkenness), the rest of the Bible locates the cause of poverty in external factors: "the exploitation of the poor by elite groups that dominate and oppress them." In the Old Testament the poor are opposed not so much to the rich but to the wicked, the haughty, and the powerful who exploit them, deceive them, and deprive them of their rights. The situation of the poor varied at different periods of Israel's history. Exploitation worsened as they passed from the relatively egalitarian tribal society of the premonarchical period to the monarchy where nobility owned the land and controlled society, and then to the periods of exile when poverty became so widespread that all Israel was seen as poor. In the New Testament, conflict and exploitation receive less emphasis. The poor are contrasted not with the wicked but with the "rich" whose greed and preoccupation with material wealth leave them indifferent to the poor (for example, Dives and Lazarus). But the New Testament clearly shows that God intends to reverse their situation — as indicated in the Magnificat and the Beatitudes.

Third, the Bible presents the poor not as a group of passive victims who can only hope for deliverance. "They are given a significant role in biblical history." In the Old Testament Soares sees the dynamic noted by Lohfink. The people of Israel are not only liberated from slavery in Egypt but called at Mount Sinai "to form the free, just, nonexploitative community that will serve as a 'contrast community' to the oppressive, violent, and power-hungry city states among which Israel lives."[31] The strong social legislation enacted by Israel witnessed to God's plan; the denunciations of the preexilic prophets witness to Israel's failure to live up to this plan; but the dream of one day realizing this contrast community remains and is reflected in the postexilic promises of "a new heaven and a new earth." In the New Testament, the poor continue to be the bearers of salvation and hope. Jesus identifies with the poor and preaches good news to them; the early church thought of itself as a church of the poor (1 Cor 1:26–28).

Soares concludes ultimately that despite analogies with Marx's view of the proletariat, the biblical poor include all the marginalized of society (who also put their hope in God); hence they do not fit into Marx's definition of the proletarian working class.

CHRISTOLOGY AND THE MISSION OF JESUS

The person, the words, and the work of Jesus quite clearly lie at the heart of Christian faith and Christian theology. If questions about the nature(s) and person of Jesus have traditionally occupied the attention of most theologians, liberation theology would focus most especially on the mission of Jesus, on the message he brought to the world. Jesus initiated his public life by proclaiming that "the kingdom of God is at hand," and that proclamation holds a place of central importance in liberation theology.

Leonardo Boff and Contemporary Christology

In *Jesus Christ Liberator* Leonardo Boff presented one of the first efforts by a liberation theologian to establish a christology with characteristics distinctive of Latin America. He articulated as distinctive traits: one that focuses on the human person rather than the church; one that stresses utopian hopes for the future; one critical of ecclesial institutions; one that emphasizes the social dimension; and one that gives primacy to orthopraxis over orthodoxy.[32]

Some would criticize Boff's claim that the christology he developed really constituted a distinctive Latin American development. Certainly this initial work does have much in common with the christologies articulated in Europe in recent decades. Boff himself acknowledges the extraordinary output of scholarly works about Jesus by Rahner, Kasper, Schillebeeckx, Pannenberg, Küng, Moltmann, and many other European theologians. He devotes the first chapters of his book to these new formulations of christology. Theologians will be quite familiar with these developments, but a very brief summary may prove useful for other readers.

Throughout most of the history of the church, Christians have built their faith on what modern theologians now call a "descending christology." The Gospel of John provided a main basis for this christology. "In the beginning was the Word; the Word was with God, and the Word was God" (Jn 1:1). Jesus was/is the second person of the Blessed Trinity who became human in order to redeem us. Faith in the divinity of Jesus became the chief focus of Christian belief. In recent decades an "ascending christology," which seeks to supplement the descending christology with greater attention to the humanity of Jesus, has become more dominant. It affirms the divinity of Jesus but, for example, tends to view Jesus' consciousness of his mission and of his own person as developing gradually and humanly rather than as total divine knowledge from the outset.

Along with this emphasis on the humanity of Jesus have come voluminous studies about the history of the New Testament itself: the dating of the different gospels and epistles, the oral or written sources that fed into a given gospel, the theological concerns that led the four evangelists to select and order their stories about Jesus in different ways, the influences of changing problems faced by the early church on the composition of the gospels, and similar issues.

These theological developments, all too briefly summarized, have unquestionably influenced liberation theology. It clearly stresses an "ascending christology," which dwells on the historical Jesus, the Jesus who defended the poor. Its theologians seek to distinguish between what Jesus emphasized in his teachings and action, and how the church in subsequent decades and centuries came to interpret his message.

For Boff, as for most other liberation theologians, the central message of Jesus lies in his preaching of the kingdom of God. Boff's statement about

the kingdom merits citing in full because it captures many of the characteristics, noted at the beginning of this section, that Boff sees as distinctive
of a Latin American christology:

> Initially, Jesus preached neither himself nor the church, but the king-
> dom of God. The kingdom of God is the realization of a fundamental
> utopia of the human heart, the total transfiguration of this world, free
> from all that alienates human beings, free from pain, sin, divisions,
> and death. He came and announced: "The time has come, the king-
> dom of God is close at hand!" He not only promised this new reality
> but already began to realize it, showing that it is possible in the world.
> He therefore did not come to alienate human beings and carry them
> off to another world. He came to confirm the good news: this sinister
> world has a final destiny that is good, human, and divine.[33]

In the body of his work, Boff presents a view of Jesus quite different
from the picture some critics attribute to liberation theology. Jesus, says
Boff, was not a revolutionary and did not preach rebellion; "he demands
a conversion of persons," and a love of friends and enemies alike. The
kingdom he preached promised the realization of the utopian society cher-
ished by human hearts, but would be "brought about by God and only by
God."[34] Boff speaks clearly, however, about Jesus' attacks on the Pharisees
who oppressed consciences with the unsupportable regimentation of legal
prescriptions, and he notes that conversion must affect not only persons
but structures of legalism and authoritarianism.[35]

In commenting on images of Jesus as a dissenter, revolutionary, and
liberator, Boff states that up to a certain point there is truth in these, but
that Christ is not defined by any "against." He is "in favor" of love, justice,
and hope. He preached a kingdom that looked to a global transformation
of the structures of this world, but Jesus "is not a revolutionary in the
emotional and ideological sense of a violent and rebellious action against
the socio-political."[36] In an epilogue, written six years later (1978) as an
appendix to the English edition of his work, Boff writes in much more
revolutionary tones, not rescinding anything he wrote before but speaking
of Jesus almost entirely in a context of conflict and struggle.

In *Passion of Christ, Passion of the World*, Boff takes up christological
questions about the meaning of Jesus' suffering and death. I will reserve
some reflections on this work, however, for the section on spirituality, for
it also falls under that category and because I discuss the meaning of
Christ's death in presenting Jon Sobrino's contributions to christology.

One very harsh critic of Boff's work, a Brazilian biblical scholar Fr. J.E.
Martins Terra, S.J., claims that the Vatican's problems with Boff arose
precisely over his christology. The Vatican investigated him and then silenced him, says Terra, not "as a liberation theologian" nor even primarily
for his controversial writings on the church, but because he commits the

same doctrinal errors found in German, liberal-Bultmannian christology.[37] What Boff writes as a liberation theologian poses no problem; "in none of his writings does he use Marxist analysis." But his treatment of the consciousness of Christ (having no foreknowledge) makes it impossible to explain how Jesus could have instituted the eucharist and the other sacraments, or how he founded the church. Boff, Terra adds, uses the historical Jesus when useful—for example, Jesus' preaching of the kingdom—but denies at other times that we can really know the true historical Jesus.[38]

Terra's remarks represent a type of critique aimed not at liberationist themes directly but at a whole trend in modern christology, concerned with the question of the "humanity" of Jesus. Any adequate response to Terra's criticisms would involve a defense not only of Boff but of Bernard Lonergan, Karl Rahner, Schillebeeckx, and many others who have developed new interpretations of the consciousness of Christ, how much foreknowledge he possessed, and on other questions related to his humanity.

Other critics, however, more sympathetic to the newer christologies, nevertheless question the accuracy and consistency of some liberation writings on christology. A Mexican theologian, Carlos Ignacio Gonzales, assesses Boff's christology in a generally favorable light but finds inconsistencies in Boff's statements about the historical Jesus. Boff asserts that we cannot reconstruct the path of the historical Jesus, since the writings of the New Testament are all theological interpretations. But at the same time he gives "scientific" value to "facts" about Jesus (for example, that the Sanhedrin perceived him as a threat to their authority or that Pilate perceived immediately that Jesus was not a Zealot).[39]

Jon Sobrino on Jesus' Mission

From El Salvador, Jon Sobrino brought his own distinctive questions to the common concern in Latin America for a christology of liberation. Christologies of the past asked most frequently about Jesus: "Who is he?" The question that prompted Sobrino's search was: "What did he try to do?," a question about his mission in life. This question ties in with elements Sobrino shares in common with other liberation theologians. He shares clearly in liberation theology's stress on a methodology that arises "from within a context of praxis."[40] He seeks to develop a christology that begins not with church dogmas about Jesus, nor on the preaching of the early church, but on the historical Jesus. He focuses on "those christological elements that serve to constitute a paradigm of liberation."[41] Three themes, I believe, stand out as distinctive contributions of Sobrino's christology, his reflections on (1) the preaching of Jesus about the kingdom and its implications for sin; (2) the faith of Jesus; (3) the death of Jesus. These reflections draw chiefly from his *Christology at the Crossroads* but with some important additions from his other writings.

The Preaching of the Kingdom. "The most certain historical datum about

Jesus' life is that the concept which dominated his preaching, the reality which gave meaningfulness to all his activity, was the kingdom of God."[42] Jesus preached not about himself primarily or even about God in general, but about the kingdom of God. Sobrino shares with Boff and most liberation theologians this conviction about the centrality of the kingdom. Mention of it remains important, however, because Sobrino's whole christology builds on Jesus' preaching of the kingdom. Sobrino sees the kingdom as a total restructuring of human relations. He sees the kingdom also as grace, coming from God's initiative, with Jesus' miracles and forgiveness as signs of liberation. He sees the kingdom not just as good news for the poor but as a revelation of who God is and what God values and wants for human society. Sobrino believes that Jesus called his disciples first to preach the coming of the kingdom and then, when failure came, to live as suffering servants in imitation of him. Of the poor Jesus asked for hope and trust; of his disciples he asked for service.[43]

Sobrino further develops his views on the kingdom in an essay, "The Centrality of the 'Kingdom of God' in Liberation Theology." Liberation theology has as its primary concern the liberation of the poor, and this primacy finds hope given in Jesus' proclamation of the kingdom. The kingdom also offers a "totality" for theological reflection, for it includes transcendence and history, salvation and liberation, hope and human practice, the personal and the social, and it points to sin as the chief obstacle to its realization. There is, however, a problem: Jesus never says *what* the kingdom is, only that it is near. Sobrino then offers and evaluates three approaches for understanding the content of the kingdom: by looking at how contemporaries of Jesus saw it, by looking at the praxis of Jesus (his cures, his forgiveness, his expulsion of demons and the compassion he manifests), and by looking at those to whom the promise of the kingdom was given ("blessed are the poor, for theirs is the kingdom of heaven").[44]

The kingdom calls for a response of human effort and praxis, but these do not deny the gratuity of God's gift. Sobrino recognizes the relativized character of any human movement toward liberation. Liberation theology, he says, does not reject an "eschatological reserve"; it does not identify the fullness of the kingdom with any human effort. But it does judge that some forms are better than others in realizing the will of God.[45]

In *Christology at the Crossroads* Sobrino links to the call of the kingdom his reflections on sin. According to Sobrino, Jesus views sin not simply as saying no to God, "but as saying no to the kingdom of God." Sin must be not just pardoned but taken away, and taking it away means eliminating oppression. Jesus does stress the personal character of sin, but he denounces primarily the collective, social, and structural aspects of sin: the Pharisees who put legal concerns over human need, the lawyers who lay burdens on persons, the rich who refuse to share their wealth with the poor. Sobrino sees sin above all as use of power to oppress others.[46]

In an article, "Liberation from Sin," Sobrino dwells especially on the acceptance of the gratuity of God's forgiveness. The proclamation that Jesus has liberated us from sin, says Sobrino, is essential to Christian faith. But we have difficulty in recognizing our own sinfulness. The social sciences, for example, can diminish our sense of sin: psychology by attributing it to neuroses, the social sciences by so focusing on structures of sin that we lose all sense of personal responsibility. But a sense of sin depends above all, says Sobrino, on the experience of pardon, a pardon that comes from the gratuity of God's love. A true experience of forgiveness requires faith in God's gratuitous love. It involves not just being absolved but experiencing oneself "as accepted," as loved by God. Forgiveness restores our dignity. It makes us recognize our sin, but it also calls us to forgive others and to ask what we can do for the suffering peoples of the world. He concludes his essay with a story of his visit to a refugee camp in El Salvador. The poor there could have rightfully viewed outsiders as offenders, but they received him and others with openness and hospitality because they have experienced God's gratuitous love and acceptance.[47]

The Faith of Jesus. Sobrino's treatment of the faith of Jesus and of its relevance to Christian morality remains for me the most insightful and personally enriching discovery in liberation theology. Sobrino boldly challenges St. Thomas Aquinas who argued that because Jesus had perfect knowledge of God he could not have faith which assumes lack of knowledge. But the letter to the Hebrews, says Sobrino, states that Jesus "leads us in our faith and brings it to perfection" (Heb 12:2). Jesus was made perfect, through suffering; he has been through temptation with us; "he was faithful to the one who appointed him" (Heb 2:10, 18; 3:2). When Jesus first preached the kingdom, he relied on his inherited faith from Judaism. When he realized his efforts were meeting with failure, and above all when he hung from the cross, his faith took the form of pure trust in God.

Jesus was perfect, but perfection did not entail knowing all things (as the Greek and consequently Aquinas' view implied). Jesus' faith reflected rather the Jewish biblical sense of persevering fidelity. He remains faithful to the mission his Father gave him, faithful to the work of the kingdom. This very human dimension of Jesus' faith comes as truly good news for the poor, for they see Jesus as one with whom they can truly identify in their own sufferings and their struggles to retain hope.

The basis of Christian morality proceeds from our faith in Jesus. Compelled by love and gratitude for the gift of Jesus in our lives, we feel an urgent need to be like Jesus. To love him and to desire to be like him means that we too wish to establish the kingdom of God in history and to undertake the actions that will concretely fashion the kingdom.[48]

The Death of Jesus. Sobrino speaks boldly also about the death of Jesus. He sees the "scandal of the cross" not simply in the fact that the Son of God suffered an ignominious death, but that God allowed him to feel abandoned and the work of the kingdom to appear lost. Following the work of Jürgen Moltmann, Sobrino also believes that we should not hesitate to speak of *God suffering* on the cross. Again the Greek notion of God as perfection has led the church to conceive of God as immutable and therefore beyond suffering. But, Sobrino asks, can we truly believe that God loves humans without being affected by their misery?

Sobrino's major point about the crucifixion, however, the one that relates most directly to the cause of liberation theology, deals with the reason for Jesus' death on the cross. Jesus suffered the crucifixion not, as St. Anselm argued, because God willed it as payment for our sins. Jesus' death was intrinsically connected to the mission and work of his life. In proclaiming the kingdom, Jesus held forth a true image of God, a God who seeks to liberate the poor from oppression and to have all persons live in solidarity. In doing this, says Sobrino, Jesus also denounced those who "manipulated" religion, using the idea of God to oppress others and to justify their oppression as law. Jesus was accused of blasphemy because he unmasked the Pharisees' idea and use of God. He was condemned as a political agitator (suffering crucifixion, the punishment imposed on political agitators, rather than the religious punishment of stoning) because he challenged their use of power.[49]

Sobrino writes also of the resurrection as showing the power of God over death, as confirmation in justice of Jesus' fidelity, and as inaugurating a new liberating hope for the future. In his later work, *Jesus in Latin America*, Sobrino stresses the "hope against hope" that the resurrection offers most especially to those who are "crucified" by injustice in the world: who suffer oppression from idolators of wealth, or who literally are tortured and killed in the name of national security.[50]

Sobrino became a very specific target of Cardinal Ratzinger's March 1984 essay discussed in the last chapter. He also came under a formal investigation by the Vatican. Fr. Juan Alfaro, a Jesuit theologian in Rome, was appointed to evaluate his orthodoxy. In a foreword to Sobrino's *Jesus in Latin America*, Alfaro notes that Sobrino himself recognized possible dangers and misunderstandings occasioned by some texts in his earlier book on christology, which Sobrino said "may be the fault of limitation, precipitation, or imprecision in (their) formulations." Sobrino used the *Jesus in Latin America* book to clarify his positions. Alfaro judges Sobrino to be fully "orthodox" on the four fundamental truths of christology. Sobrino, he says, expressly and repeatedly asserts his faith in the divinity of Christ; he acknowledges his belief in the normative, binding character of christological dogmas as defined by the councils of the church; he asserts his faith in Christian eschatology; and he professes his faith in Christian liberation as "integral liberation." He asserts these, Alfaro adds, "without any ambiguity." Moreover, "Sobrino never resorts to the Marxist analysis of society, nor does he ever draw his inspiration from any ideology alien to Christianity."[51]

In addition to questions of orthodoxy, however, some have challenged

Sobrino's use of biblical exegesis. I will consider one such critique after a discussion of Segundo, for the critique targets them both.

Juan Luis Segundo and the Political Dimension

Segundo brings his own distinctive method and style to the discussion of christology in his *The Historical Jesus of the Synoptics*. He speaks rather disparagingly of Boff's and Sobrino's christologies as more European than Latin American. He says that his own effort might better be designated an "antichristology" because he wants to liberate theology from inauthentic presentations of Jesus, so that even nonbelievers and atheists can see what Jesus really represented: a witness to certain human values and to a more humane and liberated human life.[52] We would never have theologized about Jesus, Segundo remarks, had he not attracted the interest of his contemporaries by the values he stood for. Clearly, then, the humanity of Jesus serves as the focus of Segundo's christological reflections.

The factor of "interest" figures prominently in Segundo's approach. We respond to Jesus, as did his contemporaries, not because we believe his words come from God (though in faith we may later come to believe this also). Rather we respond because Jesus speaks to us; he is of interest to us; he stirs and revives our spirit. Segundo covers himself against the charge of secularizing the gospel: "I believe that Jesus was the Word of God made human, God's very self."[53] But the real power of Jesus shows itself in the witness he gives and in the witnesses he inspires in addressing different human problems. The synoptic gospels made concern for the poor the interest Jesus addressed primarily. St. Paul felt that Jesus spoke also to the issues and interests of the people of Corinth and Rome, "so he feels free to create his own gospel."[54] Segundo believes, moreover, that we can legitimately create new gospels today so that Jesus may speak, and awaken our interest, in our day. Any claim to preach the gospel must, however, show its consistency with the gospel Jesus preached, and Segundo sets forth hermeneutical rules or criteria for getting at the historical Jesus.

Segundo devotes a special chapter to the "political dimension" of Jesus' life and ministry (a dimension stressed by many other liberation theologians as well).[55] Jesus posed a serious threat to the leaders of his day; the Pharisees, Saducces, and Herodians all wanted to get rid of him; and he died as a political agitator. Segundo believes that the postpaschal Christian community downplayed this political dimension and emphasized the spiritual. Jesus did not agitate for political or social change in a modern sense, and it would be anachronistic, says Segundo, to speak of class struggle in the first century A.D. But Jesus' actions did, in fact, sharpen conflicts in society.

In the chapter on the political dimension, Segundo again takes up a problem he addressed in *Faith and Ideologies*, which I discussed in chapter 2. Critics of liberation theology argue that Jesus shows himself concerned primarily, if not exclusively, with "conversion of the heart." Segundo takes a different tack in responding to this than do other liberation theologians. There is overwhelming evidence, says Segundo, for this view. Jesus does focus on interpersonal relations with God and with others, not with changing structures. If, however, we wish to respond with "effective love" in today's world, we must transpose the values Jesus stood for and find efficacious means for actualizing them. Interpersonal charity will not change unfair trade relations.

In subsequent chapters Segundo takes up various points about Jesus' preaching. He argues, for example, that Jesus aroused interest not as a founder of a new religion but as one who presented religion with a political dimension. Jesus promised a kingdom *for* the poor, not based on their worthiness but simply from love of the poor. Luke's first beatitude, "Blessed are the poor," expresses God's promise to the poor, "for *theirs* is the kingdom of heaven." Matthew's first beatitude, "Blessed are the poor in spirit," does not change this option but expresses the virtue and attitude that Jesus' disciples must have.[56] In Mark's Gospel, says Segundo, Jesus places no demands or exhortations on the poor. He demands radical conversion, on the other hand, from those who oppress others, and he demands certain prophetic qualities and virtues from his disciples.[57]

Criticism and Assessment

U.S. biblical scholar John P. Meier presented a rather scathing critique of both Sobrino and Segundo in an address to the Catholic Theological Society of America (June 1988). Meier focused his critique on the works in christology I have discussed: Sobrino's *Christology at the Crossroads* and his *Jesus in Latin America* and Segundo's *The Historical Jesus of the Synoptics*. He faults both theologians for their dealing with the question of the "historical Jesus." Sobrino, says Meier, cites very few important exegetes at any length, and he has no extended, critical discussion of the meaning of the historical Jesus nor of criteria for dealing with this topic. Meier asserts that the historical Jesus means that which the methods of historical criticism enable us to retrieve about Jesus of Nazareth. These historical reconstructions cannot be identified, however, with the "real" Jesus. Sobrino glosses over this and sometimes equates the historical Jesus with the humanity of Jesus and at other times with Jesus' earthly career. Segundo gives much more extensive treatment to the historical Jesus, says Meier, and he offers criteria for determining historicity. But he frequently fails to follow his own criteria in practice.

In terms of application, Meier criticizes both liberation theologians for their handling of Jesus' concern for the poor. Sobrino lumps together the poor, the oppressed, and sinners as objects of God's favor. Jesus created scandal by forgiving sinners, Meier asserts, but not all sinners were poor (for example, Zaccheus). There is no proof that Jesus' concern for the economically poor caused him to be persecuted or was grounds for his crucifixion. Segundo likewise lumps many diverse categories together, according to Meier. Segundo uses the parable of the Pharisee and the publican to illustrate Jesus' partiality to the poor, but publicans were not poor. Jesus was criticized for his association with sinners, not for his concern for the poor.

Finally, Meier faults both Sobrino and Segundo for their "oversimplified" view of Judaism in Jesus' time. Exegetical studies have shown, says Meier, that the Pharisees probably had little to do with Jesus' death. The polemics against the Pharisees in Matthew's Gospel reflect the period of A.D. 70 and do not accurately reflect the Pharisees' teachings or behavior in Jesus' time. Meier claims admiration for liberation theology, but his critique descends to a level of demeaning, invective language ("woefully ignorant" of scholarship about Judaism, "simplistic," "naive," substituting "unsubstantiated generalizations for the hard work of Jesus-research").[58]

In response to Meier's critique several points might be noted. First, Meier may be correct in judging that Sobrino's and Segundo's scholarship, with respect to biblical interpretation, falls short of the standards set by Schillebeeckx and others. But they are hermeneutical theologians trying to draw attention to dimensions of Jesus neglected in traditional christologies; Meier judges them by his own field, which bases interpretations on what most, or the most recent, exegetes have said. He also assumes his own definition of "the historical Jesus" as definitive. Secondly, and most importantly, Meier criticizes their generalizations and insists on accuracy, but his own criticisms fall short of these norms. He says, in respect to Sobrino, that there is no proof that Jesus' concern for the "economically poor" caused the conflict that led to his being crucified. But Sobrino does not present Jesus as dying in defense of the economically poor. He speaks rather of Jesus proclaiming a kingdom to end all forms of oppression, which leads to conflict with those who would use religion to defend privilege (not necessarily or even primarily the privileges of wealth). Similarly, when Segundo uses the parable of the Pharisee and the publican, he explains clearly in two endnotes (*The Historical Jesus of the Synoptics*, p. 201) that he is *not* talking about the economic status of the Pharisee and the publicans. Jesus' poor, he says, take in all who are suffering and marginalized, and hence would include the publicans. Finally, Meier's point about oversimplifying the role of the Pharisees in Jesus' death appears quite valid in the light of recent scholarship. But even on this point, the particular work he cites (E. P. Sanders, *Jesus and Judaism*) was published after Sobrino and Segundo had completed their works.

Assessments made about the level of biblical scholarship reflected in liberation theology will differ according to the particular work in question. Pixley's work on exodus appears much more careful in its interpretation than the earlier commentaries of Croatto and Richard. Further assessment of the works in christology would require much more expertise in biblical studies than I possess. One obvious problem, however, stems from the amount of *emphasis* given to socio-political emancipation in liberation theology. For example, Gutiérrez speaks of three levels of liberation but the first half of *A Theology of Liberation* deals almost exclusively with the issue of socio-political emancipation and most of the discussion about liberation from sin deals with eliminating unjust structures caused by sin. Croatto's interpretation of exodus does not deny the religious aspects of the covenant but focuses on the political act of liberation. Segundo's christology acknowledges the interpersonal aspects of Jesus' teaching but dwells almost exclusively on the political dimension of his ministry. Thus while liberation theology never "reduces" faith to politics, it has directed most of its energy to socio-political liberation.

Liberation theologians tend at times to use scripture in the way traditional Catholic apologetics once did to "prove" Catholic doctrines (e.g., the primacy of Peter). They select the particular facts of interpretations that most favor a liberation position. The same criticism, however, would also apply to conservative theologians who promote a "theology of reconciliation" or who emphasize only Jesus' teachings in respect to interpersonal relations.

In defense of liberation theology, it swung strongly in its emphases to counteract a centuries-old tradition that almost exclusively equated Christian life with personal devotions and obtaining personal forgiveness from sins to the neglect of the social miseries that have afflicted the vast majority of Latin Americans. It does not intend to give "all" that theology might say about God and the preaching of Jesus. It presents itself as a "corrective" to past theology. Liberation theology has also matured and developed over the years, creating a fuller, more integrated theology. This will become more evident in the next chapter on spirituality and on efforts to include issues raised from feminist perspectives.

As a transition to the theme of spirituality and popular religion in the next chapter, and as an illustration of why liberation theologians feel compelled to challenge traditional views on religion, I might conclude this chapter with some brief reflections about a book of essays, *The Faces of Jesus*. Several of the essays describe the "alienating" images of Jesus long prevalent in Latin America: for example, the image of a suffering, dying Jesus, which could inspire courage in the face of suffering but too often reinforces fatalism and projects Jesus as "defeated" and powerless to do anything; or Jesus as a helpless infant in the hands of Mary; or Jesus as a "heavenly monarch," an image too easily used by those in power to legitimize their authority.[59] To counteract these images liberation theologians seek to present Jesus as a liberator, one whose words and actions challenge the prevailing order. Still, none of the theologians in this book attempt to picture Jesus as a "political revolutionary." They reject such a description explicitly. Jesus was not "a guerilla Christ," a Che Guevara of his day; Jesus rejected the political messianism of the Zealots; he was not a political leader proposing a program and strategy of change; he was a religious leader.[60] The book also contains a useful and balanced synthesis of the political implications of Jesus' life, presented in a series of "theses" by Segundo Galilea.

Chapter 5

Two Special Themes:
Spirituality and Women

Controversy over issues about Marxism, social analysis, and political readings of scripture has created a distorted image of liberation theology. In terms of quantity, especially if one examines liberation theology in the 1980s, writings about liberation *spirituality* far outweigh works in all the areas that arouse debate. I would clearly designate spirituality as *the* dominant theme of contemporary liberation theology. This spirituality involves both a call to follow Jesus in working *for* and *with* the poor, but also profound reflection on what all Christians can learn about God *from* the poor. Because so many liberation theologians have written about spirituality, any selection of works will prove somewhat arbitrary. I have focused especially in this chapter on some works by Galilea and Gutiérrez, and have also included a section on the spirituality expressed in "popular religion."

The second special theme of this chapter deals with "women and liberation." Women constitute a central force in the whole movement of liberation, but they have not generally had much opportunity to play this role "on center court" as prominent theologians or as a major focus of concern. Some new developments have emerged, however, and I will examine them in the second part of this chapter.

As a conclusion to the chapter, but touching on many of the theological issues discussed in previous chapters, I have singled out an important work by Gutiérrez—a work still not available in English as I write—written in defense of liberation theology and in defense of his own works in particular.

SPIRITUALITY AND POPULAR RELIGION

To commit oneself to the process of liberation is for a Christian a new way of identifying himself or herself with Christ and constitutes a novel Christian experience, full of promise and possibility, but also of difficulties and disappointments. In fact for many Latin American Christians, liberating commitment corresponds to an authentic spiritual experience in the original, biblical sense of the term: it is living in the Spirit who causes us to acknowledge ourselves in a free and creative way to be sons and daughters of the Father and brothers and sisters to each other.[1]

This quote, whose language I modified to make the language more inclusive, comes from Claude Geffré, a French theologian who edited and introduced one of the first volumes in English of essays by liberation theologians. In the first essay of this volume, Segundo Galilea wrote an essay on politics and contemplation, articulating this "new way of identifying with Christ," this "authentic spiritual experience," which involved "living in the Spirit." With dozens of works on spirituality Galilea holds a special place among liberation theologians who have written about liberation spirituality. It would seem appropriate, then, to begin this section with Galilea and with this early essay. Galilea insists especially on the integration of political commitment and contemplation, so that neither would be sacrificed to the other. Frei Betto and Jon Sobrino make similar points. The first part of my discussion on spirituality includes these three theologians and looks to reflections that assume, for the most part, a perspective of those working *with* the poor, though this would include pastoral agents and leaders who may themselves come from the ranks of the poor.

Gustavo Gutiérrez's works have focused increasingly on spirituality but with a special concern to "enter into the world of the poor." I will look at his work and this perspective as a second part of this section on spirituality. As a third section, reflecting a different type of entering into the world of the poor, I will consider studies that have investigated and evaluated "popular religion," the forms of spirituality long practiced by the peoples of Latin America.

Integrating Commitment and Contemplation

Galilea began his essay on politics and contemplation noting the problems that can and have occurred when Christians commit themselves to the struggle for liberation. The very expression "commitment to liberation," he wrote, because it has been used for ideological or party political ends, can give the impression that Christians who make this commitment are identified with some revolutionary group or with those who accept Marxist analysis as a basis for action. Commitment itself can also engender a crisis of faith. The traditional categories of faith — sin, salvation, charity, prayer — do not inspire or illuminate sufficiently one's commitment. "The commitment to liberation in the Christian must be a place of encounter with God and therefore a source of inspiration" to one's theological and contemplative life.[2] But too easily do Christians become divided into camps: the militant and the contemplative. The contemplatives see only the strictly religious values — prayer, liturgy, transcendence — to the neglect of the politico-social. The militants begin to distrust these "vertical" elements and can risk losing their faith entirely.

An authentic integration needs to occur, and Galilea believed it was beginning to occur more frequently with those who might once have lost their faith but have now discovered the value of prayer. They see the need for a faith that guarantees that their actions are motivated and governed by love, and a faith that inspires Christian hope in them. We encounter God in Jesus, which Galilea sees as the root of all the conversions to faith in the New Testament, and we encounter God in our neighbors, particularly those in greatest need ("I was hungry . . .," Mt 25:31). Encounter with Christ in prayer leads us to go out of ourselves and to serve others, and encounter with others brings us back to prayer.[3]

Galilea further develops this concern for an integrated spirituality in his work *Following Jesus*. The gospel teaches us that "to be a disciple of Jesus is to follow him, and that this is what Christian life is."[4] We must learn from Jesus and reach out to our neighbor, especially those most in need as Jesus taught (for example, the Good Samaritan and Mt 25). Jesus calls us especially to enter into the world of the poor and to become spiritually poor ourselves, detached from material goods and using money in the service of justice.[5]

Galilea sees prayer, which is a gift from God, as essential to Christian spirituality. "What gives quality to any commitment is the mystique that inspires it, or the motives for this commitment." It is in contemplation, "not in a revolutionary dialectic," that believers find strength for their work of liberation; "if Christianity does not 'go into the desert' in order to get away from the 'system,' it will never be free or prophetic and able to liberate others."[6]

Following Jesus involves embracing his mission and his fidelity to the Father; the cross has no meaning except in fidelity to a mission. "The identification of the oppressed with the cross is not their identification with the humiliation of Christ, but with his crucified power, which calls them to a certain task."[7] We are called to follow Jesus in his work of liberation. His message of liberation, says Galilea, "contains no program or strategy of political liberation." But his preaching of the kingdom "implants in a society values that will allow for the criticism of all forms of social and structural sin, including all forms of domination and exploitation."[8]

In his final chapter, Galilea seeks to bring forth the importance of Mary in the life of the poor. Recent theology has emphasized the humanity of Jesus; so now must we stress the human qualities of Mary, a humanness that was often lost in the past with theological emphasis on the privileges and titles of Mary. Like the poor of today, Mary experienced poverty, suffering, flight, and exile. Mary is important to the people of Latin America; she is "part of our profane history, both popular and heroic"; she is not just a doctrine but "the great adopted one of the Latin American people."[9] At Guadalupe and in other appearances revered by the peoples of Latin America, Mary revealed herself to the poor. If the new base community movement stresses community, rather than juridical aspects of the church, and affectivity, rather than rationalistic thought, these owe much to the influence of Mary, in Galilea's judgment.

Frei Betto also addresses an issue discussed by Galilea in the first essay we considered. Galilea spoke of a crisis of spirituality and of the danger of setting aside prayer or even losing one's faith when one enters into a commitment to political liberation. Betto takes up this same concern, reflecting on the actual experiences of many pastoral agents in Brazil in their work with base communities. These pastoral agents, Betto observes, function as "organic intellectuals" in their relation to base ecclesial communities. Too often the spirituality they grew up with showed itself indifferent to the world of political concerns. In that spirituality one found Christ by "leaving" the world. Spirituality meant something done in silence, apart, and inside cloistered walls. Thus many pastoral agents, fired with concern for political liberation, often neglected prayer both in their own personal lives and in organizing groups of the poor, or they might "baptize" group discussions by calling them prayer.

The people in the base communities often lost confidence in pastoral agents as a consequence. Many felt that the agent did not seem to value the world of faith. Many in the base communities had joined together precisely because they wanted a deeper experience of God; they wanted God to strengthen them. Social reflection, Betto asserts, cannot substitute for the experience of God that many of the poor desire. Pastoral activity cannot limit itself to a "Christian view of the world" and to political tasks; it must help develop a conscious adherence to the person of Jesus Christ. People join base communities because of their adherence to Jesus and to the church. They should be encouraged to join with popular movements and to struggle for liberation, but the "properly political" tasks and the defining of goals and tactics belong to these movements, not to the church.[10] This emphasis on prayer and spiritual reflection does not diminish the commitment to liberating practice. Rather, as Leonardo Boff comments, prayer sustains us in struggle and guarantees our Christian identity in the process of liberation.[11]

Jon Sobrino, in his *Spirituality of Liberation,* emphasizes this last point made by Boff and the integration stressed by Galilea and Betto. Christian existence contains a certain bipolarity. The historical element focuses on working for the kingdom, for justice, and on service to others. The transcendent element involves knowledge of God and faith in God. We cannot, however, truly confess faith in God without service to the kingdom. But we are called upon, says Sobrino, not just to imitate the liberating praxis of Jesus, but also to discover and to take on the *spirit* of his praxis. We must, as the beatitudes teach us, be poor in spirit. We must have purity of heart and not let egoism in pursuing some cause dictate our actions. We must be open always to the word of God.

This spirit does not involve a choice between action or contemplation, but an integration of both. A spirituality of liberation calls for a spirit of courage in the face of persecution, a spirit of quest for the truth (especially in theology), a spirit of fidelity, and a spirit of holiness.[12]

Entering into the World of the Poor

In recent years, Gustavo Gutiérrez has devoted much of his time and writing to the question of spirituality. In the ranks of academia spiritual theology does not generally rate the importance given to christology, ecclesiology, and other areas of systematic theology. In liberation theology, however, and for understanding Gutiérrez in particular, spirituality holds a place of great importance. Gutiérrez considers the very purpose of theological reflection as helping Christians to become better followers of Jesus. Thus he believes that "all theology is spiritual theology."[13]

In *We Drink from Our Own Wells,* Gutiérrez reflects theologically on the spiritual journey of the poor in Latin America and the journey of those who have attempted to walk with the poor. When liberation theology first emerged, Gutiérrez wrote about the "revolutionary ferment" alive throughout Latin America. The revolutionary excitement has dimmed, but Gutiérrez finds a deeper, more faith-centered hope still strong. He sees an "irruption of the poor" into history, such that society will never be able to ignore the poor as it did for so long. "Ours is a land of premature and unjust death, but also an ever-stronger assertion of the right to life and to the joy of Easter."[14]

"How shall we sing to the Lord in a foreign land?" Gutiérrez asks in part 1 of *We Drink from Our Own Wells.* How is it possible to find joy and hope when conditions remain so wretched? The situation in Latin America remains one of suffering, poverty, and death. Traditional views often treated spirituality as the special domain of those with religious vows or as an individualistic, purely interior life; such views no longer suffice. A new emerging spirituality finds God in the midst of suffering. Harshness and suffering are not new, but what is new is that the people have begun to recognize the causes of their situation and seek to release themselves. They have also discovered a new faith in a God who liberates. Thus Latin America is now experiencing a time of solidarity, a time of prayer, and a time of martyrdom:

> The struggles of the poor for liberation represent an assertion of their right to life. The poverty that the poor suffer means death: a premature and unjust death. It is on the basis of this affirmation of life that the poor of Latin America are trying to live their faith, recognize the love of God, and proclaim their hope. Within these struggles, with their many forms and phases, an oppressed and believing people is increasingly creating a way of Christian life, a spirituality.[15]

Gutiérrez then examines the basic elements in all true forms of Christian spirituality. "A spirituality is walking in freedom according to the spirit of love and life."[16] It begins with experiences of encounters with the Lord, and Gutiérrez recounts how the first disciples of Jesus were encountered and called by the Lord. It involves "walking according to the Spirit" (Rom 8:4), and Gutiérrez notes that St. Paul's theology treats the human person as a whole, not as a soul in conflict with body. It involves the journey of a people, and a way of life "that gives a profound unity to our prayer, thought, and action."[17]

This new spirituality, while seeking effective means to bring about change, also recognizes the gratuitousness of God's love. "It is surprising to see a people becoming increasingly better organized and more effective in the struggle to assert its right to life and justice, and at the same time giving evidence of a profound sense of prayer and of a conviction that in the final analysis love and peace are an unexpected gift of God."[18] In spite of great suffering, this new spirituality also affirms and experiences joy. The believing poor, says Gutiérrez, have never lost their capacity for having a good time and celebrating, despite the harsh conditions in which they live. This new spirituality requires humility and a sense of spiritual childhood, especially for those who are not poor but who seek to cross into the world of the poor. Finally, this spirituality involves a solitude needed to avoid the dangers of scattered commitment and unmitigated activities, but a solitude that leads one also to value the support of a faith community.[19]

Gutiérrez takes up this spirituality of the poor again in his meditative, theological reflection *On Job*. The questions he poses again come out of his experience of work with the poor. "How are we to talk about a God who is revealed as love in a situation characterized by poverty and oppression?" "What words are we to use in telling those who are not even regarded as persons that they are daughters and sons of God?"[20]

These disturbing questions led Gutiérrez to meditate on the book of Job. The poor of Latin America have done no injustice to bring on their misery and oppression. Theirs is the suffering of the innocent. So also was the suffering of Job. Job once had everything, and so Satan challenges God. Satan wagers that if Job lost his earthly blessings, he would turn against God. The issue, as Gutiérrez presents it, concerns whether a "disinterested love of God is possible," or whether, as Satan believes, humans adhere to God and to religion only out of fear of punishment or hope of reward.[21] Though Job curses the day he was born, he does not turn against God. He does not possess an adequate theology with which to counter his friends and those who try to convince him that he must have sinned against God and others. But Job knows he is not at fault.

Gutiérrez draws a number of spiritual insights from this mediation on Job. It points up a special suffering the poor experience in being treated as nonpersons in society; the poor, like Job, often feel that no one cares to listen to them. The most important lesson of the book of Job, however, concerns the "gratuitousness" of God's love. God's love is freely bestowed, not given as a reward.[22] The book of Job also reveals how true love of God leads one beyond oneself to concern for others. We see this in the discourses of Job, which turned from an initial concern only about his own suffering to concern for all who are poor. This Gutiérrez sees as the true path to God.[23]

In lectures, Gutiérrez often adds spiritual insights that he has learned from the poor themselves. Thus an elderly woman responding to a question about her feelings as she came toward the close of her life commented: "In Peru, it is the children who are closer to death" (a reflection on the high infant mortality rate in the country). Another person observed that suffering and joy can coexist. "One cannot be joyful and sad at the same time, but one can experience joy in spite of suffering."

Assessing Popular Religion

Segundo Galilea, in a book on popular religiosity and pastoral responses to it, notes that a study undertaken in the early 1970s showed that 80 percent of Latin Americans practice what writers on the subject refer to as "popular religion" or "popular religiosity."[24] Latin Americans thus already possess a type of spirituality formed over the centuries. Writers on this subject generally agree on certain prevalent characteristics of this popular spirituality.[25] It stresses veneration of sacred images. Devotion focuses not just on Jesus and Mary, but on Jesus as "the Lord of the Miracles" or the "Lord of Huanca," and on Mary as "Our Lady of Carmen," "Our Lady of the Apparition," or "Our Lady of Guadalupe," and so on. The same system of patronage that has long characterized Latin American social and political life carries into its religious life. The saints are viewed as special friends of God who can bring protection to the family, help in sickness, or in finding a job. Each saint has his or her own "proven efficacy" for bringing help: St. Anthony for those looking for a husband, St. Peter for fishers, St. Joseph to bring rain. Shrines to Our Lady draw thousands in search of help or to offer thanks for favors received. Fiestas and processions serve as the focus of community celebration, though Galilea does not find them as central or significant as commonly believed.[26]

We might add to Galilea's work some reflections on popular spirituality drawn from various other sources. Certain sacraments play an important part in this spirituality, baptism most especially and many rites connected with death (Christian burial, memorial Masses, memorial shrines to honor the deceased). Marriages in the church are desirable but sometimes occur years after the couple has lived together. Blessings and holy water, considered only "sacramentals" in the Catholic tradition, have great symbolic value. If one were to judge, however, by the standard of Mass attendance used most often in the United States and Europe to measure religious practice, Latin Americans would appear "nonpracticing." Perhaps 10 percent, and in some areas less than 1 percent, attend church regularly. Most live their lives with only marginal connection to the church.

Many other factors complicate any effort to give a generalized description of popular religion. Syncretism affects religious beliefs and practices in some areas. In Brazil and Haiti especially, elements of African "animism" (worship of spirits) enter in. In Peru, Bolivia, Mexico, and other countries where Indian populations remain large, elements of traditional Indian worship fuse with Christianity. T. Matt Garr offers a fascinating study, for example, of popular religion among the Quechuans in the regions near Cusco, Peru. Relations with God among these people often take on a quid pro quo basis: if you honor God, God will bless you; if you do not, God will punish. Christian-Quechuan religion includes offerings to mother earth, Pachamama, who is not seen, however, as separate from the Christian God.[27]

I have been describing mostly Roman Catholic religiosity. But Protestant religion has made increasing inroads into the practice of religion in Latin America. Most of the growth has occurred in church groups other than "mainline" Protestant denominations, in the Assembly of God and other pentecostal churches especially, but with strong missionary activity by the Mormons, Jehovah's Witnesses, and Seventh-Day Adventists.

Urbanization creates further complexities, as Galilea discusses in the third chapter of his book. Many of the rituals that fitted rural life — for example, fiestas connected with the harvest — lose their meaning in the city. The secular atmosphere of the city can easily erode traditional religious beliefs and practices.

The pervasiveness of popular religiosity creates a special problem for liberation theology. Many elements in popular spirituality reinforce passivity and fatalism. We have seen this discussed in the section on christology, which dealt with alienating images of Jesus in Latin America: the "defeated" Christ on the cross, the "heavenly monarch" who assures order. Raúl Vidales and Tokihiro Kudo, in a study published in 1975, concluded with a very negative picture of religion in Latin America. "Popular religion," they noted, does not really express the values of the poor, but is defined by the "system" (dependent capitalism) that dominates Latin America. This religion is ritualistic and overvalues rites; it overvalues private property and Christian education; it puts institutions over persons; it stresses "vertical" relations (to God in heaven) and neglects the horizontal (God in history and the world). It encourages passivity, servility, and resignation.[28]

In recent years, however, many liberation theologians have come to value popular religion more highly and to recognize its positive features. Liberation theology wants liberation for the poor. But it also stresses respect for the poor. It wants them to experience their dignity as persons, to be proud of their identity, and to be — as Gutiérrez repeatedly states — the historical agents of their own liberation. Denigrating their religious beliefs and practices, even if some elements did originate from dominating cultures, does not advance this other side of liberation theology. Consequently many recent studies have looked for the positive, potentially liberating aspects of popular religion. Diego Irarrazaval argues that devotion to the Lord of the Miracles, to Our Lady of Carmen, or to the saints, gives the poor a strong sense that God is on their side. They venerate Our Lady of Guadalupe because she appeared to a poor Indian peasant and showed herself their protector. The celebration of fiestas allows the poor to experience something of the joy of the resurrection.[29]

Ricardo Falla, investigating popular religion in Guatemala, makes similar observations about the significance of saints and fiestas, and about the great importance of baptism for the poor. He also uses two interesting examples to show why those working with the poor must learn to respect their devotions. In Holy Week a pastoral agent wanted the poor community in which he worked to see the link between Christ's sufferings and human sufferings in the world today. So he showed slides of present-day sufferings. The people themselves expressed disappointment. They had hoped to see pictures depicting Jesus and his passion. More successful was a Good Friday procession that followed the traditional stations of the cross but noted some contemporary sufferings in connection with each one.[30]

Galilea, in his work, sets forth some criteria of evangelization that would combine respect for popular religion while moving it toward a more liberating perspective. To make it more liberating the human side of Jesus and Mary should be stressed so that they are seen as models with whom the poor can identify, and not just as powerful patrons. (The centrality of the Bible in base community meetings, we might add, has done much to make this change.) Devotions of the poor should be respected, but the way the poor "interiorize" these devotions, the attitudes they bring to them, can change.[31]

To these studies on spirituality many others might be added, including José Comblin's meditations, *Jesus of Nazareth* and *Sent from the Father.* Leonardo Boff has produced a number of works on spirituality, with books on St. Francis of Assisi, on the Lord's Prayer, on the way of the cross, and an award-winning study, *Passion of Christ, Passion of the World.* This last book, as noted earlier, could also qualify as part of christology. Like Sobrino, Boff presents Jesus' death as a consequence of his mission. He studies different interpretations of Jesus' death among primitive Christian communities and by later theologians. Then, toward the conclusion of his work, he reflects on "How to Preach the Cross of Jesus Christ Today." Jesus' cross was the consequence of his mission to liberate the poor and oppressed. To preach the cross today entails committing oneself to creating a new world of community, peace, and love. This commitment will involve confrontations with unjust structures and situations. It entails solidarity with the crucified of this world, being persecuted, and even suffering martyrdom for God's cause in the world. To preach the cross is to preach the following of Jesus, but through the cross, justice and love will eventually triumph. "Good, and good alone, shall reign."[32]

Works on spirituality do not receive much attention from critics because they contain little that is controversial. They show, however, why liberation theologians believe they represent a truly "integral" theology. These writings certainly challenge Richard Neuhaus's sweeping judgment, noted in the last chapter, that the dominant liberation theologians "exclude the transcendent as a matter of principle."

WOMEN AND LIBERATION

Liberation theology set as its goal from the outset to rethink and reformulate the Christian message to serve in the struggle for liberation of the poor and to reflect on the praxis that would promote that liberation. In contrast to the multiple issues that characterize political and social life in the United States, liberationists in Latin America have stressed the single issue of poverty and oppression. The liberation philosopher Enrique Dussel has for years spoken about a triple oppression (rich over poor, men over women, parents over children or those treated like children),[33] but even his work focuses primarily on economic domination. Many cultural historians have written about machismo in Latin America and males have clearly dominated in the life of the church, including liberation theology itself as the list of authors I have cited thus far should make evident. The preoccupation of liberation theology with the poor remains unchanged, but greater consciousness of the special oppressions suffered by women (and also by Indians and blacks) has begun to emerge more clearly, and the role of women in liberation theology itself has developed as well.

For some critics the changes thus far have been quite inadequate, but my purpose in this final section of the chapter will be to discuss what has occurred. I will consider first a study done by women social scientists about the oppression and liberation of women in poor barrios in Peru. Then I will look at some theological writings by feminist-liberation theologians in Latin America, and finally will consider reflections by the more prominent male liberation theologians about machismo.

Oppression and Liberation

In 1985 Peruvian sociologist Carmen Lora and two other women colleagues published a work entitled (in translation) *Woman: Victim of Oppression, Bearer of Liberation*. The study formed part of a "daily life" series for the Bartolomé de Las Casas Institute in Lima-Rimac; Gutiérrez asked that the first of this series deal with the issue of women and oppression. The study resulted from extensive interviews with women living in poor barrios in the Lima area, women who were also active in the pastoral activities of the church.

Carmen Lora articulates the problem in part 1 of the book. "Women live an experience of oppression by the very fact of being women"; at the same time women of the popular sector suffer oppression as members of a lower social class.[34] Lora then explores the issue of this dual oppression (with race sometimes adding a third oppression) by examining the writings of several prominent feminists: for example, Letty Russell, Alice Ross, Juliet Mitchell, and Carol Gilligan (all U.S.A.); Branca Moreira Alves (Brazil); and Flora Tristan (a 19th-century, European, Marxist feminist). Some Marxist-socialist feminists consider class oppression as more fundamental; radical feminists believe that sexism itself is the fundamental oppression. Lora avoids opting for one as more fundamental than the other and calls for efforts to change both. Economic oppression must be overcome, says Lora, but the experience of socialism has shown that a socio-economic reorganization of society does not change the dominance of patriarchal ideology into egalitarian thinking or practice.

In part 2 of the study Lora outlines some characteristics of the women included in the study (87 households in 7 popular sectors of Peru) and the socio-economic conditions in which they live. Some of the statistics merit noting because they reflect similar situations in much of Latin America. In some of the older, more developed barrios, 70 percent of the homes have water; in one of the newer barrios none of the homes has potable water. The average house has two rooms to accommodate an average of about six persons. In 90 percent of the households the men were the main income winners, working most often as factory workers, bus and taxi drivers, clerks, or independent artisans. About half of the women worked part-time (3–6 hours a day) in mostly domestic jobs: washing, sewing, making clothes. Lora cites family income figures in 1982, when $500 to $700 a year would be fairly typical. None of the families owned a car. Thirty percent of the women interviewed were illiterate; another 25 percent had only 1–3 years of schooling. Fifty-four percent of the women interviewed were married; another 26 percent lived in a monogamous relationship with a mate; 96 percent of these relations constituted a first marriage or first commitment. The average woman had most commonly 3–4 children; some had six or more.

In part 3, Cecilia Barnachea relates these women's experiences of sex and their own sexuality. Many had never talked about sex openly before and were nervous in doing so, but they were willing to talk in private interviews. In almost all cases, they viewed sexual relations as necessary to meet the demands of their spouse or to bear children, but with little relation to their own needs or desires. They had received no sex education, even about sexual maturing (menstruation, breast growth, etc.). Their first experiences of sex were generally quite negative, marked by fear and ignorance. One said: "It was terrible; I bled; he emitted a strange, ugly substance." Their first experience was often forced on them or submitted to with the hope of winning the man by becoming pregnant. For most women the only function of sexuality was maternity.

Fryné Santisteban picks up on this note of maternity in a continuation of part 3. For nearly all these women motherhood was the most important experience of their life. To become a mother is to feel recognized, esteemed, and valued; men at least do respect motherhood. Santisteban comments, however, that this very idealization of the maternal role becomes an expression of oppression, for it makes the woman valuable only as a mother and not as a woman or person. A mother is what a woman "should be," so that all other activities or interests are seen by the man as taking her away from "her role." This reduces her possibilities of contact with other persons and of learning new things (many husbands demand that the woman get "permission" to leave the house). It reinforces her timidity and sense of insecurity. Her preoccupation with the material needs of her family becomes the whole focus of her life and the cause of suffering.

In the fourth and final section of this study, Cecila Barnachea narrates the positive, liberating changes that these women experienced through participation in the "popular movements" developed in the barrios by the community with the assistance of pastoral church agents. Many participated in mothers clubs (concerned with providing food, education, and health services for children), in communal soup kitchens, in base Christian communities, and in similar groups. For most the motivation for joining such groups was to help in their role as mothers: to provide better nutrition, to save money, to learn to read in order to better guide their children. They often met with opposition from their husbands-mates who wanted them to "stay with their children," but who frequently changed when they recognized the benefits of these efforts.

Barnachea then notes the "liberating effects" of this participation. It opened up for the women new relationships with other women; it made them feel useful; it enabled them to speak with other women about their problems; it gave them new ideas and opened up new horizons. Their personal lives changed. They felt more secure; they gained some independence from their spouses.

They found that they could develop their own views and express them (which helped them relate more confidently with their spouses as well); they experienced making their own decisions. They experienced themselves as able not only to better meet needs in their own family but to contribute to the social liberation of the whole community. They have begun to sense their own oppression, but also to deal with it.

Barnachea recognizes that all this has not changed the machismo still pervasive in these barrios. It would not occur to these women, she says, to ask the man to share in household work or to think of abandoning their role as mothers. But the worst oppression they had experienced was silence, the inability to form opinions of their own and to express them, and this oppression they have begun to overcome.[35]

This study impressed me, as one might surmise from the space I have given to it. It does imply, however, a definite attitude and strategy toward social change. The authors believe in a gradual development, accepting and starting with the women "where they are" with the values they place in motherhood, and from this helping them to gain a stronger sense of their dignity as persons.[36] (I might add that the catechisms widely used by the church in Peru, Chile, and some other countries, include a special discussion-lesson on the dignity of women.) Some feminists (two Maryknoll sisters) with whom I spoke in Lima, sharply disagree with this approach. They feel that "patriarchy" is the fundamental oppression and that it must be attacked directly and aggressively. They feel that the Christian liberation movement in Latin America, as it is now constituted, will never truly lead to liberation because it has sexism built into it.

A Feminist Way of Doing Theology

In 1985 a group of twenty-eight women theologians and social scientists convened in Buenos Aires to discuss and share papers on Latin American liberation theology from a woman's perspective. One of the participants, Elsa Tamez, edited a collection of the theological papers, which appeared in English with the title *Through Her Eyes*. I will consider first what several of them wrote about the characteristics or distinguishing notes of theology done by women, and then look at some of the themes addressed in their essays.

In a lead essay Ivone Gebara observes that we need to speak of woman as theologian because she brings a different cultural dimension, a different way of relating and thinking, which the church needs. In addressing the characteristics of doing theology as a woman, Gebara mentions as fundamental the context in which she works as a theologian. My situation, she writes, is marked by the social conditions of northeastern Brazil, conditions that mold my being, actions, outlook, and feelings. I write, she continues, as a woman who lives in privileged conditions that allow me to reflect and write, but I write as a woman trying to transport myself into the world of the poor who live in a situation of misery and exploitation. Gebara thus tries to develop a theology that comes from the experience of life itself, drawing upon the profound intuitions of many poor women, some of them illiterate, when they relate their experiences of God. She writes as a woman in a church with a strong machismo tradition, helping other women to discover the closeness of Mary and Jesus to the problems of women and to show her own experience of God in a way that involves more than just "reason."[37]

Feminist theology, she continues, expresses life. It is a theology with a poetic dimension, a sense that the mystery of God can best be expressed by analogy, in poetry, in symbols. The purely rational does not take into account all the feelings, pain, pleasure, and mystery of life. The ministry of women also leads to questioning the authority that men have exercised with theological formulations that are markedly macho and that serve as masculine legitimation for "the way things are." We need, she concludes, not to replace the masculine model of theology with a feminine one, but to achieve a new synthesis of complementarity.[38]

Consuelo del Prado entitles her essay "I Sense God in a Different Way." The feminine perspective, Prado says, is an accent, not a polarization. It expresses the right of a woman to feel and to articulate the experience of God in a different way. Women tend to live in a more unified way and to value the everyday. We need "to break through enslaving and paralyzing machismo with feminine gifts and creativity." We need, with the poor, to show a new way to live love as an efficacious service with Mary as a model.[39] Alida Verhoeven sees as the vocation of the woman theologian to generate a new consciousness of God as a creative spiritual force, and she sees women as having a special capacity for recognizing the creative force within nature.[40] María Clara Bingemer, in her essay, seeks to find the feminine in God, integrating the problematic of woman with the struggle to liberate the poor.

We might begin with Bingemer's essay on the Trinity as an example of this feminist way of doing theology. The mystery of God, Bingemer observes, has been polarized by markedly masculine images. Woman may mirror God in her soul, but not in her body. The traditional images of God take on a masculine body form: father, king, husband, lord. Yet despite these images, reflecting the patriarchal society of the authors of the Bible, God is revealed in scripture as one with "feminine" qualities, as one who consoles and protects. God is not a solitary patriarch, but a trinity of persons in which the masculine is enriched and complemented by the feminine. God's "mercy" (*rachamim* in Hebrew), which is a dominant concept in scripture, has as its root meaning the innermost parts of a woman. "Spirit" (*ruach*) in scripture is expressed in feminine terms, and it represents not just one person of the Trinity (the Holy Spirit) but a bond within a community of persons. In the New Testament, John the Baptist's ministry looked to men; Jesus' ministry makes women an important part of his concern and discipleship. Jesus uses, moreover, female images to describe God's love (the woman in search of a lost coin) and of his own love (as a mother hen gathers chicks under her wing).[41]

Tereza Cavalcanti explores the ministry of women in the Old Testament. Though the Bible reflects clearly the context of a patriarchal society, women stand out in many instances for their wisdom and valor (Hulda, Deborah, Miriam, the wife of Isaiah). Moreover, many women played prophetic roles that had significant repercussions on the social, political and religious life of Israel: for example, Judith, Esther, Ruth, Tamar, and Anna. They drew their authority not from any institutionalized role of power, or through arms, but as witnesses to a God who takes the side of the oppressed.[42]

Other essays explore the feminine in the popular religion of the Andean Indians in Peru, Jesus' special concern for women, and a spirituality of beauty.[43] The essays challenge the maleness of traditional theology and seek to bring to theology a distinctive and different perspective of woman's experience of God.

Male Theologians Speak about Machismo

The cover of the book reads a bit like the front page of the *National Enquirer*: "For the first time Rubem Alves, Leonardo Boff, Gustavo Gutiérrez, José Míguez Bonino, Juan Luis Segundo . . . and others talk about the struggle of women" (*Against Machismo*, interviews by Elsa Tamez). But the book serves an important purpose. It not only gathers in one volume the thoughts of various liberation theologians on the topic, but the interviews also prodded the theologians (and prod us) to confront the issue of women's oppression. The delightful, often playful, personal comments that Tamez uses to set the context of each interview serve as concrete examples of the values Tamez stresses in her interview with Gutiérrez:

> Gustavo, for some time feminists reacted against and rejected certain values like tenderness and self-denial that society assigned to women par excellence. We considered them to be stereotypes. They were commonly held to be inferior to values like rationality, calmness, objectivity. But I have noticed that recently Latin American women, in search of their identity, want to appropriate or reassert tenderness, play, affection, as profoundly rich traits of women, and to link these with strength, courage, bravery, which are also, in fact, rich traits of women.[44]

Tamez asks each theologian, directly or obliquely, whether they think that women are oppressed in Latin America. All clearly did think so, but Hugo Assmann and Enrique Dussel are especially expansive and concrete in their responses. Assmann addresses the general oppression that affects women in every class of society and the very tragic dimensions of oppression of women in the lower classes. He illustrates this latter dimension with a description of the treatment of *bioafria* women who work on Brazilian plantations. They are paid less than men for the same work, are treated more cruelly by bosses, are oppressed by husbands at home, and their very language of expression is destroyed. Dussel, who traces his own awakening on the issue to a discussion group in the late 1960s, looks at the historical roots of the problem of male chauvinism and illustrates his observations with examples throughout history.[45]

All the theologians likewise acknowledge machismo within the churches. Dussel comments sharply about the Catholic Church, noting that we cannot find documents from councils or synods that even bother to say that a woman cannot be a priest or become pope. The councils see this as too obvious even to mention. Leonardo Boff speaks of rectifying the church's "historical sin" of marginalizing women from the earliest centuries until today. Women are excluded from the priesthood and top levels of decision-making, nevertheless they run parishes and make possible much of the pastoral activity of the church. The people often prefer, he adds, the sisters' liturgical services because they are much livelier. Segundo sees the exclusion of women from the priesthood as part of a general theological error that tries to make everything Jesus did in his time as normative for all times. Pablo Richard links his comments on the church to the issue of politics. Politics in Latin America has been exceedingly male-dominated and chauvinistic because it is obsessed with taking power, whereas women ask more often "what for." The church, in its Christendom form, likewise concerns itself with exercise of power, in contrast with the church of the poor, which emphasizes community.

The Protestant theologians recognize inequality in their respective churches, though they differ considerably in their evaluations. José Míguez Bonino notes that women have at times been excluded in the Methodist Church, but that in the Methodist Church today, at least in Argentina, women are numerically fairly represented and no discrimination exists with respect to the ordained ministry. Jorge Pixley asserts that the Baptist Church traditionally puts women in second place in leadership functions. At the far end of the spectrum, Rubem Alves describes the situation of women in the Protestant churches as "very ugly," with a religious ideology that does not permit women to be themselves. In the Presbyterian Church, he notes, women's groups are called "women's auxiliaries"; they serve lunches for visitors.

In response to questions about doing theology from a woman's perspective, Segundo believes that "suspicion," used to unmask cultural elements in traditional interpretations of scripture, can be used profitably by women theologians. The challenge comes, however, in completing the hermeneutic circle so that the message does not get rejected with its ideological (male) encumbrances. Leonardo Boff speaks of the need to include the "feminine dimension" in christology (a dimension he identifies with the Jungian *anima* — compassion, tenderness — in contrast to the masculine *animus*). He briefly indicates also some of the points he makes in his book *The Maternal Face of God*. He sees Mary as the "temple of the divine." She receives the Holy Spirit before she receives Jesus, and from her feminine humanity the Holy Spirit creates the humanity of the eternal son. Pablo Richard speaks of the vision of "totality" that he has especially learned from women.

In a concluding commentary, Tamez weaves together (as I have also selectively done) the issues and insights that emerged in the interviews. The final point she touches on concerns inclusive language. The male theologians who did speak to this had diverse opinions. Alves finds it annoying to speak of God as He/She at the same time; Richard looks with favor on speaking of God as She. Segundo believes that you should not try to change the language of biblical references to God. Gutiérrez (on a somewhat different point) stresses the importance of using inclusive language in theology; and judging from lectures I attended at Ann Arbor in 1986, he now very consciously uses inclusive language himself.

As Tamez acknowledges, however, "the problem of exclusive language has not been vigorously addressed by women in Latin America," in contrast to the First World, she adds, where "as I understand it . . . it is an almost obsessive battle."[46] This comment helps to explain why even in the works by the women theologians, cited in the last section, the use of inclusive language is not consistent.[47] In the whole struggle for liberation from machismo, "there is much yet to be done." But, Tamez concludes, "the important thing is that now we know there is a journey to be undertaken."[48]

GUTIÉRREZ IN DEFENSE OF LIBERATION THEOLOGY

In 1986 Gutiérrez published an important work in defense of his own theology and of liberation theology overall. In this work, *La verdad los hará libres* ("The truth will make you free"), Gutiérrez responds to most of the major criticisms brought against him and against liberation theology.[49] Even critics like Bishop Ricardo Durand, who still condemn him for his earlier writings, acknowledge the orthodoxy of the views he presents in this work. The book has four parts. It includes a summary presentation of his views submitted to the faculty of theology at Lyons (France) where he was awarded a doctorate in 1985, with already published works serving as his "thesis." The book then records an ensuing discussion with faculty members who served on his thesis defense board. It also contains an important essay, published earlier, on theology and the social sciences. In this essay Gutiérrez discusses at length his views on dependency theory, Marxist analysis, and class struggle. (These points I will take up later, in chapters 7–9). The final major part of the book responds to points raised by the 1984 and 1986 Vatican instructions.

In the summary form that follows, I have drawn mostly from this final essay. As a format, I have stated in thesis form different criticisms raised against liberation theology, and then noted Gutiérrez's responses. Gutiérrez himself approaches the criticisms more indirectly. He gives frequent references, however, to his own earlier works to show that positions stated here do not represent changes in his positions but views he has consistently held. To avoid excessive endnotes, I have indicated page numbers next to the text cited.

1. Liberation theology makes praxis the criterion for truth. In response, Gutiérrez writes that the word of God constitutes the decisive criterion for judging any understanding of the faith (p. 129). "The ultimate criteria come from the revealed truth that we accept in faith, and not from praxis itself. It would make no sense, and would be a tautology among other things, to say that praxis is criticized 'in the light of praxis' " (p. 140). It is the word of God and the teaching of the church that guarantee whether praxis is

indeed Christian (p. 141). (Clodovis Boff, as noted in chapter 2, stresses this same point.)

In *A Theology of Liberation* Gutiérrez defined the method of liberation theology as "a critical reflection on Christian praxis in the light of the word of God." In the statements made above, he reemphasizes the "in the light of the word of God" as an ultimate criterion. In the opening pages of *La verdad,* however, he adds a dimension to the definition that had not been explicit before. Theology has as its source, he says, the mystery of faith revealed "in contemplation and commitment." This living of the faith is the first act; theological reflection follows as a second act (p. 12). This new formulation, with equal emphasis given to contemplation (an addition he first made in 1981 in a work, "The God of Life"), does not affect what he said above about faith or the word of God as an ultimate criterion. But it does give a broader base for the source of theological reflection. One could perhaps view contemplation itself as a form of practice (Gutiérrez's works on spirituality certainly add dignity to the poor, which helps them in their struggle for liberation), but I think one should concede that the very use of the expression "contemplation and commitment" suggests a change. On the other points that follow, his statements appear quite consistent with his earlier writings.

2. Liberation theology reduces human development to socio-political change. Gutiérrez repeats what he wrote in various earlier works. There are three levels of liberation, distinct but not separate: socio-political liberation, full human and psychological liberation, and liberation from sin. In short, a total "integral" liberation (p. 173). Socio-political liberation is important but not sufficient for full liberation. Changing social structures may aid in changing humans but such change does not occur automatically. "Change of structures is necessary, but it is not the all" (pp. 187–90, 173).

3. Liberation theology reduces salvation history to temporal history when it speaks of "only one history." Gutiérrez claims that the unitary perspective he wants to affirm comes from the global character of the gratuitous gift of God's love. It affects all areas of human life. We can and should distinguish between the natural and the supernatural, but there is only *one* actual order of salvation, not one of the history of grace and a separate history of nature. This view of the unity of salvation history, Gutiérrez adds, is shared by many modern theologians: Rahner, de Lubac, von Balthasar, Alfaro and others (pp. 175–80).

4. Liberation theology reduces faith to politics. Gutiérrez again repeats what he stated in *A Theology of Liberation.* "Politics" has two senses: one, the global and historical efforts of the human race to realize its potential (or the broad sense of Aristotle's polis in which each of us affects society and is affected by it), and two, politics in the narrower sense of orientation toward power. Only in the first sense, Gutiérrez asserts, does liberation theology say that "all is colored politically" (pp. 184–85).

5. Liberation theology identifies the kingdom of God with human prog-

ress and liberation movements. The kingdom of God, Gutiérrez writes, is not reducible to human history or human progress. They are not identified (pp. 207–8). Liberation is in its roots a gift of the Lord. We cannot equate the coming of the kingdom with historical realizations of human liberation; on the other hand, without historical liberative events there would be no growth in the kingdom. A historical liberative event is a salvific event, but it is not the coming of the kingdom or total salvation (pp. 26–27).

6. Liberation theology locates sin in sinful structures, neglecting personal sin. Sin, Gutiérrez responds, is the "ultimate root" of all injustice, and sin is the result of a personal, free act (pp. 26, 185, 193–94). But we need also to speak of sinful structures and the need to change them. On this point he cites Pope John Paul II and the documents of Puebla (pp. 195–97). He could now strengthen his case with the many references John Paul II makes to "structures of sin" in his encyclical *Sollicitudo Rei Socialis*.

7. Liberation theology equates the biblical poor with one socio-political class. Liberation theology does clearly speak to and for the poor. But the poor, Gutiérrez notes, cannot be limited to any one determined social class. Any interpretation that reduces the poor to a purely economic-social base is mistaken. God's message is universal, though it gives preference to the poor (pp. 20–21).

8. Liberation theology eliminates the transcendent and vertical relations with God. Gutiérrez writes: "We are convinced that without songs, without thanksgiving for God's love, without prayer, there is no Christian life" (p. 21). "The contemplative dimension is an element essential to Christian existence" (p. 133).

Some critics may still quarrel with these responses; others will argue that they represent a change of positions. His defense may still not answer criticisms about the biblical interpretations used by other liberation theologians and may not satisfy objections against the amount of "political" emphasis found in liberation theology. His defense, nevertheless, presents a strong argument for the "orthodoxy" of his views and of liberation theology overall, and seems a fitting way to end these chapters on theological issues.

SOCIO-POLITICAL ISSUES

Chapter 6

Understanding Latin America: Modes of Analysis

Liberation theology looks to the social sciences for analyses that will prove most fruitful in struggles to overcome poverty and underdevelopment in Latin America. Critics of liberation theology believe that it has relied too heavily on Marxist analysis and dependency theory as sources of social analysis. Chapter 7 will consider what liberation theologians, and their critics, have said about social analysis. This chapter will examine some of the competing forms of social analysis used to explain conditions in Latin America, but we will do so in the light of Latin America's distinctive historical heritage.

Social scientists make use of various models or theories to explain problems of underdevelopment. Conventional economic theory tends to view underdeveloped countries as locked into traditional cultures and institutions, and hence needing to adopt the modern ways that led advanced industrial countries to their present status. Classic Marxist analysis follows this view when it argues that "backward" countries must first move into a capitalist stage before pushing on to socialism. But Marxist theories of imperialism also see these countries as exploited by capitalism in its drive for new markets. In reaction to the conventional modernization paradigm, and spurred in part by the Marxist critique of imperialist exploitation, many social scientists in Latin America developed or made use of new paradigms to explain conditions in their countries. The new paradigms stress the dependent status of Latin American countries as "peripheral" parts of a world capitalist system.

Any effort to understand contemporary problems in Latin America must, however, take into account its own unique historical development (recognizing also some of the distinctive factors in different countries). In my own efforts to understand Latin America and its problems, study of Latin American history, and in particular its colonial heritage, has proven more insightful than the application of any abstract model or theory of social analysis. Hence this chapter begins with a look back at Latin America's colonial heritage and the continuing impact of that heritage into the present. A portion of one chapter can hardly do justice to the whole history of Latin America. It can serve, however, to highlight factors that may help in assessing the causes of problems confronting Latin America. The occasional use of comparisons with U.S. history should indicate why we cannot judge Latin America by norms drawn from the U.S. experience.[1] The historical part of this chapter looks chiefly at the Spanish-Portuguese influence on Latin American history. The influence of U.S. investments in Latin America, treated only briefly in this chapter, will be considered in much more detail in chapter 8, which includes a lengthy assessment of arguments for dependency.

LATIN AMERICA'S HISTORICAL HERITAGE

Colonization in Latin America developed quite differently from colonization in the United States. The Spaniards and Portuguese often brought with them a high level of culture, a spirit of daring, and great loyalty to their Catholic faith. One could recount the history of their conquests in terms of bravery, discipline, and religious zeal. They also brought with them, however, many institutions and patterns of lifestyle that would prove detrimental to Latin America in the long run. They encountered, moreover, some significantly different conditions from those found in what is now the United States and Canada.

Anglo-Saxon colonists did not face the temptation, or the opportunity, to make quick fortunes from the gold and silver available in South America. They had to build up a livelihood gradually through their own efforts at work in farming and trades. The availability of land to all, however, made such efforts fruitful. British rule also provided more constitutional structures that could evolve into self-rule. With the notable exception of Native American Indians, black slaves, and indentured servants, those who settled in the North experienced equality of opportunity.

In contrast, many Spanish and Portuguese came with hopes of striking it rich through acquiring mines or vast stretches of land. They often brought with them strong class distinctions and the attitudes of the aristocracy toward work. Lands were not available to all but "bequeathed" by the crown to a few; work in mines and on farms was carried out by the forced labor of native Indians. Authoritarian, centralized political rule would not easily lend itself to gradual democracy and self-rule.

The Colonial Heritage

Many Latin American writers have underscored the negative impact of their colonial past. The renowned Mexican essayist Leopold Zea views the colonialist heritage as the most important factor in explaining Latin America's continuing problems. Spain bequeathed to Latin America problems it still has not solved. "If the Hispanic Americans wished to be completely free, they must renounce everything that was Spanish."[2] Latin America began as a colony, dependent on a reality—Spanish (or Portuguese) culture, government, and institutions—not its own. Even when Latin American countries gained their independence from Spain, they continued to live by Spanish rule and customs. "Hispanic America had gained its independence from the Spanish crown, but never from Spain."[3]

The new independent countries wrote constitutions and spoke of democracy, Zea observes, but new names only disguised old forms of government. Spanish habits and customs remained firmly rooted: independence brought only a change of power. "Each Hispanic American caudillo . . . only aspired to occupy the place abandoned by the conquistador."[4] Zea sees Latin America as still a colony, though now the struggle focuses on a new mother country, the United States. He admires the spirit of the United States and its lack of dogmatism, but does not see "anglicizing" Latin America as a solution. Latin America must find its own solutions.[5]

Enrique Dussel, prominent liberation philosopher and historian, underscores the economic aspects of this heritage:

Spain chose the easy way: exploiting the American mines with the Indians rather than taking the narrow road that England chose, namely, the hard work of an industrious people. The Spanish lack of economic vision was catastrophic for Spain and also for the Latin American countries. Spain could easily have had coal and steel in Europe, but this would have signified an austere, simple, daily industrial effort. Spain preferred to mine only gold and silver, which in the short run produced an ephemeral splendor, but in the long run produced economic catastrophe from which Spain as well as Latin America has never recovered.[6]

The aristocratic Spanish attitude toward work was captured in an oft quoted comment made by the famous conquistador Hernando Cortes. When he arrived in the new world he declared: "I came to get gold, not to till the soil like some peasant."[7] He gained not only gold but was given by the Spanish crown some hundred thousand Indians in a domain of nearly 25,000 square miles. If the extent of Cortes' rewards was exceptionally large, the pattern of enrichment was common. The Spaniards and Portuguese brought some of the riches of their culture to the new world, but their goals and methods of conquest set patterns that would affect not only the Indians they conquered but a whole way of life for the colonizers themselves.

Their treatment of the native Indian population created an economy and social life built on oppression and exploitation from the outset. They encountered a much larger number of Indian inhabitants than did European settlers in the North: perhaps 50 million in Latin America as opposed to one million in the North (estimates of Indians in Latin America prior to the conquest range from 8.5 million to 110 million).[8] Some critics have perhaps romanticized the Indian cultures and exaggerated the destruction brought by colonization. The culturally rich Mayan civilization had already declined before the Spanish arrived; the Aztecs ruled despotically with a religion that called for massive numbers of human sacrifices; the Incas had their own caste system. But much that was admirable was destroyed. The Incas, if paternalistic and rigid in their class structures, provided food and care for their sick and aged so that no one went hungry. They shared land and work as a community.

The first settlers in the Caribbeans forced natives to bring in tributes of gold dust four times a year, in return for a copper token to be worn around their necks. If they failed to bring in the gold, they faced punishment by death or by having their hands amputated. Thousands chose suicide as an escape.[9] More commonly, the native population was forced into tilling the land and working the mines of their conquerors. They had little choice. When the Spaniards moved into a new territory, they read a *requirimiento* informing the Indians that they could either submit to the rule of the Spanish king and the authority of the pope, or be responsible for the alternatives—to be killed or taken by force. Some missionaries strove to defend the Indians; Spain passed laws prohibiting their enslavement; the *encomienda* system, in which Indians were entrusted to colonizers, was intended for their protection. In fact, such legislation was widely disregarded and the Indians became forced into tribute or labor.

Imported slaves from Africa became an even lower and more oppressed class, with the great bulk of the slaves concentrated in Brazil and the Caribbeans.[10] Their enslavement also set in motion the pattern of one-crop dependencies that would plague Latin America throughout its history. Sugar cane was introduced in Barbados in 1640. It required larger acreage and cheap labor. Twelve thousand independent farmers were eliminated, and in their place 745 plantations were established with labor provided by eighty-two thousand slaves.[11]

In its treatment of Indians and blacks, the United States could hardly claim superiority. The United States made equality of all persons a basis of its democracy. All persons, however, meant all whites, with voting rights restricted to white, male property owners. The United States dealt with its "Indian problem" simply by eliminating them or by corralling them into reservations. The United States dealt with black slaves by denying them constitutional rights. Latin America, while locked into a hierarchical class system, at least integrated nonwhites into sociey.

The Spanish domination of America, writes one historian, rested on three main pillars: (1) direct control of the Indian labor force through the encomienda system; (2) the sharing out of land; (3) the ownership and exploitation of copious mineral resources, in Peru and Mexico especially. The latifundio (large estate) became the basis of agriculture. While most latifundios did not originate from royal land grants, they soon developed through the appropriation of Indians' lands (the encomiendas technically gave colonizers control over only the Indians themselves and not their lands) or from public sale of lands. Ownership of mines was also highly concentrated, with silver mining in the sixteenth century controlled by eighty owners and some three hundred managers, using some fifty-three thousand Indians, about a fourth of whom were forced laborers.[12] These owners of land and mines reaped rich personal benefits, but all of Latin America would eventually pay a heavy price for the patterns set by these get-rich-quick schemes.

José Carlos Mariátegui, whom some have called the most creative Marxist thinker in Latin American history, underscored many of the points I have noted thus far: the destruction of the Indian economy and failure to replace it with any truly productive new system; the Spanish nobility's disdain for work; the exploitation of silver and gold mines to the neglect of agricultural development; and the bequeathing of land to an aristocracy. In North America, Mariátegui wrote, colonization planted the seeds of the spirit and economy of a new system; the Spaniards brought to America the effects and methods of a feudal system in its decline. Quoting from a work by José Vasconcelos, Mariátegui continues, explaining rapid growth in the North and the slowness of growth in Latin America:

In the North, there were no kings to dispose of another's land as though it were their own. . . . The colonizers of the North proceeded to develop a system of private property under which each one paid the price of his own land and occupied only as much as he could cultivate. In place of encomiendas, there were farms. . . . The newly won lands were not turned over to the king for him to give away at his discretion and thereby create a nobility with double morals: a lackey of the sovereign and an insolent oppressor of the weak masses.[13]

This economic pattern described by Mariátegui, with land as patrimony and work done by others, had enormous consequences. Ownership became concentrated from the outset in the hands of a wealthy elite, blocking the vast majority of the population from advancing by work on property of their own. "The great plantations profited those who owned them but impeded the colonial economy. The plantation system kept the masses in varying degrees of serfdom, stifled inventiveness, retarded technical advance, and held back production."[14]

A Spanish writer of the late eighteenth century, Gaspar Melchor de Jovellanos, noted what he believed were the causes of poverty and industrial backwardness in Spain and in its colonies alike: (1) agricultural property treated as an aristocractic privilege to the detriment of the laboring masses and the true wealth of the country; (2) public and communal lands used only for pasturing cattle; (3) excessive amounts of amortized church properties, which prevented redistribution into small holdings and a free economy; (4) a monopolistic system of ownership by idle rich who did not cultivate the land regularly, causing landless, unemployed peasants to migrate into the cities.[15] This pattern of landownership continues to this day, as I have noted before, with an estimated 1.3 percent of the landowners in Latin America controlling 71.6 percent of all land under cultivation.[16]

Latin America also developed from the outset a rigidly stratified class society. Spaniards stood at the top; they occupied the top positions in government and in the church, and they held the most wealth. The creoles of Spanish blood, but born in America, occupied the next highest rank. They became landholders and business leaders but were looked down upon socially by the *peninsulares* from Spain. Below the creoles stood the mestizos, products of Spanish-Amerindian intermingling, and below them black slaves. Blacks in Latin America, concentrated mainly in Brazil and the Caribbean area, stood at the bottom rung of the social ladder, though racial prejudice was less overt than in the United States. Given this heritage, one should hardly be surprised by Gutiérrez's claim that "class struggle" is a fact in Latin America.

Machismo also perdures, creating what liberation philosopher Enrique Dussel calls a triple violation of women from the poorest classes:

> The woman of the people, the woman within a peripheral culture, ends by undergoing a threefold attack, a triple violation: violated for being from an oppressed culture and nation, for being a member of a dominated class, for being a member of a dominated sex. She is a poor woman of the poor ... victim of imperialism, of class struggle, and of macho ideology.[17]

The colonizers sought not only wealth but the prestige of living like lords on the toil of others. They built cities in imitation of the best in Europe and to evoke wonder, fear, and respect from the Indians. They sought to rival the lordly pomp and circumstance of the best in Spain and Portugal: ornate cathedrals, military parades and festive church celebrations, families with their special seals and coats of arms. The cities stood in sharp contrast to the impoverished rural villages populated by Indians and mestizos. Even within the church hierarchy, class distinctions and enormous inequalities stood out glaringly. An archbishop might have a salary equivalent to $100,000 or more in modern terms, while many rural priests had to make ends meet on $75 to $100 a year.[18]

Government in Latin America also reflected Spain and Portugal. It was authoritarian, elitist, hierarchical, and patrimonial. It defined by law the social stratifications found in society. It reflected a "corporatist" view of society in which socio-political dealings took the form of patron-client relations. The king stood atop the hierarchy as the ultimate patron. Rulers in the new world served as agents of his royal authority. While centralized in the line of commands, the viceroys and captains-general or presidents under the viceroys enjoyed considerable latitude in interpreting and implementing the law. Protection under the law most often depended on the goodwill of some official, or friend of an official, within the structure of government. This patron-client relationship remains strong in Latin America and may account for much of the corruption in countries like Mexico and Brazil.[19] It seems also reflected in the popular religiosity discussed in the last chapter, with saints viewed as patrons having special access to God. To their credit, the Spanish and Portuguese did succeed in establishing order and relative stability over a 300–year period. The type of order it established, however, set a pattern for the future.

The Age of Independence

Latin Americans experienced a love-hate relationship with Spain and Portugal. They imitated their culture but grew increasingly resentful of their rule — or more accurately of the wealth that they lost in trade and taxes to them. Latin American intellectuals took up ideas on political liberty from the European Enlightenment and from the U.S. revolution against England. The struggle for independence began, however, with reactions over Napoleon's occupation of Spain and Portugal. Napoleon put his own brother Joseph on the throne of Spain in 1808. If Latin Americans resented Spanish rule, rule by France proved too much. Within two decades, even though the deposed Spanish king returned, almost all of Latin America had gained its independence.

The struggle for independence brought pride, but the new regimes fell back into old patterns of domination. Brazil opted at first for monarchy; other countries proclaimed themselves democratic republics. The political reality proved somewhat other. Democratic hopes fell prey to new forms of authoritarian rule. "We are independent, but we are not free," wrote the Argentinian poet Esteban Echevarria; "The arms of Spain no longer oppress us, but her traditions still weigh us down."[20] Military leaders of the independence movement sought to represent all classes and races. But once independence came, the creole upper class assumed power, though even it had difficulty in maintaining control. "Economically, socially, and politically, power had fallen into the hands of a small oligarchy, which found effective government impossible because it could not control the military" who during the revolution had learned to live off the land and its people.[21] How long a government would last depended on the will of the army. The failures of strong central government led to regionalism. Local, strong-armed caudillos carried on the same authoritarian and class-structured rule established by Spain.

In the nineteenth century, the indigenous Latin American oligarchies concentrated their main efforts on landownership, while control of commerce and industry became increasingly controlled by foreign investors. The large estates, the latifundios, continued to dominate the use of land. The most commercial of these latifundios, the plantations, used labor the most ruthlessly and concentrated on single products for export (coffee, sugar, bananas, rubber). The latifundio ranches of Argentina and Uruguay raised cattle and sheep. The most fundamental of the latifundios, however, were the haciendas. The haciendas sometimes produced cash crops for export, like the plantations, but they formed more self-sustaining units. They pervaded most of Latin America, and in the estimation of one historian they determined the quality of Latin American culture throughout the nineteenth century and up to World War I.[22]

The haciendas in many ways resembled the manors of feudal society. They were self-sufficient units, closed societies with their own stores, their own supply of food, and their own government. The wealthy owners spent most of their time and wealth in the city, leaving the management of the estate to a majordomo. The owners, comfortable with their wealth, made little effort to make the haciendas more productive or efficient. The Indian or mestizo workers lived in virtual serfdom. They were given their own small plot of land to provide food for themselves; in return they worked on the owner's estate. Most lived in unending debt, a peonage that remained binding for their offspring. It was an immobile system that resisted any kind of reform, and it stunted agricultural development.[23]

A number of contributing factors led to foreign domination of commerce and industry in the nineteenth century. Spain and Portugal set a pattern of dependency by impeding industrial ventures in Latin America and by maintaining a mercantile system that kept trade restricted to themselves and their colonies. The Latin American creoles thus lacked business experience; they also inherited the Spanish disdain for competitive business. Latin American countries, moreover, found themselves in a situation of economic chaos and ruin after the wars of independence. They had become heavily indebted in efforts to finance the wars. Their main economic bases of agriculture and mining had eroded. They badly needed capital to regenerate the economy. The British, for their part, had capital and needed new markets. Business and industry thus "fell by default" to foreign investors, or as liberation philosopher Enrique Dussel puts it, "for lack of other possibilities."[24] British textiles provided cheaper goods than those produced by local weavers; local producers went out of business.[25] Liberation theologian Pablo Richard views the end of the nineteenth century as a critical moment in Latin America's history, a time when Latin America might have moved toward economic independence but moved instead toward a new dependence. (I will take up his views after completing some comments about the new dependency.)

This pattern of landowning oligarchies and foreign domination of business carried through the nineteenth century and into the twentieth. Concentration of landownership increased in the last half of the nineteenth century as Liberal governments confiscated church properties and Indian lands and turned them over to already large estate holders. (The Indians enjoyed at least some protection under the colonial system; they lost this with the coming of independence.) Mineral resources became increasingly the property of foreign owners. More and more production in Latin America became concentrated on primary goods destined for export to the North. Each country became dependent for its income on one or two commodities. One study of Latin America prior to World War II showed several countries "dangerously dependent" on one or two export commodities: tin in Bolivia constituted 71.4 percent of its total exports; coffee in El Salvador, 89.2 percent; bananas in Honduras, 82.3 percent; sugar and tobacco in Cuba, 78.6 percent; coffee and cotton in Brazil, 64.6 percent; coffee and bananas in Nicaragua, 83.5 percent. The author speaks of these countries as "dangerously dependent" because a sudden drop in the price of these exports, a tariff rise, or a crop failure "was often tantamount to financial calamity."[26] Even when balance of trade was favorable, as it was through much of the nineteenth century, little was done to reinvest in production of domestic goods, and the majority of Latin Americans gained few benefits.

From 1870 to 1913, British investment in Latin America increased ninefold. By 1914 most of the mining interests in Latin America, and much of the real estate, ranching, plantation agriculture, and manufacturing had come into the hands of foreign investors. Latin America became integrated into the world economy, but its integration came through borrowing capital and technology rather than developing these locally. The United States soon became the dominant foreign investor. From 1898 to 1923, exports to the United States rose from 9.5 percent to 39.7 percent, while exports to England declined by 25 percent. Imports from the United States went up from 10 percent to 38.9 percent; those from England dropped by 24 percent.[27] By the 1920s, U.S. companies controlled 80 percent of the copper mines in Chile; 50 percent of all the capital invested in Cuban sugar came from the United States; U.S. companies gained control of banana plantations and exports in Central America.

Pablo Richard analyzes the whole history of Latin America in terms of its dependency. He sees Latin America as part of a world capitalist system from the very beginnings of its history, providing gold and silver at the outset and various raw materials later to serve the needs of developing capitalist countries in the North. Its dependency on Spain and Portugal during the colonial period was transferred after independence to dependency upon Britain and then on the United States. The critical turning point in this new dependency occurred in the second half of the nineteenth century. Most historians of Latin America, Richard observes, focus on the political struggles for power waged by the Conservative and Liberal political parties. The Conservative Party represented the interests of traditional landowners and mercantilist capitalists who sought to maintain values and structures from the past. The Liberal Party embraced new capitalist interests and called for a transition to modernity. However this division masked a more important conflict, in Richard's judgment. The Liberal Party included two very distinct groups of capitalists: a dependent "European party," which favored free trade to enhance its interests in mining and export crops from agriculture, in opposition to an "American party," which wanted protectionist policies to safeguard and encourage small businesses and an autonomous industrial development. With the temporary exception of Paraguay, which could have served as a model of independent development for all Latin America, the European party won out. Europe itself did not "impose" this new dependency; the "European party" in Latin America fought for it and created a "new colonialist pact."[28]

This new dependency would become the focus of attack in the dependency theories that emerged in the 1960s and exercised a significant influence on liberation theology in its initial development. Chapter 8 will examine the issue of dependency in detail, but some initial data drawn from decades past will indicate why opponents of dependency targeted foreign investment for special criticism. One historian, writing about foreign ownership of copper mining companies in Chile, noted that only 11 percent of the revenues gained from copper remained in that country. Another writer claims that barely 10 percent of oil profits ($600 million of $5 billion) remained in Venezuela during the 1950s. The North American Marxist economist Paul Sweezy noted that in the heyday of British imperialism (1870–1913) the flow of income *to* Britain exceeded the flow of capital from Britain by 70 percent. Foreign investments by U.S. corporations (1950–1963) showed an almost identical percentage of profits: net flow of capital from the United States, $17.4 billion; flow of income to the United States, $29.4 billion.[29]

Concern about the effects of foreign investment, and about deteriorating terms of trade, created—prior to the emergence of dependency theory—an effort on the part of many Latin American countries to develop domestic industrialization through "import substitution." I will take up this move in discussing models of social analysis in the second part of this chapter. Before concluding this historical section, however, we need to discuss briefly some significant political changes in Latin American history.

Political Traditions

If staying power constitutes a criterion of political success, the Latin American empires created by Spain and Portugal would have to be judged successful. They left, however, a legacy of authoritarian, absolutist rule. The government was rigidly hierarchical and bureaucratic. It was based on a strict chain of command, which ran from the king and the Council of the Indies at the highest level, through the viceroys or governors in the colonies themselves, and down to officials at a district level. Appeals to higher authorities and periodic inspections from above served as checks against abuses of power.

With independence came a new political philosophy of liberalism, with its view that sovereignty rests in the consent of the governed, with balance achieved by separating the three essential powers of government (legislative, executive, and judicial). But the pattern of political behavior that developed after independence did not match these ideals. Caudillos swept aside constitutions and legislatures they believed were ineffective, and many governments became more despotic than the monarchies they had replaced. Some countries, such as Chile, Uruguay, and Costa Rica, did achieve reputations for respect of constitutional legality; most other countries alternated between constitutional civilian governments and dictatorial rule, often controlled by the military. Liberal and Conservative parties vied for power, but both generally represented dominant oligarchies. Hacienda owners would mobilize their tenants and employees to vote as the owner told them, and candidates counted on local bosses (*caciques*) to deliver votes.[30]

In the nineteenth century the right to vote was generally restricted to male property owners (as was the case in most northern countries of the world). Some countries still keep suffrage limited by making literacy a necessary condition for voting. But widening of electoral rights gradually gave labor and other lower-class groups greater political voice. Juan Perón, in the late 1940s and 50s, mobilized this new bloc of worker voters and won election in Argentina. The late 1950s witnessed an upsurge of populist movements that seemed to hold promise for widespread reforms and democracy.[31]

More radical or reactionary developments occurred instead. In Cuba, Castro's forces overthrew Batista and a new socialist government took over. In Brazil, the reformist Goulart government was overthrown and military rule was established. In Chile, the reformist Frei government, which ruled through much of the 1960s, gave way to a Marxist socialist government under Allende, which in turn became the victim of a military coup (1973). In its formative years, liberation theology seemed clearly more favorable to the socialist ventures, skeptical about reformist measures, and sharply opposed to right-wing military rule. To conclude this historical section, we might look at the military rule of this period using liberation theologian José Comblin as one of our principal sources.

In the past, the military had often stepped in to restore order. In the 1960s and 70s, a new type of military intervention occurred, one that contained its own plan of government. The Brazilian military led the way with its takeover in 1964, followed by Argentina (in 1966 and again in 1976), Uruguay (1973), Chile (1973), and Bolivia (1976). With this new wave of military coups came a new doctrine of military rule, articulated most clearly in Brazil and Chile: a national security state. In Brazil, the military who took over brought with them a professional training developed at their Escola Superior de Guerra. The training included a vision of how society should be governed, based on what the military claimed were neutral, scientific concepts from the social sciences, but modeled, says José Comblin, after ideas and strategies developed by the National War College in the United States.[32]

This vision included five central ideas: (1) it stressed national security as necessary for achieving national goals and for controlling hostile pressure groups with conflicting goals; (2) it saw the state as the expression of the nation dedicated to the common good and responsible for ensuring order and stability; (3) it placed high priority on protection of the state, not only against outside enemies but against internal subversion as well, with Marxism as its principal enemy; (4) it set self-determination, economic independence, and prosperity as major national goals; and (5) to achieve these goals it would require national power, achieved through a combination of military power and gaining popular support, and through control and direction of the economic, political, and social resources of the nation.[33]

Since the military viewed the state as representing the true, higher interests of the people, any political or social group that organized protests was seen as subversive. Consequently the military rule became strongly repressive, including the use of systematic torture (see chapter 2). It viewed civilian rule as too weak and inefficient to combat communism, and it viewed every citizen as vulnerable to Marxist influence. The national security state presented itself also not only as representing the nation's best interests but as the defender of "Western Christian civilization" against the threat of communism. Hence it expected the church to support it. It used Christian symbols, quoted church social teachings, and promised to maintain the prestige of the church in exchange for its support. To read the principles of the military junta in Chile, says Comblin, one would believe that no government in the modern world had ever shown itself so devoted to Christian goals.[34]

In the early stages of military takeovers, church officials often rallied behind the military, believing that they had indeed averted Marxist threats. This was particularly true in Chile after the overthrow of Allende in 1973. As human rights' violations mounted, however, many bishops—with Dom Helder Câmara leading the way in Brazil—became more outspoken in opposition to government policies. Over the past decade or so the failures of the national security system have led to a return to civilian rule in many countries, but the problems of social inequality created in the past continue to plague Latin America in the present, and the military continue to set the parameters of government action in many fields.

Some may dispute this data on the colonialist heritage or its importance for understanding Latin America today, but the sources used represent a wide spectrum of authors, many of them writing well before disputes about liberation theology arose. Others will accept the data, but use it selectively to reinforce their own positions. The history does bring out the Spanish and Portuguese "exploitation" of Indians and of the natural resources of Latin America. It can be used to show the "dependency" of Latin America first on Spain and then on other nations of the North. It certainly indicates why the "class analysis" urged by Gutiérrez applies at least historically in Latin America, and that elitest concentration of ownership and political power still exists. But it confirms as well arguments by Michael Novak and modernization theorists that Latin America failed to develop a broad system of free enterprise and the attitudes needed for successful business ventures.

THEORIES AND MODELS OF SOCIAL ANALYSIS

Over the past several decades, social scientists have attempted to explain and offer solutions to problems of underdevelopment in the Third World. The debate that ensued in Latin America brought into conflict several contending, though sometimes overlapping, theories about development. Dependency theory figured prominently in liberation theology at the outset. The very concept of liberation, as I have noted, arose as a reaction to a conviction that Latin America could not achieve true development unless it freed itself from dependency on the United States and Western Europe. Dependency "theory" as such no longer plays a central role in liberation theology, as we shall see in the next chapter, but much of its language and some of its contentions do remain quite operative. Most liberation theologians would still define the situation of Latin American countries as "peripheral nations dependent on capitalist center nations within a world system of economy." While use of Marxist analysis also remains operative in liberation theology, statements about its use have become more nuanced and critical. For understanding the debates in Latin America about underdevelopment, we certainly need to consider both dependency analysis and Marxist analysis, but also to see them in contrast to conventional economic theory.

As a way of proceeding in this second part of the chapter, I have linked the various models of social analysis in a way that corresponds, roughly speaking, to the process of debate that developed in Latin America over recent decades. Thus I will look first at conventional thinking about underdevelopment, then at Marxist analysis, followed by dependency theory and more recent "worldsystem" analysis, and conclude with a brief discussion of the terms "dialectical" and "functional" analysis that occur frequently in recent works of liberation theology.

The Modernization Paradigm

Most North Americans, if asked to explain why there is so much poverty in Latin America, would very likely point to the absence of features that have apparently made the United States successful: a business ethos that stresses productivity, competition, profit, available capital, a stable political system, and successful technology. From this perspective Latin American economy would seem to need updating. Such a view was the conventional wisdom after World War II when attention turned to considering the problems of Third World countries. Dependency theory would develop as a reaction against this conventional "modernization" model (or "developmentalism" as liberation theologians would more often call it).

According to this model, Latin America faced the same problems that Europe encountered before its industrial revolution: scarcity of capital, undeveloped technology, and a lack of entrepreneurs seeking to make profits through more efficient production. To achieve development, underdeveloped nations must break out of traditional mores, adopt a profit incentive, and discover newer ways to become productive. There are stages that all countries must pass through, though time spans may vary considerably. W. W. Rostow, in *The Stages of Economic Growth* (1960), spelled out the steps.[35] Advanced industrial countries had all passed through a necessary "takeoff" stage in their drive toward maturity. Underdeveloped nations would have to do the same, and they needed certain preconditions for the takeoff to occur. Development was taken to mean primarily economic growth, and to achieve growth constraints and obstacles (e.g., traditional cultural mores) must be overcome. Advanced countries could play an important role in supplying some of the missing components needed to "prime the pump" of development. Most of the arguments in defense of multinationals (or transnationals) are based on the modernization model of development. Multinationals bring the technology and managerial know-how needed to break through old patterns of production. They bring needed capital for investment; they create new jobs and train both workers and local managers with requisite skills. They help countries to specialize in what they can do best (comparative advantage), and through multinationals developing countries can penetrate new markets in advanced countries. Some theorists believed that economic growth would also create the conditions needed for democracy; economic growth and democratic political stability were seen as mutually reinforcing.

Dependency theorists would resist this linear model of progressive modernization as inadequate for explaining Latin America's problems. Marxists had argued that imperialist capitalist nations exploit workers in poor nations. The Marxist theory of imperialism would significantly influence dependency theory, but the critique that led to it most directly came from the United Nations Economic Commission on Latin America (ECLA) and its director Raul Prebisch.[36]

Raul Prebisch and ECLA

Prior to World War II, social sciences were themselves quite underdeveloped in Latin America.[37] But they developed quickly after the war, and were used effectively by ECLA. Prebisch did not attack modernization as a whole, but he did challenge an important modernization thesis. ECLA studies done after the war seemed clearly to show that the conventional wisdom about international trade was contradicted by its effects on Latin America. Conventional theory saw trade as mutually benefiting both trading partners, and believed contact with advanced productive centers would spur productivity in underdeveloped countries. In contrast, ECLA studies indicated that Latin American countries suffered from short-term instability due to fluctuating prices and long-term deterioration in terms of trade. Prebisch sought to explain why. Latin America's thrust had been outward for many decades, relying on its export of primary goods (e.g., bananas, coffee, minerals) to provide income to finance the buying of imported industrial goods. But Latin American countries were running a deficit balance of payments, caused by the rising costs of imported manufactured goods and the decreasing, unstable prices of exported primary goods. (To use a later example: in 1960, three tons of bananas could buy a tractor; in 1970, the same tractor costs the equivalent of ten tons.)[38] One reason for this, ECLA argued, was that the advanced "center" countries had nearly full employment and a highly organized labor force; the "peripheral" nations of Latin America had masses of unemployed and underemployed workers. As a consequence, productivity gains in the periphery only led to cheaper commodities and a net loss. The oligopolistic nature of center corporations also gave them greater power.

Prebisch and ECLA sought to counter this situation by an inward industrialization thrust. They urged import substitution and state protection and subsidy of national industries. To build up domestic industrialization, however, "controlled" foreign investment was needed to provide capital equipment and technology. They also noted that social issues (e.g., land and income distribution) created power struggles that impeded economic growth. ECLA policy recommendations had a very concrete impact, influencing the strategy of import substitution and encouraging the reforms undertaken in Chile (1960s), Brazil (until 1964), and Argentina (until 1966).

Economists would later challenge the statistical basis of the ECLA studies about terms of trade, saying that the terms improved in contradiction to ECLA forecasts. The strong role of the state and reformist strategies stirred even stronger reactions on the right. The left argued that adherence to capitalist principles had only increased the power of foreign investors and had made conditions worse for most Latin Americans. Thus, for example, A. G. Frank showed that the deteriorating effects of trade continued into the 1960s. The growth rate in per capita income had declined from 4.8 percent in 1945–49 to 1.9 percent in 1950–55, and then to 1.2 percent in 1960–66.[39] But Prebisch had set in motion a new way of thinking about Latin America's problems and he introduced a framework of analysis that would become part of all dependency theory: the division of the capitalist world into dominant "center" nations and subordinate "peripheral" nations such as those of Latin America. Where Rostow and modernization theorists tended to treat each national economy in isolation, arguing that each must pass through certain stages, Prebisch and the ECLA argued that this analysis ignored the *relation* between the economies of developing nations and the economies of the center nations, which already enjoyed economic advantages in respect to capital, technology, and control of markets.

Marxist Analysis

Marxism emerged in the nineteenth century as a response to conflicts between labor and capital in the more advanced industrial nations of Europe. Lenin, Rosa Luxemburg, and later Marxists would develop a theory of capitalist imperialism to explain the relationship between capitalist nations and underdeveloped nations. Liberation theologians and other Christian liberationists would use dependency theory to explain Latin America's position in the world economy but would complement it with insights from Marxism about praxis, class struggle, and the role of ideology. In an earlier work I dealt more extensively with the various components and varieties of Marxism,[40] but if we are to evaluate liberation theology's use of Marxist analysis, we need to recall the main ideas that fall under the heading of Marxist analysis.

Marxism includes several components, all of which bear upon Christian use or rejection of Marxist analysis. The two components of Marxism most usually intended by the phrase "Marxist analysis" are Marx's materialist perspective on history and Marx's critique of capitalism. A third component of Marxist analysis became prominent in the twentieth century, thanks especially to Lenin: an analysis of capitalist imperialism. We need also to discuss briefly some neo-Marxist trends and the relationship of Marxist analysis to its philosophical worldview and to Marxist strategies.

Marx's Materialist View of History: Historical Materialism. Marx believed that economic factors are most decisive in shaping society and creating change in history. Most studies about social, historical change assume that new ideas or the important political leaders of the day give rise to change. Marx thought otherwise. The key to understanding history, and the particular form a society takes at some point in history, can be found in the way humans produce—that is, their "modes of production." The modes of production depend on the natural resources, labor skills, and tools available at a given time; but more importantly they depend on how work is socially organized—that is, the "relations of production." The relationships developed in organized work, with some owning and controlling the means of production, while others work under them, create certain social classes. The state and its laws, and the cultural or religious ideas that prevail, reflect and serve the interests of the dominant class. "The mode of production in material life determines the general character of the social, political, and spiritual processes of life."[41] This last point—the influence of socioeconomic conditions on dominant ideologies—constitutes one of Marxism's main contributions to liberation theology.

Thus in medieval society, the principal mode of production involved agriculture with peasant serfs tilling the soil for wealthy landowners. The landowning lords were the dominant class, and the serfs the most oppressed class. The laws protected the owners; the prevailing political, cultural, and religious ideologies all served to justify the established order. The king ruled by divine right. God intended that some persons should be rulers and some ruled, some rich and some poor. Humans should accept their status in life, knowing that eternal salvation counts far more.

Change occurred as new modes of production developed. Industrial production became more important and lucrative than farming. Manufacture of goods shifted from hand-made to factory-made. The owners of the factories and bankers, the capitalist class, became dominant; the workers, the proletariat, became the new most oppressed class. The capitalists or bourgeoisie, in turn, use the state for their purposes with laws protecting private property and the free market system. New ideologies prevail—for example, the view that one's position in life is determined by hard work and initiative.

History thus moved through a dialectical process of change. As new modes of production arose, they conflicted with old ways of organizing society. "At a certain stage of their development the material forces of production in society come into conflict with the existing relations of production."[42] Class struggles intensify; the once-dominant class is overthrown; a new stage of history comes into being. Marx believed that capitalism would give way to socialism; the capitalists would be overthrown by the working class they had created. The capitalist mode of production produced wealth effectively, but the wealth benefited only a few. The workers, forced to subsist on minimum wages and often pushed into unemployment by capitalist crises, would revolt and usher in a new age of socialism.

Marx's Critique of Capitalism. If Marx's materialist view of history gave an overview of change over time, his more focused economic critique sought to uncover the secrets of capitalist production. Using a dialectical method—going from "appearances" to a deeper grasp of reality—Marx challenged the basic assumptions of the prevailing economic theory. He sought particularly to demonstrate "scientifically" that exploitation is *intrinsic* to capitalism, that profit can be explained only by the surplus value created by workers. Surplus value is the uncompensated labor the wage worker gives to the capitalist without receiving any value in exchange. What workers receive in wages is determined not by the value of their work, or the time they put in (labor time), but by the amount they need to sustain life (labor power). The difference between the two, the value created by work and the amount the worker needs in order to subsist, is surplus value. Marx stated his position quite graphically: "Suppose the working day consists of 6 hours of necessary labor and 6 hours of surplus labor. Then the free laborer gives the capitalist every week 6 x 6 or 36 hours of surplus labor. It is the same as if he worked 3 days in the week for himself, and 3 days in the week *gratis* for the capitalist."[43] Where Marx focused most on the exploitation of the working class in a given country, dependency theorists and liberation theologians will speak most about the "theft" of surplus value by the whole capitalist "center" from peripheral nations.

Marx did not intend, however, simply to make a moral judgment on exploitation. He argued that the internal contradictions of capitalism create crises that will eventually lead to its collapse. Marx considered overproduction, combined with lack of buying power, as the ultimate cause of all economic crises. Capitalism is driven by a law of constant expansion. Its natural dynamism pushes it to seek ever-greater profits by producing more and by producing more cheaply (for example, by intensifying labor and by replacing human labor by machines). Competition also drives capitalists to save on labor costs, reduce wages, and push smaller capitalists out of business. But this very expansion contains the seeds of capitalism's destruction. For less wages to pay and fewer small capitalists to compete with also mean less buying power. Consequently, factories must be closed when goods lie unsold, and mass unemployment results. Crises wrack the whole system; eventually the jobless masses will revolt, if only to subsist.

Marx's views on the inevitable collapse of capitalism left him quite vulnerable to critics who respond that he has been refuted by history. Workers have not revolted, at least not in the highly developed capitalist countries where revolution was predicted. Workers' wages have not remained at a subsistence level; union negotiations have taken the place of revolution; long-range corporate planning has diminished problems of unforeseen overproduction. Neo-Marxists have offered various explanations for the continuance of capitalism: heavy investment in military weapons, the stimulation of false needs through massive advertising, the intrusion of the state to subsidize private business and placate the masses. Lenin, however, made popular the most frequently used explanation: the investment of surplus and the creation of new markets through foreign imperialism.

Lenin's Theory of Imperialism. The dependency theory, which Gutiérrez and other liberation theologians would adopt at the outset, sees capitalism as impeding development in poor countries. Ironically Marx believed that colonialism was a brutal but historically necessary step if backward countries were to develop.[44] Since these countries lacked the inner dynamism to develop spontaneously, they would have to be jarred out of their stagnation. Advanced countries would have to provide them with the economic and technological components they needed. Moreover, Marx believed that capitalist modes of production were highly successful in creating wealth and would have to run their course before socialism could emerge.

Lenin's study of imperialism did, however, contribute to the development of dependency theory.[45] Lenin claimed that capitalism had entered a new but final stage: imperialism. Lenin noted five characteristics of this new stage, five changes that had prolonged the life of the capitalist system. First, it had concentrated production through the erection of monopolies that gave capitalist countries more control over markets and prices, reducing the chaos that had led to recurring crises earlier. Second, banks merged to create greater control over investment. Third, foreign countries provided not only new markets for goods but a new locus for investing surplus capital. Fourth, international cartels formed and reached agreements on spheres of interest that permitted giant corporations to avoid price wars and loss of profits. Fifth, the most striking and obvious "imperialism" took the form of direct political conquest of colonies. European powers took over 90 percent of Africa during the last quarter of the nineteenth century. Colonies gave assured control over raw materials, provided a guarantee of new markets, and permitted surplus population to resettle in colonies.

Lenin did not write with a view to explaining underdevelopment in the nations affected by imperialist expansion. He sought rather to explain why capitalism persisted and why workers had not revolted (they were even supporting their capitalist countries in World War I). His theory of imperialism, however, pointed to a new form of exploitation — companies in rich, developed nations exploiting workers in poor nations of the world. This point would find emphasis in dependency theory. Communist Party strategies, on the other hand, ran counter to the strategies of the more radical dependency theorists. In the 1950s and 60s, communist parties in Latin America urged support of ECLA-type reforms, believing that Latin America first had to develop an autonomous capitalist industrialization before it could contemplate socialism.[46]

Two North American Marxists, Paul Sweezy and Paul Baran, developed new adaptations of the Marxist analysis of imperialism, adaptations that would challenge this communist party position and would directly influence dependency theory. In particular, a major thesis developed by Baran, in his work *The Political Economy of Growth* (1957), became central in the dependency theory proposed by André Gunder Frank. Baran argued, as would Frank, that no Third World country could hope to develop on a competitive basis as long as it remained in a state of economic dependence within the world capitalist system.

Key Issues: The "Other Components" of Marxism. Had Marxism remained only a method of analysis, a way of understanding history, and of critiquing capitalism, it might never have generated the intense support and fierce antagonism that have marked its development. Scholars might have debated the validity and adequacy of its positions, and political leaders or groups might have supported or opposed its proposals. But Marxism was more than a set of ideas. It linked its analysis of what it viewed as wrong in society with a revolutionary praxis that sought to overthrow capitalism and replace it with socialism. It linked its analysis also to a materialist-atheist worldview with which it hoped to replace religion. It succeeded, moreover, in carrying out its revolutionary praxis in several countries.

Marx and Engels wrote about praxis and set down some ideas on how revolution might occur. But the revolutionary praxis most identified with Marxism came from Lenin. Lenin insisted that class struggle was an essential of Marxism and that socialism could only come about through revolution. He argued also that the revolution itself required the leadership of a "vanguard party," and that a "dictatorship of the proletariat" would then be needed to build up socialism and to suppress counterrevolutionary forces. He insisted also that a materialist worldview was essential to Marxist socialism and that materialist philosophy was "relentlessly hostile to religion."[47]

With victory in Russia, Lenin became the most authoritative interpreter of Marx. The Communist Party fulfilled the role of vanguard party and "represented" the workers in the dictatorship of the proletariat. Atheist materialism became not only the official philosophy of the party but the basis of education in the Soviet Union. Marxist analysis thus became linked with revolutionary praxis as defined by Lenin. The history of Marxism, however, suggests that it does not necessarily entail all that Lenin considered essential. The immediate followers of Marx, the German Social Democrats, moved away from revolutionary tactics and began to rely on elections and reforms as a way to socialism. Eurocommunists in Italy, France, and Spain have adopted this same parliamentary strategy in recent decades.

In chapters 7–9 I will consider where liberation theologians stand on the specific tactics embodied in Lenin's view of revolutionary praxis. We will see that they do not espouse Leninist tactics and certainly do not "promote" violent revolution, but we need to explore what they do hold in respect to revolutionary praxis.

The other significant component of Marxism concerns its atheistic worldview. Marx espoused atheism. Engels systematically developed a materialist philosophy that sought to explain not only history but the origin of the universe and the evolution of human life from pure matter alone without the need for God. Liberation theologians believe that one can separate Marxist analysis from its atheistic ideology. They draw upon several neo-Marxists to support this claim, and they have found other points in neo-Marxism fruitful in doing analysis and developing praxis.

Some Important Neo-Marxist Thinkers. In the early stages of liberation theology, some theologians cited the French Marxist Louis Althusser in support of the separation of atheist philosophy and scientific analysis. Althusser distinguished between Marxism as a scientific method and Marxism as a philosophical worldview—though Althusser himself believed both were needed. As noted in chapter 2, Clodovis Boff also made use of Althusser's ideas on how scientific thought is produced.

In more recent years, liberation theologians have drawn more often on ideas from the Italian Marxist Antonio Gramsci. Gramsci rejected philosophical materialism as an adequate basis for Marxist analysis. He differed also with other Marxists in respect to religion. Marx generally treated religion with disdain and Lenin viewed it an abomination. Gramsci, while critical of religion, saw it as an important cultural factor in the life of the Italian people. He analyzed especially the relationship between intellectuals and the masses throughout the history of Catholicism. Out of this analysis he developed some key concepts that liberation theologians have appropriated: the idea of "hegemony" (which includes winning the battle for control over the ideas, values, and institutions that dominate in society) and the concept of "organic intellectuals" (who share life with the masses and help them to articulate their views—a role liberation theologians try to fulfill).[48]

The Peruvian Marxist José Carlos Mariátegui supported the separation of atheism from Marxist analysis and his thought influenced liberation theology and Gutiérrez in particular. Mariátegui contended that historical materialism did not require philosophical materialism and that it represented a very flexible method of interpreting society. Going beyond Gramsci, Mariátegui believed that any movement must be inspired by some "myth" that gives hope and inspiration, and he believed that socialism must respect the deep cultural influence of religion on the people of Peru. He also believed that Peruvian and Latin American socialism must be truly "indigenous," incorporating the values of its Indian population and not imitating any existing models of socialism. He favored a decentralized form of socialism over a heavily state-directed form.[49] To this group of neo-Marxists who have influenced liberation theology we could also add Ernst Bloch who wrote extensively about the social dynamism of Judeo-Christian religion and about the hope it engendered.

These points about neo-Marxism have diverted us briefly from our discussion of models of social analysis, but they will prove significant in our later attempts to assess use of Marxism by liberation theologians. At this point, however, we need to return to our investigation. Having discussed the forerunners of dependency analysis (the Prebisch-ECLA analysis and Marxist analysis), we turn now to dependency theory itself.

Dependency Analysis

Marxist theories about imperialism focused on the dominant capitalist countries and how they forestalled their own downfall by exploiting poorer nations. Latin Americans looked for a method of analysis that would focus more on how such domination affected them. Brazil, in the 1960s, had the largest concentration of foreign investment in all Latin America. Not surprisingly the most important formulations of dependency theory (including all the persons discussed in this chapter) either came from Brazil or used Brazil as a subject for analysis. The new analysis rejected modernization arguments that centered criticisms on weaknesses within Latin America. Using Prebisch's "core-periphery" framework, the new analysis sought to show that the weaknesses resulted from policies controlled from the center, from the United States and Europe. Helio Jaguaribe blamed advanced nations for imposing economic servitude on underdeveloped nations. Celso Furtado sought to combine the insights of traditional economics with

Keynesian thought and Marxist analysis. He employed a historical method that would become typical of most dependency analysis.[50] Theotonio Dos Santos articulated the principal theses of dependency theory in an oft quoted definition of dependency:

> Dependency is a situation in which a certain group of countries have their economies conditioned by the development and expansion of another country's economy. The relationship of interdependency between two or more economies, and between these and world commerce, assumes a dependent nature when some countries (the dominant) can expand and be self-starting, while at the same time the others (the dependent ones) can only act as a reflection of this expansion, an expansion that can have positive or negative influence on the dependent countries' development. In whatever form, the basic situation of dependency produces a global situation in which the dependent countries are placed in a backward situation and under the exploitation of the dominant countries.
>
> The dominant countries thus impose a dominant technology, commerce, capital, and socio-political values on the dependent countries (to varying degrees in various historical moments) that permits them to impose conditions of exploitation and to extract part of the surplus produced by the dependent countries. Dependency, then, is founded on an international division of labor that permits the industrial development of some countries and limits this same process in others, submitting them to conditions and restraints imposed by the centers of world domination."[51]

Two Approaches to Dependency. Many different versions of dependency developed, some that seemed to place almost the entire blame for underdevelopment on capitalist countries of the North (the "center") and others that gave equal weight to internal factors and class struggles within Latin America. André Gunder Frank represented the stronger view. Latin America is underdeveloped *because* it has supported the development of Western Europe and the United States. Fernando Henrique Cardoso represented a more nuanced version, one that I believe is more distinctively Latin American in origin and more defensible. Dos Santos' description tends toward the stronger version, but speaks of peripheral countries as being "conditioned" rather than determined by dependency.

When dependency theory is discussed in the United States and Europe, one commentator observes, it most often refers to the work of André Gunder Frank "who is not a Latin American at all, nor a representative member of the school."[52] Frank was raised in the United States and studied economics at the University of Chicago. But he taught and did research in Latin America in the early 1960s. His experience there led him to reject the conventional views on development that he had learned at the University of Chicago. His ground-breaking work on dependency, *Capitalism and Underdevelopment in Latin America*, was first published in English in 1967. Frank acknowledged his debt to North American Paul Baran and affirmed Baran's argument that no Third World country could hope to become a competitive equal with advanced countries as long as it remained dependent in the world capitalist system.

Frank asserted the thesis most often associated with dependency theory, that underdeveloped nations were made and kept underdeveloped to support the development of advanced capitalist countries: "the development of underdevelopment" represented two sides of the same coin. He used Brazil as an example to show how foreign transnational investors, far from stimulating growth, drained off capital from Latin America. He cited a U.S. Department of Commerce study, showing that between 1950 and 1961 U.S. investment amounted to $2,962 million; U.S. remittance of profits and interest during that decade amounted to $6,875 million—or an outflow of $3,913 million lost by Brazil. He argued also that what Brazil lost in terms of trade between 1955 and 1961 offset all the aid given by the United States to Brazil since World War II.[53]

Spurred by the success of the Cuban revolution, which declared itself socialist without waiting for progressive capitalism to prepare the way, Frank called for a revolutionary breakaway from the whole capitalist system. Latin America would remain stagnant and could not develop if it remained in the world system of capitalism. Frank further argued that Latin America had been "capitalist" from colonial times on; it was not feudal or precapitalist now or even then, as both modernization and orthodox Marxism suggested. Latin America was capitalist because it used exploited labor to accumulate surplus value (capital); even the sixteenth-century encomiendas were tied to mercantile capitalism because they sought profits for goods produced for foreign markets. Latin America manifested no progressive development and remained stagnant because the accumulated capital was not reinvested for growth in Latin America but appropriated by foreign monopolies or consumed by domestic elites. Only through socialist revolution could it hope to develop.

Critics have attacked Frank from all sides and on many counts.[54] Marxists have criticized him for attempting to define capitalism simply as any exploitation and appropriation of surplus value, ignoring all differences in modes of production. Other critics say that his stagnationist thesis was empirically contradicted in fact by growth figures in the 1960s and 70s. Others say that, while insisting on the specific nature of Latin American development, Frank ends up with a generalized, mechanistic explanation of underdevelopment. His array of statistical studies, however, lent power to dependency arguments.

Some Latin American dependency theorists have developed neo-Marxist views similar in many ways to Frank's, most notably Ruy Mauro Marini (revolutionary like Frank) and Theotonio Dos Santos (more reformist). Dos

Santos, as noted, modifies the development-of-underdevelopment thesis with the words "conditioned by." He also criticizes Frank, stating that external factors are not the whole cause of the problem, though they do determine the limits and possibilities of action available.

Fernando Henrique Cardoso represented a dependency approach more distinctively Latin American in origin, and far more modest and nuanced in its claims than Frank's. Together with Enzo Faletto, Cardoso published his *Dependencia y Desarollo en América Latina* in 1969, from manuscripts written prior to the publication of Frank's work.[55] Many view this work as the *locus classicus* of dependency literature.[56] In a later essay, Cardoso insisted that when he wrote his earlier work he never claimed or intended to present a new paradigm or a "theory" of dependence. He sought rather to criticize weaknesses in prevailing methods and to explain what Latin Americans had for years experienced and discussed—the "fact" of dependency.[57]

In common with all dependency theorists, Cardoso believes that external factors are important, that one cannot understand Latin American development without considering its dependent position in relation to advanced capitalist nations. But his primary focus is internal, on the social process through which, under the impact of external forces, different classes, alliances, and conflicts are formed. Indeed so much of his original work focused on internal dynamics that he felt obliged, in response to Marxist critics, to *add* to the English edition of his work (1979) a section on U.S. interventions not treated in his original book.[58] Cardoso avoids general theorizing and insists on studying "situations of dependency" in their specifics. Even with a given country, he finds very different dynamics at work in enclave economies (formed with foreign capital and producing goods for external markets), nationally owned economies, and multinational economies. He also stresses that new factors must be studied. Thus, for example, he believes that manufacturing for domestic Latin American needs had become a new goal of the multinationals.

As the dependency debates continued, Cardoso clearly and sharply distinguished his views from Frank, stating with Faletto that "we do *not* see dependency and imperialism as external and internal sides of a single coin."[59] He finds several of Frank's theses to be erroneous—for example, that capitalist development in Latin America is impossible (it *has* developed), that domestic bourgeoisie are no longer a significant force, and that the only options available to Latin America are socialism or fascism. Though socialist in vision, Cardoso is generally classified as a moderate nationalist, and he became a senator in Brazil's new government. Critics focus on the vagueness of his socialist vision and the weakness of empirical data.

Many critics have simply dismissed dependency theory. Peter Evans, who has written extensively about development issues, reaches a quite different verdict:

"Dependency theory," if such a thing ever existed, may well have had its day, but the rich tradition of work that has been associated with the concept of dependency continues to thrive and expand its horizons, both substantively and theoretically.

The label may disappear, says Evans, because it became too identified with simplistic hypotheses about external domination and the impossibility of either capitalism or democracy in the periphery. But the dependency approach has established itself as one of the "primary lenses" through which scholars, both in North America and Latin America, analyze issues of underdevelopment. Evans cites Cardoso's historico-structural model as the one that has proved productive.[60]

World System Analysis

Many liberation theologians, as we shall see, now speak more critically of dependency theory as such. They continue, however, to speak of Latin American countries as a peripheral part of a worldwide capitalist system. We might, with this in mind, consider a more recent world system analysis pioneered by Immanuel Wallerstein of the State University of New York (Binghamton). Like dependency theory, it uses a core-periphery framework of analysis, which it studies historically. But unlike Cardoso's analysis, which stresses particular nations or situations, world system analysis views the present world economy as one entity with a history that has shaped the history of the modern world. It takes as a basic assumption that "the history of the modern world is the history of capitalist accumulation; and the capitalist development is the development of a single system, the modern world system."[61] Wallerstein's own major studies trace this modern world system from its origins in the sixteenth to eighteenth centuries.[62] Other world system studies focus on the histories of particular nations: for example, how Mexico became a peripheral nation and how it has moved up to the status of a semiperipheral state.[63]

The history of capitalism in advanced countries is well known. The study of peripheral nations calls for the same attention now, showing how they were incorporated into the system: usually, says Wallerstein, over a 50–75 year period, and often through the establishment of a new product like sugar. World system analysis studies the structures of capitalist accumulation, the division of labor created in the two productive zones (center-periphery), the cycles of capitalist expansion and stagnation, and the growth of state systems to protect the system. On this last point, Wallerstein sees the state as playing an essential role, protecting capitalism from its own self-destructive tendencies.

Like dependency analysis, world-capitalist thought sees this system as creating a stratified class system. The world system is organized around basic inequalities of political power and wealth. Even workers fall into very different class structures: relatively free, high-wage, skilled labor in the center; relatively low wages and politically-coerced labor in the periphery; with interclass struggles most acute in semiperipheral countries. Any country that succeeds in moving up the ladder of mobility does so at the expense of others. Despite similarities with Marxist thought, we might add, world capitalist analysts do not see themselves as Marxist.

Dialectical versus Functional Analysis

In the early years of liberation theology, dependency theory served as a critique of modernization or developmental models, and Marxist analysis served especially as a critique of ideology and as a source for understanding class conflict. In recent years, as already noted in chapter 2, the Boffs, Míguez Bonino, and other liberation theologians speak more often about opting for "dialectical" over "functional" analysis. But apart from some very broad statements—that dialectical analysis sees conflict in society and functionalism presumes equilibrium—the descriptions of each remain quite generic. A 1980 essay, "Analysis of Society" in the Mexican periodical *Christus*, gives at least some added details.

Functional analysis, the author comments, is a form of global analysis that originates in a comparison of society with living organisms. As an organism has diverse functions, so also does society. A social function is the contribution of each individual to the organization and operation of the whole of society. A basic postulate of functionalism is that functional unity and organization are required to achieve the internal equilibrium that makes possible the continuation of a given social system. The U.S. sociologist Talcott Parsons, a leading representative of this school, understands the social structure as a totality of relatively stable roles and behavior based on institutional norms. Functionalism, the author continues, views conflicts as "deviations" and dysfunctions, and hence does not consider conflict as able to transform society structurally. Change can occur only *within* already existing structures. Functionalism thus contains an implicit political bias, which rejects a radical, global transformation of society.

Dialectical analysis (dialectical-structural) does not make the pretended claim to neutrality implied in functionalism. It places itself at the service of the majority of Latin Americans who are exploited and oppressed. It seeks to construct a society that will eliminate the structural roots of exploitation and will make possible a more just society and true democracy. It conceives reality as a structure, containing diverse substructures, but it rejects the view that these substructures all result from or are simply reflections of the economic. It studies the dialectic interactions of humans with society; they affect society but are also conditioned by it. But this dialectical analysis, while recognizing the historico-social conditioning of humans in society, affirms human freedom. Humans are the active historical subjects of social change. (The points about the economic not being determinative and about human freedom seem clearly intended by the author to distinguish this form of dialectical analysis from classical Marxist analysis.)[64]

Functionalism comes under attack also in a work by Raúl Vidales and T. Kudo on popular religiosity. They describe the functionalist model in terms quite similar to those expressed in the *Christus* article, but they make explicit reference also to Roger Vekemans' theory of marginality. Vekemans, as noted in chapter 3, considers the basic problem in Latin America the exclusion of the poor (the marginal) from the resources and advantages enjoyed by privileged groups. The needed change would involve integrating these marginalized poor into society and enabling them to participate more fully. Vidales and Kudo acknowledge the usefulness of functionalism for statistical studies on health care, unemployment, and the like. But they believe that functionalism, and marginality theory, assume that society itself is healthy, that the poor (or poor nations) are backward and must be integrated into societies considered normal.[65]

This final section on dialetical analysis offers a natural transition to the next chapter and its discussion of what liberation theologians have said about social analysis and more broadly about socialism and capitalism.

Chapter 7

Social Analysis and Options
in Liberation Theology

Liberation theology sees liberating praxis as a primary source for theological reflection and as a desired outcome of theology. But praxis always involves some underlying social analysis. The link between social analysis and praxis is precisely what disturbs many critics of liberation theology. They see use of Marxist analysis as generating a revolutionary praxis, which, while claiming to liberate the poor, leads to violence and to the creation of new and often worse forms of domination. Critics like Michael Novak find use of dependency theory as equally misguided. They argue that it leads to placing blame for Latin American problems on external factors and ignores the positive features of "democratic capitalism" that could serve as a better system to achieve justice and freedom. More sympathetic critics have serious misgivings about the *extent* to which liberation theologians seem to rely on Marxist analysis and dependency theory, and also about their advocacy of an often unclearly defined socialism. Coming to this study, my own misgivings centered mostly on these latter points. The last part of this chapter will consider some representative criticisms of liberation theology with respect to its economic and political views. Subsequent chapters will attempt to assess the criticisms. This chapter, however, first investigates what liberation theologians have in fact said about dependency and capitalism, and about Marxist analysis and socialism.

Some Initial Observations

The world of liberation theology is significantly different today than it was in the 1970s. Not until I had come to the very end of final revisions on this book, however, did the extent of the change become evident. Nearly all the controversial texts cited by critics come from writings in the 1970s, often from the early 70s, and most of the works I cite also come from the 70s though some English translations of them appeared much later. But as I survey an array of books published in the 1980s by the most prominent liberation theologians, I am struck by how little they contain that would stir strong controversy on the socio-political level. Gutiérrez, as noted, has focused on questions of spirituality. Segundo's five-volume series, "Jesus of Nazareth, Yesterday and Today," contains only very nuanced views about social analysis and political options. Leonardo Boff has made some public statements in denunciation of capitalism and in support of socialism, but his written works in recent years have been almost entirely theological (on the Trinity, on Mary, on the passion of Christ, etc.). Even his *When Theology Listens to the Poor* makes only brief reference to favoring a "dialectical" approach to social analysis. The specific changes he calls for would fit squarely into church social teachings: defense and promotion of the rights of the poor and of a minimally decent standard of living.[1] Galilea, Sobrino, Comblin, and others have all focused their main efforts on the spirituality of liberation. Some works out of the Ecumenical Center of Investigations (Departamenta Ecuménico de Investigaciones-DEI) in Costa Rica continue to offer sharp critiques of capitalism, and liberation theology certainly continues to focus repeatedly on the poor in Latin America, but it uses little of the "revolutionary" language of the early 1970s.

Princeton scholar Paul Sigmund speaks of two distinct trends in liberation theology, reflecting two distinct phases in its development: an earlier Marxist phase and one that now focuses its attention on Christian base communities.[2] A significant change has, indeed, occurred. But I would modify his judgment in respect to both phases. References to Marxism did appear with much greater frequency in the formative years of liberation theology. But Gutiérrez and others held nuanced views even in this period (as we will note in this chapter and in the "assessment" chapters). Also liberation theology cannot be simply identified with activist groups like the Christians for Socialism. (Gutiérrez resisted forming a CFS group in Peru because he rejected "baptizing" any political movement with the name "Christian.") With respect to the more recent phase, liberation theology has become more pronouncedly "theological" with many fewer inclusions of radical analysis; in fact, it now contains very little of any kind of social analysis. But liberation theologians remain, nevertheless, fundamentally anticapitalist and still convinced that Latin America suffers from a dependency on a world-capitalist economic system with its center in the North. Consequently they continue to defend a critical "borrowing from" Marxist and dependency analyses.

When Gutiérrez first wrote *A Theology of Liberation* he noted that Latin America was in the midst of a full-blown process of revolutionary ferment. That ferment has clearly subsided, though it could rise again. Even in this period, however, liberation theologians did not equate their call for radical change with armed revolution. Some Christians joined armed guerilla groups, but liberation theologians have never called for the creation of any violent Christian revolutionary groups. Even the most militant expressions of liberation theology came in support of a democratically elected Allende government in Chile, and later in support of a broadly based overthrow of the Somoza regime in Nicaragua. Armed struggle continues in Central America, but no South American nation appears likely to undergo revolutionary change in the near future. In Brazil, where the praxis of liberation theology may have its greatest impact, civilian-democratic rule has replaced military-authoritarian rule. Its new democracy may still feel the heavy-handed influence of the military and the new civilian government has failed to meet many popular demands. But even the "left" in Brazil operates within the context of democracy, and this new context has influenced the "praxis" espoused by liberation theology.

An initial observation might also prove useful with respect to the "level" of analysis most prominent in liberation theology and its influence on Latin America. Most of the politico-economic positions held by liberation theologians deal with "macroanalysis": they offer rather global critiques of the capitalist system and dependency, and support for socialism. The importance attributed to these positions, both by liberation theologians and their critics, led me to extensive treatment of them in this book. Indeed, they remain serious issues. But the tension produced by these issues, reflected especially in discussions about Marxist analysis, often implies a very exaggerated view of the power of liberation theology. One can begin to believe that the positions espoused by liberation theologians may well determine the directions their countries will take. But liberation theology does not command troops or control mass organizations. Even its influence on public opinion in Latin America remains quite small; most Latin Americans have probably never heard of liberation theology. It struggles simply to give some voice to those who have remained powerless and oppressed. At the "microlevel," in a particular area where land rights or peasant union organizing have become volatile issues, the influence of the church and of liberation theology may take on much greater importance. Chapter 10 will study in more detail how those who support liberation theology have translated it into "practice." We need to study seriously the economic-political views found in liberation theology, but the influence of these views has too often been overdramatized.

Liberation theologians are first and foremost theologians, not social scientists. While social analysis serves as a context for liberation theology, some theologians like Sobrino say very little about such analysis. Others, like Gutiérrez, Assmann, and Míguez Bonino in their early works, speak about the types of analysis needed and discuss dependency in some detail, but they do not present social analyses of their own. Some other "liberationists," like Franz Hinkelammert (an economist-theologian), Otto Maduro (a lay sociologist), or Enrique Dussel (a liberation philosopher) have developed certain types of analysis. Most theologians, however, rely on social scientists and simply stress the "need" for scientific analysis. Thus Hugo Assmann argued that theology in Latin America starts from an analysis of reality and therefore seeks "the most appropriate scientific instrument the secular sciences can provide."[3] Gutiérrez stressed that the conclusions liberation theology reached about the causes of misery in Latin America are "based on studies of the most rigorous scientific exactitude."[4] Sergio Torrres, in an opening address to an Ecumenical Congress of Third World Theologians (Brazil, 1980) called for an analysis of capitalism done "with scientific rigor."[5] As we have already seen in chapter 2, Clodovis Boff and José Míguez Bonino argue that social sciences are a constitutive part of liberation theology. Inasmuch as dependency theory played a significant role in the early stages of liberation theology, I will look first at what liberation theologians said then, and have said more recently, about it.

Dependency

For Hugo Assmann the major contribution of the social sciences to liberation theology came from their critiques of developmentalism, critiques that showed the real problem in Latin America as one of dependency on the capitalist nations of the North. "Underlying liberation theology is the historical experience of the actual nature of *under*development, as a form of dependence."[6] The very term "liberation" drew its political significance from this conviction about Latin America's dependence. The language of Marxism and of leftist revolutionary movements exercised an influence, said Assmann, but the major influence was a new awareness that Latin Americans are "not merely underdeveloped peoples ... but peoples 'kept in a state of underdevelopment.' "[7] Míguez Bonino concurred: "Northern development is built on third-world underdevelopment."[8] Leonardo Boff spoke in similar terms: "The affluence and advanced scientific and technological development of the Northern hemisphere ... has meant the impoverishment and marginalization of the dependent, underdeveloped nations."[9] Each of them spoke not only of the fact of dependence but used André Gunder Frank's formula that blamed Latin American underdevelopment on Northern development. However, a closer look at the thought of Gustavo Gutiérrez and of Leonardo Boff will indicate some important qualifications in the use of dependency theory.

In *A Theology of Liberation* Gutiérrez wrote extensively about the problem of dependency, explaining Latin America's disillusionment with development policies, and tying the concept of liberation to the fact of dependency. He also spoke of underdevelopment "as the historical byproduct of the development of other countries."[10] Even in this first major work, however, Gutiérrez took up some of the important qualifications made by Fernando H. Cardoso about dependency theory. Latin American countries are constitutively dependent on rich nations, "but we are not dealing with a purely external factor."[11] Leninist theories of imperialism, said Gutiérrez, do not take into account the experiences of peripheral countries. Much needs to be done to work out an adequate theory of dependency, to eliminate ideological factors that impede a true scientific understanding. He cites Cardoso's warning that "one can have recourse to the idea of dependence as a way of 'explaining' internal processes of the dependent societies by a purely 'external' variable . . . which is regarded as the real cause."[12]

In *The Power of the Poor in History*, Gutiérrez returned to the issue of dependency. "External dependency and internal domination are the marks of the social structures of Latin America."[13] Looking back on the early theories of dependency, Gutiérrez felt that their analysis had been, by and large, a boon.[14] But they sometimes failed by focusing too much on the conflict between nations (center versus periphery) and not enough on class analysis.[15] In the meantime, Gutiérrez observed, a new form of domination had developed, one that required new instruments of anticapitalist analysis. This new form of domination included great expansion of foreign investment in manufacturing, an even greater draining off of capital, fiscal stability achieved by "brutally devaluing the contribution of the world labor force," and greater control of technological, political, commercial, and even 'food' power in the clutch of a few countries headed by the United States.[16] The gap between the rich and the poor had only widened; political repression, together with persecution of the church, had intensified.

Shortly after the Vatican 1984 instruction on liberation theology, Gutiérrez published an essay, "Theology and the Social Sciences." If Gutiérrez spoke earlier of "rigorous scientific exactitude," in this essay he stresses the provisional and transitory nature of social science studies. To say these disciplines are scientific "does not mean that their conclusions are definitive and beyond discussion." Liberation theology needs to be attentive to the many variations of dependency theory and to criticisms made of it; it should avoid generalizations and be enriched by other types of analysis. Gutiérrez considers Cardoso the most important figure in dependency analysis and he notes that Cardoso considers his theoretical attitude as situated at the "opposite ends" (*antípodas*) from Marx.[17]

In a new introduction to a revised (1988) edition of *A Theology of Liberation*, Gutiérrez all but abandons dependency theory:

> It is clear that the theory of dependence, which was so extensively used in the early years of our encounter with the Latin American world, is now an inadequate tool, because it does not take sufficient account of the internal dynamics of each country or of the vast dimensions of the world of the poor.[18]

Leonardo Boff, in *Liberating Grace*, reflected earlier liberationist views on Latin American dependency. In describing dependency Boff used the language of A. G. Frank: "Latin America stands on the periphery of the big-power centers and is dominated by them." "Development and underdevelopment are two sides of the same coin."[19] As evidence, Boff offered a brief account of Latin American dependency, beginning with the key stages of its economic dependency: the plunder of its resources by Spain and Portugal, production determined by Europe in the postcolonial period, the newest dependency shaped by multinationals, which determine Latin America's productive system and priorities. Boff voiced, however, his own serious reservations about dependency theory:

> It is only a theory, not an established truth. It is one stage in an ongoing investigation and has its own intrinsic limitations. It offers a good diagnosis of the structure of underdevelopment, but it does not do much to offer any viable way out.[20]

Expanding on this last point, Boff expressed skepticism about the revolutionary type of breakaway advocated by Frank. "More moderate advocates of the theory of dependency showed greater historical sense" and recognized the need to work for change within the system.[21] Citing José Comblin, Boff claimed that one cannot choose both complete autonomy *and* development. Compromise is necessary. If development is the goal, one has to work within the international system. Remarkably, Boff even mentioned, as a "more pragmatic and immediately viable" option for Brazil, the acceptance of a "Canadian" form of dependency with its promise of economic growth.[22] His views are thus far more nuanced than many have popularly supposed liberation theology to be.

I noted in the last chapter that while dependency analysis continues strong, the label "dependency theory" carries connotations of simplistic hypotheses no longer accepted as valid. (These hypotheses were, however, expressed by several liberation theologians, as we have seen.) In recent years, some liberation theologians, like Gutiérrez, have all but disavowed dependency "theory." J. B. Libânio acknowledges that liberation theology at the outset was very much bound up with dependency theory. But he finds many difficulties with it as a continuing basis for social analysis. It offered no solution to Latin American problems. Rupture with the capitalist North might bring independence, but not development. Dependency theory offered no direction for creating new structures. It oversimplified the problem, and even involved a kind of Manichaeism, with all in the center as evil and all in the periphery as good. The simple divisions of dominated and oppressed, metropolis and periphery, center countries and dependent ones, do not correspond to reality in Libânio's judgment.[23]

In interviews, Clodovis Boff and Peruvian economist Javier Iguíñiz (who works with Gutiérrez) acknowledged similar problems. Boff noted that one finds little study of dependency theory now in Brazil. Iguíñiz made several interesting comments. First he noted that the *more* developed countries in Latin America tend to be the more dependent ones. Second, he said that in the 1980s focus has shifted away from external factors to internal issues — for example, "what forces do we have to build up our nation?" Third, and most interesting, Iguíñiz observed that liberation theology really stood in

conflict with dependency theory from the outset, because dependency theory viewed structures as controlling people, whereas liberation theology
sees the poor as subjects of their own liberation.[24]

Capitalism

While liberation theologians now give less credence to dependency "theory," they still see the "fact" of dependency as a major problem. They state
the problems of Latin America more often, however, in terms of "dependent capitalism" with the accent on capitalism, which they uniformly oppose.
One could conceive of poor countries creating their own strong capitalist
enterprises and gaining independence through successful competition. But
this was the very strategy of the developmental model, which Gutiérrez saw
as discredited. Dependency studies lead one to conclude, said Gutiérrez,
"that autonomous Latin American development is not viable within the
framework of the internationalist capitalist system."[25] Gutiérrez devotes
surprisingly little time to critiques of capitalism, but his references to it are
unqualifiedly negative. The situation of dependency is rooted "in the structures of capitalist society"; reforms will not work; a social revolution is
needed.[26] Other church groups, in the early years of liberation theology,
spoke in a similar vein. A new liberated society "cannot be reached by
capitalist paths"; poverty, injustice, and exploitation are elements characteristic of capitalist society.[27] While Gutiérrez rejected capitalism as an
internal basis for Latin American development, his main target remained
the worldwide system of capitalism that produces dependency. His concern
about local, indigenous capitalism appears secondary when he comments
that liberation "also" implies confrontation with the capitalist countries'
natural allies, "their compatriots who control the national power structure."[28] On the other hand, his many references to complementing dependency theory with class analysis and study of internal factors suggest
that changing the system within Latin America remained an important
priority.

Leonardo Boff, though he suggests caution about breaking away from
capitalism internationally, speaks harshly about capitalism itself. In report-
ing on a national meeting (1978) of delegates from base communities in
Brazil, Boff affirms, "On two points opinion was unanimous: (1) the main
root of this oppression is the elitist, exclusive capitalist system; and (2)
people resist and are liberated to the extent that they unite and create a
network of popular movements."[29] A few pages later he repeats that the
base communities, in identifying the causes of the miseries they suffer, "see
the main one—not the only one, but the main one—as the capitalist system." "There is no cure for the system. It must be overcome."[30] Boff might
also have cited a pastoral letter by the Brazilian bishops of the Amazon
region, a letter that contained a searing indictment of capitalism. "We must
overcome capitalism. It is the greatest evil, the rotten root, the tree that

produces those fruits we all know: poverty, hunger, sickness, and death of the majority. The vast majority work to enrich the few."[31]

Leonardo and Clodovis Boff wrote at some length for the *National Catholic Reporter* (August 28, 1987) in response to the U.S. Catholic bishops' pastoral letter on the U.S. economy.[32] While praising the letter for confronting problems created by the U.S. economic system, the Boffs faulted the bishops for not calling into question the very system of capitalism itself. The bishops treat the system as one that "works" but needs some fixing and improvement. They use, said the Boffs, an implicit "functionalism" that sees contradictions only as dysfunctions able to be corrected. They avoid even the use of the word "capitalism"; they fail to recognize the U.S. system as part of a dominant worldwide system. In dealing with U.S. relations to the Third World, the bishops speak only of "interdependency," not of Third World dependency. They fail to discuss multinationals' exploitation of poor nations. The contradictions of capitalism may be less apparent in the United States "in large part because they are simply transferred to the Third World." The Boffs praise the bishops' letter for condemning abuses, but they criticize it for ignoring the structural failings of the very system of capitalism. The Boffs' strongest statements on this score were omitted from the shortened NCR article. "Capitalism can be more or less *immoral*; it can never be more or less *moral*. You do not eliminate the ferocity of a wolf by filing down its teeth." "It is just as impossible to create a moral market system as it is to build a Christian brothel."[33]

If the Boff's speak in uncompromising terms, their comments pale in comparison to Franz Hinkelammert's theological critique of capitalism. Using Marx's critique of "fetishism," Hinkelammert portrays capitalism as a system that has brought destruction and death to the majority of those who have fallen under its power. "Hundreds of millions of unemployed and underemployed persons within the global capitalist system are living in extreme poverty."[34] Capitalism makes the production and sale of commodities its sole purpose. Money is its only God. Workers have no say in what is produced or in how products should be shared. Capital "exercises the right to decide over the worker's life or death"; it sucks the blood of living labor.[35] It sows death on the earth, taking its own life from the life of human beings. "Capitalist industry has committed mass murder among the working classes."[36] Those who try to defend capitalism, like the economist Milton Friedman, reduce humans to commodities. For Friedman, "the freedom to murder is a vital part of his reasoning."[37]

When Pope Leo XIII wrote his encyclical *Rerum Novarum* (1891) he criticized the abuses of capitalism, but rejected socialism as false in principle. Many liberation theologians would reverse this judgment. Thus, for example, Míguez Bonino views the basic ethos of capitalism as anti-Christian: "it is the maximizing of economic gain, the raising of man's grasping impulse, the idolizing of the strong, the subordination of man to economic production."[38] Míguez then makes explicit the reversal of judgments about capitalism and socialism:

> Humanization is for capitalism an unintended by-product, while it is for socialism an explicit goal. Solidarity is for capitalism accidental; for socialism, it is essential. In terms of their basic ethos, Christianity must criticize capitalism radically, in its fundamental intention, while it must criticize socialism functionally, in its failure to fulfill its purpose.[39]

Marxism

It is difficult to gauge whether this strong anticapitalism led to the use of Marxist analysis or whether the use of Marxist-oriented social sciences created the conviction that capitalism was to blame. Certainly the prevailing economic system, which Latin Americans view as capitalist, has failed to meet even the basic needs of most Latin Americans. Given the conviction that the capitalist system constitutes the root cause of the problem, it should not be surprising that liberation theologians viewed Marxist analysis as a useful tool.

Hugo Assmann noted that liberation theology confronts problems arising from dependence, exploitation, and imperialism. "For most of those who use this language, this implies the use of a sociological analysis derived from Marxism."[40] In the early years of liberation theology, Assmann was considered one of the most Marxist of the liberation theologians. Gutiérrez was not, though his opponents accused him of Marxism chiefly because of his statements on class struggle. He insisted that "class struggle is a fact" and that the church must take a stance and opt for the poor in their class struggle.[41]

Gutiérrez's *A Theology of Liberation* contains very few references to Marxism. He briefly noted Marx's contribution to social analysis: "Marx created categories which allowed for the elaboration of a science of history."[42] Gutiérrez felt that Marxist analysis could be separated from Marxism's atheistic worldview, and he cited José Carlos Mariátegui, the Peruvian Marxist, who viewed historical materialism as a very flexible "method" of interpreting society. He referred also to Althusser's distinction between Marxism as a science and as an ideology.[43] Apart from a few endnotes, his only other comments on Marxism in the book dealt with its influence on modern theology (showing the need for transforming the world) and on the challenge of Marx's critique of religion.[44]

In April 1971 Gutiérrez gave a talk on "Marxism and Christianity" to a group of Christians supportive of socialism in Chile. Even in this context of Christians enthusiastic about the election of a Marxist president (Salvador Allende), Gutiérrez spoke quite cautiously about Marxism. He warns of the danger of using Christianity to justify revolutionary actions or making

Christianity itself into a revolutionary doctrine. Marx, Gutiérrez believes, had a valid "intuition" about capitalism, but Marxism can lose its scientific character and become a messianic socialism. You cannot simply mix Marxism and Christianity. Gutiérrez cautions also against placing too much reliance on the French Marxist Louis Althusser's distinction between ideology and science. (Many Christians in the early 1970s declared themselves Christian in faith and Marxist in analysis.) Althusser's Marxism is theoretically an antihumanism, says Gutiérrez, and Marxism in real life is more than science. Marxists have their own faith.[45]

The bulk of this talk dealt more with the issue of liberation and salvation than with Marxism. But at the conclusion Gutiérrez again distances himself from both classical Marxist analysis and Althusser's views. Science can become ideological and lead to a religious faith. Faith should not appropriate science directly. A level of utopia, of sociological imagination, is needed to mediate between faith and science.[46] (On this point Gutiérrez would also call into question Clodovis Boff's description of the direct relation between theology and science, a description I discussed in chapter 2.)

Gutiérrez spoke directly to the issue of Marxist analysis again in a 1984 essay on the social sciences and theology. In the essay, he stresses that the presence of elements of Marxist analysis does not mean identification of social science with Marxism. He notes the conflicts between Marxist analysis and dependency theory on many issues (noting Cardoso's opposition to Marx); he insists that liberation theology involves no use of Marxism that would deny human liberty; he agrees with warnings made by the magisterium about uncritical use of Marxism; and he asserts that there has never been any proposal in liberation theology to synthesize Marxism and Christianity.[47]

José Míguez Bonino wrote extensively about Marxism in the mid-1970s. In a work on Christianity and Marxism he noted that Christians in Latin America had come to recognize "the unsubstitutable relevance of Marxism" in their effort to make their faith historically relevant.[48] He then gave the reasons for this decision for Marxism. It is an option "for structural over purely individual change, for revolution against reformism, for socialism over against capitalist development or 'Third' solutions, for 'scientific' over against idealistic or utopian socialism."[49] This quote suggests that the appeal of Marxism may have been closely connected with the options that it stood for. If Christians are serious about commitment to the poor, they need some instrument for analyzing society, and Marxism offers "a scientific, verifiable, and efficacious way to articulate love historically."[50]

If Míguez defends liberation theology's indebtedness to Marxist analysis, and sees it as "the best instrument available,"[51] he also cautions about Marxism. Marxists often insist on the necessity of dialectical materialism and become dogmatic in their beliefs.[52] He believes also that Marxist materialism provides no real basis for ethics.[53] Most seriously Marxism as a historical movement shows many failures. Though Míguez views Cuba and

China more positively, he recognizes the atrocities of Stalinism and he believes that most communist countries have lost their credibility.[54]

The Boffs, in their work on introducing liberation theology, assert that liberation theology uses Marxism "purely as an instrument" and that it "maintains a decidedly critical stance" in relation to Marxism. Marx can be a companion, but never *the* guide, who is Christ.[55]

Juan Luis Segundo writes at some length about Marxist analysis in *Faith and Ideologies*. While he finds Marxist analysis useful as a method of "suspicion," he challenges it on several scores. He challenges Marxist claims to explain change "materialistically." Modes of production are not "material" factors. They involve conscious activity by spiritual persons, and they involve interactions between persons. Scientific analysis can never determine what "ought to be," and what Marxists really mean by "materialist" in describing their method of analysis is really epistemological realism. Segundo criticizes also the so-called laws of dialectical materialism. He sees the greatest fault of Marxism, however, not in the weakness of its scientific method (the focus of many critics) but in its failure to use the humanist values that first inspired it as ethical guidelines for constructing socialist societies.[56]

Liberation theologians who appeal to Marxist analysis offer different justifications for its use: that its pervasiveness in Latin American social sciences makes some use of it inevitable; that it can be separated from the Marxist worldview; that it offers a useful scientific instrument for understanding conditions in Latin America; and that it represents the analysis espoused and used by "popular movements." These last two points were unified in a talk by Luis A. Gomez de Souza at an Ecumenical Congress of Third World Theologians meeting in Brazil (1980). He was called upon to set the stage for a day devoted to analyzing the problems of Latin America. He began by making his own a statement from a Nicaraguan comrade: "We need a method of social analysis, and Marxism is the scientific method the people's movements possess to understand their practices."[57] (Note: though I was not able to interview Gomez de Souza when I visited Brazil in March 1988, two colleagues who work with him at the IBRADES center in Rio said that he would never make such a statement today, and that he has become highly critical of Marxist analysis.)

Most statements by liberation theologians speak only of the usefulness of Marxist analysis, without references to any current specific works by Marxists on Latin America. Occasionally one finds popular catechisms conveying a social analysis that borrows from Marxist analysis. In visiting Nicaragua and Mexico (1981) I found catechisms, for example, that presented Marx's economic base/superstructure model in symbolic pictures. A tree trunk symbolized the economic base of society; the branches represented politics, and the leaves ideology. The popular catechisms used in Peru (1988) and its neighboring countries, on the other hand, contained nothing similar to this. At a professional level, works by Franz Hinkelammert, Otto

Maduro, and Pablo Richard demonstrate applied uses of "adapted" Marxist analysis by Christian liberationists.

Franz Hinkelammert, a German economist and theologian, taught for a decade in Chile (1963–1973) and continues to teach and write in Costa Rica. His work *The Ideological Weapons of Death*, cited in the last section on capitalism, builds upon Marx's critique of fetishism. Marx used, as a consistent tool of criticism, a dialectical mode of thinking that sought to penetrate the "appearances" of things to get at their true reality. Conventional economics treats only of "things" (commodities, wages, prices, exchange), failing to recognize the dehumanizing social relations that underlie these economic categories. Marx's best known critique dealt with workers' wages, which he argued gave the appearance of paying workers for the true value of their input but in reality provided them only with bare subsistence. In precapitalist societies, Hinkelammert notes, the dominant class used very obvious forms of exploitation — slavery and serfdom. Under capitalism the exploitation created by the division of labor remains more hidden and needs to be unmasked.[58]

In *Capital* Marx also challenged the whole process of fetishism by which commodities, money, and capital take on a life of their own, again masking their dehumanizing impact on human beings. In his treatment of fetishism Marx often compares this fetishism to religion in which humans project their real life into imaginary gods. Hinkelammert's work begins with this Marxist analysis of fetishism, embodied in a threefold form by capitalism: fetishism of commodities, of money, of capital. Commodities take on a life of their own. Produced goods "battle" each other in competition; they appear autonomous. As a result of this autonomy humans refuse to accept responsibility for the consequences of their actions. Hinkelammert sees this fetishism as the real core of Marx's critique of religion as well. Humans relegate their decision-making power to a commodity market system. They accept no responsibility for the consequences of their action, and project responsibility onto God or the gods of private property, armies, or history itself.[59] Money becomes not only a god but the Antichrist of the Apocalypse, the beast that has caused humankind to lose its freedom.[60]

Hinkelammert charges Milton Friedman and other capitalist apologists with justifying the murderous consequences of capitalist fetishism. In doing so, he follows not only Marx's method but also his style of invective and derision. In final chapters of the book he accuses Catholic social thought — and the French Jesuit Pierre Bigo in particular — of legitimizing capitalism by defending private property as the morally right way to ensure access to the goods of the earth.[61] Hinkelammert does criticize Marx on one point: Marx concluded that the ultimate "realm of freedom" was not fully achievable. A true theology of life, says Hinkelammert, must affirm utopian hopes beyond what is humanly achievable."[62]

Otto Maduro, a Catholic layman and sociologist, offers a more self-critical use of Marxist analysis in behalf of a Christian commitment to liberation. In his *Religion and Social Conflicts*, Maduro seeks to understand the role Christian religion has played both in supporting dominant regimes and in struggling against them. He does not offer a history of the church, as does Enrique Dussel; rather he presents a systemic analysis based on his own critical reformulation of the Marxist theory of religion. In the past, Marxists have often purported to give *the* scientific truth about the "laws" of history and the role of religion. Maduro approaches his topic "with the consciousness of not having a monopoly on *the* scientifically infallible method."[63] We need, he says, "epistemological vigilance," a permanent, critical consciousness of the limits of our capacity to know reality. Every analysis reflects some bias. We cannot escape partiality, but honest analysis will involve "deliberate and ongoing self-critique."[64] Maduro repeats this caution throughout his study.

His method throughout involves showing how religion is situated in a particular social context. He argues, from a Marxist perspective, that a society's mode of production constitutes its central structure because no society can survive without the production of goods to meet basic human needs. Maduro broadens the classic Marxist view of factors that determine modes of production (for example, he notes the importance of traditional customs). He highlights two very distinct models of social relations within modes of production: a communitarian model, which involves an egalitarian labor force and equal access to means of production, and an asymmetric model in which a permanent minority controls the principal means of production.[65] He then applies these to show how they have affected religion in Latin America from pre-Columbian times to the present. Asymmetric modes of production produce class societies, and religion will tend to express one class view or another. The dominant class will seek to use religion to ensure its hegemony over society; oppressed classes will seek autonomy from this hegemony. Maduro recognizes religion itself as "relatively autonomous"; it is not, as classic Marxist analysis tends to make it, simply an ideological reflection of society. Much of the book then deals with how contending forces in Christianity—the traditional church and the new liberationist movement—seek to exercise religious power in society—though they may not consciously intend such power. Maduro's highly original adaptation of Marxist analysis echoes, or perhaps influenced, ideas found in other liberation theologians: ideas about "hegemony," opposition to functionalist analysis, and control over the "spiritual means of production."

Pablo Richard's *Death of Christendoms*, an interpretive study of church history in Latin America, also uses a modified form of Marxist analysis based on two main principles: the superstructure of society (politics, religion, ideologies) is *fundamentally* determined by the economic infrastructure, but the infrastructure itself is *relatively* determined by the superstructure. This second principle allows Richard to maintain that the church and religion have a relative autonomy; the faith, hope, and love they represent transcend pure historical analysis.[66] Richard also rejects the

Marxist view that consciousness is merely a product of material conditions.

Finally, worth noting, liberation philosopher Enrique Dussel is at work researching little-known manuscripts written by Marx in the mid-1860s, manuscripts that Dussel believes will lead to a thorough revision of traditional explanations of Marx's method.

In recent works of liberation theology, one finds very little direct appeal to Marxism and reference instead to "dialectic" social analysis in opposition to "functionalist" analysis (see the final section of chapter 6). Functionalist analyses or sociologies treat society as an organism in which social groups and classes should function harmoniously; conflicts appear as maladjustments to be resolved. Dialectical analyses or sociologies view society as complex, full of contradictions and conflicts; they look for the structural bases and dynamics of these conflicts. Liberation theologians argue for the dialectical approach because it explains Latin American reality more adequately and because it relates better to the needs and struggles of the poor.[67]

I have focused in this section only on those liberation theologians or Christian liberationists who use or discuss Marxist analysis. If one looks at the bulk of writings by liberation theologians, Marxism plays a relatively small part. For many liberation theologians Marxism serves, if at all, only as *one* method of understanding conditions in Latin America. For example, none of the essays by thirteen theologians in *Frontiers of Theology in Latin America* speaks of Marxism as an essential tool of analysis. Writers like Juan Luis Segundo and Enrique Dussel use a broad range of social theories and theorists in their analyses. Even a theologian like Míguez Bonino who stresses the importance of Marxist analysis does not really employ it to any extent other than saying it is right in its judgments about capitalism. In one of his earlier works, Míguez wrote at the conclusion of a description of conditions in Latin America that "it is not difficult to detect the Marxist frame of reference implicit in this diagnosis."[68] But if one reads even this account, it comprises a long list of social problems (unemployment, landless peasants, failure of development policies, alienated workers, etc.) but little that reflects a strict Marxist analysis of modes of production or use of the most "scientific" components of Marxist analysis (crises of overproduction, falling rates of profit, etc.). I observed in chapter 2 that many liberation theologians do use Marxist ideas "heuristically," as a way of gaining new insights into the Latin American reality. The analyses they rely on, however, might be better described as radical anticapitalist rather than Marxist. (I will return to discuss this point in the next chapter.)

Some liberation theologians adopt very critical positions regarding Marxism. All of them criticize certain forms of Marxist analysis (mechanistic, deterministic, dogmatic). All of them find significant deficiencies in Marxist analysis, particularly in respect to the Marxist critique of religion, but also for inadequacies in dealing with issues of racism, the problem of indigenous Indian populations, and the status of women.

From within the ranks of liberation theology, José Comblin offers perhaps the strongest critique of Marxism. He warns against ideologies that "appear" scientific while imposing their own values and programs.[69] He criticizes at length "idealist" philosophies that replace free human activity with some underlying "movement" shaping history. He applies this critique explicitly to Marxism. "The so-called Marxism of many Latin Americans ... is simply an expression of an idealistic philosophy, drawn from one or more of its European authors." He rejects, moreover, the distinction between Marxist methodology and its worldview: "the Marxist categories, in interpreting social justice issues, use the whole system and cannot be separated from it."[70]

José Porfirio Miranda appears to have changed radically his views on Marxism. His best-known work, *Marx and the Bible*, drew close parallels between Marxist analysis and the prophetic critiques of the Bible. In *Marx and the Marxists* he defended Marx but rejected his followers (Engels, Lenin, et al.) as distorters of true Marxism. In a more recent essay he simply rejects Marxism, arguing that Marxist analysis is based on a false reductionism that separates work from conscious activity.[71]

Otto Maduro summarizes what he perceives as the position of Latin American liberation theology in respect to Marxism. First, liberation theologians use Marxist ideas only as "tools," picking and choosing what they find fruitful (as one might take ideas from Freud or Sartre). This borrowing takes no account of what Marxists may say are essentials that need to be kept in a unified framework. Second, liberation theologians reject the Marxist claim to have discovered "laws of history" that point to the inevitable triumph of socialism. Third, liberation theologians view Marx's critique of religion not only as inadequate but as a "white, male, European ideology" that treats the poor condescendingly as victims of an illusion in their maintenance of religious faith. Moreover, a pluralism of approaches is needed to account for all the important cultural factors and values that Marxists neglect or disparage. Fourth, liberation theologians reject Marxist-Leninist attempts to impose elitist, "vanguard" leadership on the poor. Elitism only reinforces passivity and dependency in the poor. Liberation theology believes that the poor must be agents of their own destiny, using their own creativity, initiative, and leadership. Fifth, liberation theologians reject all models of authoritarian government, including Marxist models. Again, liberation theology stresses participation and shared leadership.[72] Maduro's summary represents, in my judgment, an accurate picture of liberation theology's position in respect to Marxist analysis and programs.

Socialism

Given liberation theologians' uniform opposition to capitalism, one should not be surprised to find a rather uniform conviction that some form of socialism offers the best hope for the poor in Latin America. In a frequently cited essay, "Capitalism versus Socialism: Crux Theologica," Juan Luis Segundo argued strongly that the church must make a choice, and that it should opt for socialism. Liberation theologians do not give much detail on what socialism would involve. Segundo himself asserted that he did not mean by socialism a project based on any particular ideology or philosophy: "I simply mean a political regime in which the ownership of the means of production is taken away from individuals and handed over to higher institutions whose main concern is the common good."[73] In answer to a question someone might ask about spelling out the model more fully, Segundo answered that theologians cannot foresee what exact form it might take, nor can they control the future.

In *Faith and Ideologies*, Segundo shows himself much more critical of socialism, especially of Marxist-socialist regimes. Both capitalism and socialism, he says, have proven failures, producing inhuman results. Capitalism favors the privileged; critiques of it deal with the very core of its system. But socialism in practice has involved repression and state control. It needs bureaucracy and harsh repression to sustain itself. Even Marxists recognize that expropriating the means of production has not led to any earthly paradise. Marxist regimes have failed to incorporate ethical guidelines and flexibility into their rule.[74]

When liberation theologians speak about socialism, they nearly always advocate something new, something that fits Latin America and does not simply imitate existing models. Thus Míguez Bonino, in one of his earlier works, wrote about a "Latin American socialist projection of liberation," which he said would include: a breaking away from domination from the North; transforming the social structure of Latin American societies; nationalizations; a sense of participation by the masses; a transfer of political power; the forging of a truly authentic "Latin American socialism" (not one based on Marxist dogmas or existing models); and a process that would lead to the emergence of a new humanity.[75] In a later work on political ethics Míguez included socialism in his Christian "utopian" vision of society: "Socialist in the organization of its economy, democratic in terms of the political participation of the people, and open in the sense of ensuring the conditions for personal realization, cultural freedom and opportunity, and mechanisms of self-correction."[76]

José Comblin speaks most openly about the failures of existing Marxist socialist systems. He believes that the same antidemocratic ideology characteristic of Latin American national security states operates in Marxist countries as well. The Marxist system has shifted from the idea of class struggle for liberty to an emphasis on national security. "At present, nothing is more like the national security ideology than the ideology of the Soviet Union."[77] Like national security states in Latin America, the Soviet Union seeks control over all parts of society through censorship, elimination of dangerous persons, and control over all civilian activities. The weakness of Marxism shows when it attempts to build a new society. It claims to have a scientific understanding not only of the old society but of the new as well. But its so-called new society has no reference to any science: "it is the society created by the party." It treats power as more important than freedom. "Consequently, in Marxist revolution there is no freedom for the people, only for the party."[78] In the name of science it expels freedom, just as it expels God.

In *A Theology of Liberation* Gutiérrez stressed the need for "a radical change of structures, a social revolution."[79] He spoke, however, rather cautiously about socialism. For achieving liberation socialism appears to represent "the most fruitful and far-reaching approach."[80] Participation in the liberation process "can even mean taking the path of socialism." Then in speaking of eliminating the causes of class struggle he adds: "it is a will to build a socialist society, more just, free, and human."[81] But Gutiérrez also argues, in another essay, that liberation "is not identified with any social form, however just it may appear at the time."[82]

In *The Power of the Poor in History*, in a chapter first written in the early 1970s, Gutiérrez spoke more directly in favor of socialism. The revolutionary struggle of the poor questions the very roots of the existing social order. "Hence we speak of social revolution, not reform; of liberation, not development; of socialism, not modernization of the prevailing system."[83] More significantly he spoke also about eliminating private ownership of the means of production.[84] I will return to this point in chapter 9 after considering the sharp criticism of Gutiérrez by U.S. socialist John Cort. I will then consider also some of the "new" socialist thinking in Peru and other parts of Latin America. I might end this present discussion of Gutiérrez's views, however, with a significant comment he made to me in an interview in February 1988. "Socialism," he observed, "is not an essential of liberation theology; one can support liberation theology or do liberation theology without espousing socialism."

Most liberation theologians favor some form of socialism. Even Comblin's critiques deal with the dangers of a Soviet-style socialism, not with a more democratic socialism. I have yet to find any liberation theologians who do not favor some form of socialism. Phillip Berryman says that he sees the socialism advocated by liberation theologians as having three characteristics: (1) people's basic needs will be met; (2) ordinary people will themselves be active in building a new society; and (3) what is created will not be a copy of existing socialisms but a genuinely Latin American creation.[85] His summary of what liberation theologians hope for appears quite accurate.

These three characteristics, however, represent socialist "ideals" rather than descriptions of socialist institutions. We will need to consider this difficulty more closely in the assessment chapter that follows, and we will want also to consider the controversial issue of socialism in Nicaragua. First, however, I will conclude this chapter with an overview by liberation philosopher Enrique Dussel, and finally with a discussion of some represent-ative critics of liberation theology on issues related to social analysis.

A Concluding Overview: Enrique Dussel

Differences certainly exist among liberation theologians and among other Christian liberationists. Yet certain common convictions stand out: that Latin American countries are dependent, periphery nations in a dom-inant and dominating world system; that this world system is a destructive capitalist system that offers no hope for true liberation; that Marxism, while inadequate especially in its materialist philosophy and critique of religion, provides important insights into the causes of Latin America's poverty and dependent situation; that Latin American countries must liberate them-selves through some form of their own self-determining socialism. Enrique Dussel's *Philosophy of Liberation* offers a unified exposition of these views, especially as an expression of liberation views from the 1970s.

Dussel sees Latin America as one of the periphery areas of the world (along with Africa and most of Asia) dominated by a geopolitical center (the United States, Western Europe, and now Japan). He believes that this center has imposed itself on the periphery for more than five centuries. He highlights three eras of colonialist domination: 1500–1850, during most of which period Latin America was dominated by Spain and Portugal; 1850–1940, with the English most dominant in southern areas of the world; World War II to the present, with the United States and its transnationals as dominant.[86] The center dominates not just economically and politically, but philosophically and culturally as well. Its philosophy reflects its domination. Just as Aristotle thought of the Greek male as the truly human, with slaves, women, and European barbarians as less than human, so have philosophers of the modern center reflected the hegemony of their dominant classes. Consequently, those who remain "other," exterior, and on the periphery are treated as less than human. "In the opinion of the North Atlantic ontology, the inhabitants of the periphery are not human"; they can be corrupted and killed like laboratory guinea pigs.[87]

This dominant center is capitalist. Dussel, though not a Marxist, often describes its functioning in Marxist language. The capitalist center operates through its division of labor by absorbing the surplus value of productive labor. This "theft" of surplus value, achieved at the expense of the periph-ery, accounts for the structured dissymmetry in the system as a whole. The economist Samir Amin, Dussel notes, claims that 80 percent of the benefits that the center realizes in its commercial interchanges come from the pe-riphery.[88] Capitalism destroys natural resources, creates a class system within the peripheral nations, and generates crises. "The capitalist system, unable to distribute overproduction, cannot make use of its mammoth pro-ductive capacity. It instead produces unemployment; unemployment re-duces buying potential; fewer sales further reduce production."[89] The wretched who live on the periphery must work like animals to produce goods that others will use; they eat less than do animals; they cannot express their own culture; the fruit of their labor is alienated from them. Quite clearly, then, "a new mode of production is necessary in dependent nations"; the system of capitalist enterprise can no longer be imitated in the periphery.[90]

All of the above statements echo Marxist critiques, but Dussel makes explicit the main contribution and the incompleteness of Marxism. Marxism allows one to discover the theft by the center of the surplus value earned by the periphery, but it does not always link its analysis to the concrete situation and history of a peripheral people. Dussel also criticizes the philosophical worldview of Marxism, which reduces everything to matter.[91]

Dussel sees only three options open to Latin America: a dependent capitalism (with fascist politics), an independent capitalism, or a socialism led by the popular classes. Dussel clearly opts for the latter and cites as models of liberation the popular socialisms of China, Vietnam, Cuba, Angola, and Nicaragua. He sees the hopes that some place in "populism" as a temptation, without promise of real change.[92] Many other liberation theologians today speak less confidently of socialism and use less radical language, but the anticapitalist convictions remain strong.

Critics of This Social Analysis

This section will focus on three criticisms of liberation theology, criticisms related to different issues discussed in this chapter. The 1984 Vatican instruction concentrates its attack on the use of Marxist analysis by certain liberation theologians. Michael Novak criticizes dependency theory and the starting points of liberation theology's analysis, which he believes rest on faulty assumptions and lead to a misguided desire for socialism. John Cort singles out a Gutiérrez comment about doing away with private ownership of the means of production, which Cort takes as an espousal of Marxist-Leninist socialism.

In describing conditions in Latin America, the 1984 Vatican instruction sounds very much like liberation theology itself. The instruction speaks of the shocking inequality between the rich and poor, and the lack of equity in international transactions, causing a widening gap between rich and poor nations[93] (from part 1, nn. 6–7). The instruction then asserts:

> In certain parts of Latin America, the seizure of the vast majority of the wealth by an oligarchy of owners bereft of social consciousness, the practical absence or the shortcomings of a rule of law, military dictators making a mockery of elementary human rights, the corruption of certain powerful officials, the savage practices of some foreign capital interests constitute factors which nourish a passion for revolt among those who thus consider themselves the powerless victims of

a new colonialism in the technological, financial, monetary, or economic order [VII, n. 12].

This statement appears as strong as any that could be found in liberation theology, but the Vatican's quarrel with liberation theology becomes evident in the sentence that follows this quote: "The recognition of injustice is accompanied by a pathos which borrows its language from Marxism, wrongly presented as though it were scientific language." By using Marxism, the instruction observes, liberation theology allows itself to become captive to Marxist ideology. The Vatican's objections to use of Marxist analysis can be subsumed under four main headings. The instruction first notes that its criticisms deal with "certain forms of liberation theology"; then it simply refers to liberation theology with these certain forms in mind.

First, liberation theology accepts uncritically the "scientific" claims made in the name of Marxist analysis. Conditions in Latin America sound similar to those that Marx criticized in the nineteenth century: "On the basis of these similarities, certain simplifications are made which ... prevent any really rigorous examination of the causes of poverty and prolong the confusion" (VII, n. 11). Before using a method one should first undertake a careful epistemological critique of the method, but such a critique and awareness of the plurality of methods in science appear missing from "more than one theology of liberation" (VII, nn. 4–5).

Second, liberation theologians are misguided in thinking that Marxist analysis can be separated from the rest of its ideology—atheism, materialism, violence, etc. "No separation of the parts of this epistemologically unique complex is possible. If one tries to take only one part, say, the analysis, one ends up having to accept the entire ideology" (VII, n. 6). Atheism and a denial of human dignity and human rights remain at the very core of Marxist theory; one cannot accept Marxist categories and analysis uncritically without compromising Christian faith (VII, nn. 8–10).

Third, liberation theologians make Marxist analysis the guiding force of "praxis," which then becomes the sole criterion of truth. For a Marxist only those who engage in the struggle to overthrow capitalism can work out analysis correctly. "There is no truth, they pretend, except in and through partisan praxis" (VIII, 1–4). Some liberation theologians make the same move. They start out with the idea that the viewpoint of the oppressed and revolutionary class—their own view of these—is the single true point of view. "Theological criteria for truth are thus relativized and subordinated to the imperatives of the class struggle" (X, n. 3).

Fourth, the main praxis called for by Marxism, and accepted by liberation theology, is one of class struggle, which leads to hatred and violence. Liberation theology accepts the theory of class struggle "as the fundamental law of history" (IX, nn. 2–3). It moves also from a legitimate defense of the poor "to a disastrous confusion between the poor of scripture and the proletariat of Marx" (X, n. 10). The conception of class struggle, moreover, "goes hand in hand with the affirmation of necessary violence"; any judgments about the morality of class struggle are implicitly denied (VIII, nn. 7–9).

As a warning against potential dangers in the use of Marxism or as a criticism of the way some Christian activists have uncritically appropriated Marxism, the Vatican instruction raises important issues. I will evaluate these points in the next chapter. The instruction met with countercriticism, however, because it appeared to "read into" liberation theologians far more than they actually say. No theologians whom I have read, for example, claim that class struggle is "the fundamental law of history" or that revolutionary praxis can be accepted without any theological criteria for judging it. (On this last point both Clodovis Boff and Gutiérrez say precisely the opposite.)

Just a month after the 1984 Vatican instruction appeared, Michael Novak published an essay entitled "The Case against Liberation Theology" in the *New York Times Magazine*. Novak focused his criticisms on liberation theology's reliance on dependency theory, a theory he judged "largely false" and now generally discredited. He argued that liberation theologians should stop "looking North in anger" and instead of blaming the United States and Europe they should look North to imitate the institutions and ethos that have made capitalist countries successful.[94] He expanded his views into a book, *Will It Liberate? Questions for Liberation Theology* (1986). It constitutes the most extensive U.S. critique of liberation theology's socio-economic analysis.

Throughout the book Novak contrasts his own analysis of Latin America's economic problems, and his recommended solution, with what he perceives as a very flawed analysis and socialist solution proposed by liberation theologians. North America has its own liberation theology, says Novak; it can be found more often in institutions and practices than in books, but it offers a more realistic hope of liberation for the poor than does Latin America's version of liberation theology.

Novak sees a difference in culture as the prime reason why Latin America has not advanced economically as the United States has. "For centuries now, Latin American humanism has been hostile to commerce and to economic dynamism, which it considers vulgar, low, of little esteem, and more than a little tainted with evil."[95] In contrast North America delights in economic inventions—the telephone, the electric light, the sewing machine—inventions that lead the way out of poverty. Latin America has also relied on the state to guide its economy and solve its problems; the United States encourages private initiative instead.

Novak acknowledges that the present order in Latin America protects the rich and offers little hope to the poor. Latin America needs a revolution. But his prescription lies in encouraging dynamic free enterprise. The elite who invent little and take little initiative should give way to the talented millions of poor who show greater imagination, initiative, and creativity. In short, Novak believes that a democratic capitalist society, which promotes discovery and entrepreneurship among the poor at the base of society, will succeed more quickly and more thoroughly than the socialist societies advocated by liberation theologians. He argues that the United States has, far more successfully than socialist societies, liberated the great majority of its people from poverty and provided political liberty as well.[96] Latin America really needs a "creation theology" that will recognize and encourage the institutions (free enterprise, democracy) and attitudes (inventiveness, work) that create prosperity.[97] The success of newly industrialized countries in the Far East (Japan, Taiwan, South Korea) show what the free enterprise system can do to advance formerly underdeveloped nations.[98]

With these points as his base, Novak attacks liberation theologians on several scores. He challenges their analysis of causes for poverty in Latin America. In directing their attacks against capitalism, they target a false enemy. "In Latin America today, I do not see a single capitalist economy."[99] The small-business sector, which ought to be the largest and most dynamic sector, is relatively small and powerless. Latin American countries are pre-capitalist and disproportionately state-directed. The business class does not dominate; rather the leading social classes are government officials, landowners, and the military.[100] Liberation theologians misunderstand capitalism. Its dynamism arises from creativity and the spirit of enterprise, not from the accumulation of capital.

Liberation theologians believe that they represent an "oppressed" class in Latin America. Novak argues that the use of "oppression" as a basic assumption leads liberation theology into its unhealthy appeals to Marxism and dependency theory. Once one assumes a situation of oppression, the responsibility shifts to others. Others are to blame for the poverty and misery that exist. Dividing the world into oppressors and oppressed forces one to view life as conflict. This in turn leads all too easily into the Marxist interpretation of history as class struggle.[101] Enrique Dussel says that he is not a Marxist. But Novak believes that Dussel's declaration of oppression as the basic problem leads naturally toward Marxism.

Novak acknowledges that the United States has intervened in Latin American affairs and conducted itself with arrogance at times, but not to a level of oppression. Novak believes that Latin America would face basically the same problems if it had experienced no contact with the United States over the past forty years. Again Novak blames Latin American elites for not pursuing discoveries and innovations. "Latin Americans have chosen to depend upon the more developed countries."[102]

Novak also questions liberation theologians like Gutiérrez who claim that their analysis of conditions in Latin America is based on "studies of the most rigorous scientific exactitude."[103] Novak does not believe such exactitude is possible in the social sciences. He particularly rejects Marxism's claim to be scientific; Marx's "scientific" predictions have been refuted by history. Novak also criticizes Gutiérrez for vagueness and ambiguity in using terms like "the poor" and "class struggle," and for equating the aspirations of the poor with socialism.[104]

Finally, Novak challenges Gutiérrez and other liberation theologians on their favoring of socialism. Gutiérrez seems to speak of socialism only in terms of its ideals: it will overcome class divisions; it will eliminate the private appropriation of wealth; it will function in behalf of the poor and the oppressed. But, says Novak, no information is given about the specific institutions that will replace capitalism.[105] Though liberation theologians say that they want to avoid the deficiencies of existing socialist regimes, they do not indicate how this will be done. In Novak's estimation, the historical failures of socialist governments speak loudly against them. Cuba stirred the hopes of Latin Americans but has proven a failure: it continues to be a dependent country, now under the sway of the Soviet Union; Cubans are less free politically than they were before; Cubans experience worse shortages and greater hardships today than they did before the revolution.

Novak raises legitimate and challenging questions. But he does so in a manner not likely to win much support beyond those who already support his positions. He makes an appeal for "dialogue" at the outset and expresses his "admiration" for liberation theologians.[106] Yet his book quite clearly presents a case *against* liberation theology, as the very title of his earlier article makes clear. In fairness to Novak, however, the *New York Times* editors chose the title without consulting him. Apart from saying that liberation theologians have good intentions and ask the right questions, Novak concedes little, if anything, to their analysis and proposed solutions. In addition, his psychological asides—for example, his comments on Dussel's "Manicheism" and on liberation theologians' "almost oedipal vehemence against their European teachers"[107]—will not help him to win converts.

More importantly, not much change is likely to occur if the battle lines continue to be drawn between capitalism and socialism. Novak presents an idealized picture of capitalism with little recognition of the injustices it has created in practice. To ask liberation theologians to accept capitalism and to emulate the United States would be the equivalent of calling on Novak or Ronald Reagan to adopt Cuba or the Soviet Union as a model. Novak also seems to suggest that Latin Americans could achieve development if they would simply "choose" to move in new directions. Changes and reforms, however, have not occurred because power elites have resisted them, often with the active support of the United States.

Novak's criticisms, nonetheless, need to be addressed. They reflect, if stated in harsher tones, the misgivings of many North Americans who find too much reliance on Marxist-dependency analysis and too little specificity about socialism in liberation theology.

John Cort, a U.S. socialist and author of a book on Christian socialism, believes that Gutiérrez and other liberation theologians advocate a Marxist socialism that would destroy democracy and the goals of a "true" socialism. True socialism, Cort believes, entails a strong commitment to democracy, and can even be defined as an extension of democracy into the economic sphere. He would favor wide distribution of property ownership and the encouragement of communally-owned cooperative enterprises (which would not be state-owned and therefore would remain a form of private property). He believes that Marxism, by eliminating private property entirely and giving power over entirely to the state, contradicts true socialism. Cort sees Gutiérrez opting for this same Marxist form of socialism.[108]

As evidence for his charge, Cort first cites two passages where Gutiérrez speaks of private property. In A Theology of Liberation Gutiérrez speaks of transforming society through "a radical change in the foundation of society, that is, the private ownership of the means of production."[109] Cort reads Gutiérrez as identifying this radical change with the total elimination of private ownership of means of production. Gutiérrez does state this explicitly in a passage cited by Cort from The Power of the Poor in History. The revolutionary struggle "insists on a society in which private ownership of the means of production is eliminated."[110] Cort also reads Gutiérrez's statements on class struggle as implying a rejection of all forms of employer-employee business other than state ownership, and he identifies Gutiérrez with a stand taken by Christians for Socialism who opposed peasants owning their own private land.

The concern voiced by Cort is quite real. Total elimination of private ownership of means of production does raise the specter of total state control. The Gutiérrez quote cited by Cort would trouble anyone concerned about maintaining democracy. Nevertheless I believe that Cort attributes to Gutiérrez a Marxist-Leninist position that does not at all represent his true views. Cort's critique, however, requires a serious response and we will take it up when we evaluate liberation theology's option for socialism as part of an overall assessment of social analysis issues in the chapters that follow.

Chapter 8

Marxist Analysis and Dependency: An Assessment

The next two chapters will attempt to assess the economic-political views of liberation theologians in the light of criticisms lodged against them. Assessments should strive for objectivity, but complete objectivity is almost impossible to attain. On complex social issues we rarely have all the pieces of information needed to make conclusive judgments, and the data we do have is subject to varying interpretations, which in turn are affected by the values we hold. Truth rarely lies with any one position or perspective. The assessments made in these chapters try to deal with this problem of objectivity by approaching issues with a dialectical questioning that looks for the partial truth and the inadequacies of any one answer.

The major issues discussed in the last chapter concerned dependency, capitalism, Marxism, and socialism. These same issues return in these "assessment" chapters, but grouped under different headings. This chapter has two main parts, one dealing with scientific method and Marxist analysis, the other looking at dependency and its effects. Chapter 9 focuses on the socialism-versus-capitalism issue, but includes an assessment of liberation theology in respect to the issues of violence and class struggle, and it offers some reflections on Nicaragua.

SCIENTIFIC METHOD AND MARXIST ANALYSIS

Before considering how and to what extent liberation theologians use Marxist analysis, it will prove useful to reflect first on how they understand "scientific method" in general. One finds frequent mention in liberation theology not only of the need for scientific social analysis but also of claims that liberation theology draws upon strict scientific investigations. Míguez Bonino speaks of Marxism as a "verifiable way" of doing love. Gutiérrez speaks of results based on studies of "rigorous exactitude." Dussel even speaks about studying church history as a science.[1]

Judged by what most U.S. Americans mean by "scientific"—namely, ideas that have been empirically tested and verified—these claims would appear unjustified. Míguez Bonino says that Marxism offers a "verifiable way," but its predictions about inevitable revolutions and the collapse of capitalism have proven wrong repeatedly. Gutiérrez makes his remark about studies of "rigorous exactitude" in *The Power of the Poor in History*, but his footnotes include only one general reference to two books on multinationals and dependency. The very concept of a scientific study of church history, that Dussel claims to offer, will strike many North Americans as strange.

There is, however, a very clear reason why intellectuals in the United States and in Latin America respond differently to "scientific" claims: Latin Americans have a very different understanding of what scientific method involves. Phillip Berryman states the difference succinctly:

A discussion of theory and practice reveals clear cultural differences between the intellectual milieux of North America (and often Western Europe as well) and Latin America. In our everyday usage "theory" is often contrasted pejoratively with "reality." We tend to take as normative the "scientific method" in which theory is the result of an empirical, self-correcting, trial-and-error process.

Among Latin American intellectuals, on the other hand, "empirical" is most often a pejorative term, denoting superficial appearance rather than the deep reality of things. Theory is regarded as a tool for cutting through appearance to get at the heart of things. Many esssays by Latin American social scientists, for example, seem to be focused largely on constructing a "theoretical framework." Concrete data often seem to take second place. What Latin Americans understand as "praxis" is poles apart from Yankee "practicality."[2]

Theory is regarded as a tool for cutting through appearance to get at the heart of things. This simple insight explains much about what liberation theologians mean when they refer to "scientific method." Even Dussel's claim to treat church history as a science becomes more understandable. He seeks to use hermeneutics, he says, "to reveal the hidden meaning of culture."[3] Little wonder that Marxist analysis engenders interest. The very heart of the Marxist dialectical method consists in penetrating through the appearances of things to get at their true reality.

If we look back at much that we have discussed thus far about liberation theology, we can see not only why the dialectical thinking in Marxist analysis and dependency theory have an appeal, but also how they are used. Latin Americans have long been dependent on how "others" have defined Christianity and defined their problems. The very use of dialectical thought proves liberating. It opens up a whole new way of understanding one's situation. As liberation theologians see it, much that had been held was false, tied in with dominant ideologies. Where ideas from modernization or developmentalist theories made Latin Americans appear backward and retarded, the notion of "dependency" opens up a new understanding of the structural impediments that block true development. The concepts of "praxis" and "structural change" give new insight into why moral appeals to individual conversion so often fail. The notion of "ideology" proves immensely fruitful for recognizing how dominant groups use selective ideas and values to justify their position in society. The concepts of "surplus value" and "exploitation" point to structural reasons underlying poverty and vast inequities of income distribution.

In treating the sociology of knowledge in relation to religion, U.S. social scientist Peter Berger explains how human constructions—language, customs, institutions—can appear over time to be a part of nature, as simply "out there" or the way things are.[4] Liberation theologians have effectively used historical criticism and dialectical thought to illustrate this point. What we accepted for centuries as *the* Christian message often showed itself, under investigation, to be a very historically conditioned interpretation. (For example, Leonardo Boff's striking insight that much of our Christian interpretation of salvation resulted, in great measure, from the personal problems of St. Paul, Augustine, and Luther.[5])

The identification of scientific method with a dialectical challenging of how things "appear" to be, carries with it, however, the risk of creating a new set of views that take on the appearance of reality itself. If challenging "the way things are" proved fruitful for liberation theology in de-ideologizing prevailing structures and traditional interpretations of the Christian message, the new models used to replace them can also become unquestioned givens. For a time in liberation theology, dependency theory served as a given, often stated in its strongest form as underdevelopment caused by developed nations. Dependency "theory" no longer holds this privileged position, having fallen into disfavor among social scientists. But for several years many liberation theologians accepted its conclusions.

Marxist ideas have a far longer history in Latin America. Long before liberation theology came upon the scene, Marxist language had become the dominant language of protest in Latin America. Liberation theologians could justifiably argue that any movement to bring about change in Latin America almost inevitably took on some Marxist ideas and language. Historians of twentieth-century Latin America have acknowledged this point. Thus one historian observes: "By the mid-twentieth century, Marxism had permeated the liberal and reforming social thought of the Latin American reform movement"[6]—and this comment referred to reform in general, not revolutionary insurrection. Liberation theologian José Comblin makes a similar point. Marxist thinking, he observes, has become so common in Latin America "that there is a temptation to accept it at least as the self-understanding of present society."[7] Many ideas in Marxist analysis, especially pointing to capitalism as the ultimate root of social problems, have become "givens" among Latin American protest groups. Ideas like the exploitation of surplus value or the imperialist domination of poor countries may be useful tools for analysis, but they can too easily take on the character of *descriptions*, as if they pictured "the way things are" rather than giving an *interpretation* of reality.

Even the option for using "dialectical analysis," as opposed to functional analysis, runs a similar risk. Many liberation theologians argue for a dialectical analysis (which significantly modifies classic Marxist analysis, as noted at the end of chapter 6) on the grounds that it best serves the poor and more accurately presents conditions in Latin America. Dialectical analysis does indeed point to serious conflicts of interest in Latin America where elite groups have exercised dominance and kept the masses of a local population from sharing any truly equitable distribution of political power or economic ownership. Functionalism does tend to assume a fundamentally "sound" system in which competing forces can restore equilibrium. But the expression "opting" for dialectical analysis (an expression used by some liberation theologians) could lead to consideration of only one type of analysis and not questioning its assumptions. Liberation theologians point up the ideological components of functionalism (for example, assuming that the prevailing system is sound), but dialectical analysis contains ideological components as well. All social sciences, José Comblin observes, contain some elements of scientific knowledge. But ideologies "choose their facts selectively and build a whole intellectual structure from partial truths."[8] Moreover, many who professed a dialectical approach when out of power will convert to some form of functionalism once they attain power. (Thus Marxists in power claim to have eliminated "antagonistic class conflicts" and they use Marxism to justify the new status quo.)

In practice, liberation theologians operate much more flexibly than the language of option suggests. Raúl Vidales, cited in the last chapter, acknowledges the usefulness of functionalism for certain types of statistical studies. Clodovis Boff, in my interview with him, observed that a functionalist approach proves more useful in studies of indigenous peoples. Many other liberation theologians make no "option" or do not address the issue of differing forms of analysis. On the score of Marxist analysis, liberation theologians have voiced numerous reservations: they clearly reject Marxism's philosophical materialism and its one-sided critique of religion; they reject any determinism or laws of history that eliminate human freedom and humans as agents of their own destiny. They see Marxism as failing to recognize the importance of cultural factors, and as inadequate for dealing with the special problems faced by Indians, blacks, and women. Roberto Oliveros, whose 1970s' history of liberation theology clearly favored those who use Marxist analysis, now appears much more critical. He observed, in an interview, that Marxism focuses on private control of the means of production. But in his own country (Mexico) the largest and most significant enterprises are state-owned.

These comments, then, simply voice a concern. The autonomy that Clodovis Boff (chapter 2) rightfully stressed in respect to theology should hold for social analysis as well. The objective of social analysis is truth, not any goal extrinsic to it. Or, to use Otto Maduro's expression, one must retain "epistemological vigilance" in using social sciences and avoid building an analysis based on "partial truths." The concern I have will become more evident when I take up the complexities of judging dependency, capitalism, and socialism.

The Use of Marxist Analysis

This chapter considers only the use of Marxist "analysis." Marxism as a system of thought involves much more. It includes a philosophical world-view and a program of tactics, strategies, and goals, as well as its social analysis. When critics attack Marxism they may criticize the shortcomings of its analysis, but the deeper concerns stem from fears that acceptance of the analysis will lead to espousal of its program. Church authorities voice an additional fear that the whole worldview will be absorbed with the analysis. Chapter 9, on opting for socialism, deals with issues related to the "program" of Marxism (class struggle, violence, and the building of a socialist system), and chapter 10 will discuss additional points about the actual practice of liberation theology. Some of the views of liberation theologians on these points have already been noted, moreover, in the last chapter. Concerns about the Marxist program of change are so central to the whole issue of Marxism, however, that some brief summary comment seems called for before moving on to further discussion of the use of Marxist analysis.

To begin with, we need to distinguish again between liberation theologians and groups like the Christians for Socialism in Chile or Christian supporters of the Sandinistas in Nicaragua. (Even with regard to these groups, the Marxist socialism supported by the CFS in Chile did not involve violent revolution, or a dictatorship of the proletariat, or the suppression of religion; and Christian supporters of the Sandinistas do not consider the revolutionary process in Nicaragua as simply Marxist.) If we speak simply of liberation theologians, I have not found any advocacy of Marxist-Leninist tactics, strategies, or espousal of Communist Party rule in their writings. They clearly reject any form of elitist leadership that would take power out of the hands of the poor, and they envision a society that promotes political liberties as well as economic redistribution of goods. Pablo Richard, who makes frequent use of Marxist analysis, clearly distances liberation theology from Leninist concepts of power. Speaking of the popular church he writes: "This church sets itself off from the popular movement in so far as that movement is politically organized and politically orientated, in particular with regard to leftist parties, and especially in regard to Marxism."[9]

In respect to the issue of the Marxist worldview, no liberation theologian accepts the materialist philosophy of Marxism. To do so would require denying faith in God, for philosophical materialism is explicitly atheistic.

Liberation theologians criticize the inadequacy of the Marxist critique of religion, but they believe Marxist analysis can be separated from its philosophical worldview. The 1984 Vatican document believes otherwise. In practice, it is true, most Marxists do not separate the two, and a danger certainly exists that at a popular level enthusiasm for Marxist analysis could lead activists into acceptance of the worldview of Marxism. But, as I have argued elsewhere, no logical or intrinsic connection binds the analysis and worldview together. They came to be linked together historically by Engels, Lenin, and Stalin.[10] Throughout history Christian theologians have taken from great thinkers the insights, methods, or concepts that they felt could be fruitful in articulating the faith. They have borrowed from Freud, Sartre and Heidegger without being captured by their atheism. The same could apply to use of Marx and Marxist analysis.

These statements lead us back to the question of Marxist analysis as such. Some liberation theologians say that they use Marxist analysis as an "instrument" for understanding Latin American society. Actually they make very limited use of Marxist analysis and rarely, if ever, cite any specific analyses of Latin America by present-day Marxists. This last comment ties in with what was said earlier about the Latin American view of "scientific method" as a form of dialectical questioning. Liberation theologians have borrowed *concepts* from Marxism: notions like praxis, ideology, and structural change from Marx, and expressions like "hegemony" and "organic intellectuals" from Gramsci. These concepts act as heuristic structures (ideas that generate new insights), which enable them to penetrate beyond surface appearances. Thus, for example, Segundo uses "ideology" to distinguish what really belongs to Christian faith from the culturally conditioned, ideological expressions the Christian message may take on. But this very example shows how distinct this use is from Marxist analysis; Marxists would not look for what is truly authentic in Christian faith. So also with Gutiérrez's use of praxis, which looks at how Christian love (hardly a Marxist concern) becomes actualized in deeds.

Liberation theologians believe that capitalism is the root cause of Latin America's problems, and they feel that Marxism has served as an effective tool for "unmasking" capitalism. This assumes, as a given, that most problems in Latin America can be reduced to capitalism (a point I will examine in the "opting for socialism" chapter). But certainly this assumption is widely held in Latin America. Even liberation theology critic Cardinal López Trujillo acknowledges that "in Latin America the refusal of capitalism is general." He even agrees, moreover, that Marxist analysis has served to point out structural injustices.[11] This last expression, "to point out" injustices, or the Boffs' expression of "methodological pointers," again suggests the very broad sense in which Marxist analysis and scientific method in general are understood. Liberation theologians rarely use, or even cite references to, specific and detailed accounts of the factors most associated with "scientific" Marxist analysis: falling rates of profits, cycles of stagnation and expansion, studies of changing modes of production, analysis of class structures, and so forth. For all the controversy over the use of "class struggle" in liberation theology, apart from some historical examples in Pablo Richard and Enrique Dussel, I have yet to find in liberation theology any specified analyses of class structures in Latin America. There are certainly no strategies based on class struggle, which one would expect to find if class struggle plays the important role that critics attribute to liberation theology.

If we look to questions of landownership, we may get a better idea of how Marxist analysis, in a very broad "heuristic" sense of the term, may operate in the minds of liberation theologians. Issues related to peasant farmers—land reform, access to land, the right of peasants to unionize, just wages—have probably preoccupied liberation groups more than any other concern in Latin America. On these issues one would hardly expect an appeal to Marxist analysis. Marx himself analyzed the mode of production most distinctive of capitalism, the factory system. He had, moreover, a rather contemptuous view of peasants and their revolutionary potential.

If, on the other hand, one uses Marx's concept of exploitation as a "pointer" or moral norm, then appeal to Marxist analysis becomes more intelligible. Exploitation has characterized farm production from the beginnings of the colonialist period to the present, from the forced labor of Indians and black slaves, through the controlled labor of peasants in haciendas, and into the present. Wealthy elites have controlled the vast majority of land holdings in Latin America. Concentration of land, wealth, and power in the hands of elites, and exploitation of peasant labor, have been and continue to be the most prominent social problems in Latin America. El Salvador, where Fr. Rutilio Grande was killed for encouraging peasants to stand up for their rights, provides a graphic example of the type of injustice that has perdured in Latin America. In 1979, just prior to the current war, 1 percent of the landowners in El Salvador owned 57 percent of the arable land. The median capital income in that year was $610. Yet the top twenty families, according to a study in the *New York Times*, had wealth estimated at $70 million to $300 million per family.[12] With workers on large plantations making 30 cents an hour and with owners accumulating vast fortunes—thanks in part to land expropriated from peasants in the nineteenth century—one can hardly avoid speaking in Marxist language of exploitation and oppression. But only by analogy does this reflect Marxist analysis. The exploitation did not arise from the introduction of a "new mode of capitalist production" but from a centuries-old pattern of land ownership by a wealthy oligarchy. Liberation theologians could justly add, however, that much of modern agriculture has become dominated by capitalist agribusiness and that the goods produced are intended for foreign markets.

If liberation theologians use Marxist analysis in any detailed way, as guiding their practice, they have certainly kept the sources a well-hidden secret. In the early years of liberation theology one could find a number of references to Latin American dependency theorists (Cardoso, Dos Santos, et al.). Today one finds some references to "ideas" from Marx, Althusser, Gramsci, or Mariátegui, but almost no references to any contemporary Latin American Marxist works. (Javier Iguíñiz has commented that there has not been any outstanding Latin American Marxist since Mariátegui.) Whatever use liberation theologians make of concepts from Marxism, I have found little evidence that they employ Marxist analysis in any concrete, empirical way.

This conclusion, however, has a flip side. In the mid-1970s, the German theologian Jürgen Moltmann commented that for all their emphasis on use of social sciences, liberation theologians do not do much social analysis.[13] That judgment appears true today also, though some liberation theologians do consult with social scientists, as do base community groups. In a real sense the method of liberation theology asks far too much of its theologians: competence in theology, involvement in praxis, and skilled use of social sciences. In addition, biblical critics of liberation theology look for exactitude in the use of hermeneutics; ethicists expect fully enunciated criteria for judgments made; and church authorities challenge any statement that veers away from inherited orthodoxy. At any rate, if the relative absence of detailed social analysis constitutes a problem, one can hardly accuse liberation theologians of striving to implement Marxist analysis.

To the extent that liberation theologians do use social analysis, or call for certain kinds of analysis, the references usually concern the "big picture," the macro-level of problems facing Latin America. Hence references are made to the ultimate problem of "dependent capitalism" or to using a dialectical approach in looking at problems. Even where one might expect more detailed, empirical studies, the battle generally remains at a level of ideas. Thus, for example, the works of the liberation economist-theologian Franz Hinkelammert offer critiques of capitalism from a Marxist perspective, but remain at the level of ideas with little empirical data. His work on the dialectics of unequal development discusses competing "theories" of development; his work on utopian reason deals with various antiutopian "thinkers"; and his work on the ideological weapons of death critiques the "values" he associates with capitalism.[14]

In earlier chapters we challenged critics who "read into" liberation theologians positions they do not hold. Hinkelammert, in my judgment, often commits the same offense. He may quite legitimately criticize procapitalist writers like Frederick Hayek and Milton Friedman for "idolizing" the free market. But he certainly distorts Friedman's thought when he writes that "the freedom to murder is a vital part of his reasoning" or that Friedman is "incapable of imagining a concept of freedom whose starting point is freedom of access to the goods of the world."[15] Hinkelammert quite thoroughly misrepresents Peter Berger's views on social order. Berger today represents a type of neoconservative thinking prominent in the United

States. However his *Sacred Canopy*, which Hinkelammert attacks, was written during an earlier period in which Berger even acknowledged Marx as contributing significantly to his model. His model *describes* the human need for order (which would certainly apply in any socialist country); it does not seek to *legitimize* the existing order as Hinkelammert claims.[16] If anything, as our earlier use of Berger suggested, Berger's description indicates why "the way things are" should not be taken as natural or unchangeable.

Even Hinkelammert, however, uses Marxist ideas in a creative, personal way. His thought does not reflect the classic, "orthodox" use of Marxist analysis. The 1984 Vatican instruction questioned the "uncritical" use of Marxist analysis. If critical and limited use of Marxist analysis is used as a criterion for judgment, I do not know of any present-day liberation theologian who would not pass the test. Critics who judge by earlier works, and interpret any use of Marxist terms in these works as an adoption of Marxism, will obviously reach a different verdict. Some fault may rest with liberation theologians for all but identifying anticapitalist arguments with Marxist analysis. At least in the United States I have found that the most forceful critiques of specific features of capitalism (where arguments prove more fruitful than global critiques) were written by non-Marxists. Most Marxist critiques, except for some critical neo-Marxist works, tend to be predictable rehashes that could have been written fifty years ago.

Finally, the importance once given to Marxist ideas in liberation theology has diminished significantly. In Peru the 1975 "summer school" led by Gutiérrez included some two hundred pages of reading material about Marxism (even then the readings included criticisms of Marxism by European scholars Jean-Yves Calvez, Gustav Wetter, and Henri Chambre). In the 1988 sessions of the same summer school, which I attended, Marxism was never even mentioned.

DEPENDENCY AND ITS EFFECTS

Few national economies in today's world operate independently. The fact of interdependency is widely acknowledged. The issue involves rather the question of *dependency*, a dependency that Raul Prebisch defined in terms of decisions taken in the center to which peripheral countries are subjected. For Cardoso and Faletto economic dependence exists "when the accumulation and expansion of capital cannot find its essential components inside the system."[17] Interdependence, they argue, becomes dependency when the partners are in vastly uneven positions of power, such that one partner has almost exclusive possession of the technology and financial sectors needed for expansion. No one of these authors would argue that peripheral nations have no power of decision-making, but they see external force as *more* determining growth and expansion than any internal decisions and policies.

The issue of dependency also involves implicit moral judgments. A healthy, prospering nation might conceivably also be dependent. But these authors, along with the liberation theologians we are studying, view Latin America's dependency as a major cause of its poverty and underdevelopment. Within this section I will attempt to assess the question of dependency under four heads: the fact of dependency, the causes of dependency, the role of transnationals, and the influence of U.S. foreign policy. The section on transnationals includes counterarguments and a special assessment.

The Fact of Dependency

Cardoso claims that he never intended to present a special new "theory" of dependency but simply to explain what Latin Americans had experienced and discussed for years, the *fact* of dependency.[18] Indeed historians wrote about Latin American dependency well before dependency theory came onto the scene. Thus, for example, a 1958 history of Latin America by a U.S. historian subtitled one of its chapters "Latin America's Decided Dependence on Foreign Trade and Foreign Capital." The chapter described the Latin American situation in language that anticipated dependency theory: "Latin America became a weak outlying segment of the great industrial economies of the West."[19]

In a more recent study, aimed at assessing dependency theory, Michael J. Francis questions the tenability of many theses proposed by dependency theorists, but finds at least two theses "easily defensible." He questions theses that claim that dependency always impedes economic growth, that benefits never trickle down to the poor, or that dependency necessarily results in authoritarian rule. He finds quite defensible, however, theses dealing with loss of control over the economy and poor income distribution.

The first "easily defensible" thesis argues that "because of their dependence on the developed 'core' countries, the peripheral countries are experiencing a growing loss of national control over their economic, political, social, and cultural life."[20] In support of this thesis Francis cites as evidence: the austerity programs imposed by the International Monetary Fund (IMF); the dependence for economic growth in underdeveloped countries on the price they can get for certain primary products; the inflation rates created by price hikes in oil and other imported goods, and the interest rates on bank loans; the impact of U.S. military assistance in supporting status quo systems; the impact of Western goods and advertising on Latin American culture.

Frances Lappé offers statistical data about these points. If prices had remained fixed at 1973 levels, Latin America and other Third World countries would not be suffering from a debt crisis. A sizeable part of the debt was caused by arms purchases (15–20 percent); military aid to Latin America jumped fourfold from 1981 to 1986 (mostly to Central America). The real "comparative advantage" of Latin American countries comes from keeping wages low and blocking unions. Most profits come from processing and marketing; for every dollar spent by consumers in the United States and Europe on foodstuffs from Third World countries, only 15 cents goes to persons in the originating country.[21]

The recession of the early 1980s and the current debt crisis show rather clearly the extent to which the well-being of Latin American economies depends on decisions and capital outside their control. Oil-exporting countries like Brazil and Venezuela may have counted too much on the oil boom of the 1970s, and other countries may have borrowed too much from banks eager to lend out the glut of dollars accumulated from the same boom. But Latin American countries have suffered dramatically from a succession of changes originating in the North. Inflation rates in the North made imports into Latin America more expensive; recession in the early 1980s cut into export earnings; floating interest rates on loans (up to 20 percent) caused many countries to spend most of their export earnings on efforts to retire debts. By 1982 Mexico used 59 percent of its export earning toward servicing the debt; Brazil used 69 percent, and Argentina 78 percent.[22]

The very language used by the International Monetary Fund and the World Bank in their annual reports for 1984 reflects Latin America's dependence on U.S. and European conditions and policies. An IMF report noted that Latin American countries, which had experienced growth rates averaging 5–7 percent annually from 1967 to 1980, experienced a dramatic drop to −2.3 percent in 1983. The reasons given by IMF are consistently *external.* "A major factor" in the problems faced by developing countries has been "the recession in industrial countries." Weakness of foreign exchange earnings and indebtedness made developing countries "particularly vulnerable" to interest rate increases in 1980. The weakness of economic activity in the industrial world had a "substantial adverse effect" on the terms of trade of the non-oil developing countries.[23]

Does the decision-making power to reverse these conditions lie primarily inside or outside the developing countries? The IMF report gives quite clear indications of the subordinate, reacting position of developing countries. Decision (center): high interest rates have greatly increased Latin American debts, but these rates are "a result of industrial countries 'newfound determination' to confront inflation." Reaction (periphery): "faced with an abrupt change of external finance, many developing countries had *no option* but to cut back sharply their current account deficits." A World Bank report reflects this same causal relationship: restrictive monetary policies used by the United States to control inflation had "a profoundly adverse effect" on the rates of growth of many developing countries. "Enormous pressures" have been exerted on the positions of countries in Latin America.[24] In better times U.S. prosperity may bolster Latin America's, but that too would show dependency. Nor can we say simply that all economies are interdependent and affect each other. If the relationship involved merely "interdependency," the U.S. economy should be as deeply affected by changes in Latin America. But this has never been the case; only a massive default on Latin American debts could produce similar effects.

The second thesis that Francis finds "easily defensible" concerns income distribution and the poor. "The current economic growth in less-developed countries is unevenly distributed among sectors of the society. Because income distribution is badly skewed, the poorest half of most societies is left relatively untouched by economic growth."[25] Brazil comes immediately to mind as an illustration of this thesis, so we might note first what dependency theorist André Gunder Frank wrote about Brazil's so-called economic miracle in the late 1960s and early 1970s.

Brazil enjoyed one of the highest growth rates of GNP in the world during this period. Frank claims, however, that both in relative and absolute terms the poorest sectors of society suffered. From 1960 to 1970 the top 5 percent of income recipients saw their annual income increase from $1,645 to $2,940, and their share of national income rise from 27 to 36 percent; the poorest 40 percent of the population endured a reduction in share of national income from 22 percent to 9 percent, or $90 per capita. The change was reflected in absolute terms as well. By 1975 minimum wages had been cut to 29 percent of the 1958 level and 45 percent of the 1964 level. The number of hours of work necessary to buy a subsistence diet for a worker and his family at the minimum wage was 5.7 hours in 1960, 7 hours in 1965, and 8.5 hours in 1970.[26]

On this question of income distribution, most analysts would agree that it is badly skewed in countries like Brazil where the lowest 20 percent of the population receives only 2 percent of the national income, whereas the top 10 percent accounts for over 50 percent of the income.[27] In Mexico, the lowest 20 percent of the population dropped from accumulating 7.8 percent of the national income in 1950 to only 1.9 percent in 1975.[28] The worsening distribution in these countries, according to one analyst, resulted from promotion of modern, capital-intensive sectors of the economy controlled by large corporations, and from deliberate government measures to prevent "premature" income and asset redistribution.[29] In Brazil, in the mid-1960s, growth (benefiting the upper and middle-class sectors) resulted in great part from a policy that reduced the minimum wage by 34 percent.[30]

A World Bank report (1986) showed that the poor in Latin America also suffered most from the 1981–1983 depression that saw the Gross Domestic Product decline on a national average of 11 percent, with an even sharper decline in per capita income. Unemployment rates in Mexico nearly doubled between 1981 and 1984. Chilean unemployment was by far the worst in the region, reaching 22 percent by 1984. In Mexico the minimum wage declined sharply and wages even more, with the rural poor suffering the greatest loss, a 31.3 percent wage decline.[31]

If the poor suffered disproportionately in the recession, many of the already rich profited, according to the World Bank report. "Those who were able to send capital abroad benefited, often immensely, in relation to the rest of society, where the poor become poorer because of the rise in unemployment and the sharp decline in real wages."[32]

This final point, that some in Latin America itself have benefited immensely from the current debt crisis, is stressed by another commentary on the debt crisis. Its author claims that one-third of the borrowed money went to finance the flight of private capital out of the debtor countries. Since 1973, residents of Argentina, Brazil, Mexico, and Venezuela have acquired nearly *$100 billion* in foreign assets.[33] Once again a wealthy elite has become immensely more wealthy; this time with an even more crushing effect on the poor who constitute the great majority in Latin America.

Many analysts, however, would dispute Frank's contention that the poor suffered even in absolute terms during the period of growth. (Even more would they dispute Frank's contention that growth cannot occur with dependency, for most of Latin America experienced growth rates of 5–7 percent annually between 1960 and 1980). Thus the World Bank report cited above claims that the growth in this period "went hand in hand with considerable social improvements"—for example, the accessibility of clean water went up 40 percent between 1960 and 1980, and life expectancy increased by eight years. The income share of the lowest 40 percent did not shrink, says the report; most of the poor improved their standard of living at about the same pace as the entire population.[34]

Other writers argue along similar lines, one even claiming that Latin America really had "thirty good years" prior to the 1980s' recession.[35] Perhaps some gains did occur, some "trickle down" of the benefits of growth, but with the great majority of persons still living with incomes under $1,000 a year, and with losses in the 1980s wiping out earlier gains, the picture in Latin America remains quite bleak.

The Causes of Dependency

As we have seen in chapter 6, many competing theories attempt to explain how Latin America failed to develop fully and became dependent on others. The strong form of dependency theory, most associated with A. G. Frank, places the blame primarily on external forces. Foreign colonialist or imperial powers used Latin America to subsidize their own development and have "kept" Latin America in a condition of underdevelopment. In sharp contrast to this position, the strong form of the modernization model would place the blame on internal factors. Michael Novak states this position forcefully: "Latin America is responsible for its own condition."[36] He believes that dependency theorists and liberation theologians deceive themselves by picturing Latin Americans as "victims" of oppression.

Cardoso offers a more nuanced dependency analysis that avoids focus on "who is to blame" and seeks to find both external and internal factors that have caused Latin America to "deviate" from the pattern of development in advanced countries. Several factors that caused Latin America to deviate appear evident to me from the study of Latin America's history: a pattern of property ownership with land concentrated in the hands of a few and the vast majority left propertyless; a Spanish culture imposed on an indigenous Indian people creating a rigid class stratification; a political system that kept power in the hands of the landowning oligarchy or the military; an economy geared for external markets to the neglect of both agricultural and industrial products to meet domestic needs; a consequent dependency on foreign markets and foreign investors, often supported in this century by U.S. political-military interventions.

These factors certainly caused Latin America to deviate from the natural path of growth that Adam Smith claimed societies should follow: first, to develop its agriculture through relatively egalitarian free enterprise among landowning classes in rural areas; second, industrial production for the urban market; third, production for international trade.[37] Latin America certainly did not begin with egalitarian agriculture, and it geared the production of its most important goods—from mining and plantations—for export *before* attending to domestic markets. The Nobel prize-winning economist W. Arthur Lewis sees a strong agricultural development geared for domestic markets as a necessary basis for industrial growth. Moreover, he believes that underdeveloped nations cannot escape from unfavorable terms of trade without greater and more efficient agricultural productivity.[38]

One could certainly assign "blame" in the first instance to Spain and Portugal. They did plunder the new lands of America, as dependency theorists stress, and the indigenous peoples were certainly victims of oppression. The Spanish and Portuguese also left a legacy of disdain for work and a failure to encourage entrepreneurial skills and incentives for productivity. Michael Novak is right on this score, but liberation philosopher Enrique Dussel and Marxist writer José Carlos Mariátegui acknowledge this as well. Spain chose, says Dussel, to take the easy way of exploiting mines with Indian labor rather than taking the narrow road that England chose—the hard work of an industrious people.[39]

In my estimation, the most damaging factor in this colonial heritage was a structural one: the concentration of ownership in the hands of a wealthy oligarchy. The concentration of landownership began in colonial times and continues to this day. In Brazil, a group of 340 owners control 117 million acres of land, though they only cultivate 11 percent of it, while hundreds of thousands of peasants are landless.[40] Had owners, through the centuries, been more efficient, reinvested in the domestic economy, produced to meet *domestic* needs and markets, and paid fairer wages, perhaps concentration of ownership would not have proved so negative. But the owners did not act in this way. More importantly, this very structure of concentrated ownership deprived the great masses of people of access to their own lands and trades, an access that was generally available in the United States and further enhanced by the Homestead Act. One could characterize this legacy in Marxist terms as lack of control over the means of production; one could also describe it as the absence of any real experience of free enterprise. The concentration of ownership, along with class structures created by Hispanic society, had profound effects on politics as well.

However one assesses the *past* causal factors, Latin America now finds itself in a very disadvantaged position. Like a poker game in which one player begins with $10 and another with $10,000, or a race between a Model T and a Mercedes, the odds of winning run strongly against Latin Americans—the poor especially. The industrialized North has enormous advantages of technology, capital, and access to markets. To compete, Latin American nations have resorted to borrowing capital, relying on imported technology, and keeping wages low, so that the burden of growth weighs especially hard on the poor.

The Role of Transnationals

For a time, the influence and power of transnationals (or multinationals) stirred public debate in the United States. In the mid-1970s, the United States Senate held hearings about transnationals, Richard Barnet and Ronald Muller warned against the growing power of transnationals in their widely-read *Global Reach*, and Raymond Vernon responded to critiques with an aptly titled work about the *Storm Over the Multinationals*. In the United States the storm subsided, except for protests against U.S. investments in South Africa. In Latin America, however, transnationals remain a provocative issue.

Those who defend transnationals use arguments that reflect the modernization paradigm. Transnationals, they say, bring needed capital, technology, and managerial skills to Third World countries. They provide jobs, train professionals, create orders for local suppliers, and open up new markets for the host countries. Critics of transnationals claim they impede and distort true development in the Third World. I will condense their criticisms under three main headings: the draining of capital from developing nations through excess profits; distortion of development through inappropriate goods and technology; and loss of national autonomy.

Draining Off of Capital. Dependency theorists, and liberation theologians who cite them, charge that transnationals keep Latin America underdeveloped by taking capital *out* of their countries. They cite studies showing that for every dollar invested by foreign companies, they take out two to four times as much in profit.[41] When Chile nationalized U.S. copper companies in 1971, the Allende government claimed that the companies had taken out of Chile wealth estimated at $10.8 billion over a sixty-year period. Chile refused compensation on the grounds that the copper companies had already been compensated by exorbitant profit rates. Kennecott, Allende claimed, had an average annual profit rate of 52.8 percent from its Chilean operations from 1955 to 1970; Anaconda averaged 21.5 percent in profits from Chile during the same period, as opposed to 3.6 percent from their investments elsewhere.[42]

Even where profit rates appear more reasonable, transfer pricing can dramatically increase actual profits. A study made of transnationals in Colombia showed an overpricing of imports by 25 percent in chemicals, 40 percent in rubber, and 155 percent in pharmaceuticals. A similar study in Colombia showed that average profit rates in the pharmaceutical, electric, and rubber industries increased from 15.8 percent to 52 percent when transfer pricing was included.[43]

Critics also charge that transnationals do not rely on their own capital for investment. One study of investment patterns in Latin America showed that when transnationals established companies in Latin America only 17 percent of the investment came from the TNCs themselves; the remaining capital was raised among local investors.[44] Most critics acknowledge that transnationals generally do pay higher wages than local companies, but these wages still run one-sixth to one-seventh the wages paid in the parent company. Moreover, far from creating a great number of jobs, the TNCs employ less than 2 percent of all potential workers in Latin America.[45]

Inappropriate Goods and Technologies. In discussing the history of Latin America we have seen that it did not follow the "natural path" of modernization laid out by Adam Smith. It did not build a strong agriculture based on free enterprise and geared to meet domestic needs first. Many Latin American countries have long depended on one or two cash crops for income—for example, bananas, sugar, or coffee. Transnational agribusinesses, allied with local landowners, continue this process. They often produce luxury crops such as asparagus or strawberries to meet needs in rich nations rather than producing basic staples needed by the local population.[46]

In the decades after World War II foreign investment turned more toward manufacturing. The share of manufacturing in the total value of U.S. investment in Latin America rose from 13.3 percent in 1946 to 50.5 percent in 1976.[47] Critics argue that transnationals tend to bring with them large-scale, labor-saving, and capital-intensive technologies that are inappropriate for Latin America, which needs labor-intensive production. The transnationals have no interest in sharing their technologies with potential competitors, and they keep research and development within the home country. Critics also charge that TNCs aim their products at the middle and upper levels of society, with goods such as automobiles, colored television, and processed foods that the poor cannot afford. In doing so, they only reinforce the inequitable distribution of income and goods so long characteristic of Latin America.[48]

Loss of Autonomy. Dependency connotes subordination and loss of autonomy. Resentment against transnational companies involves national pride. The people of the United States fought a revolutionary war because it believed that "taxation without representation is tyranny." Americans should understand, then, why many in Latin America chafe at foreign companies playing a dominant role in their economies. National pride becomes especially significant when foreign companies control the major resource of a country as once held true for Cuba (sugar), Guatemala (bananas), and Chile (copper).

I mentioned earlier Chile's nationalization of U.S. copper companies under Salvador Allende. The nationalization did not result from some arbitrary edict by Allende; it passed *unanimously* in the legislature, caused by a long buildup of aggravating factors. Theodore Moran's detailed study of U.S. copper companies in Chile indicates these factors. Despite great copper shortages during World War II, the United States, acting in collaboration with U.S. companies in Chile, held prices down and kept prices low after the war. Chile had the worst terms of trade in all of Latin America except for Bolivia; low prices caused a loss of somewhere between $100 to $500 million for Chile. In 1950 the United States set a low price on copper without even consulting any Chilean representative.[49] Chile was not free to trade in the free market. Its trading partners as well as its prices were determined by agreements with the United States. When Chile's share in the world market declined, it gave U.S. multinationals new concessions: lower taxes, higher profits, few controls, and preferential import rights. Kennecott's profits doubled, but it used its gains for its own multinational purposes: investing in aluminum and coal, increasing copper refining in the United States, and seeking to rely *less* on its Chilean operations.[50] In the 1960s Chilean President Eduardo Frei called on the copper companies to sell 51 percent of their shares to the government. By the time of the 1970 elections every major candidate called for nationalization of copper.

During this same time (1970) foreign companies had gained majority control of many leading industries in Latin America. In Brazil, foreign companies controlled 50 percent of all manufacturing, including 81 percent of the rubber industry, 83 percent of electrical machinery, and 88 percent of transportation equipment. In Peru and Colombia, foreign companies controlled 43–44 percent of all manufacturing.[51] In many instances — 42 percent of the time, according to one study of the 1960s — the foreign control came not through new enterprises but by buying out local companies, by "denationalizing" the economy.[52]

Resentment of foreign companies involves more than just profits or percentages of ownership. Executives of these companies often live in luxurious "enclaves," with swimming pools and tennis courts, creating an anger-provoking contrast with the slums surrounding them.

Counterarguments and an Assessment. The draining off of profits — or "theft of surplus value" as some liberation theologians put it — serves as the linchpin for the strong form of dependency theory: that corporations from rich countries have financed their own development by taking out more in profits than they invested, and that the loss of these profits has kept poor nations underdeveloped. Defenders of the transnationals challenge the assumption that profits in excess of investment proves that poor countries suffer a net loss in the process. Defenders claim that this argument ignores the creation of new wealth. Chile might not have developed a copper industry, at least not at the same level of productivity, without the capital and technology invested in it from outside companies. Even with the high profit rates cited earlier, copper companies in Chile paid more in taxes after World War II than they took out in profits.[53] If Chile's copper mines had remained untapped, Chile's national wealth might have remained at a level below what it actually attained.

Raymond Vernon questions the selectivity of examples used to argue that transnational profits have been excessive. The transnational manufacturing firms that he investigated fell under 15 percent profits, which he considers reasonable.[54] Theodore Moran argues that the "bargaining power" of host countries becomes greater over time. He acknowledges that in the initial stages of investment, transnationals often do gain concessions heavily weighted in their favor. But once established, the transnationals usually have too much invested to pull out. The host country can take advantage of this and change the original contract, calling for higher taxes, greater employment of local executives, joint ventures, and other benefits.[55]

As for inappropriate technologies, defenders argue that often the host countries demand the more labor-intensive technologies that also may provide better quality products at lower prices. As to goods produced, some defenders argue that they do not distort development but constitute a natural pattern of development as nations become modernized and industrialized. Advertising and marketing provide ordinary persons with more variety in product choices. As for the power of U.S. transnationals creating loss of autonomy, some would argue that their investments have declined sharply in recent decades. The U.S. share in exports from its Latin American affiliates fell from 40 percent in the 1960s to 20 percent in the 1970s, and continues to go down.[56]

These counterarguments serve as a caution against oversimplified analyses and solutions. U.S. foreign investment did not cause the problems confronting Latin America; the pattern of dependency began in colonialist times. In many ways, however, transnationals have aggravated conditions in Latin America. They tend to reinforce the maldistribution of wealth and power there. The "bargaining model," Moran acknowledges, works only for countries that reach a strong bargaining position. Even then it does not take into account whether the *people* of a given country benefit when bargaining power does become more equal. Anastasio Somoza in Nicaragua and Ferdinand Marcos in the Philippines—to use extreme examples—may have gained in bargaining power. But the benefits—wealth estimated in the hundreds of millions for Somoza and as high as $10 billion for Marcos—accrued to them, not to their people.

Analysts I cited earlier acknowledge that foreign borrowing and investment have gone, in countries like Mexico and Brazil, into capital-intensive modern sectors, with government policies agreeing with foreign investors in keeping wages deliberately low and impeding labor unionizing. The goods produced by most multinationals look to the same levels of affluence found in the United States and Europe. They do not fulfill the basic needs of the vast majority in Latin America. Presence of U.S. transnationals has also significantly influenced U.S. foreign policy in favor of maintaining the status quo.

The withdrawal of all transnationals, on the other hand, would be un-realistic and would not solve Latin America's problems. Governments in Latin America, if they truly had the good of their citizens at heart, could stipulate terms of investment that would look to the common good of the vast majority of citizens. A stronger political voice on the part of the popular masses may have to develop, however, for this to occur.

U.S. Political and Military Interventions

The United States does not determine government policies in Latin America; governments there do not "depend" simply on the whim of U.S. decisions. The United States has intervened frequently enough, however, especially in Central America and the Caribbean area, to arouse great resentment among many Latin Americans. In recent decades the United States has almost always justified its actions as security measures to stop communism. U.S. interventions, however, began long before communism came onto the scene. The United States sent troops on six occasions to Panama to insure that it remained open to "our" right to build a canal.[57] It sent warships on numerous occasions to protect U.S. property. It sent marines to Nicaragua in 1912 (and kept them there for nearly twenty years) to insure a government favorable to the United States. U.S. marines went into the Caribbean region some twenty times between 1898 and 1920.[58]

Since World War II the United States has intervened in the name of democracy, judging dictatorships to be "on the side of democracy" if they oppose Marxism, and helping to overthrow democratically elected govern-ments if they gave any leeway to Marxists. If Ronald Reagan most clearly exemplified this attitude, it has dominated U.S. foreign policy throughout the post-World War II period. John F. Kennedy aptly articulated U.S. objectives in respect to Latin America, shortly after Trujillo was assassi-nated in the Dominican Republic: "There are three possibilities in descend-ing order of preference—a decent democratic regime, a continuation of a Trujillo-type regime, or a Castro regime. We ought to aim for the first, but we can't renounce the second until we are sure that we can avoid the third."[59]

The United States has gone to great lengths to avoid the third. In 1954 the United States organized the overthrow of a democratically elected gov-ernment in Guatemala. The United States justified it, Secretary of State Dulles would later say, to stop the "intrusion of Soviet despotism."[60] Even later studies made to substantiate this threat showed no evidence of Soviet designs. The offenses that President Jacobo Arbenz did commit were: initiating a land reform that included the expropriation of lands owned by U.S.-based United Fruit, allowing the Communist Party (with only three to four thousand members) to have legal status, and using some young Marxist labor leaders as part of his advisory team.[61]

In Brazil in 1964, the United States sent clear messages of support for the military overthrow of a democratically elected government. Lyndon Johnson sent an aircraft carrier, helicopter, tanker, and six destroyers to back up the military. U.S. aid to Brazil soared from $15 million in 1964 to $122 million the next year.[62]

In the summer of 1965, President Johnson sent 25,000 marines to the Dominican Republic. He first justified it as an action to protect U.S. lives; and then added, to prevent another communist takeover like Cuba. Juan Bosch had been elected president in 1963; he was overthrown by a military coup in 1965; his supporters staged a rebellion to reinstate him as president. Though less than a hundred communists lived on the island, their presence was used to justify blocking the return of a democratically elected president.[63]

In the early 1970s, the United States through the urging of ITT and other U.S. multinationals intervened in yet another democractically elected government. The United States sought first to block the election of Salvador Allende (a Marxist), then helped finance terrorists who assassinated his chief military supporter, General Schneider. The United States cut off aid to Chile, influenced international banks to cut off credits and loans, and sought, in President Nixon's words, to "make Chile's economy suffer."[64] If in the 1980s the Reagan administration argued that the proximity of Nicaragua made it a special threat, in the early 1970s Nixon argued that the United States cannot allow a "red sandwich" to develop, with Chile on one end and Cuba on the other.

In Nicaragua, in the 1980s, the U.S. government supported the "Contras"—judged by Americas Watch as the second most brutal terrorist group in Latin America—and proclaimed them "freedom fighters." It judged Nicaragua's elections in 1984 to be fraudulent, though parliamentarians from Europe who observed the elections judged them fair; it violated international law; it violated amendments passed in the U.S. Congress; it engaged in a deliberate "disinformation" campaign about Nicaragua; and it helped to finance the killing of more than twenty-five thousand Nicaraguans.

The United States also conveniently forgets the aftermath of its efforts in these countries. When Vice-President Nixon visited Guatemala after the overthrow of Arbenz he proclaimed: "This is the first instance in history where a Communist government (sic) has been replaced by a free one. The whole world is watching to see which does the better job."[65] In fact, most of the world stopped watching. Agrarian reform was reversed and less than one percent of the peasants retained the plots of land gained under Arbenz.[66] Voting rights were taken away from all who were illiterate, namely about 70 percent of the population. Amnesty International estimated that more than thirty thousand civilians were abducted, tortured, or assassinated between 1966 and 1981.[67] Thousands more were killed in the Rios Montt regime that followed. Hundreds of thousands became refugees.

In Brazil, democracy was replaced by military dictatorships, which its own court documents show engaged in thousands of cases of torture to repress dissent (see chapter 2). The military overthrow of Allende in Chile ended one of the longest standing democracies in Latin America. The military rule, described by a U.N. commission in 1976 as "barbaric sadism," has involved mass executions, arrests, and torture.

Many in the United States believe that liberationists in Latin America are naive in not recognizing the dangers of Marxism. The liberationists might well reply that anyone who believes their country will be better off after a U.S. intervention must indeed be naive.

Chapter 9

Opting for Socialism:
An Assessment

Chapter 7 summarized what liberation theologians have said about capitalism and socialism. They rather universally and staunchly oppose capitalism and favor some sort of socialism. Critics of liberation theology, and many who support it overall, share some common concerns about this option. The major concern involves a fear that the socialism, whose form liberation theologians leave quite undefined, would simply repeat existing Marxist-Leninist regimes.

Use of the word "fear" to describe this concern about Marxist socialism creates its own grave consequences. The U.S. government has played on this fear to justify numerous interventions in Latin America. As we have seen, the presence of Marxist "advisors" in Guatemala sufficed to justify the overthrow of a democratically elected government there; the perceived danger of a few dozen Marxists in the Dominican Republic lent justification to the sending of U.S. marines; fear that communists might eventually end up on the borders of Texas was used to dramatize U.S. support for the Contras against the Sandinista government in Nicaragua. Latin American military governments have used the threat of communism to justify repression of movements for land reform, peasant rights, and labor unions. Catholic bishops who spoke out for reform, or even to protest torture, have been denounced as "communist subversives." General Pinochet in Chile played upon fears of communism to impede a return to democracy. Fears about Marxist socialism, on the other hand, do have a basis in historical experience. Many of the worst atrocities of this century have been committed under the banner of Marxism: Stalin authorized massive executions of kulaks and purges that took millions of lives in Russia; one to two million were executed in the first years after the communist takeover in China; the Khmer Rouge and Pol Pot undertook genocidal policies in Cambodia. Moreover, from the time of Lenin on, the Communist Party has exercised single-party control in almost every Marxist government. The party may claim to rule "in the name of the proletariat," but the workers' Solidarity

177

movement in Poland shows how shallow this claim can be. Promises that some new Marxist regimes "will be different" evoke strong skepticism. Any true assessment of movements in Latin America must determine how real or how exaggerated these fears may be.

Far too often the labels "Marxism," "socialism," and "capitalism" polarize discussion of issues and impede thoughtful evaluation. I adverted to this in the introduction to the book; my own aversion to assessments based on labels will become especially evident in this section. The label "Marxist analysis," as used by critics, ignores nuances in its use and takes on all the worst connotations associated with the classic Marxist worldview and Leninist tactics. The Sandinista government in Nicaragua gets prejudged once the label "Marxist-Leninist regime" is placed upon it. For some critics, any advocacy of "socialism" implies state-controlled, one-party rule. For some adherents of liberation theology, on the other hand, a rather undefined socialism becomes the bearer of all the hopes and ideals connected with liberation. Capitalism, without any differentiation of its components, becomes simply the evil to be overcome. Careful assessment requires examining and going beyond these labels.

Opposition to Capitalism: The Main Argument for Socialism

One reason liberation theologians opt for socialism stands out above all others: their abhorrence of the prevailing capitalist system. If, as many liberation theologians stress, capitalism cannot be reformed to meet the basic needs of the poor or to give them true participation in society, then socialism would seem to be the only real option. U.S. defenders of capitalism point to its record of achievement: the high standards of living achieved by most Americans. But if one uses the same "realistic" criterion for judging Latin America's system, the record of capitalism there would lead to a quite negative judgment. The desire for radical change on the part of many Latin Americans seems quite justified.

We need to examine, however, the use of the term capitalism to designate Latin America's economic system, past and present. In terms of the past, liberation sociologist Otto Maduro dates the development of capitalism in Latin America to the end of the nineteenth century.[1] This would fit with a definition of capitalism as a new mode of production most characterized by industrialization in privately owned factories that employ wage laborers. Gutiérrez, on the other hand, speaks of the initial sixteenth-century conquerors of Latin America as "the first representatives of capitalism."[2] Pablo Richard takes this point much further. He believes that Latin America constituted a capitalist society from the outset: "The position I adopt here is that Latin America was inserted into the expanding worldwide capitalist trading system ever since the Spanish and Portuguese conquest. From the very beginning, starting with its discovery and conquest, Latin America has developed with a capitalist social pattern."[3]

Richard bases this assumption on arguments by dependency theorist A. G. Frank who considers "exploitation of surplus value" from the labor of others as the hallmark of capitalism. Some points in Richard's argument have validity; the label "capitalist," however, obfuscates the problem. The native population of Latin America and the resources of Latin America were clearly "exploited"; Latin America had a relationship of dependency imposed upon it by Spain and Portugal; Latin America was inserted into a wider world market from the outset; "backwardness" was not the main cause of Latin American underdevelopment through the centuries that followed. Latin American countries, however, were not "capitalist societies" from the outset. Even if one assumes that countries in northern Europe had "begun" a form of mercantilist capitalism that would eventually lead to industrial capitalism, Spain and Portugal by any definition remained feudal in character, and Latin America took on their societal traits. Even Marxist critics have sharply criticized Frank's description, which they say ignores the whole question of modes of production.[4] Mariátegui's writings consistently describe Latin America's economy as a carryover from feudalism, and he faults it for *not* adopting the methods and spirit of capitalist productivity.[5] If one makes exploitation of surplus value and serving external markets the defining norms of capitalism, even the ancient Roman empire would fall under the classification of capitalist. To call Latin America capitalist in its very origins may help to fuel moral outrage against the capitalist system, but it greatly oversimplifies analysis.

Through most of its history Latin America has had a hybrid form of economy that defies simple classifications. The haciendas, for example, have been described as semifeudal, semicapitalist: feudal in their internal structures and use of coerced labor; capitalist in having external markets.

Even the application of the term capitalism to many present-day economic systems in Latin America raises some questions. In some respects the dominant economic system in some countries resembles more closely the socialist "state capitalism" of the Soviet Union and Eastern Europe than the capitalism of the United States and Western Europe. According to one study, the state in Mexico accounts for 65–70 percent of the GNP. In Bolivia the state accounts for 92 percent of the GNP, higher than in Poland. The same study claims that 50–60 percent of Latin Americans work for the state.[6] Another study reports that the 25 largest nonfinancial corporations in Brazil are state-owned.[7] These figures, however, refer to the monetized sector of the economy and do not take into account the subsistence level at which many of the poor live.

None of these observations diminishes the substantive critiques of Latin American systems as externally dependent and exploited, and internally elitest and exploitative, so that even many opponents of liberation theology judge capitalism a "dismal failure." But these observations do warn against simply reducing the problem to a struggle between capitalism and socialism. The term "capitalist" has entirely negative connotations in liberation theology: foreign domination, exploitation of workers, human needs subordinate to the drive for profits, and concentration of power and wealth. Capitalism historically is unquestionably linked with many injustices and inequities; a strong case can be made against many features of capitalism.[8] The worst problems with capitalism, in my estimation, are linked to concentration of power and wealth, to what Leonardo Boff captures with his reference to "elitest, exclusivist capitalism."[9]

Capitalism, however, includes a variety of components: it includes small businesses as well as giant corporations; it includes a free market system; it uses self-interest and profits as motivating factors, but its ethos also involves hard work, productivity, creativity, and inventiveness. A sweeping rejection of capitalism fails to distinguish these components or structures, which need to be weighed separately. A true dialectic process would involve assessing each of the structures within the system. Marx himself recognized this, even though he sought to replace capitalism with socialism. Above all he recognized the immense productive capacities of capitalism. In fact, he argued that socialism could not or should not take over *until* capitalism had run its course, producing enough goods for all.

Trotsky argued that the state-controlled, bureaucratic system that developed in the Soviet Union under Stalin resulted from the undeveloped state of its economy when socialism took over. Trotsky cites Marx who insisted that full development of productive forces was absolutely necessary for socialism. Without this development, capitalist-type struggles would emerge again: "with want, the struggle for necessities begins again, and that means that the old crap must revive."[10]

If a system is to provide for the basic needs of a people, it must develop productivity, along with the virtues of hard work and inventiveness that make productivity possible. At a time when socialist countries have begun to question whether some of its structures may impede growth — in Nicaragua the government has moved away from collectivist farm efforts to allow peasants to work for themselves — liberation theologians need to consider what might be fruitfully retained from "capitalist" structures. Private farms and small businesses have helped greatly in achieving equitable economic growth. The free market system fails when wealth and income are vastly unequal; the market then responds to money, to those who can pay, not to individual preferences. It acts blindly in respect to social costs. But a market *can* work where purchasing power is more widely dispersed, and measures by socialist governments to replace the market have led to significant failures.[11]

Socialist Ideals and the Socialist Option

In recent years many liberation theologians have spoken more cautiously about socialism. Some, like Segundo, have become more critical of existing socialisms. Gutiérrez, as I noted, does not consider an option for socialism essential to liberation theology. J. B. Libânio says that liberation theology has modified its position and now speaks of an "alternative system" to capitalism rather than of socialism.[12] Liberation theologians remain, nevertheless, generally quite positive about socialism. If opposition to capitalism offers the strongest argument for socialism, three related reasons also stand out: socialist ideals fit closely with Christian ideals; socialism offers a utopian vision as does the "kingdom of God"; socialism stresses important, basic-needs priorities.

Christianity stresses — one could say, above all else — love of others. The great commandment ("love one another as I have loved you"), the last judgment scene in Matthew 25 ("what you do for the least of these"), the parable of the good Samaritan, and countless other passages all emphasize concern for one's neighbor. The first Christian communities tried to live out this ideal, sharing goods in common and making certain that no one was left in need (Acts 4:32). Socialism emphasizes these very same ideals. It strives to create a system that will meet the basic needs of all, that will allow ordinary persons to be active agents in building up a new society, and will stress cooperation and community rather than competition and individual self-interest. Liberation theologians express their vision of society in just such terms, in terms of ultimate goals and ideals. Moreover, strong moral judgments about the value of community (a Christian socialist ideal) and the evils of individual self-seeking (viewed as the capitalist spirit) recur frequently in liberation writings.

Critics respond with arguments that we have seen earlier. Theological critics argue that socialism ignores the factor of original sin, that any system that hopes to succeed must take into account the reality of self-interest as a motivating factor. Other critics say that goals and ideals do not translate into reality simply through espousing them. The greatest fear is that Marxists will control the building up of a socialist society by imposing one-party rule and control over every aspect of life. John Paul II warns that collectivist socialism only takes power from a wealthy capitalist elite and transfers it to a new bureaucratic elite.[13]

Critics of Marxist socialism fault Marx not for designing a totalitarian system — he was in fact radically democratic in what he envisioned — but for not giving much thought at all to how the political or economic structures of socialism might work. Lenin supplied the realism through one-party communist rule, but its results have been less than praiseworthy. If significant change occurs in Latin America, it will come as the result of some group's already developed plan. Liberation theologians have argued that Christianity contains no master plan and that Christian liberation should identify instead with the praxis of "popular movements." But the specific plans and goals of such movements call for critical evaluation.

The concept of "utopia" also plays a significant role in respect to envisioning a new socialist society. The Bible itself inspires utopian thinking with the prophet Isaiah's rich language of hope for a new society, but above all through Jesus' preaching of the kingdom of God. If the kingdom will only come in its complete realization as a gift from God, it holds forth an ideal of the kind of society God wills, one in which the poor are treated with dignity and find their fulfillment. Liberation theologians could also cite Pope Paul VI who called specifically for creative utopian thinking to go beyond present systems and ideologies.[14]

The concept of utopia figures prominently in the writings of many liberation theologians.[15] Gutiérrez gives great importance to utopian thinking. It expresses the not-yet, but something also in the process of becoming. It helps the poor to challenge and denounce dominant ideologies. It serves to question and correct systems and ideologies that claim to be "orthodox" and "realistic" — and these include both politically conservative positions and dogmatic communist ones. Utopia mediates between the realms of faith and political action. It humanizes the first level of liberation (the politico-social) and prevents translating the political into a Christian ideology or messianism.[16]

Critics, especially those who draw on Reinhold Niebuhr's thought, want to see utopian ideals translated into realistic "approximations," and again they fear that without critical evaluation of socialist and capitalist models liberation movements will follow existing socialist programs. Liberation theologians have not given much specificity to how a socialist society might operate other than describing the ideals they hope to see it fulfill. They do recognize in principle, however, the need for translating ideals into concrete forms. We need, says Leonardo Boff, to choose historically viable mediations.[17] If liberation theology once spoke in uncompromising terms of radical transformation and creating a "new person," realism has now become more evident. We must look, says Segundo, for creative possibilities "however limited" they may seem. We must try to carry out changes "on the scale that is possible for us." The quality most needed for this, he says, is flexibility.[18]

Writing in the concrete context of El Salvador, Ignacio Ellacuría observes that realism dictates that El Salvador cannot expect to create a new society. But it can hope to transform existing structures by reducing violence and outside military interventions, by guaranteeing human rights, and by allowing popular movements to organize so that they can play a more effective part in the political life of the country. Some critics view liberation theologians as giving unquestioned support to revolutionary groups. Ellacuría takes a different position. He says that the revolutionary groups in El Salvador cannot claim to represent the majority. They represent many aspirations of the people and they must become part of a political solution to the present conflict, but they cannot claim that their programs express the popular will.[19]

Liberation theologians do tend, however, to give existing socialisms much higher marks than most North Americans would give. Hence they would see some socialist countries as reasonable "approximations" of Christian-socialist ideals already. Cuba inspired hopes in the early stages of liberation theology; Nicaragua revived hope for liberation in the 1980s. Enrique Dussel cites China, Vietnam, and Angola as other examples. Most liberation theologians who talk about socialism usually have some critical remarks to make about socialism in the Soviet Union and Eastern Europe. But Leonardo Boff returned from a short visit to the Soviet Union and proclaimed it a "clean, healthy society," which inspired his group to think about the kingdom of God being actually realized.[20] (Even supporters of Boff in Brazil found this a bit much.) Boff judges the U.S. capitalist system as immoral and cites the 15 percent living in poverty as a scandal, but 50 percent of Soviet citizens would fall below the U.S. poverty line.

The attractiveness of socialist models seems to derive from two factors. First, socialist countries have broken away from a capitalism viewed as the root problem of poverty and domination. Cuba and Nicaragua, moreover, have taken stands against U.S. domination and interference. Second, socialist countries give high priority to addressing the basic needs of the poorest sectors of society. Countries like China and Cuba have dramatically improved medical care, basic food supplies, and literacy among the poor. For many Latin Americans such gains constitute an important achievement.

Socialism has not scored well, however, in terms of *continued* productivity and growth, nor in respect to political freedom. In *Liberating Grace*, Leonardo Boff commented that Brazil and other Latin American countries might have to choose between liberation from dependency and development (see chapter 5). No system produces only positive or only negative effects. Either-or choices between capitalism and socialism ignore the possibility of building structures that take the best from each and reject what is worst in each. One can certainly learn from socialist models, but also from more positive aspects of capitalism—looking not to the United States but perhaps to Sweden, or to the successes of Taiwan and South Korea. These latter, formerly underdeveloped countries have not been models of democracy, but thanks in part to significant land reforms they have high rates of growth and also rank near the top of all countries (Taiwan especially) in levels of equal income distribution. They have done this also without stressing the individualism usually associated with capitalism.[21]

Finally, it is interesting to note that Mariátegui based his arguments for socialism in Peru—a socialism based on community ownership, not state control—on the special situation of the large Indian population there. Mariátegui acknowledged the success of competitive free enterprise in the North, with its broad opportunities for private ownership of farms. But the Indians, he argued, do not thrive under competition and individualism; they need the bonds of community.[22]

Private Property and Democracy

Many critics believe that existing socialisms have sacrificed political democracy to economic goals; this carries over to a concern that liberation theology's favoring of socialism could lead in the same direction. I have linked this issue of democracy with the question of private property because critics like John Cort believe that total elimination of private property, and making it state-owned and controlled, would effectively destroy democracy and the goals of "true" socialism as well. I will consider in this section some reflections about Catholic social teachings on private property, respond to Cort's criticisms of Gutiérrez in respect to property, and then discuss the place of democracy in liberation theology.

In the first great social encyclical, *Rerum Novarum* (1891), Pope Leo XIII spoke of the "natural right" of every person to possess property (no. 5). Even this encyclical spoke about the abuses of this right, and one could use its emphasis on *every* person's right to own as a norm for judging that systems excluding the vast majority from ownership are immoral. Wealthy owners have cited this "right," however, in defense against any attempts at land reform or nationalization of industries. In Brazil, I was told, private and corporate owners of vast, uncultivated lands (100,000 acres or more) still argue that their ownership constitutes an inviolable natural right.

Latin American theologian Ricardo Antoncich argues, in response, that the church has consistently defended the right of *access to property by all*, not for some absolute right on the part of those who already possess property.[23] If humans have a right to property, according to natural law, this right is violated when access is denied. The right of all to the goods of the earth takes priority over ownership by some. Applying the teachings, Antoncich concludes that a "mixed ownership" of the means of production (some private, some social ownership) fits best with conditions in Latin America and is consistent with church views.

Franz Hinkelammert also argues for right to access by all. He views Catholic social teachings—wrongly, in my judgment—as supporting one particular type of property—that is, capitalist private property—and his initial treatment suggests total opposition to private property as such. Later in this same work, however, Hinkelammert speaks favorably of "true private property" characterized by full employment, decent pay, affable owners, and the like.[24] Thus neither of these liberation theologians calls for elimination of private property, but they stress the right of access.

The Pontifical Justice and Peace Commission in Rome confirms this position. A 1977 document, in which the commission claimed to give the true intent of Catholic social teachings on property, argues that access to the goods of the earth by all is the most fundamental principle of church teachings. The commission puts in question form a criterion for judging property relations: "Does the existing regime, and the development it is undergoing, still enable all to exercise their 'natural' (hence valid for all) right to have access in one form or another to some power over things, a power to be exercised in responsible freedom?"[25]

Pope John Paul II, in *Sollicitudo Rei Socialis*, likewise states as the characteristic principle of Christian social doctrine that "the goods of this world are originally meant for all." This does not negate, says the pope, the right to private property, but it places it under a "social mortgage," which means that it falls under the more general principle of the universal destination of goods. The pope speaks of respect for "economic initiative" and he warns against "total collectivization." Total collectivization, however, does not mean rejection of all forms of socialized ownership. In *Laborem Exercens* John Paul II not only accepts "truly socialized" forms of ownership, but favors "proposals for joint ownership of the means of work."[26]

If we accept John Cort's critique, noted in chapter 7, Gutiérrez goes beyond these norms and calls for the total collectivization of all property and putting it into the hands of the state. Gutiérrez does indeed, in a passage cited by Cort, say that revolutionary struggle "insists on a society in which private ownership of the means of production is eliminated."[27] Cort draws far too much, however, out of this quote. Gutiérrez has never, to my knowledge, called for nationalizing all property, nor for placing all property in the hands of one party or the state. If these really did represent his positions, one would expect to find them stated somewhere in his many works. Even his statements on eliminating private property are directed against concentrated private control over property, and Gutiérrez insists in the same passage that the *masses* (not the state) appropriate the means of production. Gutiérrez nowhere condemns all employers as enemies (as Cort claims is implied in accepting the concept of class struggle), nor does he repudiate peasants for wanting to own their own lands (as Cort claims).

In *La verdad los hará libres*, Gutiérrez clarifies his position. He discusses the church's social teachings on property with their *double* concern: the danger of an individualistic conception that stresses profit as the motor force of economic activity, and a totalitarian vision that fails to respect the liberty of each person. His statements about social appropriation of the means of production (which does not necessarily mean state property) responded, says Gutiérrez, to the first concern or danger. He acknowledges, however, the second danger of denying personal liberty to all members of society. "Justice and liberty are two exigencies of human society." Many, says Gutiérrez, believe that a healthy equilibrium between private property, social property, and state property would best serve to protect against these two dangers.[28]

Gutiérrez clearly does not discount the importance of democracy. The struggle of the poor for liberation includes the desire for "an effective share in the exercise of political power" and the desire "for a truly democratic society."[29] One can justly argue, however, that liberation theologians have stressed far more the issue of socio-economic transformation and have not dwelled at any length on the importance of the political institutions and structures needed to ensure the "liberty" that Gutiérrez noted above.

This seems, however, to be changing. One of the most significant political turns in the liberation movement in recent years concerns democracy and how to make best use of the new political openings in countries formerly

under military rule. The reintroduction of formal democracy in many countries has not led to any simple "trust" in the democratic process, for the
history of most Latin American countries offers little reason to hope for
substantive social changes simply through the election of new government
officials. But the political change has allowed for greater development of
popular movements through which the poor can be mobilized to gain
greater strength and voice.

At an international assembly of liberation theologians, meeting in Mexico in December 1986, the theologians listed *first* among the present challenges in Latin America a preoccupation with the type of democratic
organization the peoples of Latin America might develop. In the 1960s and
70s, the theologians commented, "democracy" was associated with bourgeois rule and institutions. The question of democracy, however, has taken
on a new significance: "How to articulate a political order that permits an
opening to attain better levels of life?" This concern does not mean accepting a return to bourgeois domination, but "the popular sectors want to
participate decisively in the history which belongs to them to shape." The
new evaluation of democracy involves creating or occupying "spaces" where
various political projects can be conjoined, and the forging of a new political
order that will include the participation of the majority.[30]

Hugo Assmann, long considered the most Marxist of the liberation theologians, also spoke in the mid-1980s of the "redemocratization of Latin
America" as an essential priority. While Assmann insists that democracy
must go beyond the preservation of political liberties to include the incor-
poration of the large masses into the whole of society, he affirms with the
bishops of Brazil that "political democracy is a form and a prerequisite,
whose very definition and destination is social democracy."[31]

During my 1988 visit to Latin America, I found a great deal of discussion
about political participation and democracy among liberation theologians
and their supporters. The expression "building or occupying spaces" provided by democracy came up repeatedly in discussions and interviews. I
will discuss this important topic still more in the next chapter.

Violence and Class Struggle

Richard Neuhaus claims that some liberation theologians "advocate violent revolution,"[32] and other critics voice a similar concern about liberation
theology promoting violence. Though I have tried to search out writings
that deal with the question of violence, I have yet to find any statement by
a liberation theologian calling for violent revolution or declaring it necessary for bringing about social change in Latin America. One might expect
to find some statements to this effect at least in the early years of liberation
theology. With that in mind I read through a collection of testimonies
(*Signos de liberación*) from Christian activist groups and liberation theologians covering the years 1969 to 1973. In 290 pages I found no statement

that encouraged violence. Many liberation theologians did speak of the need for "social revolution" or for a "revolutionary change." But calls for the radical restructuring of society do not imply use of violent means. Priests for the Third World, one of the groups cited in this collection, did face precisely the charge that their call for social revolution implied the acceptance of violence. They replied that their movement had never "preached, proposed, or adhered to any form of violence" and they went on to say that violence is non-Christian and can be justified only, as the church itself teaches, in cases of extreme and prolonged tyranny.[33]

Among Gutiérrez's writings I found two statements that some critics might claim imply possible use of violent means. In his 1970 "Notes for a Theology of Liberation," Gutiérrez called for a profound transformation of society and then stated that "for many in our continent, this liberation will have to pass, sooner or later, through paths of violence." But this hardly constitutes an endorsement of violent revolution, especially since he adds that "it is hard to weigh its possibilities in terms of political effectiveness" and that "the reverses it has suffered have obliged it to rethink its program."[34] A second statement, in *The Power of the Poor in History*, says only that "we cannot say that violence is all right when the oppressor uses it to maintain or preserve 'order,' but wrong when the oppressed use it to overthrow this same order."[35]

In *The Liberation of Theology*, Segundo claimed that "all the remarks we find in the Bible about violence or nonviolence are ideologies" and that Jesus' adoption of nonviolent resistance is a question of ideology (means) and not a matter of faith.[36] But again these reflections do not suggest that violent means should or must be used in Latin America.

Some statements occur in liberation theology noting the church teaching about justification for use of arms as a last resort, and many wrote about "institutionalized violence" and how it can provoke armed resistance. Some in the early days of liberation theology spoke positively of Camilo Torres and Nestór Paz who joined with guerilla groups. The early commentators on Exodus, discussed in chapter 4, come closest to affirming the necessity of violent means. But even these fall far short of "advocating" or promoting the use of violent means in Latin America. In contrast, theologians like Segundo Galilea, Ricardo Antoncich, and Leonardo Boff speak out explicitly against violence and urge pursuing change through nonviolent means.[37] Gutiérrez has spoken out against the violence of the Shining Path group in Peru. It must embitter Latin Americans to be lectured on violence when the United States justifies, with little moral debate (other perhaps than "hope of success"), the arming of Contras to carry out the violent overthrow of Nicaragua.

Critics also come down strongly on the concept of "class struggle" in liberation theology. Much of the criticism has focused on Gutiérrez's discussion of class struggle in *A Theology of Liberation*. Most of his comments on class struggle simply stress that class conflict constitutes a "fact" of reality in Latin America. But Gutiérrez does say that neutrality is impossible, for to deny the existence of social divisions would mean accepting the prevailing system. "To accept class struggle," he says, "means to decide for some people and against others" and he calls upon the church to "opt" for the oppressed.[38] Similarly, in *The Power of the Poor in History*, Gutiérrez again stresses the fact of class struggle and adds that "an option for the poor is an option for one social class against another."[39]

The question then arises: "do these statements constitute an acceptance of a *Marxist* view of class struggle?" In a commentary on the issue of class struggle, Gregory Baum notes four aspects of Marxist class struggle that the church has consistently rejected: seeking victory by one class over another, promoting resentment and hatred in place of love, an implied encouraging of violent means, and viewing class struggle as the driving force of history.[40] If one accepts these as norms, Gutiérrez's statements do not constitute any endorsement of "Marxist" class struggle. He calls for opting with the poor against oppressing classes, but makes clear that what he seeks is a restoration of true unity in society, not the victory of one class over another. Far from advocating class hatred, the very problematic he wrestles with in *A Theology of Liberation* is how to preserve "universal Christian love" in the midst of class conflict. He does not endorse violence, and he nowhere says or even implies that class struggle is the driving force of history.

The problem remains that the expression "class struggle" has become so much identified with Marxism. Consequently opponents of liberation theology have linked the use of this phrase with acceptance of the whole Marxist program and tactics of social change. In the new edition of *A Theology of Liberation*, Gutiérrez acknowledges the misunderstandings that have arisen. To clear up these misunderstandings, and in light of new documents by the magisterium of the church, he has rewritten the section on class struggle, entitling it "Faith and Social Conflict." Probably with a view to justifying his earlier version, Gutiérrez cites papal encyclicals and church documents that refer explicitly to the fact of class struggle, and he gives several passages where John Paul II writes about social conflict. In the new edition he avoids expressions such as "combatting the oppressive class" and "to participate in class struggle"; he speaks rather of "opposing certain groups of persons" (who violate human rights) and of "solidarity with" or a "preferential option for" the poor.[41]

Ricardo Antoncich distinguishes between class conflict as a "fact" and Marxist "programatic class struggle." To acknowledge the fact, he observes, does not mean to favor or promote struggle as a method or strategy.[42] Gutiérrez might have avoided some of the difficulties he confronted if he had made a similar distinction in his first writing of *A Theology of Liberation*. Conflict does evoke struggle, and calling for the church to opt for the poor in their struggle could still be used legitimately. This call, however, should also involve a serious discussion of ethical norms to determine what "means" of struggle might be justified in resistance to injustice and what means could not be justified (for an obvious example, terrorist killing).

The Case of Nicaragua

Throughout the 1980s, no other country in Latin America has created more controversy or awakened more Christian interest than Nicaragua. From this perspective Nicaragua would certainly call for a separate chapter and could serve as the subject of an important book. A poll of liberation theologians would almost certainly show strong, if not unanimous, support for the "revolutionary process" in Nicaragua. It has represented the kind of hope for liberation of the poor that we associate with liberation theology. On the other hand, one could hardly view Nicaragua as a "product" of liberation theology. Liberation theologian Juan Hernández Pico and others have reflected on Nicaragua from a Christian perspective, but it has not served as a major subject in the works of liberation theology.[43] Too much emphasis on Nicaragua might also reinforce a wrong impression that liberation theology seeks to "overthrow" existing regimes through armed revolution.

Responding to the problem of how much attention to give to Nicaragua, and where to include it in this study, I will take up certain points about the "nature" of the Nicaraguan revolution as a conclusion to this chapter, and deal with the history of base communities in Nicaragua, and their relationship to the hierarchical church, as part of the next chapter on the church and ecclesiology. This concluding section will look especially to socialism in Nicaragua, taking up four points: an idealized Nicaragua as a socialist-liberation model; conflicting views of the reality in Nicaragua; the issue of democracy and social revolution; and some reflections on U.S. support for the Contras. The historical situation may obviously change significantly by the time this book is published.

An Idealized Nicaragua as a Socialist-Liberation Model. For most of the poor in Latin America liberation has remained a distant hope. In Nicaragua that hope seemed about to be realized with the overthrow of the Somoza dynasty in July 1979. Hopes soared after this victory, which many Nicaraguans proudly call "the Triumph." Unlike most previous revolutions, the victors did not avenge their sufferings with new violence. Instead they outlawed capital punishment and proclaimed a bill of rights that went far beyond traditional political rights. The new government proclaimed the right of every Nicaraguan to adequate food, to work, to an education, and to medical care. Somoza had piled up a $300 million fortune and had absconded with millions of dollars from the banks when he left. The country was saddled with a $1.6 billion debt. Still hopes ran high. Thousands of Nicaraguans joined in a vast literacy campaign that dramatically reduced illiteracy from 52 to 13 percent. Lands taken over from the Somoza family— some 20 percent of all the farmland—went into the creation of cooperative or state farms. The production and distribution of basic foods received a priority status. Significant gains were acheived in health care and education. Pax Christi, Amnesty International, and other human rights groups gave high marks to the Sandinista government in the first years after the "Triumph."[44]

If we could imagine Nicaragua without any negative features of Marxism, and could focus only on the Sandinistas' professed goals and some of the changes they have effected, we would have, I believe, an accurate picture of a society that liberation theologians and their more supportive critics would both embrace. It would be a country in which land reform was carried out, giving landless peasants new opportunities. It would be more autonomous by expanding its export markets to more countries and by adopting a nonaligned foreign policy. It would be self-determining by diversifying its production, while maintaining income from some exports. It would be a "mixed economy" with state banks and with some collective and state enterprises, but it would also retain and encourage private ownership and free enterprise. Socio-economic rights and basic needs would receive a high priority. Production of staple foods would be stressed, along with free or low-cost medical care for the poorest sectors, and efforts to eliminate illiteracy. At the same time political rights would be safeguarded. There would be open and fair elections, pluralism of political parties, an absence of government repression, allowance for trade unions, freedom of the press, and guaranteed freedom of religion.

Conflicting Views on the "Real" Nicaragua. Supporters of the revolutionary process believe that much in this idealized picture of Nicaragua matches the reality, and that the approximation would be much closer if the United States had allowed it freedom to develop. A surprise witness in favor of the process in Nicaragua came from John Cort who, as we have seen, strongly distrusts Marxist socialism. Cort returned from a visit to Nicaragua in 1986 and wrote quite positively about what he had seen.[45] Certainly the Sandinista government has had the very active support of the Catholic priests who took on important government positions: Fr. Miguel d'Escoto (Maryknoll) became foreign minister; Fr. Ernesto Cardenal (a Trappist-trained diocesan priest) served for several years as minister of culture; Fr. Edgar Paralles (Franciscan) first served as minister of social welfare and later as ambassador to the OAS; Fr. Fernando Cardenal (Jesuit) headed the literacy campaign and later became minister of education. Still other priests worked with the government in advisory capacities.

The Reagan administration quite obviously viewed the Sandinista government in a different light. It charged that the Sandinistas had betrayed the revolution by not permitting political freedom, and that they were self-proclaimed Marxist-Leninists who sought to subvert other Central American countries, constituting a threat as well to U.S. security. The United States used these arguments to justify financial aid to the Contras. In the early 1980s, the Reagan administration stressed chiefly the subversion-security arguments. Initial aid to the Contras came on the grounds that the Sandinistas were a major supplier of arms to guerilla forces in El Salvador. The U.S. administration viewed the buildup of the Nicaraguan army as motivated by aggressive aims. It judged the presence of Cuban and Soviet advisors and supplies as signs of communist domination. A visit of Nicaraguan President Daniel Ortega to Moscow was seen as a clear confirmation of these communist ties.

By the mid-1980s Reagan administration arguments focused much more on issues of democracy and political freedom. Aid to the Contras and a U.S. economic boycott would "pressure" the Sandinistas into making changes. The administration charged the Sandinistas with suppressing freedom of the press (the opposition paper *La Prensa*), with violations of human rights, with mistreatment of Miskito Indians in the northeast of Nicaragua, and with not allowing opposition candidates fair terms of operation in the elections of 1984. The United States would cite Cardinal Miguel Obando y Bravo and other members of the Catholic hierarchy who believed that the Sandinistas were undermining freedom of religion. The United States also pointed to discontent in Nicaragua brought on by deteriorating economic conditions with shortages of supplies and an inflation rate that soared to 20,000 percent in early 1989.

A thorough assessment of these conflicting views would require investigation of the factual basis of the charges, interpretation of the data, and determining how much of the violations that occurred stemmed from "Marxist" rule and how much from "war conditions." The Republican platform in 1980 called for "rolling back" the Sandinista rule. This goal preceded specific charges, and the Reagan administration used a "disinformation" strategy to gain support for its position. David MacMichael, who worked for the CIA studying arms flows from Nicaragua into El Salvador, testified that evidence was lacking to justify U.S. claims. The Sandinistas do have close ties with Cuba, but the buildup of the army and military resources could certainly be justified as defensive given the United States and Contra efforts to attack them. If Ortega's visit to Moscow put Nicaragua in the Moscow camp, a similar judgment could have applied to India's President Gandhi who visited Moscow and obtained arms supplies shortly before Ortega's visit. Violations of human rights have occurred, and the Sandinistas acknowledge failures in treatment of the Miskito Indians.[46] But these have taken place under war conditions, and they have not occurred at a level even approaching the tens of thousands executed in Guatemala and El Salvador (which also have no opposition presses to suppress). A group of European parliamentarians who observed the 1984 elections judged them fair, certainly in relation to elections elsewhere in Central America. A deeper issue, however, underlies the controversy about Nicaragua. It concerns the "real" aims of the Sandinistas, which opponents see as totalitarian and supporters believe really intend the good of the vast majority of Nicaraguans.

Democracy and Social Revolution. Opponents of the Sandinistas believe that they really disguised their true goals to win international support by proclaiming their support for political pluralism, a mixed economy, and freedom of religion. Many in the church hierarchy believe that the Sandinistas, while initially promising freedom of religion, really intend to displace religion with a Marxist form of "Sandinismo." This view of the Sandinistas' "real aims" was strongly voiced in Humberto Belli's work *Breaking Faith.* Belli had taken part in the Sandinista front from 1973 to 1975. He broke with the Sandinistas, converted to Catholicism, served as an editor of *La Prensa* and as an advisor to Obando y Bravo, left Nicaragua for the United States, and then wrote his book.

Belli claims to speak with authority as a former insider and he cites the Sandinistas' own documents to substantiate his charges. His major thesis can be briefly stated. The Sandinistas intended from the outset, and still intend, to impose the type of Marxist-Leninist rule characteristic of the Soviet Union and Eastern Europe: total political control by one party, a state-controlled, collectivist economy, the exclusion of any real pluralism, and toleration of religion only for religious groups that go along with the revolution. Belli argues that the Sandinistas' espousal of a mixed economy, of a plurality of political parties, and of freedom of religion only form part of a "transition plan" to give the appearance of democracy until the hard-line Marxist goals can become operative. Belli's attack also contains chapters dealing with evidence he believes shows widespread violations of human rights and of democratic freedoms even in this first stage. He sees the priests involved with the government as middle- or upper-class intellectuals out of touch with the people.[47]

Given Marxism's historical record, one can appreciate the distrust that opponents experience in respect to the Sandinistas, a distrust that Belli finds substantiated by the Sandinistas' own documents. A question arises, however, about interpretation of the documents. The secret Sandinista platform, cited by Belli, does speak of a tactical transition stage until socialism can be openly pursued: "Factors of a tactical and strategic order do not allow us to state, in this phase . . . [the goal of] socialism in an open manner . . . [but this] does not imply that we are for a bourgeois-democratic revolution."[48] But does this mean, as Belli goes on to claim, that the Sandinistas intend the same kind of rule that one finds in Cuba and Eastern Europe? It may mean this, but it may also mean that the Sandinistas do not want to sacrifice "social revolution" for the type of "democracy" so often characteristic of Latin American countries, where wealthy elites replace each other in elections and resist any significant social reform.

When the United States presses for political democracy in Nicaragua, it has in mind political elections, freedom of the press, and respect for private property. The United States has certainly not insisted that any government that might replace the Sandinistas must "guarantee" respect for the land reform policies now in place, must give first priority to the most basic needs of the majority (in food production, medical care, education, and housing), and must also guarantee proportionate representation of the peasants and workers in the legislative assembly of the government. But these goals, which concern the vast majority of Nicaraguans, constitute the very heart of a social revolution. They are goals that Sandinistas and their supporters fear would be lost if elections and traditional political rights comprised the only criteria for a free and just society.

Obviously the reverse of this, sacrificing political freedom to social goals, constitutes an equally serious problem. The traditional Leninist model in Marxist socialism gives power almost exclusively to the Communist Party; it establishes a "temporary" dictatorship of the proletariat to build up socialism and to exclude groups considered counterrevolutionary; and it promises that once the social transformation has occurred state power will wither away. In practice, the last step never comes. The question then becomes: "Is this the model being followed by the Sandinistas?" Some Sandinistas proclaim themselves Marxist-Leninists and the Sandinistas do speak of themselves as a "vanguard party." But "Sandinismo" involves much more than just Marxism. It involves Sandino's own vision (non-Marxist) of nationalism and *popular* control of economic resources and the political process. It also involves recognition of the basic religious beliefs of the people and input from Christianity.

The theme I heard and saw most discussed in Nicaragua among pro-Sandinista social scientists was the "necessity" for building democracy into the process. Democracy cannot be postponed. The dictatorship of the proletariat model, they argue, has proven ineffective for achieving true socialism in other countries. Open political participation *must accompany* the process of socio-economic transformation.[49] Supporters believe that this represents the Sandinistas' "true goals" and that the Sandinistas consider responding pragmatically to the people as more important than ideological faith in classic socialist goals. Thus, to cite an example noted to me, the Sandinistas have responded to peasant demands for their *own* land and have turned over some state farms. As a consequence state-controlled farms represented only 13 percent of the agriculture in Nicaragua in 1988; the rest was privately owned (some of it by cooperatives).

U.S. Aid to the Contras. In these last few paragraphs I have tried to present the Sandinista goals in a more favorable light. Unlike enthusiastic supporters of the Nicaraguan revolutionary process, however, I still retain some serious misgivings. In the late 1980s Nicaragua's economy deteriorated badly. The cost of the war against the Contras, U.S. efforts to force Nicaragua into failure, and the natural disaster of hurricane Joan certainly played major parts in this deterioration. But Sandinista policies and poor administration undoubtedly contributed also. On a political level, Nicaragua could become more repressive and adopt hard-line Marxist-Leninist tactics (though I did not see anything approaching totalitarianism in my visits there). But to move from this possibility to supporting aid for the

Contras violates, in my judgment, the moral principles of the "just war" theory.

For most of the 1980s the U.S. Congress debated the issue of aid to the Contras mostly on the grounds of "hope for success." Had the Contras demonstrated a clear ability to win, congressional opposition to aid might have withered. But far more is involved ethically. Certainly one could hardly argue with any objectivity that military war constitutes a "last resort," that the United States has exhausted every effort to achieve a peaceful solution. The Contadora plan and then the "Arias" plan showed clearly the presence of alternatives to a military solution.

More decisive, however, are considerations of "proportionality" — whether the good to be achieved outweighs the bad. *If* the Contras had won, one has to show clearly that their rule would be significantly better for Nicaragua than present Sandinista rule. Given the military leadership of hated ex-Somoza guards and the Contra record of rape, torture, and brutality, faith in their good intentions seems hardly plausible. But proportionality also involves much more; it asks whether the costs of victory outweigh victory itself. The Nicaraguan people had lost twenty-five thousand lives by 1987 in the fight against the Contras. Given the population of Nicaragua (about 3 million), this means that the Nicaraguans have already suffered more losses proportionately than the United States did in *all* its wars of this century (World War I, World War II, Korea, Vietnam). Moreover, even military defeat of the Sandinistas would not bring an end to violence but only the likelihood of new guerilla warfare. One has to picture the Sandinistas as incredibly evil to justify such sufferings.

This rather long discussion of Nicaragua has drawn us away from liberation theology proper, but it does relate importantly to the question of socialism and liberation goals. The case of Nicaragua, however, can create the wrong impression, as we noted earlier, that liberation theology envisions the overthrow of existing regimes. Even in Central America, liberation theologians I met hope for peaceful solutions achieved in a way that will enable social transformation to occur. In South America, as we will see in the chapter to follow, a strategy of involvement in the political process appears clearly dominant.

ECCLESIAL ISSUES

Chapter 10

A New Way of Being Church

In planning this book I tried to follow a logical progression within liberation theology: from an awareness of poverty and the faith response it
elicits, to social analysis about the structural causes of poverty, and then to
calling upon the church to break away from its traditional alignments and
to place itself with the poor in their struggle for liberation. If we look,
however, at the original impetuses for liberation theology, we might well
have begun with the church. It was the church, represented by the bishops
at Medellín, which first gave public expression to liberation themes. Moreover, Gutiérrez's ground-breaking work *A Theology of Liberation* seemed
clearly addressed to the church in Latin America and not just to interested
individuals. In the introduction to his work Gutiérrez asserts that the theological meaning of liberation is a question "about the very meaning of
Christianity and about the mission of the church." Christian faith and the
church are being radically challenged, said Gutiérrez, to show what significance they have to the liberation process underway in Latin America, and
"the greater part of our study is concerned with this aspect."[1]

Gutiérrez's message was clear. The church must become politically involved with the poor and with their struggles to liberate themselves from
poverty and oppression. The church cannot evade involvement by claiming
that its mission deals with the spiritual and not with the temporal. The
"two-planes" distinction, which relates the church only indirectly to the
temporal through the inspiration of its moral teachings, breaks down in
practice and too often conceals the church's real political option—support
for the status quo. The very presence of the church has "an inescapable
political dimension."[2] The church needs to rethink its mission. Its purpose
is not simply to "save" in the sense of guaranteeing heaven; the work of
salvation occurs in history. Humans have a single fulfillment, which involves
an integration of the spiritual and the temporal, of this world and the next.[3]
Consequently, "in Latin America, the church must place itself squarely
within the process of revolution . . . its mission is defined more by the political context than by intraecclesial problems."[4] It must express its presence
by denouncing unjust and dehumanizing situations in the present order,

197

and by announcing a utopian vision of what society should be. It must denounce "sinful situations" and reject any use of Christianity to legitimize the present order, and must announce the need to transform society.[5] To do all this the church must also recognize the fact of class struggle and opt for the side of the poor. "The class struggle is a fact, and neutrality in this matter is impossible."[6]

When Gutiérrez first wrote about the need for the church to become involved, the word "church" most often signified the institutional church: its bishops, priests, religious men and women, and pastoral agents. This church, Gutiérrez hoped, would become a church "for" the poor. Gutiérrez desired from the outset, however, to move beyond efforts to convert the institutional church to service of the poor. Support from this church had to come as a first step, but Gutiérrez affirms in the conclusion to *A Theology of Liberation:*

> We will have an authentic theology of liberation only when the op-
> pressed themselves can freely raise their voice and express themselves
> directly and creatively in society and in the heart of the people of
> God, when they themselves "account for the hope," which they bear,
> when they are the protagonists of their own liberation.[7]

In the years since Gutiérrez first wrote these words, significant changes have occurred in the church in Latin America. Within society as a whole the poor still lack sufficient voice and strength to act as "the protagonists of their own liberation." But they have succeeded in far greater measure to "express themselves directly and creatively" within the church, in the "heart of the people of God." A major embodiment of this new voice within the church has come through the extraordinary development of basic (or base) ecclesial communities.

The first part of this chapter will focus on these basic communities. Brazil will serve as the principal model in discussing the historical development of basic communities and their distinguishing notes. Base communities in Nicaragua followed a very different path of development and they will receive special attention. This chapter will also take up the political signif-icance of base communities and how they translate liberation theology into "praxis" in various countries. The following chapter will then study a new ecclesiology that draws upon the base community experience. It will also include discussions about the relation of base communities to the church and of the church in relation to society.

Basic Ecclesial Communities

In recent years liberation theologians have directed their attention in-creasingly to the growing phenomenon of basic communities, which express a new presence of the church among the poor. Since the formation of the first such communities in Brazil, in the mid-1960s, their numbers have expanded dramatically. Estimates about the numbers vary considerably. In Brazil they probably number some eighty-thousand to one hundred thousand groups, with one to two million members. The Brazilian communities represent perhaps half of the communities in Latin America overall.[8]

Base communities, it should be noted at the outset, constitute only a small part of church involvement with the poor. In Peru, for example, only a fraction of church work with the poor concerns formation of the type of base communities one finds in Brazil. In the poor barrio of El Augustino on the outskirts of Lima, church efforts involve work with literally hundreds of organizations—mothers clubs, youth groups, education centers, workers groups, etc.—some of them church inspired and organized, others part of "popular movements" supported by the church. The same would hold true for parishes and church groups in many other parts of Latin America. Even in Brazil many groups do not fit neatly into the base community model. Consequently, some liberation theologians use the phrase "base communities" as a generic term to refer to all types of Christian-based, grass-roots groups among the poor rather than as a specific term referring to the small, Bible-centered, reflection groups treated most explicitly in this chapter.

The models of involvement differ from country to country, but the evangelizing and organizing efforts remain similar. The stress in base communities on community faith-sharing and community organizing, with responsibility taken on by the poor themselves, characterize the modes of operation found in Peruvian parishes and in other popular Christian groups that function in the spirit of liberation theology. ("Popular" denotes "of the people," not "a current fad.") In a broad sense, then, the basic ecclesial communities can be considered as a general expression of liberation theology in practice. Liberation theology and the base communities grew together out of the same impetus to reach the poor, but now one can quite generally say that the communities embody the spirit of liberation theology (certainly in its broadest sense). In turn they provide theologians with a major source for theological reflection.

The Development of Basic Ecclesial Communities in Brazil

The formation of the first base communities in Brazil occurred about 1963. Their creation, however, came as a result of pastoral initiatives in preceding years. As in many other countries in Latin America, the Catholic Church in Brazil ended the nineteenth century with serious internal weaknesses and very limited influence on society. The new century brought new hope and new efforts to revitalize the church. The 1930s especially marked a time when the church sought to "regain the world for Christ" and to christianize society. Catholic Action groups formed, along with groups modeled after the organizations created by Canon Joséph Cardijn in Belgium: the Young Christian Workers, Young Christian Students, Catholic University Youth, and others. To unify the efforts of the church a Brazilian national conference of bishops was created in 1952, through the initiative of Dom Helder Câmara who would become one of the strongest prophetic voices for the poor in decades to follow.[9]

A shortage of priests prompted many efforts to use the laity more effectively in evangelizing society and in attempting to counter the inroads made by Protestantism and the influence of spiritism and Marxism among the poor. Accounts of the origins of the base community movement tell one story (perhaps somewhat apocryphal), which indicates the pastoral concerns that prompted a response from the institutional church. According to the story, an old woman spoke to the bishop during a pastoral visit in her area. She lamented that at Christmas the Protestant churches were lit up and crowded, while the Catholic Church remained closed and in darkness because no priest was available.[10] Moved by this comment, the bishop of Barra do Pirai, Dom Angelo Rossi, organized a lay missionary movement to provide "Masses without a priest" and other religious services in the area. He mobilized lay catechists who would gather Catholics together to pray and listen to scripture. Many catechists served also as community coordinators and organized teaching of religion, basic literacy skills, and trades.

In the state capital of Natal (northeastern Brazil) a similar movement was launched with an added goal of creating treatment centers for diseases and malnutrition. The "Natal Movement" made special use of radio programs designed to teach basic literacy, to raise the consciousness of the population about problems, and to instruct in the faith. By 1963 some 1,410 radio schools had formed in the diocese of Natal alone.

Paulo Freire initiated a new method of popular education in the northeast of Brazil during the late 1950s and early 60s. Working at first out of the University of Recife, Freire used ideas and techniques of adult education that would gain world renown. His "pedagogy of the oppressed" stressed respect for the popular classes and their abilities. Freire insisted that educators serve as facilitators, enabling the poor to develop their own ideas in confrontation with their living situations, rather than simply "imparting" knowledge to them. Learning must be an active process through which the poor could come to their own decisions and gain greater control over their lives.

In 1961 the church launched its own Movement for Grass-roots Education (MEB). Like Paulo Freire's method, the guiding idea behind the MEB approach to popular education stressed enabling the poor to become agents of their own destiny. It rejected elitist approaches that made traditional politicians or leftist "vanguard parties" the principal agents of change. But it also stressed the importance of a "conscientization" process that encouraged persons to see their problems as part of issues in the larger society, and it declared itself in favor of a radical transformation of society.[11]

The beginnings of the base community movement certainly owed much to these efforts in popular education. The communities did not start, however, as part of any determined plan. Historians of the movement give 1963 to 1964 as the time when base communities began to form, but with little detail as to where or how they were formed. (Significantly, their beginnings coincided with the 1964 meeting of theologians at Petrópolis that initiated the process of liberation theology.)

Political events in Brazil significantly affected the first stage of base community development and the more general development of a "popular church." The spirit of reform and calls for radical change fit well with the politics of the Goulart government in the early 1960s, but came to a screeching halt with the military takeover in 1964. Paulo Freire was forced to leave the country; conservative bishops took over leadership positions in the national bishops' conference, and they reined in the politicizing of the MEB. The Young Christian Workers movement (JOC) dwindled from twenty-six thousand members in 1961 to 654 by 1968. The once influential Popular Action group of the Catholic left slowly disintegrated. It had become strongly Marxist in orientation by 1964; in the early 1970s the remaining members formed a Maoist party and later joined the Communist Party of Brazil.[12] The hierarchical church gave initial support to the military regime, thanking it for rescuing the country from the threat of communism. The base communities remained too incipient to have any significant voice.

As evidence of brutal repression by the military government became more evident in the late 1960s and early 70s, the Catholic Church began again to assert itself. With almost every other source of dissent suppressed, the church became the lone voice able to speak out against human rights violations and to protest conditions of the poor. If many bishops condemned torture and repression, others spoke out forcefully in defense of landless peasants—including peasants driven off lands they once farmed. In 1973 the bishops of the Amazon region and bishops in northeastern Brazil produced documents that historian Scott Mainwaring claims "were probably the most radical statements ever issued by a group of bishops anywhere in the world."[13] They condemned the violence perpetrated against Indians and peasants, and judged the capitalist system as the root of the poverty, hunger, and death inflicted upon the poor in their area. The per capita income in northeastern Brazil was barely more than one-fourth of that in the rest of the country. The church itself became a victim of brutal repression. According to one report, from 1964 to 1978 some 347 religious leaders were arrested in Brazil, including two bishops and 185 priests. Three priests were assassinated, many were tortured, and twenty seven expelled from the country. Bishop Adriano Hypólito was taken, stripped, and sprayed with red paint.[14] The church, however, grew stronger and the number of base communities grew dramatically.

Characteristics of Basic Ecclesial Communities

The basic communities developed in various locales, but predominantly in rural areas or in the slum peripheries of large cities. The communities vary in size, usually between ten to thirty persons in a group. They come together about once a week to read scripture, to pray, to sing hymns, and to discuss problems and how to act upon them. In the beginning many referred to the groups simply as base communities or as Christian base communities. But the expression "basic ecclesial communities" became more accepted to stress their relation to the church as a whole. Each word in their title has special significance, as Marcello Azevedo explains in his study.

The groups are "communities," not just weekly discussion groups. They strive to form a mutual support group, sharing in each other's cares and struggles. In some cases they represent the principal life of the church, though they generally retain a linkage to a parish center for important occasions like baptisms, weddings, funerals, and full eucharistic liturgies.[15]

The communities are "ecclesial." While they sometimes become politically involved, faith constitutes their common base and their reason for forming. In Brazil, says Azevedo, they owe the initiative for their founding to the bishops. The 1984 Vatican instruction on liberation theology cautioned about base communities becoming divorced from the church and growing into a "popular church" in opposition to the official, institutional church. As we shall see, the church in Nicaragua has struggled with this tension because of division in the church over support for, or opposition to, the Sandinista government. In Brazil, while some church divisions exist, the bishops and base communities appear more closely allied. As for the church in Latin America as a whole, the documents from Medellín and Puebla, while voicing some cautions, expressed clear affirmation of the base communities. Medellín called for more ecclesial base communities to be formed.[16] Puebla affirmed: "We are happy to single out the multiplication of small communities as an important ecclesial event that is particularly ours, and as the 'hope of the church.' "[17]

These communities are "of the base" in a sociological sense primarily. They constitute the poor, simple, marginalized persons in Latin American society. Thus the poorest sectors of society have the "good news preached to them," or more accurately they share actively in discussing the word of God in their lives — as opposed to being more passive listeners. They also begin to recognize their potential for organizing together to work for social change.

Azevedo sees the basic communities in Brazil as initiating several important shifts in the way the church operates: a shift from clerical hegemony to the active presence of lay persons and religious women in the evangelical and apostolic work of the church; a shift from an overly spiritualist approach to a broad comprehensive view that incorporates human material needs as well; a shift from treating persons as objects of evangelization to respecting them as active subjects of their own spiritual development; a shift from a hierarchical, institutional church playing a protective role to the model of a church of service; a shift from seeing transformation as something always effected from the top down to endorsement of creativity from the bottom up; and a shift from an emphasis on starting with theory to using reality and experience as the basis for reflection.[18]

Guillermo Cook organizes his study of the base communities under the headings of four "fundamental orientations": (1) a new way of seeing reality; (2) a new way of being church; (3) a new way of approaching scripture; and (4) a new way of understanding mission.[19]

A new way of seeing reality involves conscientization, along the lines first developed by Paulo Freire. Traditionally the poor have felt fatalistic about their situation. Pastoral agents help the poor to recognize the structural causes of their poverty and to believe that working in solidarity as a community they can effect change. This often involves suspicion and criticism of prevailing ideologies: for example, not accepting what landowners or government officials say to legitimize their authority. The Marxist critique plays some role in this, says Cook, but Brazilian theologian J.B. Libânio makes greater use of Peter Berger's "sociology of knowledge," showing how certain ways of thinking become dominant in society. As Paulo Freire recognized, this process carries with it a risk. Pastoral agents should act as facilitators, enabling the poor to develop their own ideas and praxis; but the agents have sometimes violated this, injecting what they think the poor should think or do.[20] Pastoral agents acknowledge this difficulty and know that enabling the poor to take responsibility lies at the very heart of the movement.

The new way of being church involves many of the "shifts" noted by Azevedo, above all giving the poor a sense that they are the church. They take an active role in liturgies and in evangelizing each other. The church becomes less of a "sacrament-instrument" offering grace to them; it becomes instead a "sacrament-sign" of Christ working salvation within the community. The second part of this chapter, on ecclesiology, will say more about this new way of being church.

The new way of approaching scripture lies at the heart of the base community movement. Faith constitutes the bond of a base community. A group that meets only to discuss and act on problems would not qualify as a base ecclesial community. Members meet to discuss their problems, but "in the light of scripture." They recognize the stories of the Bible as dealing with persons like themselves in situations like their own. Carlos Mesters has pioneered in translating Bible stories and teachings into the language of the poor, and of raising questions that will open up scripture for them. Pastoral agents may help in raising questions, but the process depends on members themselves seeing the relation between scripture and their own lives. Cook cites examples of how this occurs. A reading of Luke's account of the nativity provoked a discussion on the humiliations and hardships that mothers in the group had experienced. A question about why Jesus chose to be born poor and humble led a young woman to observe that "he chose to be poor like us so that we can realize that we are important."[21]

The new way of understanding mission relates closely to the "preferential option for the poor" given priority by the bishops at Puebla. The base communities have certainly become a major focus of this option, but interpretations of what this should involve differ. The more conservative bishops stress evangelization as the primary sense of this mission; progressive bishops and liberation theologians want to ensure that conscientization and liberation remain integral to the process of evangelization.[22] In Brazil and elsewhere the tension in emphases remains, along with tension between hierarchical control over the movement and allowing broad participation in planning from the bottom up. These tensions are most clearly evident in the case of the church in Nicaragua.

The Church and Base Communities in Nicaragua

Relations between the church hierarchy and the base communities appear most affected by cohesion or conflict over political positions and relative harmony or dissent on authority issues. In Brazil, while a few bishops oppose political involvement in general, the national conference of bishops has voted for strong pastoral letters on human rights, land reform, and other social issues, with nearly unanimous voice. In addition, no real fear of a Marxist-oriented government has threatened a division in the ranks, at least not since the early 1960s. The Brazilian bishops also look upon the base community movement as a product, in part at least, of their own initiatives. Many bishops have theological views closely attuned to those of liberation theology, and many in the base communities, in turn, revere many bishops as champions of their cause. In Nicaragua, in contrast, the church is sharply divided about the Sandinista government. The hierarchy generally views it as Marxist-Leninist, while base communities tend to view it as the defender of a revolutionary process in which they feel very much a part. In terms of origins and development the base communities and popular church movements never had the same kind of endorsement in Nicaragua that they had in Brazil.

The origins of the base communities in Nicaragua have a much clearer starting point in Nicaragua than in Brazil. In 1966 Father José de la Jara created a base community in the parish of San Pablo in Managua and it became a "mother church" and model for others. The Medellín conference inspired a small group of young priests to create more base communities and to direct the work of the church toward the poor. Base communities were formed in Managua, along the Atlantic coast, in rural areas in the north of Esteli, and on the island of Solentiname.[23]

Nicaragua also had its equivalent of Brazil's politicized Catholic youth groups. In 1970 a group of students at the Catholic Central American University (UCA) challenged the university's curriculum for failing to address Nicaragua's socio-economic problems. They attempted a takeover of the school, and this led to other takeovers and protests against human rights violations by the government. A group of students and some priests occupied the cathedral in Managua as an expression of protest. The government arrested more than a hundred students and had them expelled from the university. Out of this student movement the Revolutionary Christian Movement was formed, with Fr. Fernando Cardenal as one of its founders. Fr. Uriel Molina, who would later become head of the ecumenical Antonio Valdivieso Center, integrated students into his work with base communities in the Barrio Rugiero in Managua, and after a time they forged contacts with the Sandinista Front.

Other "popular" Catholic movements developed in the 1970s, geared toward serving the poor. The Capuchins working along the Atlantic coast began training delegates of the Word: lay ministers who could coordinate and provide religious services to communities in the absence of priests, and who also helped to provide health services and to teach vocational and literacy skills. On the west coast, the Jesuits created a Center for Agrarian Education and Promotion (CEPA), using delegates of the Word for religious instruction and to teach agricultural skills. Soon CEPA's work turned more toward conscientization and organizing peasants to promote their rights. It kept some of its Christian character but became independent of the Jesuits and of church affiliation after 1977.

On the isle of Solentiname in the late 1960s, Fr. Ernesto Cardenal developed a faith-sharing community of persons from different walks of life. They became increasingly politicized during the 1970s, and in 1977 members of the Solentiname community joined in an attack on a national guard post near the Costa Rican border. Ernesto Cardenal declared his allegiance to the Sandinista front. In retaliation, the guard attacked Solentiname and burned it to the ground.[24] Others from these different groups also joined with the Sandinistas or lent their support to anti-Somoza protests. After the overthrow of Somoza, members of the base communities and persons trained in the groups noted above would become active supporters of the Sandinistas and of the new revolutionary process.

The base communities at the time of the overthrow numbered only about three hundred with some five thousand members.[25] They have remained relatively small in number, but they represent some of the most committed Catholic activists.

The Catholic hierarchy in Nicaragua had traditionally served as a support for the government. The bishops there had declared in a 1950 pastoral letter that "when you obey the government . . . you perform acts that constitute obedience to God."[26] But they became more critical as evidence of repression and corruption in the Somoza government became more evident. In 1977 they published a letter denouncing torture and repression, enumerating specific cases, and they criticized the inequitable distribution of wealth in the country. Opposition to Somoza became widespread in the late 1970s and many church figures became more involved. Frs. Miguel d'Escoto and Fernando Cardenal formed part of a group of "Twelve" leading citizens who sought Somoza's removal. Pedro Joaquin Chamarro, editor of *La Prensa*, belonged to the Twelve. His assassination in 1978 turned public opinion dramatically against Somoza.

Bishop Miguel Obando y Bravo opposed Somoza in his final years in power, and shortly before the overthrow he declared that in the judgment of some moral theologians armed insurrection could be justified. The bishop's distrust of the Sandinistas, however, appears to have been present from the outset. Prior to the July 1979 triumph, Obando y Bravo traveled to Caracas to support a U.S. plan that would give power to a non-Somoza, non-Sandinista government. When the Sandinistas did assume power, the bishops adopted as an official stance that the church should retain its independence from the government, free to approve or criticize its actions. The bishops believed that having priests in the government compromised this independence. The enthusiastic support of the base communities for the new revolutionary government also impaired the church's position, in the judgment of the bishops.

In November 1979 the bishops issued a pastoral letter warmly supporting the hopes and aspirations a new socialist program might fulfill. Even this initial letter, however, warned of the dangers of a "false socialism" that might manipulate persons and depend on totalitarian rule. The fears of the bishops appeared focused especially on suspicions that the Sandinistas intended to establish a Marxist-Leninist state. The last chapter spoke about Humberto Belli's *Breaking Faith*, which claimed that the Sandinistas were disguising their "real aims" (Marxist-Leninist rule) with a transitional plan that claimed to respect religious freedom and political pluralism to gain international support. The bishops seemed to share this view. (Belli served for a time as an advisor to Obando y Bravo; critics of the bishop say that he also relies on views of leaders in the wealthier business community.) The bishops feared that the whole system of education, in particular, would become infected with Marxist ideas, and that Sandinismo would be used as a substitute for faith in Christianity.

In October 1980, addressing these fears, the Sandinista front published a statement on religion. It praised bishops who had taken stands against Somoza and affirmed that Christians had been an "integral part" of the recent revolutionary history of the country. It asserted that freedom to profess a religious faith is an inalienable right, which the revolutionary government would fully guarantee. The bishops responded with skepticism, however, expressing concern about Nicaragua's becoming a one-party state guided by atheistic values.[27]

The presence of priests in the government (see chapter 6) served to legitimize the Sandinista government, in the eyes of the bishops, who also felt that the base communities were more committed to the government than to the church. Both of these raised problems, they believed, with maintaining church authority. The bishops first called on the priests to resign from the government in May 1980; the Sandinista government sent a delegation to Rome to lobby for their retention. In June 1981 the hierarchy again called for the priests' resignation; later that year an agreement was reached allowing the priests to remain in the government but not allowing them to celebrate Mass and administer sacraments. (In 1984 Fernando Cardenal was told that he must either leave his position or quit the Jesuits; he chose to remain in his government post and withdrew officially from the Society of Jesus but he still lives out his vows in a Jesuit community.)

Pope John Paul II focused on the authority issue both in a 1982 letter to the church in Nicaragua and in his visit to Nicaragua in 1983 when "obedience to your bishops" became the principal message of his homily. The Nicaraguan bishops and church authorities at CELAM clearly influenced his perceptions about Nicaragua. They sent a memo to Rome to instruct the pope about conditions in Nicaragua in preparation for his 1983 visit. The memo, leaked to a journal in Spain, judged the Sandinistas to be a Marxist-Leninist government, "in short, an enemy" of the church with whom no accommodation was possible.[28]

Numerous issues created tension between the government and the Catholic hierarchy: a letter of the bishops condemning Sandinista treatment of the Miskito Indians (though the bishops rejected an invitation by the government to visit the Atlantic coast and judge the situation first hand); a Holy Week sermon in which Obando y Bravo referred to Judas as a *compañero* (the favorite term of solidarity used by the Sandinistas); a scandal or frameup (depending on whose story one believes) involving Fr. Bismark Carballo, director of Radio Católica; the bad feelings engendered during the pope's visit in 1983; the expulsion of Bishop Pablo Antonio Vega for statements made in support of the Contras during a trip to the United States; the government closing or censoring of Catholic radio broadcasts, and so forth. The bishops' criticism of compulsory military service created special conflicts. The government claimed that all governments in time of war require military service; the bishops claimed that the army represented the Sandinistas and not the nation as a whole.

While Cardinal Obando y Bravo may have intended to remain an independent critic, his words were used in the United States to gain support for Contra aid. Many Contras and Contra supporters, moreover, viewed him as a hero. The Sandinista government did agree, however, to naming him as a mediator with the Contras in the first phase of Sandinista-Contra negotiations in 1987. (Early in 1988 they moved to direct negotiations.)

Protestant conflicts with the government have been less pronounced. Mainline Protestant churches have maintained a fairly flexible attitude. Many remain "critically supportive" of the government. A Committee for Aid and Development, first created to aid victims of the 1974 earthquake, developed many additional social projects that have assisted government social goals. The Moravians, concentrated among the Miskito Indians on the East coast, have tried to resolve problems with the government. More underlying conflict exists in respect to Pentecostal and fundamentalist groups that have accounted for most of the dramatic growth of Protestantism in Nicaragua since 1979. Protestants, together with groups like the Mormons, Jehovah Witnesses, and Seventh Day Adventists, have grown from about 3 percent of the population in 1979 to over 15 percent in 1985. The more fundamentalist groups tend to be strongly anti-Marxist but express this more in the form of otherworldly religious indoctrination rather than in antigovernment political protest. Their very growth would seem to testify to the absence of religious persecution. One Episcopal bishop has testified that he does not find any religious persecution.[29]

The Catholic hierarchy's suspicion and opposition to the Sandinistas revolve nearly always, as we have seen, on questions regarding Marxism and its perceived threat to religion and political freedom. Christians who support the revolutionary process in Nicaragua believe that the label "Marxist," with all its negative connotations, does not accurately describe all that is distinctive of the Sandinistas and their goals. Fr. César Jerez, the Jesuit president of the Central American University in Managua, argues that the Sandinistas pay far more attention to Nicaraguan history in forming their policies than to doctrinal Marxism. He acknowledges that the Sandinista directorate includes some dogmatic Marxists who would welcome an end to religion, but he says the majority of Sandinistas hold varying views of religion ranging from pragmatic acceptance of it (even if they personally remain atheists), through nonpracticing believers, to some with a fervent faith in Christianity.[30] The Sandinistas have publicly guaranteed freedom of religion; they have subsidized Catholic schools; they printed coins with "In God We Trust" (with Sandino on the other side). Certainly no typical Marxist regime has ever included priests in key government roles, especially not in the influential position of minister of education held by Fr. Fernando Cardenal.

The future may resolve questions as to the real nature and intentions of Sandinista rulers, but they also may leave the questions in doubt. If Nicaragua becomes more totalitarian, present supporters of the Sandinistas could argue that U.S. hostility and church opposition forced them in this direction; if Nicaragua becomes more democratic, present critics may argue that U.S. pressure and church criticism of the Sandinistas moved them to be more open.

In all of this, liberation theology plays only an indirect part. It has not directly influenced events in Nicaragua, but the hopes engendered by the revolutionary process in that country have reflected the hopes of liberation theologians as well.

The Political Context: Praxis and Influence of Base Communities

One writer, in analyzing the new dynamic of grass-roots Christian community movements in Latin America, offers three models of how they relate to society. In countries like Brazil, during the period of its authoritarian military rule, the church and popular religious movements have acted as surrogates for political activism in the absence of other agents for change. In Central America, popular religious movements began as protests but have seen some of their activists cross over, in frustration, into insurrectionist movements. In countries with conservative hierarchies and relatively stable governments, like Colombia and Mexico, popular religious activism has been greatly contained.[31]

These classifications provide a helpful starting point for looking at different situations in Latin America, but they can also indicate the limits of any attempts at generalization. Not only do conditions change, but the response of the church is often quite different in countries with very similar political contexts. In Brazil, the church (both the hierarchy and the base community movement) did indeed act as a surrogate for other political groups during the late 1960s and through the 1970s. The church finds itself in a different position now with the restoration of civilian government. In Argentina, however, a very conservative hierarchy remained silent in the face of an authoritarian military rule despite the arrest and disappearance of thousands of Argentinian citizens. The socio-economic situation of Argentina also differs considerably from Brazil. Argentina does not have a massive, landless peasant population or any significant number of indigenous Indians. Hence popular activism has its roots there in the traditional working class. In Chile, the hierarchy has spoken out on human rights violations, but not with the force of bishops in Brazil. Church groups have significant involvement with the poor—half of the women religious in Chile work with base community groups—but the government suppresses efforts at popular mobilization or exerts its own control in the popular sectors by creating or taking over programs dealing with health, education, and housing for the poor.[32]

In Central America, the pattern of radicalization that developed in Nicaragua during the 1970s occurred in other countries as well. El Salvador certainly experienced the phenomenon of priests, delegates of the Word, and base community members strongly engaged in land reform and other social issues, and this involvement led some to join with armed revolutionary forces.[33] Some base communities remain very much in sympathy with these forces, but a longing for a peaceful, just resolution of conflict seems quite evident now. The popular Christian movements in Nicaragua, as indicated earlier, have shifted from opposition against Somoza to support for the Sandinistas with all the church conflicts that shift has entailed. In sharp contrast to these, Costa Rica represents the exception in Central America, with a stable democracy and a generally "centrist" social consensus and no strong political forces at either extreme (radical left or right-wing reactionary).

Colombia merits very special attention because relations between the church and society there reflect the influential thinking of Cardinal López

Trujillo and CELAM, and may quite possibly also reflect the Vatican's views on how base communities should operate and how liberation theology should express itself. The hierarchical church in Colombia speaks of an option for the poor and claims it has great numbers of base communities. The church is well organized and has a large network of religious and social programs. These programs, however, are also very carefully administrated, monitored, and controlled by the institutional church. Authority and unity are important concepts in the structuring of church activity. The hierarchy guides the choosing and training of pastoral agents. Its conception of the church is traditional: pastoral agents serve to carry out the mission of the bishops. Using an implied "Christendom" model, the church sees itself as the guardian of the morals and values of society. Its view of social change, a view shared by the government, emphasizes harmony and cooperation between social classes and abhors "class conflict." Its base communities do not arise "from the people" nor are they encouraged to exercise any autonomous self-determination. Many of them, in fact, are simply older organizations that have been renamed.[34]

The church in Mexico would fall under the same classification as Colombia with a conservative hierarchy reluctant to disturb church-state relations, fearing a return to the virulent anticlericalism and open persecution of the church that marked relations earlier in the century. Base communities, on the other hand, flourish and have more autonomy than in Colombia, and many liberation theologians (Dussel, Vidales, Miranda, and others) have made Mexico a home.

Many other Latin American countries would be difficult to fit into the tripartite division noted at the beginning of this section. Ecuador and Bolivia have fairly strong base community movements. Peru, the home of Gustavo Gutiérrez and of a summer school of liberation theology that draws upwards of two thousand persons each year, certainly remains an important base for liberation theology. Its political situation differs considerably from other countries noted thus far. It had its recent period of military rule (1968–1975), but its military were leftist in orientation and they nationalized some foreign corporations and introduced land reform programs. The changes, however, which liberation critics considered too "top-down" in nature, left the economy even weaker and it has not recovered since. Peru has its insurrection groups, the Shining Path and Tupac Amaru, but organizations and communities inspired by liberation theology have opposed them. The election of a charismatic, popular president, Alan García, spurred hopes initially but economic and social conditions deteriorated after he took office.[35] The church in Peru also presents a very different picture. Some bishops have actively supported liberation theology; others have vigorously denounced it. For a time, in the mid-1980s, it appeared that the Peruvian bishops, under the urging of Cardinal Ratzinger, might condemn Gutiérrez and liberation theology. Instead they published a document that affirmed liberation theology, though it included as correctives points made in the two Vatican instructions.[36] The conflict did not end there, however; critics prevailed and the pope issued new stern warnings during his May 1988 visit to Peru.

Peru has a great number of popular Christian organizations, and many priests, religious, and laity work with the poor. The church has not concentrated as much on small base communities as they are understood in Brazil, but its groups have much the same spirit and dynamics.

In discussing the issue of "democracy" in the last chapter, I noted the new direction this has given to the praxis of liberation theology. The assembly of Latin American theologians meeting in Mexico in 1986 singled out building up a new form of democracy and using the "space" created by democracy as important priorities. Peru and Brazil both illustrate the form this new direction has taken. In Peru, the political left (noninsurrectionist) emphasizes the building up of popular sectors through participatory democracy at community levels. Socialist-oriented groups criticize "centralized" models of government.[37] The Peruvian economist Javier Iguíñiz, a consultant to Gutiérrez and the principal author of the government plan of the United Left, stresses building up the power of the poor to exercise their own decision-making so that they can learn to participate politically as well as economically at every level of society. The pastoral practice of priests, religious, and lay leaders focuses increasingly on programs of "self-help" through mobilizing popular organizations and not looking to the government or the church to "provide" basic needs and assistance.

In Brazil, Clodovis Boff noted in my interview with him, the main project at present consists of building and occupying "spaces" where the poor can have their own say at a community level and can begin to gain political experience to represent their interests at a higher level.

In an essay reflecting on the changes underway in Latin America, Charles Reilly describes the new dynamic as a form of "religious populism," which he compares to grass-roots agrarian protests in the United States toward the end of the nineteenth century. This religious populism, he notes, differs considerably from the state-heavy, top-down, charismatic-leader type of change that the term "populism" usually suggests in Latin America: for example, the populism of Juan Perón in Argentina or Getulio Vargas in Brazil. The religious populism derives not from the state but comes out of *society*. It involves organizing "excluded" sectors of society through cooperatives, base communities, and other popular organizations that operate with considerable autonomy.[38]

In extended trips to Latin America in 1981 and 1988, one of my principal objectives was to determine how communities and groups that espouse liberation theology translate their commitment into practice. Contrary to stereotyped pictures of liberationists stirring up revolutions, the actual practice most resembles what North Americans would call "community organizing." The problems most often addressed turn toward the communities' needs for clean water, sewage disposal, electricity, paved roads, food and education for children, health care, and job skills. In areas where land reform is a key issue, the process of conscientization and organizing can lead to strongly conflictual situations. At some point the efforts at "self-help" run into unjust structures that block the possibility of further development. Conflict becomes inevitable if owners refuse to change. In labor union organizing and other spheres where vested interests stand opposed to change, conflict may also occur (usually initiated by those in power). Most work of base communities, however, involves cooperative efforts of members rather than struggles of conflict, and the groups clearly opt for nonviolent methods of change.

The political influence of base communities would be difficult to judge. To picture them as a powerful new socio-political force would be to misjudge and misinterpret their significance. Even with their rapid growth they constitute less than 2 percent of the population in Brazil where they are most prominent. Many communities, moreover, remain at a low level of political awareness.[39]

Critics of the base communities fear that "outside" intellectuals and agents will manipulate them and lead them into radical activism. Scott Mainwaring, writing about Brazil, believes the danger lies in almost the opposite direction. He sees the base communities, and the pastoral agents who work with them, as so protective of their autonomy that they resist linking with any group that might manipulate them, including political parties. Mainwaring believes that base communities and popular Christian movements must establish links with broader political parties if they hope to achieve real structural change. Despite general criticisms of both capitalism and socialism, says Mainwaring, "the popular church has not conceptualized a model of the way to promote social change." It overestimates the capacity of grass-roots organizations to transform society, and it underestimates the importance of political parties and institutions.[40] Marcello Azevedo expresses a similar concern, arguing that the base communities will need to form coalitions, and must collaborate and compromise with groups in different sectors of society if they hope to effect broader social changes.[41]

Both commentators support the base community movement and see the valuable contributions it already makes: giving the poor a sense of their dignity, allowing them to participate actively in decisions that affect their lives, and preparing them for a more active role in society as a whole. They encourage, however, as I would also, a more planned and pragmatic strategy for effecting social change.

Chapter 11

Toward a New Ecclesiology

In the early years of liberation theology, discussions about the church revolved mostly around issues related to the mission of the church and the role it should play in respect to confronting social injustice and transforming the world. The citations from Gutiérrez, given at the introduction to chapter 10, focused on how the church should relate to the world. In addition to questions about the external thrust of the church's mission, however, liberation theology has also raised questions about the internal structure of the church, about the very "nature" of the church itself, and how it should function in respect to its own members. One of the earliest probings of how the church should constitute itself came from Juan Luis Segundo. In recent years works by Leonardo Boff on the church have occupied center stage. Boff's works have drawn upon the experience of the base communities discussed in the last chapter. His works have also evoked considerable controversy.

This chapter on ecclesiology will consider briefly some of Segundo's thoughts on the church, and then focus in more detail on Boff's views. In connection with Boff's work it will also take up some theological reflections by Jon Sobrino on the church and call attention to a work by a Brazilian bishop whose "praxis" of running his diocese reflects much that Boff expresses theologically. The chapter will then discuss some critiques of Boff's work, and will conclude with reflections about the external mission of the church, in particular how the church might influence social change.

Juan Luis Segundo's *The Community Called Church*, first published in the late 1960s, starts with a question about the church's mission to the world: "What can the church offer the world?" The church, Segundo believes, should not allow itself to focus on the size of its membership or rate of its growth, but should concern itself with the world. The church should be a "sign" to the world, to persons outside itself. It should be a sign of God's love and in the end it will be judged by the mutual love it has encouraged.

To fulfill its mission, Segundo argues, the church should be comprised of those willing to take seriously the demands that Jesus makes on his

213

disciples. The church should not minimize its requirements, as it now does, to include as many members as possible. Rather it should recognize that only a small number can successfully carry out the church's mission of justice and love. Only a minority can respond effectively to the raising of consciousness. Only a small "revolutionary vanguard" can resist mass tendencies to accept immediate gains and work instead for long-range goals. As the gospel attests: "Many are called and few are chosen." The church has universality as a goal, but it should concentrate its efforts on the minority ready and able to transform society.[1]

Leonardo Boff and the Way To "Be" Church

Leonardo Boff calls into question the way the church has traditionally operated. He believes that the base communities represent not only *a new* way of being church, but a better way. In his *Ecclesiogenesis*, Boff develops his ideas by contrasting two very different ways of being church: institutional and community. The traditional institutional church acts from the top down. It views itself as a juridical society in which God the Father empowers Jesus to found a church headed by a pope and bishops who transmit teachings and the sacraments through priests to the faithful below. Its very size and structure preclude it from being a true community. The new basic community churches, in contrast, develop from the bottom up. They view all members as equals, sharing with each other their special gifts and charisms. All bear responsibility for the church, not just a few; all must sanctify, not just some. The need for some hierarchy and administration does arise, but as a service to the community.[2]

Boff does not envision or desire the elimination of the institutional church in favor of the community-style church. The basic communities, while they witness to the communitarian aspect of Christianity, "cannot pretend to constitute a global alternative to the church as an institution."[3] They can, however, in addition to their own witness as church, be a ferment for the renewal of the institutional church.

If Boff's writings have proven highly controversial, the conflicts arise not from any attempt to create a separate church in opposition to the institutional church, for both are needed. Rather controversy arises from the quite negative descriptions he gives of the institutional church, and from the changes he calls for. Thus, for example, he pictures authorities in the church "as amassing all power in the church" so that the actual community is divided "between rulers and governed, between celebrants and onlookers, between producers and consumers of sacraments."[4] He sees the institutional church as centered "in society's affluent sectors, where it enjoys social power and constitutes the church's exclusive interlocutor with the power of society."[5] On this last score, he does acknowledge that interaction with base communities has led the institutional church to weaken its commitment to the power elites and to lend itself more to the service of the poor.

But the church still must decide whether it will retain its links to the rich and powerful or give itself fully to the prophetic mission of defending the poor.

Boff believes that the basic communities constitute a true and authentic church, with an explicitly conscious awareness of themselves as church, and not just as a community with "some elements" of church. They are church because they are a community based on a common faith. They participate in explicitly church activities; they feel a oneness with the parish, diocese, and universal church. The church is a mystery of communion with God and with others. But communion does not admit of degrees: it either is present or it is not. It is present in basic communities, which therefore constitute true church.[6]

To establish the authenticity of base communities as church, Boff offers also a theological reinterpretation of the founding of the church. In the traditional view, Jesus laid the foundations for the church when he named his twelve apostles (the first bishops and priests), conferred primacy on Peter (the first pope), and gave them power to perform sacraments: eucharist, when he said "Do this in memory of me"; penance, when he said "whose sins you shall forgive . . ."; baptism, "go forth and baptize all nations." Jesus thus created in embryo an institutional church.

Boff challenges this story, basing his arguments on scriptural exegesis and the study of some contemporary theologians. Jesus intended not to establish a church, but to preach the kingdom of God. The parousia he felt was imminent. He chose apostles not as builders of a new church, but as symbols of a new Israel. Peter did not receive his name "Peter-Cephas-Rock" from Jesus himself, as suggested in Matthew 16:18, but became the rock as the first witness to the resurrection of Jesus.

Only with the death and resurrection of Jesus did the church come into being. The church was born at Pentecost and even more specifically when the apostles felt called and inspired to go forth "as apostles" to convert the gentiles. During his public life, Jesus gave essential elements of the church—teachings, the eucharist, the apostles—but in its "concrete historical form" the church sprang from a decision of the apostles, enlightened by the Holy Spirit after his resurrection.[7]

However the church may have originated, Boff acknowledges that "the episcopate, the priesthood, and other functions are here for good" and that they respond to real needs "for unity, universality, and bonding with the great witnesses of the apostolic past." More important for Boff is the *style* with which one lives these functions: "whether the functionaries are *over* the communities, monopolizing all services and powers, or *within* them, integrating duties instead of accumulating them, respecting various charisms." This latter style, Boff concludes, translates the gospel attitude and the praxis that Jesus wanted.[8]

Boff would like to see this sharing of powers applied to celebration of the eucharist. The Second Vatican Council declared that no Christian community can be built up unless it has its basis and center in the celebration of the eucharist. But countries like Brazil lack the priests to provide the eucharist. Lay coordinators conduct paraliturgical services but cannot celebrate the Mass proper; the rule of celibacy for priests blocks their possibility of being ordained. Boff appeals to practices in the early church to justify his solution. The priest may indeed be the "ordinary minister" of the sacrament of the eucharist, but the early church allowed for nonordained ministers to preside if priests were not available. Boff argues that given the need for eucharistic celebration by a community without a priest, a lay coordinator could be designated as an "extraordinary minister" to celebrate the Lord's supper. Though the minister lacks ordination, the church, by its position as the root of all sacraments, could render the celebration sacramentally valid.[9]

Still another possibility for providing eucharist remains: ordaining women to the priesthood. Boff takes up the traditional arguments against ordaining women (Christ was a man; he chose twelve men as apostles; St. Paul's restrictions on women in the church, etc.) and responds to them point for point. He argues that the nonordination of women in the early church did not express any unchangeable divine law, but simply reflected the culture of the day.[10]

In *Church: Charism and Power*, Boff again contrasts the new way of being church in base communities with the institutional church. Other works of liberation theology stress the necessity of involving the church in the process of liberation. That concern forms part of Boff's work, but he focuses more sharply on relations *within* the church—and most especially on the issue of power.

Jesus relied only on the power of love. He renounced power as domination and preferred to die in weakness rather than force persons to accept his message. He did not proclaim any established order, or call others to be rulers. He liberates for freedom and calls on those in power to be servants. Open communication with others, solidarity with all, especially with the poor and sinners, and unlimited forgiveness are the ideals expressed and embodied by Jesus.[11]

The institutional church, in contrast, too often concentrates its sacred ecclesial power in the hands of the hierarchy. Just as capitalist owners control the means of production and retain all decision-making power, so the hierarchy of the church controls the "spiritual means of production" and retains decision-making power over laws, practices, and correct interpretations of doctrine. The laity remain passive accepters of the faith, in contrast to base communities where the poor learn *and* teach, and where they experience themselves as true subjects in shaping the world and forming the church.[12]

In the model of church expressed in base communities, everything revolves around the conception of church as the "people of God." Community is central. "There is a fundamental equality in the church. All are people of God. All share in Christ, directly and without mediation. Therefore all share in the services of teaching, sanctifying, and organizing the community."[13] Bishops and priests play an important function of unification, but in service to the larger community, which acts in the world as a sign and instrument of liberation.

In its social teachings about secular society, the church warns against concentration of power in the hands of any elite group. But in respect to spiritual society, the church hierarchy arrogates all power to itself. In both spheres concentration of power leads to abuses, and Boff charges the institutional church with violating basic human rights in dealing with its own members. In its teachings, the church upholds the dignity of every person; it demands that all persons be treated with fairness and justice. The bishops' 1971 document, "Justice in the World," called for lay participation in drawing up decisions, insisted on respect for rights within the church, recognized everyone's right to suitable freedom of expression and thought, and argued for fair judicial procedures in judging anyone. The hierarchical church, Boff asserts, has violated these principles. It does not treat its members with dignity. It discriminates against women and treats all the laity as passive recipients of laws and doctrines. It relegates to itself all decision-making. It suppresses dissent and open discussion of issues. It does not follow fair judicial procedures in judging its own theologians (not allowing them to know their accusers and judging them without due process).[14]

These few examples should suffice to indicate why Boff ran into conflict with Rome. The conflict appears even sharper when one compares what Boff proclaims as characteristics of a true Christian church with the four "notes" of the church as traditionally interpreted. For Boff, the true marks of the church, embodied in base communities are: a unity of equals in community, a holiness that shows itself in militant commitment to liberation, an apostolicity that ministers to those in most need, and a catholicity that struggles in behalf of a universal cause of liberation.[15] In contrast, the traditional interpretation of these notes, which Boff criticizes, may unwittingly express the priority concerns of many church officials now in Rome: "unity" as uniformity of teaching, liturgy, and laws; "holiness" as faithfulness to the hierarchy; "apostolicity" as carrying out the mission of the bishops; "catholicity" as uniformity of practices.

Boff repeats again, however, a point he insisted upon in his earlier work. The institutional church is necessary and base communities want and need relations with it. "The institutional church supports and encourages the base ecclesial communities. ... These communities, in turn, are in communion with the institutional church; they want their bishop, their priests, and religious."[16] Where conflict exists, the antagonism occurs between institutional Christianity (the church as associated with the ruling powers of a class society) and the popular church (identified with the grassroots). The base communities do not, however, stand in conflict with the institutional church as such; both expressions of church need and complement each other.

Two Other Liberation Views on the Church and the Poor

Before turning to critiques directed against Boff's works, we might look briefly at two other expressions of liberation theology's views on the church: a theological work by Jon Sobrino and pastoral reflections by a Brazilian bishop, Dom Antônio Fragoso. Neither of these men uses the strident language Boff adopts in questioning the institutional church, but both affirm as he does a "new way of being church" in the world of the poor.

Jon Sobrino, in *The True Church and the Poor*, speaks of the new church of the poor in Latin America as representing "a resurrection of the true church." It has broken away from traditional ways of being church and begun to attain a greater fullness and authenticity. Sobrino does not mean to imply by the term "resurrection" that the church had died, but that this new way of being church manifests a newness of substance and life more in conformity with the spirit of the early church. "The grace given to the first Christians has been given once again on our continent."[17] The first resurrection involved not just Jesus but the disciples as well; it launched a movement aimed at overcoming death and the wretchedness of history; the same resurrection of spirit manifests itself today in the church of the poor in Latin America.

It does so because it best reflects the spirit of Jesus struggling to liberate the world from sin and working toward the fulfillment of the kingdom of God. The expression "church of the poor" is important for Sobrino. The church is not simply "for" the poor or ethically concerned about them, but is a church "of" the poor where the poor constitute its very basis. This church of the poor offers the most Christian locus or channel for experiencing God.[18] The church of the poor also manifests the "notes" of a true church: unity in community and active solidarity in the work of liberation; holiness in seeking justice and confronting sin; catholicity in mutual responsibility and linking with other parts of the Third World; apostolicity, in making liberation a reality.[19]

Bishop Antônio Fragoso's *Face of the Church* does not present itself as a theological treatise on the church, but simply as an account of his own experiences as bishop in the diocese of Crateús, Brazil. In the course of his story, however, he gives clear expression to how a bishop and the institutional church should function. If liberation theology builds its critical theological reflection on "praxis," it could well use Fragoso's administration of his diocese as a source.

When Fragoso first arrived in Crateús in 1964, he found expectations placed upon him that conflicted with his views of service. His predecessor had been a "builder" of schools, a hospital, and a museum. Fragoso was expected to follow suit and also to live in the bishop's palace and to socialize with the leading businesspersons and government officials. When he sought instead simply to serve his people, and the poor especially, he met with opposition. He tried especially to break away from the authoritarian centralism that characterized most diocesan administration and to allow freedom for different groups and organizations to plan and run their own programs. In dealing with the poor he came to realize the structural causes of poverty and how the poor are victims of class struggle. By class struggle, he says, I do not mean some scientific theory: "I am referring to a simple fact of daily experience: there are mechanisms of exploitation at work, wielded by persons who benefit from them as members of a dominant class."[20]

The bishop, Fragoso claims, should be the servant of the people and the servant of the diocesan church. Like Boff and Sobrino, Fragoso believes that the base communities will eventually bring profound changes in the structures of the church. Vatican II had called for the people of God to assume co-responsibility for the work of the church. "I view the base community as a genuine church," exercising co-responsibility and not just receiving as passive listeners. "The spirit is not the monopoly of the hierarchy" but is shared by the base.[21]

Critiques and Comments about Boff's Works

Church authorities reacted strongly to Boff's *Church: Charism and Power*. The archdiocesan commission for the doctrine of the faith in Rio de Janeiro sharply criticized the work. Boff responded in February 1982 declaring that the criticisms made of his book misrepresented his views. The Vatican Congregation for Doctrine of the Faith took up the issue, sending Boff a letter expressing numerous reservations about the book. The congregation called for a dialogue but also said it would make public its criticisms to counter what it viewed as a harmful influence of the book on the faithful. In September 1984, Boff came to Rome to meet with the congregation, with Cardinals Aloisio Lorscheider and Paulo Evaristo Arns in Rome also to lend their support to him. The congregation made public a letter in March 1985 expressing points it claimed were "unsustainable" in Boff's work. In May 1985 Boff was "silenced" and told he could not teach, give public addresses, or publish for one year. He accepted the silencing saying that "I prefer to walk with the church rather than to work alone with my theology." Boff commented also that the congregation's notification did not judge his views heretical or criticize liberation theology as such or make any reference to Marxism. In March of the following year (1986) the silencing was lifted. This greatly abbreviated account of the affair is taken from a Catholic news service report. U.S. Protestant theologian Harvey Cox probes the whole affair in rich detail in *The Silencing of Leonardo Boff.*[22]

In its public notification (1985) the Vatican congregation highlighted four points of criticism. First, it gives Boff's position about the founding and development of the church. Boff claims that Jesus did not have in mind the church as an institution during his lifetime. The church evolved after the resurrection and over time it took on the societal characteristics of the Roman empire and later of feudalism. The church, in Boff's view, needs to change and to replace power concerns for service. In response, the congregation charged Boff with "relativizing" the structure of the church and also with justifying his views by a distorted interpretation of Vatican II's teachings on the church's "subsistence." The church subsists fully only in the one true Catholic Church; outside this true church only "elements" of the church exist. The church as such does not subsist in different particular churches, as Boff claims.[23]

Second, Boff relativizes church dogmas, in the judgment of the congregation. Boff claims that a dogma in its formulation holds good only for a specific time and specific circumstances. Dogmas must give way to new formulations proper to today's world. The congregation recognizes the need for adapting the *language* of the past, but asserts that "the sense of the dogmatic formulas remains true and coherent, determined and unalterable."

Third, Boff speaks of the church's exercise of sacred power as a "grave pathology." In the process of history the clergy and hierarchy "expropriated the means of religious production" and then exercised its power in terms of centralization and domination rather than of service. The congregation accuses Boff of impoverishing and subverting the sacraments by reducing them to "products for consumption."

Fourth, Boff denounces the church's hierarchy and institutions, claiming that such critiques are an exercise of the charism of prophecy. In Boff's view the hierarchy should function only by coordinating different charisms in the church, not by subordinating them. The congregation, in response, acknowledges that the whole people share in the prophetic office of the church but argues that to remain legitimate the prophetic voice must accept the church's institutions and recognize the hierarchy as responsible for judging its exercise.

Since Vatican II a great deal of theological discussion among Catholic theologians has centered upon questions about the nature of the church, its mission, different models for understanding the church, and the exercise of power in the church.[24] These issues have special ramifications, however, for liberation theology. The concerns of liberation theology turned first on the mission of the church. Liberation theologians called upon the institutional church (its bishops, clergy, religious, and pastoral agents) to opt for the poor and to direct the service of the church to the poor. With the development of base communities, the concern showed itself next in calling upon the institutional church to recognize these communities and the church of the poor as the most authentic expressions of true Christianity. This emphasis on the church of the poor as an authentic expression of Christianity comes through strongly in Boff's *Ecclesiogenesis* and in Sobrino's work on the church. If Christ came to preach the good news to the poor, and to identify with the poor, then indeed he remains most authentically present among the poor. The church of the poor, while not the exclusive bearer of Christianity, should stand out as the most privileged "sign" of Jesus' presence.

The exercise of power in the church, the focus of Boff's *Church: Charism and Power*, touches a much broader issue troubling theologians in many parts of the world. The traditional view of the church views power, grace, mission, and authority as proceeding from the top down. Many since Vatican II believe the church should be characterized by community, collegiality, subsidiarity, and shared responsibility. In the United States, the "liberal agenda" predominates: for example, allowing greater leeway for free theological inquiry and dissent, respecting the individual conscience, and giving women equal status in the church. In Latin America, the "liberation agenda" places much less emphasis on issues of dissent or theological freedom of inquiry. The authority issue, however, touches Latin America in a special way because at all levels of society the poor have long been subject to authoritarian, patron-client, paternalistic relationships. The guiding value of liberation theology, to enable the poor to become active subjects of their own destiny, clashes with this traditional pattern of relations, including relations within the church. In Boff's ecclesiology, Franciscan spirituality appears operative as well. St. Francis of Assisi, while not questioning the teaching authority of the church, did challenge practices in the church. He founded a group of poor, egalitarian religious with a mission to the poor and with a desire to renew the church by bringing its life more into conformity with the spirit of the gospel and of the early church.

Boff views the institutional church as stifling spirit. In contrast, many church authorities believe that permissiveness and undisciplined spirit have rather contributed to contemporary problems, causing the church to lose its identity and causing society itself to lose its moral bearings. John Paul II, Cardinal Ratzinger, and Cardinal López Trujillo, whatever their differences of socio-political perspective, appear to share a common perception about the deterioration of traditional moral values.[25] If one perceives the loss of respect for these values (as expressed, for example, in the ten commandments) as the major cause of problems in society, and if one also believes that the church by reaffirming these values with a clear, unified voice could restore them, then strong authority does take on great importance.

Unity in the church and emphasis on the primacy of its spiritual mission have become, together with the issue of authority, the critical themes of church leaders who believe that the church has risked losing its identity and departing from its true mission since Vatican II. The "notions" used to express the church have become the focus of contending ecclesiologies and differing models of the church. A notion of the church as the "people of God" gained prominence through its use in Vatican II documents. This notion carries with it connotations of greater equality and of embodiment in this world, including the conflicts and struggle that a "people" encounters in its way through life. It ties in with images of the exodus and the Israelites as the people of God whom Yahweh led out of Egypt and into the promised land. "Church of the poor" carries this image even further, identifying the church of Jesus most especially with the lives and struggles of those furthest removed from positions of power and prestige in the church.

In recent years many church leaders have sought to reverse this trend. They claim that notions like the "people of God" have given one-sided emphasis to thisworldly concerns, neglecting the sacramental gifts of the church and creating opposition between the hierarchy and the "popular church." The 1985 synod of bishops convened in Rome by Pope John Paul II moved strongly toward use of the notions of "mystery" (to stress the supernatural dimension) and "communion" (to downplay opposition) in place of "people of God," which appears only once in the synod's final document.[26] Cardinal López Trujillo, from the outset of his battle against liberation theology, recognized the importance of terms used to define the church. In a 1972 essay he defines the church precisely as "mystery of communion." Citing the Vatican II *Lumen Gentium* he speaks of the church as the "sacrament of communion"; the spirit unifies "in communion and mystery," vivifying the church as the soul of the human body.[27]

Despite conflicting views about the nature of the church and how authority should be exercised in the church, the institutional church and the base communities cannot afford to become alienated from each other. The institutional church *needs* the base communities, and in a real sense it needs liberation theology as well. While attention has often focused on the political implications of base communities, they have become very important to the church's mission of evangelization. Many of the poor have begun to truly appropriate their Christian faith. The future of the church in Latin America depends on winning the hearts of the masses to the faith, and the masses remain poor. The church cannot afford to lose them as it lost so many of the working class in Europe in the nineteenth century. The church in Latin America has also made a public commitment to the poor (the preferential option) in its declarations at Medellín and Puebla. This commitment, moreover, embraces the material needs of the poor, helping them to confront the unjust structures that impede their development. The institutional church will lose its credibility if it does nothing to address these issues.

If the church needs the base communities and even liberation theology, they in turn need the church. As Boff has clearly stated, the poor want close relations with their bishops and pastors. Moreover, Christian groups need the protection of the church. If even with the church standing behind them in Brazil, peasant unions and other activist groups suffered from government repression, their activity would become far more precarious without the support of bishops in their defense.

Liberation theologians need also to present themselves as teachers within the church. The attempts to silence Leonardo Boff and Gustavo Gutiérrez could have done serious harm for liberation theology (though the temporary silencing of Boff only augmented his status). Liberation theologians may prod the church to open itself to new interpretations, or challenge it to live out the spirit of the early Christian church. But they must do so as theologians of and in the church to be effective.

For all the problems that liberation theologians have experienced with church authorities, I suspect that no other group of theologians use as many references to church documents as do liberation theologians. They may use these documents selectively to stress their own points, but they make frequent appeals to Medellín, Puebla, Vatican II, and to writings of all the recent popes. The summer school in Lima deals extensively with church teachings, including many sessions on the writings of Pope John Paul II, and Gutiérrez has repeatedly stated that theology must always proceed from within the church.

The resolution of conflicts within the church will not come through the victory of any one model, in my judgment. The issue really comes down to how much the church will move in one direction or another — that is, more stress on authority and on nonpolitical evangelization, or more stress on subsidiarity and on evangelization that emphasizes socio-political liberation.

The Church and Social Change

As we approach the conclusion of this book, one critical issue remains. Liberation theologians and their critics alike acknowledge the need for social changes in Latin America. They differ quite clearly in how this change should be effected. This issue will occupy the final section of the chapter. First, however, we might reflect briefly on some related questions that have come up in various parts of the book. "Should the church become involved in politics?" Liberation theology's position that the church has, in fact, a political dimension seems irrefutable. The church acts politically when it performs symbolic gestures (for example, a bishop offering a blessing for a new government) and even when it distances itself from any involvement (for example, the Argentinian bishops remaining silent in the face of the military's use of arbitrary arrests and torture). The church, in addition, has frequently engaged directly in exercising its political influence: for example, to protect Catholic education, to impede laws that would permit divorce or abortion, and to instruct the faithful about how to vote on "Catholic" issues.[28] Bishops in many Latin American countries, other than Argentina, have accepted responsibility for denouncing human rights violations. The distinction between the institutional church engaging only indirectly in politics, and leaving direct political involvement to the laity, breaks down in the examples already noted. If by "political involvement" one means partisan politics and promoting one particular party or candidate over others, both the institutional church and liberation theologians reject this as an improper activity for the church.

Earlier chapters discussed the criticism that liberation theology "reduces faith to politics." If in the early days of liberation theology, great *emphasis* was given to socio-political liberation, theologians like Gutiérrez asserted from the outset that true liberation involved *three* levels of liberation (the socio-political, full development of human persons, and liberation from sin). In recent years much of the writing in liberation theology has concerned itself with a spirituality that fills out these other dimensions. All this leaves, however, the question of socio-political change, a change that many documents of Medellín, Puebla, and papal encyclicals acknowledge as an important "part" of the church's mission. I will comment first on views in liberation theology about effecting change, and then I will consider church social teachings and the views of some critics of liberation theology.

Changes have occurred in liberation theology in respect to bringing about a social transformation in Latin America. If Hugo Assmann and some Christians for Socialism argued that the church came too late to propose its own program of change and must rely on support for existing revolutionary movements, this view did not represent liberation theology overall. Gutiérrez explicitly rejected "baptizing" as Christian any specific movement. At the outset many liberation theologians did state the problems of Latin America in very global terms (dependency, capitalist domination) without very clear strategies in mind other than favoring socialism and somehow enabling the poor to become agents of their own destiny. In recent years, liberation theologians have spoken often about working within the openings permitted by legal democracy to build and occupy "spaces" so that base communities and popular movements can organize and gain experience in effecting change. This general strategy stresses working for change *in and through* society rather than leaving change to political leaders. It also involves a clear rejection of turning over the praxis of change to any Marxist vanguard party. But it falls short of any clear, feasible strategy of its own for moving beyond small community actions to the broader problems of "changing structures." The present strategy, in short, moves in a healthy direction (popular participation) but requires planning for fuller coordination of efforts and coalition building.

The social teachings of the Catholic Church have acknowledged more often in recent years the necessity of working toward "transforming structures" (for example, the 1986 Vatican instruction, and John Paul II's *Sollicitudo Rei Socialis* on structures of sin). John Paul II's *Laborem Exercens* accepts even the legitimacy of "struggle" in bringing about change (struggle for change, not struggle *against* persons). The pope has also often affirmed the right of peasants and workers to organize and to struggle for their rights. In contrast to efforts in decades past to form Catholic Action groups, the social teachings give little indication, however, of how change might be promoted *from the bottom up*. Nor do critics of liberation theology indicate, except for encouragement, how the church might aid the efforts at change. Much in the social teachings of the church still emphasizes "conversion of the heart" as the way to change.

The history of Latin America clearly shows that hardness of heart has kept those in power consistently deaf to calls for conversion (from the time of Spanish conquistadores and their treatment of Indians to modern-day Somozas). Over the centuries not many wealthy landowners in Latin America have been "converted" to distributing their land, and we would probably still have slavery if the decision to end it depended on converting the hearts of slaveholders. Ultimately conversion of the heart is *also* needed for full liberation to occur, and this liberation theologians acknowledge. Conversion has not, however, proved an efficacious means for changing structures.

Moreover, changes of heart often follow, rather than precede, changes in structures. The issue of racism in the United States provides an example. Prior to the 1950s, laws in many states legitimized racial segregation. Only by changing these laws, by "transforming sinful structures," could real progress toward justice be achieved. The segregation laws had reinforced and confirmed racist attitudes. Only by getting at the structures and eliminating segregation laws, could the attitudes be effectively addressed.

The institutional church recognizes this, at least implicitly, by its actions. Church leaders do not say that the only way to end abortions should be through conversion of the hearts of those contemplating abortions; the church lobbies to have laws imposed (structures) that would prohibit abortions. Even in the internal dealings of the church, authorities do not rely simply on conversion of the heart. The church creates canon laws, replaces bishops, and silences theologians.

Bishop Roques Adames of the Dominican Republic, in a critical assessment of liberation theology, draws attention to the weakness of Catholic social teachings in respect to *means* of social change. Even if one stresses conversion, a change on the part of one wealthy capitalist does nothing to affect the system or structures in operation. Even with conversion as a model, change must involve some method of "group" conversion. Only group actions, says Adames, can effect structural change. Adames also notes that church teachings tend to stress what *not* to do (for example, avoidance of violence) and do not give directions on *how* social change could be brought about.[29]

Latin American critics of liberation theology have proposed a "theology of reconciliation" rather than a conflictual theology of liberation as the true Christian way. At least one book articulating this theology gives no indication of how conversion of heart has brought about, or even might bring about, social change.[30] Cardinal López Trujillo, in the course of a book-long interview, gives some small clues as to his views. He speaks about concern for the poor, but the only concrete examples he offers involve reliance on the goodwill of government officials and business leaders. To counter poverty, he speaks only of the need for new small businesses and more jobs created by existing businesses; he calls on the rich to "aid" the poor, and he notes that he led visits of "people with influence" to show them the problems of the poor.[31] (In fairness, his country, Colombia, despite its present grave drug problem, has had more experience of democracy and relatively greater economic development than some other countries in Latin America.)

Liberation theologians, in the past, could be faulted for treating capitalism as *one* structure to be eliminated and replaced by socialism rather than as a complex of structures some of whose parts must be retained and complemented with democratic political structures to achieve a truly effective development and liberation. But church social teachings, especially as interpreted by critics of liberation theology, contain little evidence of realistic strategies of social change. If one takes seriously reconciliation and avoidance of conflict (which is not the position of *Laborem Exercens* and other papal encyclicals), even the type of development that occurred in Europe and the United States would be excluded, for it included long histories of often violent conflicts between labor unions and capitalist owners. Also to claim that the gospel preaches reconciliation and rejects conflict one must disregard all of Jesus' denunciations of the Pharisees and warnings to the rich.

In *Laborem Exercens* Pope John Paul II gave at least implicit support to the worker "solidarity" movement in Poland (a conflictual movement). In Latin America even the creation of such movements remains a problem. The issue of church involvement in politics deals not just with the encouraging of social change "in principle." Church leaders must ask themselves honestly whether appeals for conversion of elites will really suffice or whether the institutional church should lend its support to the formation of movements from below that might function as forces of change. Bishops in Brazil and elsewhere have accepted responsibility for the involvement of church-sponsored groups (for example, the Pastoral Land Commission in Brazil) in the *practice* of struggle for change. Without this the church may say that it has made a preferential option for the poor, while distancing itself from any truly effective means for achieving the transformations it claims to espouse.

Conclusion

The conflicts between liberation theologians and their critics will almost certainly continue into the future. Greater effort at listening and dialogue could perhaps mollify the conflicts, but ultimately very different values and very different conceptions of Christianity and the church underlie the conflicts. No degree of clarification or empirical data will change basic values and assumptions. On at least one score, however, liberation theology can claim victory. It has proven itself far more than the "passing fad" some early critics believed it would be. It has profoundly affected the life of the church in Latin America. Theology has "come alive" and become a topic of serious interest. Where the institutional church has responded to the concerns of liberation theology, it has gained respect from the youth of Latin America. In Brazil, in the early 1960s, two-thirds of university students polled in Rio de Janeiro considered themselves unbelievers and viewed the church as "on the side of injustice." The bishops in Brazil actively fought for human rights and in defense of the poor in the late 1960s and 70s. A new student poll in 1978 showed a striking change, with three-fourths of the students declaring themselves "believers" and favorable to the church.[1]

The institutional church itself has accepted many of the most important points in liberation theology. The Vatican instructions acknowledged "liberation" as a valid and even essential theme of Christian revelation. The bishops at Puebla clearly affirmed a "preferential option for the poor." If the political involvement of the church remains controversial, the church has in practice devoted much greater pastoral efforts toward the poor than it did in ages past. Even Cardinal López Trujillo rates concern for the poor the second most important priority for the church in Colombia, and he takes great pride in the forty new parishes created in poor barrios in five years.[2]

If many bishops still try to restrain their clergy and religious from political involvement, they are quite unlikely to voice the unquestioned support for the status quo that once characterized much Christian teaching. In a pastoral letter of 1915, the bishops of Brazil instructed their priests to "inculcate the spirit of obedience and submission to those who govern in civil society, in religion and in the family . . . to lead the faithful to accept their proper situation and the conditions in which they were born and not to hate the modest and difficult life in which Providence has placed them."[3] A repetition of such a statement by a group of bishops would be almost inconceivable in contemporary Latin America. In principle at least, the institutional church has recognized the dignity of the poor and accepted the value most central to liberation theology: namely, that the poor should become active, participatory agents in shaping their own destinies.

U.S. theologian J.J. Moeller credits liberation theology with some important contributions to theological method. Liberation theology, says Moeller, has shown the need for theology to consider the role that socio-economic conditions play in shaping culture and theology itself. It has shown the contribution that praxis can make to theology. It has listened to the cry of the poor, emphasizing that only by insertion into real conditions of oppression and suffering can theology be credible and the gospel realized.[4]

Throughout this book I have distinguished between liberation theology and various liberation movements (ranging from Christians who opted to join guerilla groups, through activist groups like the Christians for Socialism, to very diverse groups of Christian base communities). Both liberation theology and the liberation movements grew out of the same historical context, but they had different origins and have different identities. Liberation theology and the base community movement had parallel but distinct histories of development. Without any writings of liberation theology, radical Christian groups would still have formed in the 1960s and 1970s. In fact, groups did form in Brazil, Chile, and in Central America *before* the first works of liberation theology appeared. Certainly many Christians in the United States and Europe became politically involved in the sometimes radical movements of the 1960s without any input from liberation theology.

In Latin America, the developments in theology and in social movements cannot be separated entirely. Christian activist groups and liberation theologians often worked together; present-day liberation theologians reflect upon and give strong affirmation to ecclesial base communities. Some liberation theologians have incorporated elements of social analysis used by activist groups. A distinction, nevertheless, should still be made between liberation *theology* as such and liberation movements.

Some critics of liberation theology concentrate almost entirely on the social analysis and economic-political views they find in liberation theology. Almost all the works they cite date back to the 1970s, and works in theology are often lumped together with statements by the Christians for Socialism and other activist groups. Nearly all the criticisms focus on the dangers of using Marxist ideas or espousing socialism. These political concerns, moreover, prompt most of the criticisms of liberation theology as a whole. As noted earlier, very few recent works in liberation theology contain any extended treatment of social analysis, and whatever judgment one makes about the validity or weakness of social analysis in liberation theology, its broadly stated, politico-economic options appear to have very little impact on macroplans in Latin American countries. Many critics, nevertheless, continue to define liberation theology by the statements of social analysis found in its earliest writings, linking these statements with radical groups from the early 1970s.

Other critics focus on theology proper in liberation theology. Some target it as just one more expression of a modernist European theology, which they see as undermining the true, traditional faith. Others see it as a challenge to church authority and as going beyond "official teachings" of the church. Some quarrels with the Vatican remain over issues of orthodoxy, but most liberation theologians have consciously attempted to keep their theological views consistent with the central tenets of the Christian faith, and some have reformulated their views to avoid any conflict with church doctrines. Still other critics of the theology of liberation, critics like John Meier, question the soundness of biblical scholarship used in some liberation works. Some criticisms on this score appear valid, but do not take sufficiently into account liberation theology's principal concern to *stress* certain aspects of the gospel that theology through the ages has downplayed or neglected. A few critics, like Cardinal Ratzinger, direct their criticisms at both the social analysis and theology proper of liberation theology, but in doing so sometimes "read into" it much more than is actually stated.

Any assessment of liberation theology should also take into account the changes and developments it has undergone since its inception more than twenty years ago. Liberation theologians argued from the outset for a "contextual" theology that would reflect the culture and conditions of Latin America and not assume traditional European theology as *the* universal and unchanging theology of Christianity. But liberation theology itself has reflected changing conditions in Latin America. Its first formulations often mirrored attitudes prevalent in the late 1960s and early 70s. These years were, in Gutiérrez's words, a time of great "revolutionary ferment." Liberation theology thus called for revolutionary change. Even many in the hierarchy, however, expressed themselves in similar language. The Peruvian bishops, who a dozen years later would wrestle with a decision about condemning liberation theology, wrote a pastoral letter in 1971 calling for revolutionary change. "To construct a just society in Latin America and in Peru signifies liberation from the present situation of dependency, oppression, and exploitation in which the great majority of our people live." The people are called to shape their own destiny. "This means that the people ought to have a real and direct participation in a *revolutionary action* against oppressive structures and attitudes and for a just society for all."[5]

Aspirations for a dramatic change and liberation of the poor influenced the social analysis first used. Dependency theory, in its strong form, placed the blame for underdevelopment on advanced countries of the North; capitalism became for many the single cause and catch-all explanation for the misery in Latin America. Socialism represented the hope for change. Social analysis and solutions thus were repeatedly stated in broad, global terms of ultimate causes and ultimate aspirations. Marxism did serve as a "tool" to challenge long dominant ideologies that claimed to explain underdevelopment as "backwardness," and it pointed to "exploitation" of the poor as the true cause. The initial importance given to the exodus as a biblical theme captured the sense of a dramatic breakaway from oppression into a new world of liberation.

Even this initial period, however, did not simply represent a "Marxist phase." The initial impulse of liberation theology came from a new Christian awareness of the sufferings of the poor and a conviction that God remains present and active in the struggles of the poor to liberate themselves. In Chile, the Christians for Socialism movement, Chilean theologians like Pablo Richard and Diego Irarrazaval, the Brazilian Hugo Assmann and others were swept up by Marxist ideas and translated the "will of God" into socialist aspirations. Even then, however, theologians like Gutiérrez, Comblin, and Galilea distanced themselves from Marxist options and warned against christianizing any revolutionary ideology. Segundo has always used Marxism quite selectively, balanced with theories from a large array of other social theorists. Sobrino does little social analysis, and what he does express does not reflect Marxism. Even the critics of Leonardo Boff do not accuse him of Marxism.

As already noted in various parts of this book, liberation theologians use some elements of Marxist analysis because they see it as the principal method of critiquing capitalism (which they believe is the major cause of Latin America's problems) and because some of its ideas help to generate insights about the situation of Latin America. Liberation theology makes use of Marxist concepts but these concepts do not retain the same meanings they have in classic Marxism. "Praxis" connotes the living out of the Christian faith, not Marxist tactics of change. "Class struggle" expresses the reality of social conflict in Latin America, not a program to stir up hatred or to eliminate some ruling class. Liberation theologians speak of the "poor" of Latin America, with a special emphasis on landless peasants and those left marginalized and excluded from real participation in the economic-political life of Latin America. They do not focus on the industrial "proletariat" that Marxists have viewed as the bearer of emancipation.

One might still question the adequacy of liberation theology's identification of capitalism as *the* principal source of Latin America's problems. Some would certainly criticize the openness of many liberation theologians to collaboration with Marxists. But liberation theology clearly makes "critical" use of Marxist ideas. Otto Maduro's reflections on its use of Marxism (see chapter 7) appear quite accurate: liberation theology "borrows" from Marxist analysis but criticizes too many aspects of Marxism to consider it a guiding force of analysis.

Liberation theologians have also modified their politico-economic views in recent years. As noted in the last chapter, the new political context in many parts of Latin America has led liberation theologians to talk about building a "participatory democracy" from within civil society. Socialism no longer remains an unqualified paradigm for liberation aspirations.

In theology itself, liberation theology has turned increasingly to Jesus. It relies less on exodus and Old Testament sources. It recognizes especially the suffering and cross of Jesus, not with a traditional message of "accepting sufferings as part of one's lot in life," but as part of a painful process of struggle leading to hope, resurrection, and liberation. Liberation theology has expanded into many new areas of theology. Its emphasis on spirituality has been especially prominent. Vatican criticisms have undoubtedly made liberation theology more cautious, but the goal of creating a truly "integral" liberation theology proceeds from a deeper conviction than a simple political need for accommodation. The U.S. Catholic Press Association awarded prizes in 1988 to Leonardo Boff's *Passion of Christ,* Jorge Pixley's *On Exodus,* and Gustavo Gutiérrez's *On Job* as the outstanding books of the previous year in the categories of spirituality and biblical study. It would require incredible cynicism to perceive such works as "covers" for some political purpose.

It would require more intuitive and prescient capabilities than I possess to predict the future course that liberation theology will take or the political and religious impact it may have in years to come. Both supporters and critics alike tend to overestimate its political influence. The message of liberation theology and the development of base communities, on the other hand, have already made it possible for many poor to experience a new sense of dignity, a new awareness of God's special love for them, and an ability to work in solidarity to achieve significant social goals at community levels. "Popular movements" may indeed play a far more significant role in the future, pressing for social changes on a broader national level. But Latin American governments have proved all too adept at impeding or co-opting such movements. The United States shows no sign as yet of developing policies that go much beyond measures to make sure that "communism" does not spread.

Attitudes and decisions in the institutional church will greatly affect the future of both liberation theology and the base communities. Movements cut off from support of the church are unlikely to have great impact. Moreover, leaders in such movements may well become targets of government repression and even of elimination, if government officials see that they have no support from the institutional church. In principle, as noted above, the institutional church has stated an option for the poor and acknowledged liberation—including socio-political transformations—as important parts of the church's mission. In practice, however, an apparent trend in the appointment of new bishops raises doubts about the church's role in any new social transformations. Priorities about maintaining orthodoxy and reasserting church authority appear to outweigh social concerns. Since Pope John Paul II came to office, he has replaced progressives with conservatives in nine of Brazil's thirty-six archdioceses, with only three progressive bishops appointed during the same period. The diocese of Recife and Olinda, for years one of the most progressive dioceses in Brazil, now has a conservative bishop.[6] Peru, I am told, now has seven Opus Dei bishops. The bishop of Cusco has dismantled social centers once looked upon as models of work for change. The new head of the Bishops Conference in Peru, Bishop Ricardo Durand, is one of the fiercest critics of liberation theology. This trend in the hierarchy, combined with the worsening of economic conditions in most Latin American countries, do not presage a very promising future for the hopes expressed in liberation theology.

Some rays of hope, nevertheless, continue to break through. In 1988, reports from Bolivia and Guatemala spoke of the reawakening of social concern within the church, with bishops in those countries becoming more outspoken on social issues. In Chile, the defeat of General Pinochet in a referendum election gave new hope for democracy. But above all the remarkable capacity of so many of the poor in Latin America to keep going and even to celebrate life, joined with the continued dedication and vitality of many who work with the poor, testify that hope remains very much alive in Latin America despite disheartening conditions. To be ultimately successful, however, liberation work with the poor does require support from the institutional church (though church efforts alone will not decide the outcome). One can only hope that the church's option for the poor will, in time, override other concerns and prove a positive force for change.

On a theological level, the output of books on liberation theology continues to be impressive. Some dozen or more books have been published in a projected 50-volume series out of Petrópolis (and scheduled also for translation into English). Leonardo Boff and Juan Luis Segundo have been prolific in their output of works. Enthusiasm still runs high. On the other hand, doing creative theology from one basic paradigm (challenging and deideologizing older interpretations of Christianity and gaining new insights from the perspective of the poor) may reach a limit. European theology appears to have lost much of the vitality so evident in the epoch of Rahner, Congar, Schillebeeckx, Moltmann, and the generation of theologians who combined new biblical exegesis with the "rediscovery" of the humanity of Jesus. The liberation theologians prominent a decade or more ago remain the key figures in liberation theology today; new theologians are needed to carry forward the tradition. Women theologians could further enrich the movement.

As liberation theology moves toward the start of a new century, I would like to see innovations along several lines. Liberation theology has matured sufficiently to include greater internal self-criticism. A danger exists, certainly, that any self-criticism may be used by opponents to put down liberation theology or to give the appearance of dissension and division. But healthy, supportive criticism could enhance the vitality of liberation theology and gain for it greater support. On the level of social analysis the global "dependent capitalism" critique has limited usefulness in developing a realistic "praxis" for social change. (As I have noted, more recent works in liberation theology contain very little social analysis, even of a macro-kind.) I would hope that more specific analyses would develop with a view to formulation of concrete strategies on specific issues like land reform, but also to make popular Christian movements more politically effective at a national level. Liberation theologians and the popular movements they support need to move beyond identifying the causes of poverty and underdevelopment and give more attention to *how* the poor can become more effective agents of social change.

Part of the development of strategies of social change might include, in reflecting on the experiences of the poor, a greater articulation of the *values* and specific aspirations of the poor (over and above the ultimate goal of liberation). Theological reflection might also focus on the sources of strength that enable the poor to survive and even to celebrate despite the odds they face. To complement development of strategies for social change, liberation theology could also serve the poor and pastoral agents by developing explicit ethical norms that could guide in evaluating what "means" are appropriate to Christian change and what means are not.

It may be presumptuous to think that this work will be read by any liberation theologians. Certainly developments that do occur will come from within the movement of liberation theology and not from outside observers. The difficulties under which liberation theologians work may also greatly constrict what they can achieve. Many must work under threats from the government and opposition from church authorities. Most are already spread thin trying to meet requests from a multitude of sources; they have limited resources and only so much energy to give. What liberation theology has already achieved is of great significance. It has drawn the attention of the church, and of many persons in various parts of the world, to the sufferings of the poor in Latin America. It has challenged us to rethink the ways in which we understand and live out our faith. It has brought pride to the church in Latin America and made theology a subject of vital interest. In a very real way it has made visible the sign that Jesus gave to the disciples of John the Baptist: "The poor have the good news preached to them." Liberation theology strives to keep alive the hopes embodied in Jesus' proclamation of the kingdom of God, so that one day the great hope expressed in the book of revelations may be celebrated: "See I am making all things new" (Rv 21:5).

Appendix

Profiles of Liberation Theologians

The following are some of the leading liberation theologians in Latin America:

RUBEM ALVES is a native of Brazil. Ordained as a Presbyterian minister, he later left his church in protest against its conservatism. He studied at Union Theological Seminary (New York), and Princeton Theological Seminary. Alves wrote one of the first books on liberation theology, *A Theology of Human Hope*. More recently, he has experimented with a more poetic style of theology. He is currently a professor at the University of Campinas in Brazil. His books include *Protestantism and Repression* (Orbis Books, 1985), and *What Is Religion?* (Orbis Books, 1984).

RICARDO ANTONCICH is a Jesuit priest. He serves as a theologian for the Latin American Confederation of Religious (CLAR) and the Latin American Episcopal Conference (CELAM). An expert on Catholic social teaching, he teaches at the University of Javierana in Bogotá. He is the author of *Christians in the Face of Injustice: A Latin American Reading of Catholic Social Teaching* (Orbis Books, 1987).

HUGO ASSMANN studied theology and sociology in his native Brazil and in Europe. In 1973 he published one of the earliest volumes of liberation theology, *Theology for a Nomad Church* (Orbis Books, 1976). Although he now lives and teaches in Brazil, he has at various times been expelled from Brazil, Uruguay, Bolivia, and Chile as a result of his work in liberation struggles.

FREI BETTO (Carlos Alberto Libanio Christo), is a Dominican friar from Brazil, who works with base communities. He was a political prisoner of the military dictatorship in Brazil between 1969-73, the subject of his book *Against Principalities and Powers* (Orbis Books, 1977). More recently, he published the widely read volume, *Fidel and Religion* (Simon & Schuster, 1987).

MARÍA CLARA BINGEMER is a lay Catholic theologian from Brazil, professor at the Pontifical Catholic University of Rio de Janeiro, and regional coordinator for Latin America of the Ecumenical Association of Third World Theologians (EATWOT). She is co-author, with Ivone Gebara, of *Mary: Mother of God, Mother of the Poor* (Orbis Books, 1989).

CLODOVIS BOFF is a Servite priest from Brazil who teaches at the Franciscan Seminary in Petrópolis and who also works with base communities. His book *Feet-*

on-the-Ground Theology (Orbis Books, 1987), which describes his pastoral work among rubber plantation workers in the Amazon, won a Catholic Book Award in the U.S. Among his other books are *Theology and Praxis* (Orbis Books, 1987), and, with his brother Leonardo, *Salvation and Liberation* (Orbis Books, 1984), and *Introducing Liberation Theology* (Orbis Books, 1987).

LEONARDO BOFF, a Franciscan priest from Brazil, is one of the most prolific and influential theologians in Latin America. Educated in Brazil and in Munich, Germany, he teaches theology in Petrópolis, and serves as an advisor to the Brazilian bishops. His major works focus on christology and ecclesiology. They include *Jesus Christ Liberator* (Orbis Books, 1978), *Ecclesiogenesis* (Orbis Books, 1986), *Passion of Christ, Passion of the World* (Orbis Books, 1987), and *Trinity and Society* (Orbis Books, 1988). Boff was silenced for a year by the Vatican, following an investigation by the Congregation for the Doctrine of the Faith which focused on his criticism of church authority in *Church: Charism and Power* (Crossroad, 1985). The case is described in *The Silencing of Leonardo Boff*, by Harvey Cox (Meyer-Stone, 1988).

JOSÉ COMBLIN is a Belgian theologian and social critic. He has lived in Latin America since 1958 and now works in Brazil. In the sixties he wrote works on the theology of revolution that were influential on the later development of liberation theology. He is the author of more than forty books, including *The Church and the National Security State* (Orbis Books, 1979), *Cry of the Oppressed, Cry of Jesus* (Orbis Books, 1987), and *The Holy Spirit and Liberation* (Orbis Books, 1988).

JOSÉ SEVERINO CROATTO is a specialist in Semitic languages and biblical archeology. He teaches Old Testament and Hebrew in his native Argentina. His books include *Exodus: A Hermeneutics of Freedom* (Orbis Books, 1981) and *Biblical Hermeneutics* (Orbis Books, 1987).

ENRIQUE DUSSEL has doctorates in philosophy, history, and theology, and has made original contributions in all these areas—particularly in church history and ethics. For many years a political refugee from his native Argentina, he has settled in Mexico, where he teaches at the National Autonomous University of Mexico, and coordinates the Commission for the Study of History of the Church in Latin America (CEHILA). His numerous books include *History of the Church in Latin America* (Eerdmans, 1981), *Philosophy of Liberation* (Orbis Books, 1980), and *Ethics and Community* (Orbis Books, 1988).

IGNACIO ELLACURÍA, a Spanish-born Jesuit, has lived and worked in Central America for more than thirty-five years. He is president of the Universidad Centroamericana José Simeón Cañas in San Salvador, where he also teaches theology. Although he has written widely, his one book in English remains *Freedom Made Flesh: The Mission of Christ and His Church* (Orbis Books, 1976).

SEGUNDO GALILEA is a Claretian priest from Chile. He has served as an advisor to the Latin American Episcopal Conference (CELAM) and has worked in many countries in Latin America. Galilea was one of the earliest and most influential exponents of liberation theology, stressing in particular the centrality of spirituality and a constructive attitude toward popular religion and culture. His many books include *Following Jesus* (Orbis Books, 1981), *The Beatitudes* (Orbis Books, 1984), and *Spirituality of Hope* (Orbis Books, 1989).

IVONE GEBARA is a Catholic Sister from Brazil and professor of philosophy and theology at the Theological Institute of Recife. She is co-author, with María Clara Bingemer, of *Mary: Mother of God, Mother of the Poor* (Orbis Books, 1989).

GUSTAVO GUTIÉRREZ is probably the best-known liberation theologian, and the author of what remains the classic exposition of this movement, *A Theology of Liberation* (Orbis Books, 1973; Fifteenth Anniversary edition, 1988). Born in Lima, Peru, Gutiérrez earned degrees in philosophy and psychology (at Louvain), as well as theology (Lyons, France, and the Gregorian University in Rome). Ordained a priest in 1959, he lives and works in a poor slum of Lima, dividing his time between pastoral work and teaching at the Catholic University. His books include *The Power of the Poor in History* (Orbis Books, 1983), *We Drink from Our Own Wells* (Orbis Books, 1984), and *On Job: God-Talk and the Suffering of the Innocent* (Orbis Books, 1987). In 1989 Orbis Books published a *Festschrift* in his honor, *The Future of Liberation Theology* (Marc Ellis and Otto Maduro, eds.), with contributions from sixty bishops and theologians from around the world.

FRANZ HINKELAMMERT holds a doctorate in economics from the Free University of Berlin. He has taught at the Catholic University of Chile. Currently, he is a staff member of the Departamento Ecuménico de Investigaciones in San Jose, Costa Rica. Among his many books is *The Ideological Weapons of Death: A Theological Critique of Capitalism* (Orbis Books, 1986).

JOÃO BATISTA LIBÂNIO is a Jesuit professor of theology at the Instituto Santo Iñacio in Belo Horizante, Brazil. He is the author of numerous books and articles, including *Spiritual Discernment and Politics: Guidelines for Religious Communities* (Orbis Books, 1982).

OTTO MADURO was born in Venezuela and studied at Louvain, where he obtained degrees in religious sociology and philosophy. He has taught in Venezuela and in the United States, currently at the Maryknoll School of Theology. He has published several books on the general subject of religion and liberation, including *Religion and Social Conflict* (Orbis Books, 1982).

CARLOS MESTERS is a Dutch-born Carmelite and scripture scholar who has worked in Brazil for the last twenty-five years. He is the foremost authority on the use of the Bible among base communities, and has been a prolific author of popular biblical commentaries and other literature for these communities. His most famous work is *Defenseless Flower: A New Reading of the Bible* (Orbis Books, 1989).

JOSÉ MÍGUEZ BONINO, a Methodist minister and theologian, is one of the leading Protestant figures associated with liberation theology. Born in Argentina, he teaches in Buenos Aires but has also taught in seminaries and universities in many countries in Europe, the U.S., and Latin America. He has been active in the ecumenical movement as an observer at Vatican II and member of the Faith and

Order Commission of the World Council of Churches. His books include *Doing Theology in a Revolutionary Situation* (Fortress Press, 1975), and, as editor, *Faces of Jesus: Latin American Christologies* (Orbis Books, 1984).

JOSÉ PORFIRIO MIRANDA has degrees in economics, philosophy, and biblical sciences. He has taught at various universities in his native Mexico, where he also serves as advisor to numerous workers' and student groups. He is the author of a number of politically charged works of philosophy and exegesis, including *Marx and the Bible* (Orbis Books, 1974), *Communism in the Bible* (Orbis Books, 1982), and *Marx Against the Marxists* (Orbis Books, 1980).

RUNALDO MUÑOZ is a Chilean priest and theologian, with degrees from the Gregorian University in Rome, the Catholic Institute of Paris, and the University of Regensburg. For the past twenty-five years, he has divided his time between teaching fundamental and dogmatic theology and doing pastoral work among urban workers. He has published numerous books and articles, especially in the area of ecclesiology. His book *The God of Christians* is forthcoming in English (Orbis Books, 1990).

JUAN HERNANDEZ PICO is a Mexican Jesuit, the director of the Center of Investigation and Social Action for the Jesuits in Central America. He has lived for many years in Managua, Nicaragua and is the author (with Jon Sobrino) of *Theology of Christian Solidarity* (Orbis Books, 1985).

JORGE (GEORGE) PIXLEY was born in Chicago and raised in Nicaragua. An ordained Baptist minister, he has taught at the Seminario Evangélico of Puerto Rico and at the Seminario Bautista in Mexico City. He currently teaches in Nicaragua. He is the author of *God's Kingdom* (Orbis Books, 1981), and *On Exodus: A Liberation Perspective* (Orbis Books, 1987), which was awarded a Catholic Book Award in the U.S. for the best work in the area of scripture.

PABLO RICHARD was born in Chile. He has degrees in theology from the Catholic University of Chile, Holy Scriptures from the Pontifical Biblical Institute in Rome, and in the sociology of religion from the Sorbonne in Paris. At present he lives in Costa Rica where he teaches at the National University and serves on the board of DEI (Ecumenical Department of Research). He is the author of *Death of Christendoms, Birth of the Church* (Orbis Books, 1987), and other works on ecclesiology, sociology of religion, and biblical studies.

JULIO DE SANTA ANA is a Methodist theologian, philosopher, and sociologist from Uruguay who works as studies coordinator in the World Council of Churches department for development. His books include *Towards a Church of the Poor* (Orbis Books, 1981) and *Separation Without Hope* (Orbis Books, 1980).

JUAN CARLOS SCANNONE is a Jesuit from Argentina. He has degrees in philosophy from the University of Munich and theology from the University of Innsbruck. Currently he teaches philosophy and theology at the Universidad del Salvador in Buenos Aires. He has extensive publications in philosophy, and has contributed widely to European theological journals, including *Concilium*, focusing on his interest in popular religion and culture.

JUAN LUIS SEGUNDO is a Jesuit from Uruguay with degrees in theology from Louvain and the University of Paris. He has worked in association with the Peter Faber Center in Montevideo. Segundo has produced some of the most rigorous and weighty contributions to liberation theology, beginning with his five volumes, *Theology for Artisans of a New Humanity* (Orbis Books, 1973-74), up to his recent five-volume work of christology, *Jesus of Nazareth, Yesterday and Today* (Orbis Books, 1984-89). Other works include *The Liberation of Theology* (Orbis Books, 1976), and *Theology and the Church: A Letter to Cardinal Ratzinger and a Warning to the Church* (Winston-Seabury, 1985).

JON SOBRINO is a Spanish-born Jesuit living in El Salvador, where he teaches theology at the Universidad José Simeón Cañas, and co-directs the *Revista Latinoamericana de Teología*. He is especially known for his first important work, *Christology at the Crossroads* (Orbis Books, 1978). Since then he has also published *The True Church and the Poor* (Orbis Books, 1984), *Jesus in Latin America* (Orbis Books, 1987), and *Spirituality of Liberation* (Orbis Books, 1988).

ELSA TAMEZ, a Methodist theologian from Costa Rica, is one of the best-known women theologians of Latin America. She is professor of biblical studies at the Seminario Biblico Latinamericano in San Jose, and serves as a staff member of the Departamento Ecumenico de Investigaciones. Her books include *Bible of the Oppressed* (Orbis Books, 1982), *Against Machismo* (Meyer Stone, 1987), and (as editor) *Through Her Eyes: Latin American Women Doing Theology* (Orbis Books, 1989).

Some other liberationist authors mentioned in this book are:

TEREZA CAVALCANTI, who teaches Biblical Pastoral Studies at the Catholic University of Rio de Janeiro; JAVIER IGUÍÑIZ, an economist who has written the government plan for the United Left in Peru; DIEGO IRARRAZAVAL, a Chilean priest who investigates folk religion in Chicuito, Peru; CARMEN LORA, a Peruvian sociologist who works with Gutiérrez at the Bartolomé de Las Casas Institute in Peru; NELLY RITCHIE, a Methodist minister from Argentina; ARACELY ROCCHIETTI, a Methodist pastor in Uruguay; RAUL VIDALES, a Mexican priest who has taught theology and worked with grass-roots organizations in many countries of Latin America; ALIDA VERHOEVEN, a Methodist minister in Argentina who works with women victims of human rights violations in Mendoza.

Notes

INTRODUCTION

1. The magazine referred to is the *Family Protection Scoreboard,* a special issue on "Liberation Theology: Will it Liberate or Enslave People?," published by the National Citizens Action Network, Costa Mesa, Calif., 1988. The advertisement, by the Committee for Improved U.S.-Mexican Relations, appeared in the *Wall Street Journal,* Friday, October 7, 1988, p. C20, and was entitled "State of Insurrection in Mexico." The identical ad appeared a few days later in the *New York Times.*

2. McGovern, *Marxism: An American Christian Perspective* (Maryknoll, N.Y.: Orbis, 1980).

3. Robert McAfee Brown, *Theology in a New Key* (Philadelphia: Westminster, 1978). Phillip Berryman, *Liberation Theology* (New York: Pantheon, 1986). Leonardo and Clodovis Boff, *Introducing Liberation Theology* (Maryknoll, N.Y.: Orbis, 1987; original 1986). [Note: The "original" date refers to the Spanish or Portuguese edition; this can be significant in making assessments when the English translation comes several years after the original.] Ricardo Planas, *Liberation Theology* (New York: Paulist, 1986). Paul Sigmund, "Whither Liberation Theology? A Historical Evaluation," *Crisis,* 5/1 (January 1987): 5–14, a preliminary overview of a book on liberation theology and democracy to be published by Oxford University Press. Rebecca S. Chopp, *The Praxis of Suffering* (Maryknoll, N.Y.: Orbis, 1986), on both European political theology and liberation theology. Deane William Ferm, *Third World Liberation Theologies, An Introductory Survey* (Maryknoll, N.Y.: Orbis, 1986), contains brief accounts of several Latin American theologians. Rosino Gibellini, *The Liberation Theology Debate* (Maryknoll, N.Y.: Orbis, 1987), gives an overview of liberation theology and discusses in detail the 1984 and 1986 Vatican instructions on liberation theology.

4. Berryman, *Liberation Theology,* p. 6, presents the following as the principal elements of liberation theology: (1) an interpretation of Christian faith out of the suffering, struggles, and hope of the poor; (2) a critique of society and of the ideologies sustaining it; (3) a critique of the activity of the church and of Christians from the angle of the poor.

5. Roger S. Haight, S.J., *An Alternative Vision: An Interpretation of Liberation Theology* (Mahwah, N.J.: Paulist Press, 1985).

6. Leonardo and Clodovis Boff, *Introducing Liberation Theology* (Maryknoll, N.Y.: Orbis, 1987; original 1986).

7. Alfonso López Trujillo, *De Medellín a Puebla* (Madrid: Biblioteca de Autores Cristianos, 1980), chapter 7 (from a 1977 article); comments on Gutiérrez, pp. 188–89, and on Boff, pp. 200–201.

8. Sigmund, "Whither Liberation Theology."

9. Juan Luis Segundo, "Two Theologies of Liberation," *The Month,* 17/10

(October 1984). Segundo believes that the "deideologization" of the language used in conveying Christian truths lay at the heart of liberation theology's original purpose. This purpose extended to the whole of theology. He feels that the focus placed on the word "liberation" unfortunately distorted this original purpose and made it appear that political liberation was viewed as the very center and main content of all theology. This focus, Segundo adds, led Latin American theologians into useless battles with European and North American theologians and into conflict with church authorities. His work *The Liberation of Theology* intended precisely what its title implies, to free theology from non-Christian ideological elements. In achieving this goal, Segundo believes, liberation theology would in turn and in time affect pastoral attitudes and hence contribute to the long-range goal of socio-political liberation.

10. J.C. Scannone, S.J., "La teología de la liberación, caracterización, corrientes, etapas," *Stromata* (San Miguel-Buenos Aires), January-February 1982, pp. 18ff. Bishop Roques Adames cites Scannone's distinctions in chapter 3 of *Evangelización liberadora y doctrina social católica* edited by CELAM (Bogotá: Departamento de Pastoral Social, 1987); so also does Ignacio Palacios Videla, "El Contexto histórico de la teología de la liberación," *Todo es Historia* (March 1987), pp. 79ff.

11. Segundo Galilea, *Religiosidad popular y pastoral* (Madrid: Ediciones Cristiandad, 1979), pp. 112–13.

12. The expressions "free enterprise" and "capitalism" are often used interchangeably. I believe they *connote* different things and should be distinguished. Free enterprise suggests opportunities for individuals to begin their own businesses. Capitalism suggests ownership of factories or other large businesses with physical work done by hired laborers. Thus I view the United States as a free enterprise system from the outset—four of five white U.S. Americans owned their own farm or trade prior to 1850—but as capitalist (with a continuation of free enterprise) only from the mid- to late-nineteenth century on.

13. Ricardo Antoncich, *Christians in the Face of Injustice, A Latin American Reading of Catholic Social Teaching* (Maryknoll, N.Y.: Orbis, 1987; original 1980).

14. Alfonso López Trujillo, *Liberation or Revolution?* (Huntington, Ind.: Our Sunday Visitor, 1977), p. 101.

15. On Vekemans, see Padre J. Guadalupe Carney, *To Be a Revolutionary* (San Francisco: Harper & Row, 1985), pp. 199–200.

16. Michael Novak, *Will It Liberate? Questions about Liberation Theology* (Mahwah, N.J.: Paulist, 1986), p. 176.

1. A BRIEF HISTORY OF LIBERATION THEOLOGY

1. I have drawn especially on works by Phillip Berryman, *Liberation Theology* (New York: Pantheon, 1987), and Edward L. Cleary, O.P., *Crisis and Change, The Church in Latin America Today* (Maryknoll, N.Y.: Orbis, 1985), as well as an earlier history of liberation theology by Roberto Oliveros, *Liberación y teología, génesis y crecimiento de una reflexión, 1966–1977* (Lima: Centro de Estudios y Publicaciones, 1977).

2. Enrique Dussel, *A History of the Church in Latin America, Colonialism to Liberalism (1492–1979)* (Grand Rapids: Eerdmans, 1981), pp. 38–39. For another

"liberationist" interpretation of Latin American history and the church's place in it, see Pablo Richard, *Death of Christendoms, Birth of the Church* (Maryknoll, N.Y.: Orbis, 1987; original 1978).

3. Hubert Herring, *A History of Latin America from the Beginnings to the Present* (New York: Knopf, 1968, 3rd ed.), p. 171.

4. Ibid., pp. 171–74; see also Dussel, *A History of the Church*, pp. 47–55 on Las Casas and other church defenders of the Indians.

5. Herring, *A History of Latin America*, p. 178.

6. Mariano Picon-Salas, *A Cultural History of Spanish America, From Conquest to Independence* (Berkeley: University of California, 1963), p. 74.

7. P. Antoine Tibesar, "The Lima Pastors, 1750–1821," *The Americas* 28 (July 1971), cited by Jeffrey Klaiber, S.J., *La Iglesia en el Perú*, chapter 1 (from a manuscript later published by the Pontifical Catholic University in Lima in 1988).

8. Ibid.

9. Dussel, *A History of the Church*, pp. 87–91.

10. Ibid., p. 60.

11. Ibid., p. 81.

12. Cleary, *Crisis and Change*, p. 9.

13. Dussel, *A History of the Church*, p. 105.

14. Klaiber, *La Iglesia en el Perú*, chapter 1.

15. See José Míguez Bonino, *Toward a Christian Political Ethics* (Philadelphia: Fortress, 1983), pp. 59ff., on the growth of Protestantism in the late 19th and early 20th centuries and its links with liberalism.

16. Cleary, *Crisis and Change*, p. 9.

17. *The Documents of Vatican II*, ed. Walter M. Abbot, S.J. (New York: America Press, 1966), from *Gaudium et Spes*, no. 2.

18. Paul VI, *Populorum Progressio*, nos. 7 and 9, in *The Gospel of Justice and Peace*, ed. Joséph Gremillion (Maryknoll, N.Y.: Orbis, 1976).

19. Cleary, *Crisis and Change*, pp. 26–30.

20. Roberto Oliveros, *Liberación y teología*, p. 35.

21. See the many letters and documents collected by Alain Gheerbrant in *The Rebel Church in Latin America* (Middlesex, England: Penguin Books, 1974). Gheerbrant cites letters and manifestos from radical Christian leaders like Msgr. German Gusman Campos, Juan Carlos Zaffaroni, and Juan García Elorrio, from Colombia, Uruguay, and Argentina, respectively.

22. Leonardo and Clodovis Boff, *Introducing Liberation Theology* (Maryknoll, N.Y.: Orbis, 1987; original 1986), p. 69. The Boffs also provide a great number of names of theologians who emerged at different stages of liberation theology's growth. See chapter 5, "A Concise History of Liberation Theology."

At the initial 1964 meeting in Petrópolis, Segundo cited three issues as requiring the special attention of Latin American theology: the problems created by urbanization, the mass media, and the growth of revolutionary consciousness. Gera urged the renovation of seminaries in Latin America. Gutiérrez called for establishing a dialogue with the people of Latin America, and more specifically called for a study of the behavior and praxis of three important groups: the popular masses, the technological and cultural elites, and the conservative oligarchy. See Roberto Oliveros, *Liberación y teología*, pp. 53–57.

23. Oliveros, pp. 115–16.

24. From notes prepared by Comblin, cited in Gheerbrant, *The Rebel Church*, pp. 223ff.

25. Medellín documents found in Gremillion, *The Gospel of Peace and Justice*, "Justice," no. 1, p. 445.

26. Ibid., "Peace," nos. 3, 9, 16–19, pp. 455–61, and "Poverty of the Church," no. 7, p. 473.

27. A. García Rubio, *Teología da libertação, política ou profetismo?* (São Paulo: Loyola, 1977), pp. 41–43, notes, for example, that the document on justice tends to speak more of integral development and reform, while the document on peace stresses more radical ideas, including the conscientization method used by Paulo Freire. García's work, often quite critical of liberation theology, deals both with the history of liberation theology and its main characteristics. Ignacio Palacio Videla, "El contexto histórico de la teología de la liberación," in *Todo es Historia*, March 1987 (Argentina), pp. 79ff., makes the same point about the juxtaposition of development and liberationist language in the documents of Medellín.

28. This summary of 1970–1971 works is drawn from Oliveros, *Liberación y teología*, pp. 135ff.

29. Gutiérrez, *A Theology of Liberation* (Maryknoll, N.Y.: Orbis, 1973, original 1971), pp. 36–37, 176–78, 235–36, on the threefold liberation. All citations refer to this 1973 edition unless specific reference is made to a newer 1988 edition.

30. Paul VI, *Octogesima Adveniens*, nos. 31 and 33, in Gremillion, *Gospel of Peace and Justice*.

31. Bishops' Synod on "Justice in the World," also in Gremillion.

32. Berryman, *Liberation Theology*, pp. 98–99, and Dussel, *A History of the Church*, pp. 223–34. Eric O. Hanson, *The Catholic Church in World Politics* (Princeton: Princeton University Press, 1987) adds that Cardinal Baggio in Rome supervised López Trujillo and used CELAM to limit the influence of Cardinal Silva (Chile) and Cardinal Arns (Brazil) and other Brazilian bishops, p. 60.

33. Bishop Alfonzo López Trujillo, *Liberation or Revolution?* (Huntington, Ind.: Our Sunday Visitor, 1977), pp. 16–17.

34. See McGovern, *Marxism*, pp. 231–32. The documents referred to are found in *Christians and Socialism*, ed. John Eagleson (Maryknoll, N.Y.: Orbis, 1975), pp. 184–217.

35. Norbert Greinacher, ed., *Konflikt um die Theologie der Befreiung, Diskussion und Dokumentation* (Zurich: Benzinger, 1985), pp. 51–56.

36. Paul VI, *On the Evangelization of the Modern World* (*Evangelii Nuntiandi*), given December 8, 1975 (Washington, D.C.: United States Catholic Conference, 1976).

37. On the Puebla Conference, the speeches of John Paul II in Mexico, and the other events surrounding the conference, see *Puebla and Beyond*, eds. John Eagleson and Phillip Scharper (Maryknoll, N.Y.: Orbis, 1979).

38. Phillip Berryman, *Liberation Theology*, p. 3.

39. Congregation for the Doctrine of the Faith (Cardinal Joseph Ratzinger), "Instruction on Certain Aspects of the Theology of Liberation," published in the *National Catholic Reporter*, September 21, 1984.

40. The address by Cardinal Ratzinger appeared originally in *30 Giorni*, March 1984, and was published in *Catholicism in Crisis*, September 1984.

41. Congregation for the Doctrine of the Faith (Cardinal Ratzinger), "Instruc-

tion on Christian Freedom and Liberation" (Vatican City: Libreria Editrice Vaticana, 1986).

42. *Latinamerica Press*, May 1, 1986 (Lima, Peru), published responses from four leading liberation theologians to the 1986 Vatican Instruction. Leonardo Boff welcomed the instruction "as a legitimation of all the pastoral practice and theology . . . carried out in Brazil over the past twenty years." The document also strengthens liberation initiatives, said Boff, such as peasant struggles for land, and it calls on all Christians to make an option for the poor. Gutiérrez welcomed the instruction's placing of liberation in the context of freedom. Jon Sobrino, on the other hand, while praising some parts of the document, found it lacking in theological depth and concrete historical analysis. Ignacio Ellacuría also expressed disappointment that it did not recognize positive contributions of liberation theology to the fields of christology, ecclesiology, and spirituality, nor did it acknowledge the personal and collective sufferings of those who have acted courageously in working for liberation. For a very positive assessment of the instruction by a U.S. theologian, see Alfred T. Hennelly, "The Red-Hot Issue: Liberation Theology," *America*, May 24, 1986. I have drawn upon Hennelly's comments in my summary of the positive aspects of the instruction.

43. John Paul II to the Brazilian Bishops, 1986, published in part in the *National Catholic Reporter*, May 9, 1986.

44. The statements of Castillo Morales were reported in a news article, "Una biblia para comemorar el V centenario de la evangelización de América," in *Vida Nueva* (Madrid), February 13, 1988, p. 373.

45. The quotes from John Paul II's address to the Peruvian bishops are taken from a mimeographed copy (in Spanish) distributed May 15, 1988, by the papal nunciature, nos. 3, 5, 7.

46. Ricardo Durand Florez, S.J., *La utopia de la liberación* (Callao, Peru, January 1988). Durand, I was told, sent a copy of his book to all his priests (with a bill attached, but with the option of saying a Mass for him).

47. Penny Lernoux, "Rome sends 'warnings' to eight Brazilian bishops," *National Catholic Reporter*, November 4, 1988, p. 10.

2. A NEW WAY OF DOING THEOLOGY

1. Leonardo and Clodovis Boff, *Introducing Liberation Theology* (Maryknoll, N.Y.: Orbis, 1987; original 1986), pp. 1–2.

2. *World Development Report 1987*, Table 1, pp. 202–3.

3. Ibid., pp. 252–53.

4. *South America, Central America, and the Carribean, 1986* (London: Europa Publications, 1985), p. 161.

5. *Time*, September 11, 1978, pp. 32–37, cited by Guillermo Cook, *The Expectation of the Poor, Latin American Basic Ecclesial Communities in Protestant Perspective* (Maryknoll, N.Y.: Orbis, 1985), p. 23.

6. Michael P. Todaro, *Economic Development in the Third World* (New York: Longman, 1981, 2nd ed.), p. 260.

7. Stephen Kinzer, "The Hunger for Land Feeds the Crisis in Central America," *New York Times*, September 7, 1987, pp. 1, 5.

8. James Lemoyne, "In Long-Suffering Central America, the Workers Suffer Most," *New York Times*, September 8, 1987, p. A14.

9. Miguel Varon, "Colombia: Government Turns Blind Eye to 'Dickensian' Child Labor Problems," *Latin America Press,* January 16, 1986, pp. 3–4.

10. "Quiche People Suffer 'Genocide,' " *Latin America Press,* October 31, 1985, p. 6.

11. Penny Lernoux, *Cry of the People* (New York: Penguin Books, 1982), chapter 1 on torture, and passim.

12. Lawrence Weschler, "A Reporter at Large" (Brazil: Nunca Mas), *New Yorker,* part 1, May 25, 1987 and part 2, June 1, 1987.

13. Juan Luis Segundo, "Two Theologies of Liberation," *The Month,* October 1984, vol. 17, no. 10.

14. Gutiérrez's experiences are recounted by José Míguez Bonino in a statement for the *Theology of the Americas,* eds. Sergio Torres and John Eagleson (Maryknoll, N.Y.: Orbis, 1976), p. 278. They are cited also by Robert McAfee Brown, *Gustavo Gutiérrez* (Atlanta: John Knox, 1980), p. 23.

15. Leonardo and Clodovis Boff, *Introducing Liberation Theology,* p. 7.

16. Jon Sobrino, *Christology at the Crossroads* (Maryknoll, N.Y.: Orbis, 1978; original 1976), pp. 34–35.

17. Hugo Assmann, *Theology for a Nomad Church* (Maryknoll, N.Y.: Orbis, 1976), p. 74.

18. Alves cited by Assmann, p. 76.

19. Gutiérrez, *A Theology of Liberation,* p. 13, uses this expression. A second concept from Gramsci's thought appears also operative in liberation theology. Gramsci spoke of gaining "hegemony" in society. In contrast to the classic Marxist view that economic conditions determine ideology, Gramsci believed that socialist ideas must gain acceptance before the working class attempts to seize power. One could use this concept of hegemony to explain much that liberation theology seeks to achieve in criticizing status quo ideologies and in winning acceptance for a more prophetic Christianity and a church committed to the poor. The concept of hegemony is used explicitly in this way to explain struggles within the church and in society by Otto Maduro, *Religion and Social Conflicts* (Maryknoll, N.Y.: Orbis, 1982; original 1979), chapters 16, 30, 31, and passim.

20. Leonardo and Clodovis Boff, *Introducing Liberation Theology,* p. 19.

21. Ibid., chapters 2 and 3.

22. Gutiérrez, *A Theology of Liberation,* p. 15.

23. Ibid., chapter 1.

24. Ibid., p. 145.

25. Ibid., p. 11.

26. Ibid., p. 13.

27. Gutiérrez, *La verdad los hará libres, confrontaciones* (Lima: Centro de Estudios y Publicaciones, 1986), p. 138; English translation forthcoming, Orbis, 1990. See also the extended treatment of praxis in his new introduction to the 15th anniversary edition of *A Theology of Liberation* (Maryknoll, N.Y.: Orbis, 1988), p. xxx.

28. Pablo Richard, *Death of Christendoms, Birth of the Church* (Maryknoll, N.Y.: Orbis, 1987; original 1978), pp. 147ff. The first phase of the use of praxis, on pastoral activity of the church, can be found in Gutiérrez, *Líneas pastorales de la iglesia en América Latina* (Lima: CEP, 1986, new edition).

29. J.C. Scannone, S.J., "La teología de la liberación, caracterización, corrigentes, etapes," in *Stromata* (San Miguel, Buenos Aires), January-June 1982, p. 7,

indicates various formulas used by Gutiérrez to define the method of liberation theology. J.B. Libânio, *Teologia da libertação, roteiro didático para um estudo* (São Paolo: Loyola, 1987), p. 117, gives his view of the many ways praxis is involved in liberation theology.

30. Leonardo and Clodovis Boff, *Introducing Liberation Theology,* pp. 41–42.

31. Carlos Mesters, *Flor sem defesa, uma explição da biblia a partir do povo* (Petrópolis: Vozes, 1983), pp. 24–29; *Defenseless Flower: A New Reading of the Bible,* Orbis, 1989. For a commentary on Mesters and this work, see L. Alonso Schökel, "Exegesis y hermenéutica en Brasil," in *Biblica* (Rome), vol. 68, 1987.

32. Mesters, *Flor sem defesa,* pp. 32–33.

33. Leonardo and Clodovis Boff, *Introducing Liberation Theology,* p. 22.

34. Ibid., p. 24.

35. Ibid., pp. 24–32.

36. Ibid., pp. 32–35.

37. Ibid., pp. 39–41.

38. Clodovis Boff, *Theology and Praxis, Epistemological Foundation* (Maryknoll, N.Y.: Orbis, 1987; original, 1978), Preface.

39. Ibid., p. 10.

40. Ibid., pp. 30–41.

41. Ibid., pp. 55–58.

42. Ibid., pp. 70–77.

43. Ibid., pp. 81–88.

44. Ibid., p. 14l quote; on Exodus, p. 143.

45. Ibid., p. 167.

46. Ibid., p. 198.

47. Ibid., p. 44. José Míguez Bonino, *Toward a Christian Political Ethics* (Philadelphia: Fortress, 1983), pp. 42–43, affirms and builds upon Boff's third mediation especially. Theologians, says Míguez, find themselves in a double location. As theologians they must respect the autonomy of theology—"we intend to do theology, not sociology or politics"—but at the same time they are social agents affecting society. Their social location can determine their perspective—for example, seeing God and the world from a perspective of the poor; it can influence the questions they pose; and it can determine on whose behalf they are writing. Like Boff, Míguez affirms social analysis as "constitutive" of liberation theology, and he favors dialectical social analysis over functional analysis, pp. 45–47.

48. Juan Luis Segundo, *The Liberation of Theology* (Maryknoll, N.Y.: Orbis, 1976; original 1975), pp. 7–8. For a study of Segundo's thought, up to and including this work, see Alfred T. Hennelly, *Theologies in Conflict. The Challenge of Juan Luis Segundo* (Maryknoll, N.Y.: Orbis, 1979).

49. Segundo, *Liberation of Theology,* p. 9. The examples used to explain Segundo's method are my own.

50. Ibid., pp. 13–19.

51. Segundo, *Faith and Ideologies* (Maryknoll, N.Y.: Orbis, 1984; original 1982), chapter 1.

52. Ideology, says Segundo, deals with the structure of "means" used to make some faith structure effective. As Christianity is often viewed as faith only, though it expresses itself in ideology, so Marxism is thought of as an ideology without any reference to a faith element. But Segundo argues that Marx's thought contains both. The faith structure, which gives meaning to Marx's work, lies primarily in

wanting to create a new, more human society. Marxism has its own transcendent element: belief in a not-yet achieved society. The ideology of Marxism lies in its scientific method and program of social transformation. These are the instruments (means) to realize the values of Marxist faith. Most Marxists would consider Marx's methodology as a science, not as ideology, and would say that the ideology of Marxism is contained in its materialist philosophy and worldview. But since Segundo uses ideology as any system of means, Marxism's scientific method fits under this head; it gives technical means for achieving a new society. See Segundo, *Faith and Ideologies,* chapter 4.

53. Ibid., p. 47.

54. Ibid., p. 165, also chapter 3 on faith.

55. Segundo, *The Historical Jesus of the Synoptics* (Maryknoll, N.Y.: Orbis, 1985; original 1982), pp. 7–9.

56. Ibid., pp. 81–82.

57. For a summary of liberation theologians' criticisms of European theology, which I do not discuss at any length in this book, see Gibellini, *The Liberation Theology Debate,* pp. 13–19.

58. *The Documents of Vatican II,* ed. Walter M. Abbott, S.J. (New York: America Press, 1966), *Gaudium et Spes,* n. 42.

59. Ricardo Planas, *Liberation Theology. The Political Expression of Religion* (Kansas City: Sheed and Ward, 1986), p. 79.

3. THE CRITICS: AN OVERVIEW

1. Alfonso López Trujillo, *De Medellín a Puebla* (Madrid: Biblioteca de Autores Cristianos, 1980), p. 79.

2. Ibid., pp. 98–99.

3. Ibid., pp. 177–87.

4. Ibid., pp. 188–89.

5. Ibid., pp. 226–27.

6. Ibid., p. 330.

7. Ibid., p. 236.

8. López Trujillo, *Liberation or Revolution?* (Huntington, Ind.: Our Sunday Visitor, 1977; original 1975), pp. 37–46.

9. Ibid., p. 74.

10. Roger Vekemans, S.J., *Teología de la liberación y cristianos por el socialismo* (Bogotá: CEDIAL, 1976), p. 30.

11. Ibid., pp. 43–45.

12. Ibid., p. 161.

13. Ibid., pp. 165–69 on praxis; pp. 176ff. on use of biblical texts.

14. Bonaventure Kloppenburg, O.F.M., *Temptations for the Theology of Liberation* (Chicago: Franciscan Herald Press, 1974).

15. The International Theological Commission, "Human Development and Christian Salvation," *African Ecclesial Review,* April 1979, p. 119. A subcommittee of the commission, headed by Karl Lehmann, examined liberation theology from various angles: methodological and hermeneutical (Karl Lehmann), biblical (Heinz Schurmann), ecclesiological (Olegario Gonzáles de Cardedal) and systematic (Hans Urs von Balthasar). See Gibellini, *The Liberation Theology Debate,* pp. 42–43.

16. "Human Development," pp. 119–20.

17. Ibid., pp. 120–23.

18. Ibid., pp. 123–28.

19. Congregation for the Doctrine of the Faith, "Instruction on Certain Aspects of the Theology of Liberation," published in the *National Catholic Reporter,* September 21, 1984, section VI, nn. 5–10 (citations given by section and paragraph numbers).

20. Ibid., IV, 3 and X, 11–12.

21. The address by Cardinal Ratzinger appeared originally in *30 Giorni* (Italy), March 1984, and was published in *Catholicism in Crisis,* September 1984, p. 38.

22. Gutiérrez, *A Theology of Liberation,* p. 47.

23. Ratzinger's March 1984 address, p. 38.

24. Ibid., pp. 40–41.

25. "Instruction on Certain Aspects . . ." (1984), Introduction.

26. Ibid., IV, 2.

27. Ibid., IV, 12–15.

28. Congregation for the Doctrine of the Faith (Cardinal Ratzinger), "Instruction on Christian Freedom and Liberation" (Vatican City: Libreria Editrice Vaticana, 1986), no. 3 (citations given by paragraph numbers).

29. Ibid., nos. 52–53.

30. Ibid., no. 75.

31. Ibid., nos. 68, 75.

32. These essays appear in James V. Schall, S.J., *Liberation Theology in Latin America* (San Francisco: Ignatius Press, 1982).

33. Thomas G. Sanders, "The Theology of Liberation: Christian Utopianism," *Christianity and Crisis,* September 17, 1973, vol. 33, no. 15, pp. 167–73.

34. Dennis P. McCann, *Christian Realism and Liberation Theology* (Maryknoll, N.Y.: Orbis, 1981), p. 27.

35. Ibid., p. 113.

36. Ibid., p. 18.

37. Ibid., p. 107.

38. Ibid., p. 118.

39. Ibid., p. 157.

40. Ibid., p. 117.

41. Ibid., p. 230.

42. Matthew L. Lamb, "A Distorted Interpretation of Latin American Liberation Theology," *Horizons,* Fall 1981.

43. Richard John Neuhaus, *The Catholic Moment. The Paradox of the Church in the Modern World* (San Francisco: Harper & Row, 1987), p. 172.

44. Ibid., p. 177.

45. Ibid., p. 195.

46. Ibid., p. 184.

47. Ibid., Neuhaus's criticisms, pages 183 and 185, respectively, offer citations from Juan Luis Segundo, *The Sacraments Today,* volume 4 of "A Theology for the Artisans for a New Humanity" series (Maryknoll, N.Y.: Orbis, 1974; original 1971), p. 54 for both references.

48. Schubert M. Ogden, *Faith and Freedom. Toward a Theology of Liberation* (Nashville: Abingdon, 1979), p. 31.

49. Ibid., p. 33.

50. Ibid., pp. 71–75.

51. Ibid., pp. 86–87.

52. Ibid., pp. 89–91.

53. Ibid., p. 127.

54. José Luis Illanes, "Teología de la liberación, análisis de su método," in Roger Vekemans and Juan Cordero, *Teología de la liberación* (Bogotá: CEDIAL, 1988), p. 50.

55. Enrique Colom Casta, "Entre la opción por los pobres y el marxismo," *Tierra Nueva* (Bogotá), 1988, n. 64.

4. BIBLICAL THEMES

1. U.S. Catholic Bishops, "Economic Justice for All: Catholic Social Teaching and the U.S. Economy," *Origins*, November 27, 1986, vol. 16, no. 24, chapter 2, nn. 30–54. For a biblical commentary on liberation themes by a U.S. scholar, see L. John Topel, S.J., *The Way to Peace, Liberation through the Bible* (Maryknoll, N.Y.: Orbis, 1979).

2. John Shea, *The Spirit Master* (Chicago: Thomas More, 1987), pp. 127–28.

3. Leonardo and Clodovis Boff, *Introducing Liberation Theology*, pp. 32–33.

4. Gutiérrez, *A Theology of Liberation*, pp. 150–54.

5. In addition to other theologians cited in this section on exodus, see, for example, Gutiérrez, *A Theology of Liberation*, pp. 155–59; Hugo Assmann, *Theology for a Nomad Church*, p. 66; Rubem Alves, *A Theology of Human Hope*, p. 89; José Míguez Bonino, *Revolutionary Theology Comes of Age*, pp. 134–35; and a series of articles on exodus-liberation in *Revista Biblica*, 32, no. 139 (1971).

6. J. Severino Croatto, *Exodus, A Hermeneutics of Freedom* (Maryknoll, N.Y.: Orbis, 1981; original 1978), chapter 1, pp. 4–5, 8–11.

7. Ibid., chapter 3. Croatto deals with Genesis after his account of the exodus because he believes that the book of Genesis was written in the light of the exodus experience. Many scholars would concur with this judgment, but I have taken the liberty to put Genesis first to avoid a long discussion of this rather peripheral issue.

8. Ibid., pp. 16–18.

9. Ibid., pp. 18–23.

10. Ibid., pp. 23–30; quote on p. 30.

11. Pablo Richard, "Biblical Theology of Confrontation with Idols," in *The Idols of Death and the God of Life. A Theology*, Pablo Richard et al. (Maryknoll, N.Y.: Orbis, 1983; original 1980), p. 4.

12. Ibid., p. 7.

13. Ibid., p. 17.

14. Jorge V. Pixley, *Exodo, una lectura evangélica y popular* (Mexico City: Casa Unida, 1983), pp. 8–9; *On Exodus: A Liberation Perspective* (Maryknoll, N.Y.: Orbis, 1987).

15. *Exodo*, pp. 10ff. See also his treatment of these stages in Pixley, *God's Kingdom. A Guide for Biblical Study* (Maryknoll, N.Y.: Orbis, 1981, original 1977), pp. 19ff.

16. Pixley, *God's Kingdom*, p. 63.

17. Pixley, *Exodo*, on Moses, pp. 31 and 43, on Aaron, pp. 56–57.

18. Ibid., pp. 113–14.

19. Ibid., pp. 126–27, 171–72.

20. J. Andrew Kirk, *Liberation Theology. An Evangelical View from the Third World* (Atlanta: John Knox, 1979), pp. 147–48. In assessing liberation theology's use of the exodus story, Kirk cites Croatto often but uses passages from Miranda, Gutiérrez, Segundo, and other liberation theologians as well.

21. Ibid., p. 95.

22. Ibid., pp. 148–50.

23. Norbert F. Lohfink, *Option for the Poor. The Basic Principles of Liberation Theology in the Light of the Bible*, ed. Duane L. Christiensen (Berkeley: BIBAL, Berkeley Institute of Bible, Archeology, and Law).

24. José Míguez Bonino, *Christians and Marxists: The Mutual Challenge to Revolution* (Grand Rapids: Eerdmans, 1976), pp. 31–33.

25. José Porfirio Miranda, *Marx and the Bible: A Critique of the Philosophy of Oppression*, (Maryknoll, N.Y.: Orbis, 1974; original 1971), pp. 14–15.

26. Ibid., p. 46.

27. Croatto, *Exodus*, pp. 39–40.

28. Julio de Santa Ana, *Good News to the Poor. The Challenge of the Poor in the History of the Church* (Geneva: World Council of Churches, 1977), chapter 1.

29. George M. Soares-Prabhu, S.J., "Class in the Bible: The Biblical Poor a Social Class?," in *Vidayajoti* 49 (1985): 325–46. I am indebted to Fr. John R. Donahue, S.J., for drawing my attention to the Soares and Lohfink articles. Donahue's own study, "Biblical Perspectives on Justice," in *The Faith That Does Justice*, ed. John C. Haughey (New York: Paulist Press, 1977) also provides a valuable assessment of the themes we have been discussing. Donahue cites the renowned scholar Gerhard von Rad who claims: "There is absolutely no concept in the Old Testament with so central a significance for all relationships of human life as that of justice" (p. 68). The doing of justice, says Donahue, constitutes the very substance of religious faith; without it, God remains unknown. While New Testament statements on justice are not as rich or direct as those in the Old Testament, says Donahue, justice still remains a central concern (p. 85). In preaching the kingdom, Jesus presents it as the power of God active in the world, transforming the world, and confronting the powers in the world. The kingdom finds a special home in the poor. Donahue's own insights can also be found in the U.S. Bishops' letter on the U.S. economy, since Donahue was the principal biblical scholar working with the bishops.

30. Soares-Prabhu, *Class in the Bible*, p. 332.

31. Ibid., p. 339.

32. Leonardo Boff, *Jesus Christ Liberator. A Critical Christology for Our Time* (Maryknoll, N.Y.: Orbis, 1978; original 1972), pp. 44–47.

33. Ibid., p. 49.

34. Ibid., pp. 59, 60, 64.

35. Ibid., p. 72.

36. Ibid., p. 240.

37. João Evangelista Martins Terra, S.J., "Eco del informe Ratzinger: Fray Boff y el neo-galicanismo brasileno," *Tierra Nueva* (Bogotá), October 1987, p. 16, and a continuation of the article, January 1988, p. 54.

38. Ibid., (January 1988), pp. 51–53.

39. P. Carlos Ignacio Gonzales, S.J., *El es nuestra salvación. Cristología y soteriología* (Bogotá: CELAM, 1986), Appendix II on christologies of liberation, pp. 513ff. Gonzales follows his critique of Boff with a critique of Jon Sobrino also.

40. Jon Sobrino, *Christology at the Crossroads* (Maryknoll, N.Y.: Orbis, 1978, original 1976), p. xxv.

41. Ibid., on starting with the historical Jesus, pp. 3–9; on liberation elements, p. 35.

42. Ibid., p. 41.

43. Ibid., pp. 42–50, 55–61.

44. Sobrino, "La centralidad del 'Reino de Dios' en la teología de la liberación," *Revista Latinamericana de Teología* (San Salvador), September-December 1986, pp. 248–65.

45. Ibid., p. 276.

46. Sobrino, *Christology at the Crossroads*, pp. 50–55.

47. Sobrino, "Liberación del pecado," *Sal Terrae*, January 1988, pp. 15ff.

48. Sobrino, *Christology at the Crossroads*, chapter 4 on the faith of Jesus.

49. Ibid., chapter 6 on the death of Jesus.

50. Sobrino, *Jesus in Latin America* (Maryknoll, N.Y.: Orbis, 1987; original 1982), p. 151 and chapter 7 overall.

51. Ibid., foreword by Juan Alfaro, pp. x–xii.

52. Juan Luis Segundo, *The Historical Jesus of the Synoptics* (Maryknoll, N.Y.: Orbis, 1985, original; 1982), pp. 14–17.

53. Ibid., p. 22. On the temporal priority of human interest over religious assent, Segundo comments: "Jesus' interest for the human being comes prior to the establishment of his relationship with God of his divinity" (p. 32).

54. Ibid., pp. 19–20 on the composition of the gospels; p. 21 the quote about St. Paul; pp. 6–7 on the gospels for our day and needs.

55. Ibid., chapter 5 on the political dimension.

56. Ibid., pp. 105–9.

57. Ibid., pp. 136–40.

58. John P. Meier, "The Bible as a Source for Theology," opening address to the Catholic Theological Society of America (Toronto, June 15, 1988), to be published in the CSTA proceedings.

59. *Faces of Jesus. Latin American Christologies*, ed. José Míguez Bonino (Maryknoll, N.Y.: Orbis, 1984; original 1977), chapters 2, 4, 5, and 6 all speak about different images of Jesus in Latin America.

60. Ibid., the statements saying that Jesus was not a political revolutionary on pp. 45, 69–70, 117–18, 145. Chapter 8 of this book contains Segundo Galilea's "Jesus' Attitude toward Politics: Some Working Hypotheses."

5. TWO SPECIAL THEMES: SPIRITUALITY AND WOMEN

1. Claude Geffré and Gustavo Gutiérrez, eds., *The Mystical and Political Dimension of the Christian Faith* (New York: Herder and Herder, 1974), pp. 15–16.

2. Ibid., Segundo Galilea, "Liberation as an Encounter with Politics and Contemplation," p. 20.

3. Ibid., pp. 22–25.

4. Segundo Galilea, *Following Jesus* (Maryknoll, N.Y.: Orbis, 1981; original 1974–1975), p. 1.

5. Ibid., chapters 3–4.

6. Ibid., p. 46 (on the quality of commitment), and p. 63 (on going into the desert).

7. Ibid., p. 70.

8. Ibid., p. 103.

9. Ibid., p. 112.

10. Frei Betto, "La oración, una exigencia (también) política," in Eduardo Bonnín ed., *Espiritualidad y liberación en América Latina* (San José, Costa Rica: Departamento Ecuménico de Investigaciones, n.d. [1982]), pp. 15–26.

11. Leonardo Boff's essay appears in the same volume of *Espiritualidad*; his statement on prayer, p. 55; see also p. 49. This valuable collection contains essays by fourteen authors, including the essay of Galilea that I cited at the beginning of this section. For a synthetic overview of liberation spirituality by a Spanish theologian who spent some time in Peru, see Jesús Espeja, *Espiritualidad y liberación* (Lima: CEP, 1986).

12. Jon Sobrino, *Spirituality of Liberation. Toward Political Holiness* (Maryknoll, N.Y.: Orbis, 1988; original 1985), chapter 1.

13. Gutiérrez, *We Drink from Our Own Wells. The Spiritual Journey of a People* (Maryknoll, N.Y.: Orbis, 1984; original 1983), p. 37.

14. Ibid., p. 2.

15. Ibid., p. 28.

16. Ibid., p. 35.

17. Ibid., p. 88.

18. Ibid., p. 111.

19. Ibid., p. 129.

20. Gutiérrez, *On Job. God-Talk and the Suffering of the Innocent* (Maryknoll, N.Y.: Orbis, 1987; original 1986), pp. xii–xiv.

21. Ibid., chapter 1.

22. Ibid., pp. 87–89.

23. Ibid., p. 48.

24. Segundo Galilea, *Religiosidad popular y pastoral* (Madrid: Ediciones Cristiandad, 1979), pp. 17–18.

25. Ibid., chapter 2. See also Ernest S. Sweeney, "The Nature and Power of Religion in Latin America: Some Aspects of Popular Beliefs and Practices," *Thought*, June 1984, vol. 59, no. 233.

26. Galilea, *Religiosidad popular*, p. 26.

27. Thomas M. Garr, S.J., *Cristianismo y religión quechua en la prelatura de Ayauiri* (Cusco, Perú: Instituto de Pastoral Andina, 1972), chapter 5 esp.

28. Raúl Vidales and Tokihiro Kudo, *Práctica religiosa y proyecto histórico* (Lima: CEP, 1975), p. 107 and the pages preceding, on defining popular religion.

29. From a lecture given by Diego Irarrazaval, which I attended in Chimbote, Peru, in July 1981. Irarrazaval has a book on popular religiosity in Peru, which I was not able to locate. John A. McCoy, "Popular Religion in Latin America," *America*, December 31, 1988, pp. 533–36, cites Irarrazaval among other liberationists in his fine short piece.

30. Ricardo Falla, *Esa muerte que nos hace vivir, estudio de la religión popular* (San Salvador: UCA Editores, 1984), pp. 132–33.

31. Galilea, *Religiosidad popular*, pp. 87–89.

32. Leonardo Boff, *Passion of Christ, Passion of the World* (Maryknoll, N.Y.: Orbis, 1987; original 1977).

33. Enrique Dussel, *A History of the Church in Latin America. Colonialism to Liberation (1492–1979)* (Grand Rapids: Eerdmans, 1981), pp. 3–5.

34. Carmen Lora, Cecilia Barnachea, and Fryné Santisteban, *Mujer: víctima de opresión, portadora de liberación* (Lima-Rimac, Peru: Instituto Bartolomé de Las Casas, 1987, 2nd edition), p. 21.

35. Ibid., pp. 152–56.

36. Christine E. Gudorf, "Indigenous Moral Problems in Peru," *America*, October 24, 1987, concludes her reflections on the issue of women in Peru with a position similar to that enunciated in the *Mujer* study I have been considering. Gudorf finds "compelling" the pragmatic objections to direct attacks on the issue of sexism, p. 272.

37. Ivone Gebara, "Women Doing Theology in Latin America," in Elsa Tamez, ed., *Through Her Eyes* (Maryknoll, N.Y.: Orbis, 1989), pp. 37–48.

38. Ibid., p. 48.

39. Consuelo del Prado, "I Sense God in a Different Way," in Tamez, *Through Her Eyes*, pp. 140–49.

40. Alida Verhoeven, "The Concept of God: A Feminine Perspective," in Tamez, *Through Her Eyes*, pp. 49–55.

41. María Clara Bingemer, "The Trinity from a Woman's Perspective," in Tamez, *Through Her Eyes*, pp. 56–80.

42. Tereza Cavalcanti, "The Prophetic Ministry of Women in the Old Testament," in Tamez, *Through Her Eyes*, pp. 118–39.

43. Essays by Aurora Lapiedra on popular religion of the Andeans and María Teresa Porcile on the right to beauty in Latin America appear in the original Spanish edition, *El Rostro Feminino de la Teología* (San José, Costa Rica: DEI, 1986). Nelly Ritchie on women and christology, Anacely de Rocchietti on women and the people of God, Ana María Bidegain on women and liberation theology and a concluding essay by Elsa Tamez appear in the English translation, *Through Her Eyes*.

44. *Against Machismo. Interviews by Elsa Tamez*, John Eagleson trans. and ed. (Oak Park, Ill.: Meyer-Stone, 1987; original 1986), p. 45.

45. Because the interviews are fairly short, the reader can locate the data I have summarized under the name of the theologians interviewed; I will only give page references to specific quotes.

46. Elsa Tamez, commentary, *Against Machismo*, p. 146.

47. In *El rostro feminino*, the generic "hombres" (men) is used on several occasions by different women theologians—for example, pp. 38, 45, 47, 50; and we also find love of "hermanos" (brothers) used generically—for example, pp. 77, 81.

48. Ibid., p. 147.

49. Gustavo Gutiérrez, *La verdad los hará libres* (Lima: CEP, 1986). English translation forthcoming, Orbis, 1990.

6. UNDERSTANDING LATIN AMERICA: MODES OF ANALYSIS

1. In comparing Latin America's experience to those of the United States my purpose is not to reinforce U.S. attitudes of superiority. My intention, in fact, is quite otherwise. It stems in part from a reaction against critics who imply that Latin America needs only to "choose to imitate" the United States if it wants to develop. Latin America has a distinctive past, and it must find its own distinctive path into the future.

2. Leopold Zea, *The Latin American Mind* (Norman: University of Oklahoma Press, 1963), p. 66.

3. Ibid., p. 9.

4. Ibid., p. 42.

5. Ibid., p. 87.

6. Enrique Dussel, *A History of the Church in Latin America* (Grand Rapids: Eerdmans, 1981), pp. 77–78.

7. Hubert Herring, *A History of Latin America from the Beginnings to the Present* (New York: Knopf, 1968, 3rd ed.), p. 185.

8. Writers on Latin America give very conflicting statistics on the number of Amerindians in America at the time of the first European conquests. Benjamin Keen and Mark Wasserman, *A Short History of Latin America* (Dallas: Houghton Mifflin, 1980), pp. 30–31, offer a very helpful survey of the estimates made by various historians, ranging from 8.5 million to 110 million, with 53 million as a rather likely estimate. Simon Collier, *From Cortes to Castro. An Introduction to the History of Latin America, 1492–1973* (New York: Macmillan, 1974), p. 101, says that 13 million is a widely accepted estimate. L.S. Stavrianos, *Global Rift. The Third World Comes of Age* (New York: Macmillan, 1974), p. 80, gives the number as 50 million. Eduardo Galeano, *Open Veins of Latin America. Five Centuries of the Pillage of a Continent* (New York: Monthly Review Press, 1973), p. 50, claims there were 70 to 90 million, reduced a century and a half later to 3.5 million.

9. Stavrianos, *Global Rift*, pp. 75–76.

10. On the number of black slaves, Stavrianos cites the following statistics (1451–1870): British North America, 400,000; Spanish America, 1,550,000; the Caribbean area, 3,793,200; Brazil, 3,646,800 (p. 95).

11. Ibid., p. 89.

12. Simon Collier, *Cortes to Castro*, pp. 166–76.

13. José Carlos Mariátegui, *Seven Interpretive Essays on Peruvian Reality* (Austin: University of Texas, 1971; new paperback ed., 1988), pp. 39–40. On land as patrimony, see also Herring, *A History of Latin America*, p. 155. "The land was the king's; the right to exploit its fields, pastures, and mines was a grant of favor revocable at will."

14. Herring, *A History of Latin America*, p. 199.

15. Mariano Picon-Salas, *A Cultural History of Spanish America. From Conquest to Independence* (Berkeley: University of California Press, 1962), p. 167. Keen and Wasserman estimate that in Spain, in 1500, some 2 to 3 percent of the population owned 95 percent of the land, with ownership coming through royal decrees (*A Short History of Latin America*, p. 41).

16. Michael P. Todaro, *Economic Development in the Third World* (New York: Longman, 1981, 2nd ed.), p. 260.

17. Enrique Dussel, *Philosophy of Liberation* (Maryknoll, N.Y.: Orbis, 1985; original 1980), p. 83.

18. Herring, *A History of Latin America*, p. 182.

19. On the corporative nature of Latin American society, see Howard J. Wiarda, "Toward a Framework for the Study of Political Change in the Iberic-Latin Tradition: The Corporative Model," *World Politics*, January 1973, vol. 25, no. 2. On the effect of this corporative model on corruption, see Jeffrey Klaiber, S.J., "Etica, abusos del poder y corrupción en el Perú: una perspectiva histórica," in

Klaiber, ed., *Violencia y crisis de valores en el Perú* (Lima: Pontífica Universidad Católica del Perú, 1987).

20. Cited in Stephen Clissord, *Latin America. A Cultural Outline* (New York: Harper Colophon, 1965), p. 86.

21. Frank Tannenbaum, *Ten Keys to Latin America* (New York: Vintage, 1966), p. 73.

22. Ibid., p. 77.

23. This account of the haciendas is drawn from Tannenbaum, *Ten Keys*, chapter 5, and from Collier, *Cortes to Castro*, pp. 179–88.

24. Enrique Dussel, *A History of the Church in Latin America*, p. 77. See also Tannenbaum, *Ten Keys*, p. 118. Eugene W. Ridings renews this argument about the failure of Latin American landowners to take leadership in commerce, in "Foreign Predominance Among Overseas Traders in Nineteenth-Century Latin America," *Latin American Research Review*, no. 2, 1985. For a debate about Ridings's views, see also the *Latin American Research Review*, no. 3, 1986.

25. Collier, *Cortes to Castro*, p. 210 on the textile industry, and pp. 206–11 on British investment overall.

26. J. Fred Rippy, *Latin America. A Modern History* (Ann Arbor: University of Michigan Press, 1958), pp. 391–93.

27. On English investment, see Keen and Wasserman, *A Short History of Latin America*, pp. 202–3, and Thomas E. Skidmore and Peter H. Smith, *Modern Latin America* (New York: Oxford University, 1984), p. 47. On the rise of U.S. imports-exports, see Mariátegui, *Seven Interpretive Essays*, p. 15.

28. Pablo Richard, *Death of Christendoms, Birth of the Church* (Maryknoll, N.Y.: Orbis, 1987; original 1978), pp. 41, 53–56, 61–62.

29. On Chilean copper, see Roberto Contes Conde, *The First Stages of Modernization in Spanish America* (New York: Harper and Row, 1974), pp. 73–77; on Venezuelan oil, see John Gerassi, *The Great Fear in Latin America* (New York: Collier-Macmillan, 1968, revised), p. 370; on inflow versus outflow of capital, Paul Sweezy, *Modern Capitalism and Other Essays* (New York: Monthly Review Press, 1972), p. 18.

30. Most of my summary on politics is drawn from Collier, *Cortes to Castro*, chapter 5, "Political Traditions."

31. Ibid., pp. 57–63.

32. José Comblin, *The Church and the National Security State* (Maryknoll, N.Y.: Orbis, 1979), pp. 65–66.

33. Summary from Robert Calvo, "The Church and the Doctrine of National Security," in Daniel H. Levine, ed., *Churches and Politics in Latin America* (London: Sage, 1979), pp. 140–45.

34. Comblin, *National Security State*, p. 77.

35. Walt W. Rostow, *The Stages of Economic Growth: A Non-Communist Manifesto* (New York: Cambridge University Press, 1960).

36. My presentation of the development of dependency theory is a summary drawn from several studies and commentaries. A brief word about each may be helpful: (a) Gabriel Palma, chapter 1, "Dependency and Development: A Critical Overview," in Dudley Seers, ed., *Dependency Theory. A Critical Assessment* (London: Frances Pinter, 1981). This prize-winning essay, first published in *World Development* (July-August 1978), is the best source I found, especially in relating dependency theory to Marxism. (b) Philip J. O'Brien, "A Critique of Latin American

Theories of Dependency," in Ivar Oxaal, Tony Barnet, and David Booth, eds., *Beyond the Sociology of Development* (London: Routledge and Kegan Paul, 1975). It gives a useful account of ECLA, and of A.G. Frank and Cardoso. (c) Ronald H. Chilcote has edited or coedited several helpful studies dealing especially with the debate between Marxism and dependency: *Dependency and Marxism* (Boulder: Westview, 1982); Chilcote and Dale L. Johnson, eds. *Theories of Development* (Beverly Hills: Sage, 1983); Chilcote and Joel C. Edelstein, eds., *Latin America: The Struggle with Dependency and Beyond* (New York: John Wiley, 1974). (d) Richard C. Bath and Dilmus D. James, "Dependency Analysis of Latin America," *Latin American Research Review*, vol. 11, no. 3, 1976. They focus more on North American dependency theorists. (e) James L. Dietz, "Dependency Theory: A Review Article," *Journal of Economic Issues*, vol. 14, no. 3, September 1980, pp. 751–57, compares Frank and Cardoso. (f) Miguel Jorrin and John D. Martz, *Latin-American Political Thought and Ideology* (Chapel Hill: University of North Carolina Press, 1970), chapter 14, "Ideologies of Development," deals especially with ECLA and different ideologies in Brazil.

37. Eduardo Venezian, "The Economic Sciences in Latin America," in Lawrence D. Stifel, Ralph K. Davidson, and James S. Coleman, eds., *Social Sciences and Public Policy in the Developing World* (Lexington, Mass.: Lexington Books, 1983), notes that apart from one university in Mexico, no schools or faculties of economics existed in Latin America before the 1950s. He credits U.S. aid for spurring their rapid development. Jorge Balan has an essay on this topic in the same book.

38. Frances Moore Lappé and Joseph Collins, *Food First: Beyond the Myth of Scarcity* (Boston: Houghton Mifflin, 1977), pp. 182–83.

39. André Gunder Frank, *Lumpenbourgeoisie—Lumpenproletariat: Dependence, Class, and Politics in Latin America* (New York: Monthly Review Press, 1972), p. 93, cited by Booth in "André Gunder Frank: An Introduction and Appreciation," *Beyond the Sociology of Development*, p. 62.

40. Arthur F. McGovern, *Marxism: An American Christian Perspective* (Maryknoll, N.Y.: Orbis, 1980); chapter 1 on Marx's thought; chapter 2 on later Marxists; chapter 5 includes a section on Lenin's theory of imperialism.

41. From Marx's preface to his *Contribution to the Critique of Political Economy* (1859) in Lewis S. Feuer, ed., *Marx & Engels. Basic Writings on Politics and Philosophy* (Garden City, N.Y.: Anchor Doubleday, 1959), p. 43.

42. Ibid.

43. Karl Marx, *Capital* (New York: International Publishers, 1967) 1:236.

44. See the introduction by Shlomo Aveneri, *Karl Marx on Colonialism and Modernization* (Garden City, N.Y.: Anchor Doubleday, 1969), p. 13.

45. V.I. Lenin, "Imperialism: The Highest Stage of Capitalism" (1916) in Lenin's *Selected Works in Three Volumes*, volume 1. On Marxist views of imperialism, see also Irving M. Zeitlin, *Capitalism and Imperialism, An Introduction to Neo-Marxian Concepts* (Chicago: Markham, 1972), chapters 6 and 7, and the Palma essay already cited.

46. Palma in Seers, *Dependency Theory*, pp. 39–40.

47. On Lenin's interpretation of Marxist "essentials," see McGovern, *Marxism*, pp. 56–60, and on Lenin's atheism, pp. 263–66.

48. For more on Gramsci and Althusser, see ibid., pp. 73–75, 80–82.

49. On Mariátegui, see Jeffrey Klaibler, *Religion and Revolution in Peru, 1824–*

1976 (University of Notre Dame Press, 1977), chapter 5, and Mariátegui's own *Seven Interpretive Essays*.

50. Jorrin and Martz, *Latin American Political Thought and Ideology*, chapter 14.

51. Theotonio Dos Santos, in Helio Jaguaribe, Aldo Ferrer, Miguel S. Wionczek, and Theotonio Dos Santos, *La dependencia política-económica de América Latina* (Mexico City: Siglo Veintiuno, 1971, 3rd ed.), p. 180. Cited by Michael J. Francis, "Dependency: Ideology, Fad, and Fact" in Michael Novak and Michael P. Jackson, eds., *Latin America: Dependency or Interdependence?* (Washington, D.C.: American Enterprise Institute, 1985), p. 89.

52. Seers, *Dependency Theory*, p. 13. For a more positive, but critical assessment, see David Booth's chapter on Frank in *Beyond the Sociology of Development* and his article "André Gunder Frank" in *Latin American Research Review*, vol. 17, no. 1, 1982, pp. 115–30.

53. André Gunder Frank, *Latin America: Underdevelopment or Revolution* (New York: Monthly Review Press, 1969), pp. 150–54.

54. For critiques of Frank, see articles already cited by Palma, Booth, and O'Brien.

55. Fernando Henrique Cardoso and Enzo Faletto, *Dependency and Development in Latin America* (Berkeley: University of California, 1979).

56. Robert Packenham, "Plus ça change . . . The English Edition of Cardoso and Faletto's Dependencia y Desarollo en América Latina," in *Latin American Research Review*, vol. 17, no. 1 (1982), p. 131, cites several authors who view the Cardoso-Faletto book as the *locus classicus*.

57. Fernando Henrique Cardoso, "The Consumption of Dependency Theory in the United States," *Latin American Research Review*, vol. 12, no. 3 (1977), p. 8.

58. Packenham, "Plus ça change."

59. Cardoso and Faletto, *Dependency and Development in Latin America*, p. xv.

60. Peter Evans, "After Dependency: Recent Studies of Class, State, and Industrialization," *Latin American Research Review*, no. 2, 1985, quote p. 159; other points, pp. 149–50, 157–58. John Walton, "Small Gains for Big Theories, Recent Work on Development," *Latin American Research Review*, no. 2, 1987, reaches a similar conclusion: "Presently it [dependency analysis] dominates our domain assumptions about Third World development . . . and it continues to produce results in the hands of skilled researchers."

61. Richard Rubinson, ed., from his introduction to *Dynamics of World Development* (London: Sage, 1981), pp. 11–12. My summary of world system analysis is drawn from his introduction, and chapter 12, "Structural Transformations of the World Economy," by Terrence K. Hopkins and Immanuel Wallerstein, and also from Volker Bornscheier and Christopher Chase-Dunn, *Transnational Corporations and Underdevelopment* (New York: Praeger, 1985).

62. Immanuel Wallerstein's main works are: (1) *The Modern World System I: Capitalist Agriculture and the Origins of the European World-Economy in the Sixteenth Century* (New York: Academic Press, 1974); (2) *The Modern World System II: Mercantilism and the Consolidation of the World-Economy, 1600–1750* (New York: Academic Press, 1980); (3) *The Capitalist World Economy* (Cambridge: Cambridge University Press, 1979).

63. Rubinson, *Dynamics of World Development*, pp. 17–18.

64. On dialectical versus functionalist analysis, see Guillermo Villaseñor, "So-

ciedad, análisis de la," *Christus* (Mexico City), May 1980, no. 534, pp. 64–67.

65. On Vekemans as an example of functionalism, see Raúl Vidales and To-kihiro Kudo, *Práctica religiosa y proyecto histórico* (Lima: CEP, 1975), pp. 41–45.

7. SOCIAL ANALYSIS AND OPTIONS IN LIBERATION THEOLOGY

1. Leonardo Boff, *When Theology Listens to the Poor* (San Francisco: Harper & Row, 1988; original 1984), p. 76 on the use of "dialectic" analysis, and chapter 2 on the options for the poor.

2. Paul Sigmund, "Whither Liberation Theology?," *Crisis,* January 1987, pp. 5–14, and a book forthcoming from the Oxford University Press.

3. Hugo Assmann, *Theology for a Nomad Church* (Maryknoll, N.Y.: Orbis, 1976), p. 63.

4. Gutiérrez, *The Power of the Poor in History* (Maryknoll, N.Y.: Orbis, 1983; original 1979), p. 45.

5. Sergio Torres and John Eagleson, eds., *The Challenge of Basic Christian Communities* (Maryknoll, N.Y.: Orbis, 1981), p. 4.

6. Assmann, *Theology for a Nomad Church,* p. 37.

7. Ibid., p. 49.

8. José Míguez Bonino, *Revolutionary Theology Comes of Age* (London: SPCK, 1975), p. 16. Also published as *Doing Theology in a Revolutionary Situation* (Philadelphia: Fortress, 1975).

9. Leonardo Boff, *Liberating Grace* (Maryknoll, N.Y.: Orbis, 1979; original 1976), p. 29.

10. Gutiérrez, *A Theology of Liberation,* p. 84. Gutiérrez cites dependency theorist Osvaldo Sunkel among others.

11. Ibid., p. 85.

12. Ibid., p. 87.

13. Gutiérrez, *The Power of the Poor,* p. 45.

14. Ibid., p. 78.

15. Ibid., p. 45.

16. Ibid., pp. 83–88.

17. Gutiérrez, "Teología y ciencias sociales," appeared originally in *Christus* (Mexico City), October-November 1984; it was published also in Gutiérrez, *La verdad los hará libres* (Lima: CEP, Instituto Bartolomé de Las Casas, 1986) (English translation forthcoming, Orbis, 1990).

18. Gutiérrez, *A Theology of Liberation* (Orbis, 1988 ed., with a new introduction by the author), p. xxiv.

19. Leonardo Boff, *Liberating Grace,* pp. 65, 66; also Boff's *Jesus Christ Liberator,* pp. 276–77.

20. Boff, *Liberating Grace,* p. 66; the historical stages, pp. 67–72.

21. Ibid., p. 77.

22. Ibid., p. 78.

23. João Batista Libânio, *Teología da libertação* (São Paolo: Loyola, 1987), pp. 201ff.

24. My interview with Javier Iguíñiz in February 1988, and with Clodovis Boff in March 1988.

25. Gutiérrez, *A Theology of Liberation,* p. 88.

26. Ibid., pp. 110–11.

27. Groups cited by Gutiérrez, ibid., p. 127, nn. 53 and 55.

28. Ibid., p. 88.

29. Leonardo Boff, *Ecclesiogenesis. The Base Communities Reinvent the Church* (Maryknoll, N.Y.: Orbis, 1977), p. 35.

30. Ibid., p. 42.

31. A 1973 pastoral letter cited by Scott Mainwaring, *The Catholic Church and Politics in Brazil, 1916–1985* (Stanford University Press, 1986), p. 94.

32. Clodovis and Leonardo Boff, a commentary on the U.S. Bishops' letter on the U.S. economy appeared in the *National Catholic Reporter,* August 28, 1987.

33. The fuller draft of the Boffs' commentary, which I obtained in manuscript form, was entitled "The Church and the Economy in the United States: A Look from the Point of View of the Periphery."

34. Franz J. Hinkelammert, *The Ideological Weapons of Death. A Theological Critique of Capitalism* (Maryknoll, N.Y.: Orbis, 1986; original 1977), p. 174.

35. Ibid., pp. 29–30.

36. Ibid., p. 75, and also p. 42.

37. Ibid., p. 78.

38. José Míguez Bonino, *Christians and Marxists: The Mutual Challenge to Revolution* (Grand Rapids: Eerdmans, 1976), p. 115.

39. Ibid.

40. Assmann, *Theology for a Nomad Church,* p. 116.

41. Gutiérrez, *A Theology of Liberation,* section on "Christian Brotherhood and Class Struggle," pp. 272–79. In the revised (1988) edition, this section has been redone and retitled "Faith and Social Conflict," pp. 156–61.

42. Ibid., p. 30.

43. Ibid., on Mariátegui, p. 90, and on Althusser, pp. 97, and notes pp. 249, 277. Curt Cadorette, *From the Heart of the People, The Theology of Gustavo Gutiérrez* (Oak Park, Ill.: Meyer-Stone, 1988), chapter 4, has an extensive treatment of Gutiérrez's views in respect to Marx, Althusser, Gramsci, and Ernst Bloch. See also Michael Candaleria, "Mariátegui: Forerunner of Liberation Theology," *The Christian Century,* October 14, 1987, pp. 885–87.

44. Gutiérrez, *A Theology of Liberation,* pp. 9, 220, and endnotes, pp. 97, 242, 284.

45. Gutiérrez, "Marxismo y cristianismo," an unedited talk published in *Pasos,* 13, 1971 (Santiago, Chile), from part 1 of his talk.

46. Ibid., the concluding pages. Note: I worked from a mimeographed, unpublished manuscript. On his critique of Althusser, see also *A Theology of Liberation* (1973), p. 249, note 121.

47. Gutiérrez, *La verdad hará los libres,* pp. 85–91.

48. Míguez Bonino, *Christians and Marxists,* p. 19.

49. Ibid.

50. Ibid., p. 115.

51. Míguez Bonino, *Revolutionary Theology,* p. 97.

52. Míguez Bonino, *Christians and Marxists,* pp. 25–28.

53. Ibid., p. 100.

54. Ibid., pp. 89–90.

55. Leonardo and Clodovis Boff, *Introducing Liberation Theology,* p. 28.

56. Juan Luis Segundo, *Faith and Ideologies:* on the spiritual aspects of pro-

duction, p. 180; on the limits of social analysis and on Marxist materialism as realism, pp. 224–31; on criticism of the laws of dialectical materialism, pp. 207–10; on the loss of humanist values in the building of socialism, p. 191.

57. *The Challenge of Basic Christian Communities,* p. 13.

58. Hinkelammert, *The Ideological Weapons of Death,* pp. 2–3.

59. Ibid., p. 15.

60. Ibid., p. 19.

61. Ibid., pp. 157–58.

62. Ibid., pp. 227–28.

63. Otto Maduro, *Religion and Social Conflicts* (Maryknoll, N.Y.: Orbis, 1982; original 1979), p. 26.

64. Ibid., p. 28.

65. Ibid., chapter 9.

66. Pablo Richard, *Death of Christendoms, Birth of the Church,* pp. 9–11.

67. On favoring "dialectical" analysis over "functional," see Clodovis Boff, *Theology and Praxis* (Maryknoll, N.Y.: Orbis, 1987; original 1978), pp. 55–58; José Míguez Bonino, *Toward a Christian Political Ethics* (Philadelphia: Fortress, 1983), pp. 45–47; and Ricardo Antoncich, *Christians in the Face of Injustice* (Maryknoll, N.Y.: Orbis, 1987; original 1983), p. 71.

68. Míguez Bonino, *Revolutionary Theology,* p. 34.

69. José Comblin, *The Church and the National Security State* (Maryknoll, N.Y.: Orbis, 1979), p. 66.

70. Ibid., pp. 140 and 142.

71. José Porfirio Miranda, "Is Marxism Essentially Atheistic?," *Journal of Ecumenical Studies,* vol. 22, no. 3, Summer 1985.

72. Otto Maduro, "The Desacralization of Marxism within Latin American Liberation Theology," a circulated but unpublished paper, written by Maduro at Maryknoll, N.Y., in 1988. Maduro gives twelve points; I have reduced and reorganized them.

73. Juan Luis Segundo, "Capitalism versus Socialism: Crux Theologica," in *Frontiers of Theology in Latin America,* ed. Rosino Gibellini (Maryknoll, N.Y.: Orbis, 1979; original 1975), p. 249.

74. Segundo, *Faith and Ideologies,* pp. 254, 262, 300, 318–19.

75. Míguez Bonino, *Revolutionary Theology,* pp. 39–40.

76. Míguez Bonino, *Toward a Christian Political Ethics,* p. 77.

77. Comblin, *National Security State,* p. 132.

78. Ibid., p. 220.

79. Gutiérrez, *A Theology of Liberation,* p. 32, but also pp. 26, 83, 111, 133, 138, and passim.

80. Ibid., pp. 90 and 111.

81. Ibid., p. 274.

82. Gutiérrez, "Liberation, Theology, and Proclamation," in *The Mystical and Political Dimensions of the Christian Faith, Concilium* 96, eds. Claude Geffré and Gustavo Gutiérrez (New York: Herder and Herder, 1974), p. 74.

83. Gutiérrez, *Power of the Poor,* p. 45.

84. Ibid., p. 37.

85. Phillip Berryman, *Liberation Theology* (New York: Pantheon, 1987), p. 92.

86. Enrique Dussel, *Philosophy of Liberation* (Maryknoll, N.Y.: Orbis, 1985; original 1980), pp. 10–13.

87. Ibid., p. 72.

88. Ibid., pp. 145–47.

89. Ibid., p. 116.

90. Ibid., pp. 150–51.

91. Ibid., critique of Marxist analysis, p. 171; critique of philosophical materialism, pp. 102–3.

92. Ibid., on the three options, p. 150; on existing socialist models, pp. 74–76; on populism as a temptation, pp. 75, 150, 193.

93. The Congregation for the Doctrine of the Faith, Cardinal Joseph Ratzinger, "Instruction on Certain Aspects of the Theology of Liberation," published in the *National Catholic Reporter,* September 21, 1984. I have cited references within the chapter; the references refer to sections (in Roman numerals) and numbers.

94. Michael Novak, "The Case against Liberation Theology," *New York Times Magazine* (Sunday, October 21, 1984).

95. Michael Novak, *Will It Liberate? Questions for Liberation Theology* (New York: Paulist, 1986), p. 3; on culture as a primary factor, see p. 82.

96. Ibid., chapters 2 and 3 especially.

97. Ibid., chapter 5.

98. Ibid., pp. 90, 128–30.

99. Ibid., p. 85.

100. Ibid., p. 22.

101. Ibid., pp. 108–9.

102. Ibid., p. 138.

103. Ibid., p. 127; Novak cites Gutiérrez, *Power of the Poor,* p. 48.

104. Novak, on Gutiérrez, pp. 142–50, 169–70; on his critique of Marxism, p. 90; see also his note on C. Wright Mills, p. 276.

105. Ibid., pp. 166–67.

106. Ibid., p. 7.

107. Ibid., on Dussel, p. 197; on reactions to European teachers, p. 19.

108. John C. Cort, "Christians & the Class Struggle," *Commonweal,* July 11, 1986, pp. 400–404. Cort's recent book, *Christian Socialism, An Informal History* (Maryknoll, N.Y.: Orbis, 1988), takes up the same issues about Gutiérrez, pp. 310–24.

109. In his article, Cort cites Gutiérrez, *A Theology of Liberation,* p. 202.

110. Cort cites Gutiérrez, *The Power of the Poor,* p. 37.

8. MARXIST ANALYSIS AND DEPENDENCY: AN ASSESSMENT

1. Enrique Dussel, *A History of the Church in Latin America* (Grand Rapids: Eerdmans, 1981), p. xv.

2. Phillip Berryman, *Liberation Theology* (New York: Pantheon, 1987), p. 85.

3. Dussel, *A History of the Church in Latin America,* p. 21.

4. Peter Berger, *The Sacred Canopy,* (Garden City, N.Y.: Doubleday, 1969), pp. 11–13. Chapter 1 summarizes his longer work co-authored by Thomas Luckmann, *The Social Construction of Reality* (Garden City, N.Y.: Doubleday Anchor, 1967).

5. Leonardo Boff, *Liberating Grace* (Maryknoll, N.Y.: Orbis, 1979; original 1976), p. 23.

6. Harold Eugene Davis, *Latin American Thought: A Historical Introduction* (New York: Free Press, Macmillan, 1972), p. 184. See also Miguel Jorrin and John D. Martz, *Latin American Political Thought and Ideology* (Chapel Hill: University of North Carolina, 1970), p. 270.

7. Comblin, *The Church and the National Security State*, p. 140.

8. Ibid., p. 66.

9. Richard, *Death of Christendoms*, p. 173.

10. On the issue of separating atheist materialism from Marxist analysis, see McGovern, "Atheism: Is It Essential to Marxism?" *Journal of Ecumenical Studies*, Summer 1985, and also McGovern, *Marxism*, pp. 49–64.

11. Alfonso López Trujillo, *De Medellín a Puebla*, on capitalism, p. 246; on Marxist analysis, p. 241.

12. For per capita income in El Salvador, see *Economic Handbook of the World, 1981*, ed. Arthur S. Banke et al. (New York: McGraw-Hill), p. 140. On the twenty wealthiest families, see Paul Heath Hoeffel, "The Eclipse of the Oligarchy," in *New York Times Magazine* (Sunday, September 6, 1981), p. 23.

13. Jürgen Moltmann, "On Latin American Liberation Theology," *Christianity and Crisis*, March 29, 1976, vol. 36, no. 5, pp. 57–63.

14. Franz Hinkelammert, *Dialéctica del desarrollo desigual* (San José, Costa Rica: EDUCA, 1983, 2nd ed.); Hinkelammert, *Crítica a la razón utópica* (San José: Departamento Ecumenico de Investigaciones—DEI, 1984); Hinkelammert, *The Ideological Weapons of Death* (Maryknoll, N.Y.: Orbis, 1986; original 1977).

15. Hinkelammert, *The Ideological Weapons of Death*, pp. 78, 85.

16. Hinkelammert, *Crítica a la razón utópica*, chapter 1.

17. F.H. Cardoso and E. Faletto on the definition of dependency, in *Dependency and Development*, pp. xx–xxi. Raul Prebisch's definition can be found in "The Dynamics of Peripheral Capitalism," *Democracy and Development in Latin America*, eds. Louis Lefeber and Lissa L. North (Toronto: CERLAC-LARU, 1980), p. 25.

18. F.H. Cardoso, "The Consumption of Dependency Theory in the United States," *Latin American Research Review*, vol. 12, no. 3, 1977, p. 8.

19. J. Fred Rippy, *Latin America. A Modern History* (Ann Arbor: University of Michigan Press, 1958), pp. 389–90. In more recent histories, Gordon Connell-Smith, *The United States and Latin America* (London: Heineman, 1974), speaks of the disparity of power between the United States and Latin America, p. 2, and he adds: "Latin America is heavily dependent upon the United States as a market and as a source of investment capital" (p. 8). Similarly, Cole Blasier, *The Hovering Giant* (University of Pittsburgh Press, 1976), writes that Latin American countries have been dependent on the United States and that "in great measure dependency has been the inevitable result of disparities in economic and political power" (p. 6).

20. Michael J. Francis, "Dependency: Ideology, Fad, and Fact," in *Latin America: Dependency or Interdependence?*, eds. Michael Novak and Michael P. Jackson (Washington, D.C.: American Enterprise Institute, 1985), p. 92.

21. Frances M. Lappé and Joseph Collins, *World Hunger. Twelve Myths* (New York: Grove, 1986), p. 87 on low wages, p. 91 on percent of profits to poor countries and on the 1973 prices in respect to the debt, p. 122 on percent of debt devoted to arms purchases. Lappé et al., *Betraying the National Interest* (New York: Grove, 1987), p. 29 on the jump in U.S. military aid.

22. William P. Glade, Jr., "Latin America: Debt, Destruction, and Development," in *Latin America: Dependency or Interdependence?*, p. 37.

23. *International Monetary Fund Annual Report, 1984* (Washington, D.C.: IMF, 1984), pp. 9–11.

24. Ibid., p. 31, on center-periphery relations (these terms represent my own formulation of this part of the report). The World Bank study is given in *The World Bank Annual Report, 1984* (Washington, D.C.: World Bank, 1984), p. 32.

25. Francis, "Dependency: Ideology, Fad, and Fact," p. 95.

26. André Gunder Frank, *Crisis: In the Third World* (New York: Holmes and Meier, 1981), pp. 7, 12. See also Lappé and Collins, *World Hunger*, who say that food supplies per person dropped by one-fifth in the 1970s and wages rose at only one-half of the rate of food price increases, p. 84.

27. *World Development Report 1987*, Table pp. 252–53.

28. Werner Baer, "Growth with Inequity: The Cases of Brazil and Mexico," *Latin American Research Review* (LARR), no. 2, 1986, pp. 197–98 on income distribution in Mexico and Brazil.

29. Ibid., p. 206.

30. Jeffrey A. Frieden, "The Brazilian Borrowing Experience: From Miracle to Debacle and Back," LARR, no. 1, 1987.

31. *Poverty in Latin America, The Impact of Depression* (Washington, D.C.: World Bank, 1986), pp. 12 and 20 on employment rates; pp. 16–17 on decline of wages by Mexico's rural poor.

32. Ibid., p. 24.

33. Larry A. Sjaastad, "Where the Latin American Loans Went," in *Liberation Theology and the Liberal Society*, ed. Michael Novak (Washington, D.C.: American Enterprise Institute, 1987), p. 237.

34. *Poverty in Latin America*, p. 3.

35. Frieden, "The Brazilian Borrowing Experience," pp. 96–97, says that Brazil's GDP tripled from 1965 to 1980 and that per capita GDP doubled. Albert O. Hirshman, "The Political Economy of Latin American Development: Seven Exercises in Retrospection," LARR, no. 3, 1987, pp. 9–11, talks about the "thirty good years" with some improvement in the position of the poorest sectors, with infant mortality down from 130 per 1,000 to 50 per 1,000. Richard Webb and Guy Pfefferman, "Miguel Urrutia's *Winners and Losers in Colombia's Economic Growth of the 1970s*," LARR, no. 2, 1987, p. 209, say that this and similar studies "leave no doubt that the fruits of growth have reached the poor in Latin America" and that mass immiserization "seems to have been a figment of the social science imagination."

36. Michael Novak, *The Spirit of Democratic Capitalism* (New York: Simon and Schuster, 1982), p. 301.

37. On this natural path described by Adam Smith, see John A. Willoughby, "International Capital Flows, Economic Growth and Basic Needs," in *Human Rights and Basic Needs in the Americas*, ed. Margaret E. Crahan (Washington, D.C.: Georgetown University Press, 1982), p. 200.

38. W. Arthur Lewis, *The Evolution of the International Economic Order* (Princeton University Press, 1978), pp. 9–10, 16–18.

39. Dussel, *A History of the Church in Latin America*, p. 77.

40. Lappé and Collins, *World Hunger*, p. 67. See also Michael P. Todaro, *Economic Development in the Third World* (New York: Longman, 1981, 2nd ed.), p. 260, cited in chapter 2. Todaro states that 1.3 percent of the landowners in Latin America control 71.6 percent of all land under cultivation.

41. For a summary of arguments and studies for and against transnationals, see Thomas J. Bierstecker, *Distortion or Development? Contending Perspectives on the Multinational Corporation* (Cambridge: MIT Press, 1978), chapters 1–3; on outflows of capital, pp. 3–6. See also Richard Barnet and Ronald Muller, *Global Reach: The Power of the Multinational Corporations* (New York: Simon and Schuster, 1974), p. 161. Also A. G. Frank, *Latin America: Underdevelopment or Revolution?* (New York: Monthly Review Press, 1969), pp. 150–54.

42. From a speech given by Salvador Allende before the General Assembly of the United Nations, December 1972.

43. The Colombia studies are cited by Rhys Jenkins, *Transnational Corporations and Industrial Formation in Latin America* (New York: St. Martin's, 1984), p. 9.

44. See studies cited by Bierstecker, *Distortion or Development*, p. 4.

45. Jenkins, *Transnational Corporations*, on wages, p. 168; on percent employed, p. 165.

46. On this point see Frances Moore Lappé and Joseph Collins, *Food First. Beyond the Myth of Scarcity* (Boston: Houghton Mifflin, 1977), pp. 210, 279–81, and passim.

47. Jenkins, *Transnational Corporations*, p. 28.

48. See studies cited by Bierstecker, *Distortion or Development?*, pp. 11–18. See also Richard Newfarmer, ed., *Profits, Progress and Poverty, Case Studies of International Industries in Latin America* (University of Notre Dame Press, 1985). One study in Newfarmer shows that transnational electrical companies in Brazil use less labor per unit of capital than do Brazilian firms, and that on the consumption side they are oriented toward an elite demand locally—for example, color televisions (chapter 4, pp. 140–42). Chapter 6 on the auto industry in Latin America argues that consumers are a minority class whose use of autos is subsidized by government expenditures on roads and parking facilities to the neglect of more basic needs (pp. 224–25). Still another study in Newfarmer on manufacture of tractors shows that they favor the already large landowners and cannot be afforded by poorer farmers (chapter 9, p. 329, especially).

49. Theodore H. Moran, *Multinational Corporations and the Politics of Dependence. Copper in Chile* (Princeton University Press, 1974), p. 87.

50. Ibid., pp. 102–15.

51. Jenkins, *Transnational Corporations*, p. 34.

52. Bierstecker, *Distortion or Development?*, pp. 4–7.

53. Moran, *Multinational Corporations and the Politics of Dependence*. Moran acknowledges the unusually high profit rates of U.S. copper companies (up to 40 percent through World War II). He likewise admits that "extreme disparity of bargaining power will exist at the initiation of any concession agreement" (p. 159, note). But he notes that Chile gained more in taxes from the copper companies than the companies gained in profits. From 1945 to 1955, Anaconda and Kennecott together recorded profits of $275 million, and from 1955 to 1965, profits of $465 million. Chile gained $328 million and $909 million in tax revenues from them during the same periods, p. 55.

54. Raymond Vernon, *Storm Over Multinationals* (Cambridge: Harvard University Press, 1977), pp. 155–56.

55. Moran, *Multinational Corporations and the Politics of Dependency*, chapter 6 deals with bargaining power. A more recent discussion of his views on bargaining power can be found in *Multinational Corporations*, ed. Theodore H. Moran (Lex-

ington, Mass.: Lexington Books, 1985), chapter 5 on risk assessment.

56. Jenkins, *Transnational Corporations*, p. 115.

57. Walter LaFeber, *Inevitable Revolutions. The United States in Central America* (New York: Norton, 1983), p. 32. Gabriel Kolko, *Confronting the Third World. United States Foreign Policy, 1945–1980* (New York: Pantheon, 1988), argues that U.S. interventions since World War II have been prompted most often by fears that nationalist leaders would restrict U.S. business opportunities. Kolko includes case studies of U.S. policies toward Chile, Brazil, Cuba, and Central America.

58. LaFeber, *Inevitable Revolutions*, p. 79.

59. Richard J. Barnet, *Intervention and Revolution* (New York: Meridian, 1980, revised), p. 187.

60. U.S. Department of State, *Intervention of International Communism in the Americas* (Washington, D.C., 1954), p. 30.

61. Stephen Schlesinger and Stephen Kinzer, *Bitter Fruit. The Untold Story of the American Coup in Guatemala* (Garden City, N.Y.: Doubleday, 1982), give a full account of this story.

62. Lars Schoultz, *Human Rights and the United States Policy toward Latin America* (Princeton University Press, 1981), p. 184 on financial aid.

63. Barnet, *Intervention and Revolution*, pp. 189–201.

64. Schoultz, *Human Rights*, pp. 243–46.

65. Schlesinger and Kinzer, *Bitter Fruit*, p. 34.

66. Ibid., p. 233.

67. Ibid., p. 246–47, citing a study by Amnesty International.

9. OPTING FOR SOCIALISM: AN ASSESSMENT

1. Maduro, *Religion and Social Conflict*, p. 60.

2. Gutiérrez, *The Power of the Poor*, p. 185.

3. Pablo Richard, *Death of Christendoms*, p. 23. See also the whole of chapter 1, "A Colonial Christendom within a Capitalist Society."

4. Ronald H. Chilcote, "Issues of Theory in Dependency and Marxism," *Latin American Perspectives*, Summer-Fall 1981 (nn. 30–31), p. 4, on Marxist critics of A. G. Frank's classification of colonial Latin America as capitalist.

5. Mariátegui, *Seven Interpretive Essays*, passim (see his Index, under feudalism, p. 294).

6. Howard J. Wiarda, "Economic and Political Statism in Latin America," in *Latin America: Dependency or Interdependence?*, pp. 4–6.

7. Frieden, "The Brazilian Borrowing Experience," p. 104. See also Frederick C. Weaver, "Recent Scholarship on Industrial Growth in Latin America," *Latin American Research Review*, n. 1, 1986, p. 181.

8. See McGovern, *Marxism*, chapter 5, "The Case against Capitalism," and the sources used in the chapter.

9. Leonardo Boff, *Ecclesiogenesis*, p. 35.

10. Leon Trotsky, *The Revolution Betrayed* (New York: Pathfinder, 1972), p. 56. Marx's statement, cited by Trotsky, comes from Marx, "The German Ideology," *The Marx-Engels Reader*, ed. Robert C. Tucker (New York: Norton, 1978, 2nd ed.), p. 161.

11. For the pros and cons of the market system, see the brief summary of

Lappé and Collins, *World Hunger*, pp. 77–81. They cite Cuba as an example of a failure in its efforts to do away with the market. See this work also on the greater productivity of small farms, pp. 67ff. Charles E. Lindbloom, *Politics and Markets. The World's Political-Economic Systems* (New York: Basic Books, 1977), makes a detailed case for a market economy over centralized "command" economies, but he also sharply criticizes large corporations as not fitting into true democracy, and he makes a special case for Yugoslavia's "market socialism."

12. Libânio, *Teología da libertação*, pp. 276–78.

13. John Paul II, *Laborem Exercens*, n. 14. The text of the encyclical can be found in Gregory Baum, *The Primacy of Labor* (New York: Paulist Press, 1982).

14. Paul VI, *Octogesima Adveniens*, n. 37, in *The Gospel of Peace and Justice*, ed. Joseph Gremillion (Maryknoll, N.Y.: Orbis, 1976).

15. On utopia, in addition to Gutiérrez, see, for example, Hinkelammert, *The Ideological Weapons of Death*, chapter 6, and José Míguez Bonino, *Toward a Christian Political Ethics*, chapter 7.

16. Gutiérrez on utopia, *A Theology of Liberation*, pp. 232–39. See also Cadorette, *From the Heart of the People*, which discusses Gutiérrez's views on utopia at some length, pp. 53–56, 98–102, especially.

17. Leonardo Boff, *Liberating Grace*, p. 81.

18. Segundo, *Faith and Ideologies*, pp. 305–9.

19. Ignacio Ellacuría, "Perspectiva política de la situación centro americana," *ECA* (Estudios Centro Americano), September-October 1985, pp. 631–32, especially.

20. Leonardo Boff, as quoted in a release by the *National Catholic Reporter*, July 31, 1987, p. 6; also his report on the visit to Russia in *Vozes* (Petrópolis, Brazil), November-December 1987.

21. Lappé and Collins, *World Hunger*, p. 73.

22. Mariátegui, *Seven Interpretive Essays*, on the positive features of authentic capitalism and private ownership of land in North America, pp. 21, 39–41, 79–82; on the need for a communitarian-socialist basis for the Amerindian culture, pp. 33–36, 57–58, and the whole essay, "The Problem of Land."

23. Ricardo Antoncich, *Christians in the Face of Injustice. A Latin American Reading of Catholic Social Teaching* (Maryknoll, N.Y.: Orbis, 1987; original 1983), chapter 8.

24. Hinkelammert, *The Ideological Weapons of Death*, p. 159 and chapter 6, overall for his initial treatment, then later on "true private property," p. 262. I would argue that *Rerum Novarum*, far from intending "capitalist"-factory ownership in its defense of private property, speaks consistently in images that suggest the small farm owner ("the soil toiled and cultivated," etc.). For my own treatment of church teachings on property, see McGovern, *Marxism*, pp. 278–85.

25. The text of the papal commission document on property can be found in *Church Alert*, The Sodepax Newsletter, no. 18, January-March 1978, p. 17.

26. John Paul II, *Sollicitudo Rei Socialis,* in *Origins*, March 3, 1988: on the goods of the earth for all, n. 42; on economic initiative, n. 15. On "truly socialized" forms of ownership, see *"Laborem Exercens,"* nos. 14–15.

27. Gutiérrez, *The Power of the Poor*, p. 37.

28. Gutiérrez, *La verdad los hará libres*, pp. 220–21.

29. Gutiérrez, *The Power of the Poor*, p. 49.

30. Document of Latin American theologians from the Second Assembly of

the Ecumenical Association of Third World Theologians (Mexico, December 7–14, 1986), in *Revista Latinoamericana de Teología*, September-December 1986 (San Salvador), pp. 304–5.

31. Hugo Assmann, "The Improvement of Democracy in Latin America and the Debt Crisis," in *Liberation Theology and the Liberal Society*, ed. Michael Novak (Washington, D.C.: American Enterprise Institute, 1987), pp. 46–48, especially.

32. Richard John Neuhaus, *The Catholic Moment*, p. 171.

33. *Signos de liberación, testimonios de la iglesia en América latina, 1969–1973*, (Lima: CEP, 1973).

34. Gutiérrez, "Notes for a Theology of Liberation," *Theological Studies*, vol. 31, n. 2, June 1970, p. 250.

35. Gutiérrez, *The Power of the Poor in History*, p. 28.

36. Segundo, *The Liberation of Theology*, pp. 166 and 116.

37. On nonviolence, Antoncich, *Christians in the Face of Injustice*, pp. 39–42; Leonardo Boff and Segundo Galilea in *Frontiers of Theology in Latin America*, ed. Rosino Gibellini (Maryknoll, N.Y.: Orbis, 1979), pp. 120 and 175, respectively.

38. Gutiérrez, *A Theology of Liberation* (1973 edition), quote, p. 275, and pp. 272–79 overall.

39. Gutiérrez, *The Power of the Poor in History*, p. 45.

40. Gregory Baum, *Theology and Society* (Mahwah, N.J.: Paulist Press, 1987), p. 32, and the whole of chapter 2, "Class Struggle and Magisterium: A New Note."

41. Gutiérrez, *A Theology of Liberation* (1988 edition), pp. 156–61.

42. Antoncich, *Christians in the Face of Injustice*, p. 128. See also McGovern, *Marxism*, pp. 292–96, for a discussion of class struggle from a Christian perspective.

43. Juan Hernández Pico, "The Experience of Nicaragua's Revolutionary Christians," and Miguel d'Escoto, "The Church Born of the People in Nicaragua," in *The Challenge of Basic Christian Communities*, eds. Sergio Torres and John Eagleson (Maryknoll, N.Y.: Orbis, 1981), pp. 62–73 and 189–96, respectively. Also see Juan Hernández Pico, with Jon Sobrino, *Theology of Christian Solidarity* (Maryknoll, N.Y.: Orbis, 1985; from articles in 1982–83).

44. For a thorough, sympathetic account of the Sandinista revolution, see *Nicaragua. The First Five Years*, ed. Thomas Walker (New York: Praeger, 1985).

45. John C. Cort, "Raised Voices in Nicaragua," *Commonweal*, November 21, 1986, pp. 623, 629–31.

46. On human rights violations in Nicaragua, see *An Americas Watch Report*, "Human Rights in Nicaragua: Reagan, Rhetoric and Reality" (New York: Americas Watch, July 1985). The report does note violations but asserts that the Reagan administration description of Nicaragua as a totalitarian state "bears no resemblance to Nicaragua in 1985" (p. 6). An Amnesty International Report, "Nicaragua, The Human Rights Record" (London, March 1986) finds evidence for arbitrary arrests and mistreatment of prisoners. But it also notes government prosecution and sentencing of army officers who committed the worst offenses (p. 25).

47. Humberto Belli, *Breaking Faith. The Sandinista Revolution and Its Impact on Freedom and Christian Faith in Nicaragua* (Westchester, Ill.: Cross Way Books, Good News Publishers, 1985).

48. Ibid., pp. 35–36.

49. José Luis Coraggio, "Revolución y democracia en Nicaragua," *Encuentro* (Managua, 1984, n. 21), cites Sandinista sources in focusing on "the unity and simultaneity" between democracy and social transformation. *Transition and Devel-*

opment. Problems of Third World Socialism, ed. Richard R. Fagen et al. (New York: Monthly Review Press, 1986), contains several essays focused on the problem of socialism and democracy in Nicaragua. Donald Hodges, *Intellectual Foundations of the Nicaraguan Revolution* (Austin: University of Texas Press, 1986), studies in detail the ideas of Sandino himself, the type of "new Marxism" blended into "Sandinismo" (see especially the section "What is Sandinismo?," pp. 184–96) and the role of Christians in the revolutionary process. Giulio Girardi, *Sandinismo, Marxismo, Cristianismo: la confluencia* (Managua: Centro Ecuménico Antonio Valdivisio, 1986), also studies the interplay of Sandino's ideas, Marxism and Christianity in the process in Nicaragua. English translation, *Faith and Revolution in Nicaragua: Convergence and Contradictions* (Maryknoll, N.Y.: Orbis, 1989).

10. A NEW WAY OF BEING CHURCH

1. Gutiérrez, *A Theology of Liberation*, p. xi.
2. Ibid., pp. 49–50, 54–57, 65–66.
3. Ibid., pp. 255–56.
4. Ibid., p. 138.
5. Ibid., on denouncing and announcing, pp. 114–15, and 233–34.
6. Ibid., p. 273.
7. Ibid., p. 307.
8. Scott Mainwaring, *The Catholic Church and Politics in Brazil, 1916–1985* (Stanford University Press, 1986), p. 108, gives an estimate of eighty thousand base communities in Brazil with two million members. Edward L. Cleary, O.P, *Crisis and Change. The Church in Latin America Today*, p. 104, estimates one hundred thousand CEBs with over a million members in Brazil, and some two to three million members in Latin America overall.
9. Scott Mainwaring, *The Catholic Church and Politics in Brazil*, provided much of the material for this discussion on the church and base communities. See chapter 2 of his book on the beginnings of new efforts to "christianize" Brazil, and chapter 6 on the Young Christian Workers movement. Two other works, which will be cited often in the next section, also give short histories of the development of base communities: Guillermo Cook, *The Expectation of the Poor. Latin American Basic Ecclesial Communities in Protestant Perspective* (Maryknoll, N.Y.: Orbis, 1985), chapter 4; Marcello DeC. Azevedo, S.J., *Basic Ecclesial Communities in Brazil* (Washington, D.C.: Georgetown University Press, 1987), chapter 1 on origins. Other works on base communities include: Alvaro Barreiro, *Basic Ecclesial Communities: The Evangelization of the Poor* (Maryknoll, N.Y.: Orbis, 1982), and Thomas C. Bruneau, *The Political Transformation of the Brazilian Catholic Church* (London: Cambridge University Press, 1974) and his "Basic Christian Communities in Latin America: Their Nature and Significance (Especially in Brazil)," in *Churches and Politics in Latin America*, ed. Daniel H. Levine (Beverly Hills: Sage, 1980), pp. 226–37.
10. This story of the old woman is related by Cook, *The Expectation of the Poor*, p. 64, and by Leonardo Boff, *Ecclesiogenesis. The Base Communities Reinvent the Church* (Maryknoll, N.Y.: Orbis, 1986; original 1977), p. 3. Marcello Azevedo commented, in an interview with me, that the story appears apocryphal.
11. On Freire and the MEB, see Mainwaring, *The Catholic Church and Politics in Brazil*, pp. 66–70.

12. Ibid., chapter 4, esp. pp. 64–65 on the Popular Action groups, and p. 103 on the Young Christian Workers.

13. Ibid., p. 93 on the bishops' documents; pp. 94–95 on per capita income in northeastern Brazil.

14. Ibid., p. 155 and chapter 7. The statistics on persecution of the church come from Cook, *The Expectation of the Poor,* p. 48; he cites an Associated Press report of June 30, 1980.

15. Azevedo, *Basic Ecclesial Communities in Brazil,* chapter 2.

16. Second General Conference of Latin American Bishops, *The Church in the Present-Day Transformation of Latin America in the Light of the Council* (Washington, D.C.: United States Catholic Conference, II Conclusions, 2nd edition, n.d.), "Pastoral Care of the Masses," no. 13 (p. 106); "Joint Pastoral Planning," nos. 9–12 (pp. 200–202).

17. *Puebla and Beyond,* eds. John Eagleson and Phillip Scharper (Maryknoll, N.Y.: Orbis, 1979), no. 629, also see nos. 96, 156, 649.

18. Azevedo, *Basic Ecclesial Communities in Brazil,* pp. 245–46.

19. Cook, *Expectation of the Poor,* chapter 6. I have added the points about Paulo Freire and some other comments to the account given by Cook.

20. Paulo Freire, *Pedagogy of the Oppressed* (New York: Seabury, 1974), pp. 126, 185.

21. Cook, *Expectation of the Poor,* p. 121; chapter 7 develops in more detail the new way of approaching scripture.

22. Ibid.; chapter 8 develops the new understanding of mission.

23. For fuller accounts of the development of base communities and politically active "popular" Christian groups in Nicaragua, and their relation to the church see: Phillip Berryman, *The Religious Roots of Rebellion. Christians in Central American Revolutions* (Maryknoll, N.Y.: Orbis, 1985); Michael Dodson, "Nicaragua: The Struggle for the Church," *Religion and Political Conflict in Latin America,* ed. Daniel H. Levine (Chapel Hill: University of North Carolina Press, 1986), chapter 5; this is the most compact summary; Michael Dodson and Laura Nuzzi O'Schaughnessy, "Religion and Politics," *Nicaragua: The First Five Years,* ed. Thomas W. Walker (New York: Praeger, 1985), pp. 125–28 on early developments; Laura Nuzzi O'Schaughnessy and Luis H. Sera, *The Church and Revolution in Nicaragua* (Athens: Ohio University Press, Monographs in International Studies, Latin American Series, no. 11, 1986); Rosa María Pochet and Abelino Martínez, *Nicaragua iglesia: manipulación profecía?* (San José, Costa Rica: DEI, 1987).

24. Dodson, "Nicaragua: The Struggle for the Church," p. 85.

25. Pochet and Martínez, *Nicaragua iglesia,* p. 25.

26. Cited by Sera, *The Church and Revolution in Nicaragua,* pp. 54–55.

27. Dodson, "Nicaragua: The Struggle for the Church," pp. 95–96. On the role of the priests in the government, see Dodson and O'Schaughnessy, pp. 132–33, and Berryman, pp. 260ff.

28. This memo is cited by Betsy Cohn and Patricia Hynds, "The Manipulation of the Religion Issue," in *Reagan versus the Sandinistas,* ed. Thomas W. Walker (Boulder, Colo.: Westview, 1987), p. 117.

29. Ibid., on the Protestant churches, pp. 101–2.

30. César Jerez, S.J., *The Church and the Nicaraguan Revolution* (London: Catholic Institute for International Relations, 1984).

31. Charles A. Reilly, "Latin America's Religious Populism," in *Religion and*

Political Conflict in Latin America, ed. Daniel H. Levine (Chapel Hill: University of North Carolina Press, 1986), p. 51.

32. On Chile, see Brian H. Smith, "Chile: Deepening the Allegiance of Working Class Sectors to the Church in the 1970s," in *Religion and Political Conflict in Latin America,* chapter 8.

33. On El Salvador, see Phillip Berryman, "El Salvador: From Evangelization to Insurrection," chapter 4 in the same work (above). See also his *The Religious Roots of Rebellion* on Central America overall.

34. On the church in Colombia, see Daniel H. Levine, "Colombia: The Institutional Church and the Popular," in *Religion and Political Conflict in Latin America,* chapter 9.

35. For a study of Peru and the impact of the insurrectionist groups especially, see Raymond Bonner, "A Reporter at Large, Peru's War," *New Yorker,* January 4, 1988, pp. 31ff.

36. The Peruvian bishops' statement of October 1984 was published as "Peruvian Bishops' Message, Liberation and the Gospel," in *Origins,* January 17, 1985, vol. 14, no. 31.

37. For example, the Peruvian periodical *Socialismo y Participación* in an editorial statement called for decentralizing the government and delegating functions of government to the population (December 1987 issue, p. vii).

38. Reilly, "Latin America's Religious Populism."

39. Berryman, *Liberation Theology,* p. 72, comments on the small percentage in Brazil; Cook, *The Expectation of the Poor,* p. 74, cites J. B. Libânio on the weakness of political consciousness in many groups.

40. Mainwaring, *The Catholic Church and Politics in Brazil,* the quote, p. 229, also pp. 234–35 and chapters 9 and 10 overall.

41. Azevedo, *Basic Ecclesial Communities in Brazil,* pp. 82–88, 139–42.

11. TOWARD A NEW ECCLESIOLOGY

1. Juan Luis Segundo, *The Community Called Church* (Maryknoll, N.Y.: Orbis, 1973; original 1968), chapter 4 esp., p. 6 on universality. See also Segundo, *The Liberation of Theology,* chapter 8.

2. Boff, *Ecclesiogenesis,* pp. 26–27.

3. Ibid., p. 6.

4. Ibid., p. 24.

5. Ibid., p. 8.

6. Ibid., chaper 2.

7. Ibid., pp. 57–58.

8. Ibid., p. 60.

9. Ibid, pp. 72–73.

10. Ibid., chapter 7.

11. Leonardo Boff, *Church: Charism and Power. Liberation Theology and the Institutional Church* (New York: Crossroad, 1985; original 1981), p. 59.

12. Ibid., pp. 111–13.

13. Ibid., p. 133.

14. Ibid., chapter 4.

15. Ibid., chapter 8.

16. Ibid., p. 126.

17. Jon Sobrino, *The True Church and the Poor* (Maryknoll, N.Y.: Orbis, 1984; original 1981), p. 85.

18. Ibid., pp. 93, 134–39.

19. Ibid., pp. 106–20.

20. Dom Antônio B. Fragoso, *Face of a Church. A Nascent Church of the People in Crateús, Brazil* (Maryknoll, N.Y.: Orbis, 1987; original 1982), p. 42.

21. Ibid., pp. 67, 72.

22. The congregation's notification, together with brief details of the Boff affair, can be found in "Doctrinal Congregation Criticizes Brazilian Theologian's Book," *Origins,* April 4, 1985, vol. 14, no. 42. Harvey Cox, *The Silencing of Leonardo Boff* (Oak Park, Ill.: Meyer-Stone, 1988) investigates the affair and its implications in great detail.

23. This summary of the four points noted by the congregation is taken from the *Origins* account noted above. For more discussion on the dispute over the church's "subsistence," see Cox, *The Silencing of Leonardo Boff,* pp. 98–103, and chapter 12 overall on the issues discussed at the meeting between Ratzinger and Boff.

24. For a study on these issues, see Avery Dulles, S.J., *Models of the Church* (Garden City, N.Y.: Doubleday, 1974).

25. On Pope John Paul II's perceptions about the decline of values in society and loss of spiritual discipline in the church, see George Hunston Williams, *The Mind of John Paul II* (New York: Seabury, 1981), pp. 139, 286–87, and chapter 9 overall. On Cardinal Ratzinger's pessimistic view of human nature and conditions in the church, see Andrew Sullivan, "Cardinal Sins," the review of three books (one by Ratzinger, one on his theology, the third about the Inquisition) in *The New Republic,* July 4, 1988, pp. 29ff. On Cardinal López Trujillo, see his comments on permissiveness and the loss of religious and family values as the most serious problem in Colombia, in *Momento histórico de paz, libro reportaje del periodista Jaime Montoy Candamil, Alfónso López Trujillo* (Bogotá: Plaza and Janes, 1981), pp. 33–34, 90–91, 96–98, 126–128, and passim.

26. On the 1985 synod, see Joseph A. Komonchak, "Horizons, A Pastoral Survey, The Synod of 1985 and the Notion of Church," *Chicago Studies,* November 1987, vol. 26, no. 3.

27. López Trujillo, *De Medellín a Puebla,* pp. 21–22 and following pages.

28. On direct political involvement of the church, see Mainwaring, *The Catholic Church and Politics in Brazil,* pp. 32–33, 61.

29. Bishop Roques Adames R., in an essay for *Evangelización liberadora y doctrina social católica,* the Council of CELAM (Bogotá: Departamento de Pastoral Social, 1987), pp. 39–40. Gregory Baum, *Theology and Society,* pp. 8–9, poses the issue of social change in terms of a "soft" concept of liberation (conversion of the heart) and a "hard" view (changing sinful structures), and he indicates where both perspectives find expression in recent church social teachings.

30. Luis Fernando Figari, *Aportes para una teología de la reconciliación* (Lima: Aprodea-Fondo, 1985).

31. López Trujillo, *Momento historico de paz,* pp. 79–80 on creating new businesses and jobs; pp. 179–83 on charity and leading influential persons on visits to the poor.

CONCLUSION

1. Cited by Penny Lernoux, "In Common Suffering and Hope, the Base Communities in Brazil," *Sojourners*, December 1987, p. 26.

2. *Momento histórico de paz*, p. 175–80, on work with the poor as the second most important priority of the church, and on the forty new parishes. López Trujillo considers restoration of religious-family values as the most important priority, pp. 33–34.

3. Harvey Cox, *The Silencing of Leonardo Boff*, p. 66, citing Pedro Ribeiro de Oliveria, in *Social Compass*, vol. 26, nos. 2–3, 1979, p. 314.

4. J.J. Moeller, S.J., *What Are They Saying about Theological Method?* (Ramsey, N.J.: Paulist Press, 1984), p. 70.

5. Document of the Peruvian bishops, "Justice in the World," in preparation for the 1971 bishops' synod in Rome, in *Signos de liberación, testimonios de la iglesia en América latina, 1969–1973* (Lima: CEP, 1973), pp. 179–80.

6. José Pedro S. Martins, "Brazil: Church Uneasy Over Recent Papal Appointments," *Latinamerica Press*, May 12, 1988, p. 6. See also *Latinamerica Press*, May 5, 1988, on the change in Recife and Olinda diocese.

Index of Concepts

Index of Names